INCHBALD, HAWTHORNE AND THE ROMANTIC MORAL ROMANCE: LITTLE HISTORIES AND NEUTRAL TERRITORIES

INCHBALD, HAWTHORNE AND THE ROMANTIC MORAL ROMANCE: LITTLE HISTORIES AND NEUTRAL TERRITORIES

BY
Ben P. Robertson

Routledge
Taylor & Francis Group

LONDON AND NEW YORK

First published 2010 by Pickering & Chatto (Publishers) Limited

Published 2016 by Routledge
2 Park Square, Milton Park, Abingdon, Oxfordshire OX14 4RN
711 Third Avenue, New York, NY 10017, USA

First issued in paperback 2015

Routledge is an imprint of the Taylor & Francis Group, an informa business

BRITISH LIBRARY CATALOGUING IN PUBLICATION DATA

Robertson, Ben P. (Ben Preston)
Inchbald, Hawthorne and the Romantic moral romance: little histories and neutral territories. – (Literary migrations)
1. Inchbald, Mrs., 1753–1821 – Criticism and interpretation. 2. Hawthorne, Nathaniel, 1804–1864 – Criticism and interpretation. 3. Romanticism – Great Britain.
4. Romanticism – United States. 5. English fiction – 19th century – History and criticism. 6. American fiction – 19th century – History and criticism. 7. English literature – American influences. 8. American literature – English influences.
I. Title II. Series
823.7-dc22

ISBN-13: 978-1-138-66510-1 (pbk)
ISBN-13: 978-1-8519-6627-1 (hbk)

Typeset by Pickering & Chatto (Publishers) Limited

CONTENTS

Reader of superior rank, if the passions which rage in the bosom of the inferior class of human kind are beneath your sympathy, throw aside this little history ...

– Elizabeth Inchbald, *Nature and Art*

[By moonlight], the floor of our familiar room has become a neutral territory, somewhere between the real world and fairy-land, where the Actual and the Imaginary may meet, and each imbue itself with the nature of the other.

– Nathaniel Hawthorne, *The Scarlet Letter*

ACKNOWLEDGEMENTS

This project has received enormous support from a large number of people, both in financial terms and in terms of encouragement and assistance.

Most recently, the Troy University Faculty Development Committee provided generous funding for extensive work in Washington, DC, at the Folger Shakespeare Library and the Library of Congress. Earlier grants from the same source were just as helpful in my completing this book, even when they may have been granted for other projects. I am especially thankful to Harold Kaylor, William Thompson and Stephen Cooper, successive chairs of the English Department at Troy University who provided encouragement and letters of support. I owe many thanks to the Troy University Library and especially to Jill McLaney and Belinda Edwards for their assistance with many interlibrary loan requests.

I offer special thanks to the Folger Shakespeare Library and especially to the reading room staff. The Folger provided generous funding for a separate project that was closely related to this one, and the reading room staff has been helpful, professional and extremely competent during each of my visits. Thanks are due, also, to the Library of Congress and its staff for providing access to newer materials not available at the Folger and to the British Library and its staff for providing access to some of Inchbald's correspondence.

I would like to express my thanks to the University of Tulsa, especially to the Department of English, to the McFarlin Library, and to the Office of Research, for funding and professional development opportunities that helped this project in its earliest stages.

Much gratitude goes to Hermione de Almeida, who first introduced me to Elizabeth Inchbald over a decade ago and who has kindly and patiently helped to feed my growing Inchbald obsession in the intervening years with letters of support for grant applications and with encouragement for my continuing work. Her support, along with that of George H. Gilpin and Gordon O. Taylor, has been invaluable and without it, this project could not have materialized. All three of them commented upon early drafts of this project and helped to steer me toward stronger arguments.

Thanks go to Ken and Margaret Robertson for their enduring and enthusiastic support. They helped in a myriad of ways, including encouraging an intellectual curiosity that, I hope, will serve me for many more decades.

LIST OF FIGURES

ABBREVIATIONS

Diaries E. Inchbald, *The Diaries of Elizabeth Inchbald*, 3 vols, ed. B. P. Robertson (London: Pickering & Chatto, 2007).

EAI-1 C. K. Shipton (ed.), *Early American Imprints, 1639 – 1800* (Worcester, MA: American Antiquarian Society/Readex Microprint, [various dates]).

EAI-2 American Antiquarian Society (ed.), *Early American Imprints, 1801–1819* (Series II) (New York and New Canaan, CT: Readex Microprint, [various dates]).

ITYW A. Jenkins, *I'll Tell You What: The Life of Elizabeth Inchbald* (Lexington, KY: University Press of Kentucky, 2003).

MFN Hawthorne, *The Marble Faun, or The Romance of Monte Beni*, in W. Charvat, *et al.* (eds), *The Centenary Edition of the Works of Nathaniel Hawthorne*, vol. 4 (Columbus, OH: Ohio State University Press, 1968).

N&A E. Inchbald, *Nature and Art* (1796; Oxford: Woodstock Books, 1994).

NHHT J. R. Mellow, *Nathaniel Hawthorne in His Times* (Boston, MA: Houghton, 1980).

ODNB H. C. G. Matthew and B. Harrison (eds), *Oxford Dictionary of National Biography* (Oxford: Oxford University Press, 2004).

Remarks E. Inchbald, *Remarks for* The British Theatre *(1806–1809)*, intro. C. Macheski (Delmar, NY: Scholars' Facsimiles & Reprints, 1990).

INTRODUCTION
THE ROMANTIC MORAL ROMANCE: AN ALTERNATIVE TRANSATLANTIC SUB-GENRE FOR ELIZABETH INCHBALD AND NATHANIEL HAWTHORNE

> Every author has a right to give what appellation he may think proper to his works.
> The public have also a right to accept or refuse the classification that is presented.
> – Maria Edgeworth[1]

For a study in the evolution of Anglo-American Romantic fiction, Elizabeth Inchbald (1753–1821) and Nathaniel Hawthorne (1804–64) may seem an unlikely pair (see Figure 1, Portrait of Elizabeth Inchbald, and Figure 2, Portrait of Nathaniel Hawthorne). While Inchbald published *A Simple Story* and *Nature and Art* for a British audience in 1791 and 1796, respectively, Hawthorne published most of his books, most importantly *The Scarlet Letter* of 1850 and *The Marble Faun* of 1860, half a century later for an American audience.[2] And while Hawthorne rose quickly to occupy a position as one of the great writers of the American literary tradition, Inchbald has received less critical attention as a contributor to the British literary tradition, especially given the usual preference given to male poets during the Romantic Period.[3] Yet, despite the distinct differences between the two authors in terms of patrimony, chronology and critical acclaim, and despite the cultural differences inherent in situating their literary efforts on opposite sides of the Atlantic Ocean, an undeniable transatlantic connection binds the two writers' fiction in textual parallels that suggest a more than coincidental relationship among their books. Both writers, based on their own social, political and personal agendas, sought to develop literary vehicles that would best express their intentions and views as writers and perhaps realign and expand the literary tradition they had inherited. And, while the two authors' individual intentions were divergent in terms of the exact nature of that realignment and expansion, the results were so similar in their effects, patterns and resolutions that the two authors rightly may be classified as practitioners working within the same form of mixed genre that might be called Romantic moral romance. This sub-genre of the novel represents an important tie between the two writers and their intentions and between British Romanticism and American versions of Romanticism.

Painted by Lawrence – Engraved by Freeman.

Mrs. Inchbald.

Published by Verner. Hood & Sharpe. Poultry. July 1 1807.

Figure 1, Portrait of Elizabeth Inchbald. An 1807 engraving by Samuel Freeman after a painting done by Inchbald's friend Sir Thomas Lawrence. Inchbald wears French-style clothing in this image. *Courtesy of the Folger Shakespeare Library (Folger ART File, I37, No. 3).*

Figure 2, Portrait of Nathaniel Hawthorne. An engraving published around 1883 of
Hawthorne as he appeared at some point after 1857. He grew the moustache during his
time in Italy when he was working on *The Marble Faun. Courtesy of the Library of Congress
(LC-DIG-pga-00065).*

The Romantic moral romance was a profoundly self-reflexive sub-genre, for it provided Inchbald and Hawthorne a means of examining the very nature of fiction and of the writer's role as an artist. Inchbald wrote her fictions during a time when women novelists often were denigrated as frivolous or even immoral, so although she may have used the term *novel* in private, she avoided using it in print. Years later across the Atlantic, Hawthorne composed his works in an atmosphere that encouraged American writers to break free of British literary tradition and to avoid becoming mere imitators of the novel tradition that had developed in Britain. Paradoxically, both writers wished to write novels but felt obliged to avoid the traditions associated with the very form they wanted to produce. The solution was the Romantic moral romance, which borrowed enough from the novel tradition to be considered a sub-genre but which also borrowed elements of symbolism and an interest in moral order from the mediaeval chivalric romance and perhaps the French *conte moral*.[4]

Romantic-Period writers are well known for revising or reforming older, simpler forms, particularly the romance, which received innovative treatment from such writers as Samuel Taylor Coleridge, John Keats and Lord Byron.[5] The traditional chivalric romance focused attention on class issues, since its hero was an aristocratic knight, and on the preservation of the moral order established by the aristocracy and the clergy. A romance followed a knightly hero on a quest, usually successful, whose ultimate goal involved the knight's union with a chaste maiden, who may have been imprisoned in a desolate tower or enchanted by an evil sorcerer. Anna Shealy's entry on romance in the *Encyclopedia of Medieval Literature* begins with the 'cliché of the knight rescuing the damsel in distress' and points out the genre's preoccupation with rank, chivalry, adventure, the fantastic and light-hearted fighting on the part of the hero.[6] During his quest, the hero encountered a variety of obstacles ranging from the temptation of his immortal soul to the obstruction of his progress by natural or supernatural means. Critic Northrop Frye notices the importance of symbolism in this genre with his comment that 'allegory is constantly creeping in around its fringes'.[7] Certainly, this potential for allegorical interpretation provides ample opportunity for the chivalric romance to uphold the aristocratic social order along with established religious order. The idea of resisting temptation and overcoming obstacles (supernatural or otherwise) bears striking parallels with allegorical Christian conceptions of one's progress through life, and the male chivalric hero's trials can be interpreted symbolically as a self-reflexive exploration of faith – or as a test of faith – particularly in his responses to sin and guilt.[8]

While the traditional chivalric romance may seem conservative, Northrop Frye acknowledges it as a revolutionary form, and writing more recently, Jacqueline Labbe suggests that while chivalric romances uphold the *status quo*, they quietly and simultaneously reject social order.[9] Likewise, Krueger asserts that the traditional romance often has 'a critical perspective that calls social ideals or practices into question'.[10] Among other characteristics, it is this questioning of social practices that marks the Romantic moral romance as unique because this sub-genre overtly and daringly challenges, on multiple levels, the very definition of 'moral order' as a construct for 'correct' conduct, suggesting that the parameters established by a government, by a particular religion or by a social group for correct behaviour may be inadequate for the individual, for whom an individual moral code may be more appropriate. Hence, the hero of the Romantic moral romance written by Inchbald or Hawthorne, unlike the hero of a mediaeval chivalric romance, may exhibit 'correct' conduct that directly subverts traditional religious or social moral codes. In fact, the very identity of the hero himself may be subversive because he may be a *she* in the sub-genre, as exemplified by Miss Milner and Matilda in Inchbald's *A Simple Story* and by Hester Prynne in Hawthorne's *The Scarlet Letter*. The revolutionary nature of the romance form attracted Romantic writers like Inchbald and Hawthorne, who recognized its potential for further development, especially since they both were familiar also with William Shakespeare's Renaissance experimentation in his last plays with romance forms to create another mixed sub-genre – the tragicomedy.

Inchbald, perhaps sensing the overuse of features of the chivalric romance for morally didactic purposes that upheld traditional codes of conduct, but still inspired with a Romantic interest in the romance's earlier and simpler literary form, decided to borrow features from the mediaeval genre to create a viable tool for evoking the social and political issues that were contemporaneous with her writing.[11] In so doing, she ironically positioned the romance, no longer a chivalric form, as moral rival to the popular – and sometimes scandalously Gothic – novel. The irony is that the Romantic moral romance would only masquerade as a traditional didactic form. While Inchbald's contemporaries would consider it morally superior to the novel because of its apparent conservatism, it would simultaneously subvert contemporary moral codes. Sixty years later, Hawthorne, among the American practitioners of Romanticism, continued Inchbald's transformation of the romance form, evoking similar precedents and adapting the Romantic moral romance sub-genre to the literary imperatives and agenda of his own era. Hawthorne's experimental tales suggest closer deliberative ties with British writers like Inchbald and a continuum of literary experimentation with genre that reaches forward to the modern and symbolic novel as developed by writers like Henry James.

This study of the Romantic moral romance developed by Inchbald and Hawthorne briefly evokes some of Inchbald's plays (especially her experimental dramatic adaptation *Lovers' Vows*), her published prefaces on British drama, one of Hawthorne's short stories, his prefaces to his romances, and his three completed romances, *Fanshawe* (1828), *The House of the Seven Gables* (1851) and *The*

Blithedale Romance (1852). The discussion focuses primarily on *A Simple Story, Nature and Art, The Scarlet Letter* and *The Marble Faun* as Inchbald's and Hawthorne's best-known and most representative books. In the succeeding chapters, after discussions of the transatlantic connections between the two authors and after a discussion of the authors' intentions and motivations, the four primary texts are juxtaposed first in separate pairs and then as a group to demonstrate how Inchbald and Hawthorne experimented in such revolutionary terms with the very forms and purposes of fiction writing and how, by probing the limits of Romantic fiction in their attempts to avoid writing traditional novels in favour of writing new fiction for their Romantic Era, they can be seen as contributing ironically, but significantly, to the evolution of the modern symbolic novel.

The discussion in Chapter 1 explores the transatlantic relationship between Inchbald and Hawthorne, solidifying the connection between the two by focusing first on common influences that may have inflected the evolution of their fiction. Both were familiar with mediaeval chivalric romance forms and probably had some knowledge of the French *conte moral*, or moral tale. These older forms likely provided common sources for Inchbald and Hawthorne in terms of their allegorical potential and their use of simplified characters. Moreover, both authors knew the Gothic genre very well – Inchbald through her association with the Godwin circle, and Hawthorne through his admiration of Gothic writers like William Godwin and Charles Brockden Brown. Both authors were familiar with other Gothic novel writers such as Ann Radcliffe, Matthew Lewis and Mary Shelley, whose dark, transgressive fictions so significantly altered the Romantic spirit on both sides of the Atlantic, providing yet another common source for the Romantic moral romance. Indeed, Inchbald was a significant figure in London in the Godwin/Shelley circle, whose revolutionary ideas, promulgated particularly by Godwin and Mary Wollstonecraft, established much of the groundwork in the 1790s for the British Romanticism that so profoundly influenced Hawthorne's intellectual milieu. Finally, this chapter turns specifically to Inchbald and her popularity and influence both in Britain and America during and just prior to Hawthorne's lifetime. As first an actor and then a playwright who wrote over twenty plays, Inchbald became an important figure in British culture during the final two decades of the eighteenth century, and her ideas formed part of the current of British Romantic thought that was to influence American writers like Hawthorne in the decades that followed.[12] Most of Inchbald's plays were produced repeatedly in London, and many of them were published soon afterward, with some of them being reprinted several times within a given year. *A Simple Story* and *Nature and Art*, Inchbald's two Romantic moral romances, also achieved great success, and, in fact, as of 2009, the former book has never been out of print. Inchbald's plays and two romances were so popular that they appeared rapidly in America, where enterprising publishers reprinted them (undoubtedly without permission and without paying royalties) before the texts were sold to American readers and to the many circulating libraries that provided reading material to a large segment of the public that could not afford to buy the volumes. Even the critical material that Inchbald wrote for such collections as *The British Theatre* appeared in America, where Hawthorne and his contemporaries had ready access to them. Moreover, many of Inchbald's plays were produced in the former American colonies, particularly *Lovers' Vows*, whose inflammatory subject matter paralleled many of the themes in her two Romantic moral romances.

After this survey of common sources for the Romantic moral romance and of Inchbald's direct and indirect influence on American writers of Hawthorne's era, Chapter 2 examines the two authors' divergent intentions in experimenting with the novel and romance forms and with developing their particularly Romantic versions before moving to a tentative definition of their alternative sub-genre. Attention to both authors' prefaces and to the contexts in which they wrote reveals that Inchbald and Hawthorne, though motivated for different reasons, essentially positioned themselves in opposition to the same cultural construct – the tradition of the British novel. By the late eighteenth century, the British novel was established as a popular genre with its own traditions and broad readership – and its own critics among those who found it to be an immoral influence on impressionable young women. Moreover, although a few male writers had attained success with the genre, the novel had become associated with frivolous writing by women because women writers had been attracted to the classless freedom they perceived in the narrative structure and domestic subject matter of the genre.[13] Inchbald, conscious of the reputation of the novel as a genre and perhaps in agreement with its critics, avoids publicly labelling her books novels and instead calls them *stories* and *little histories*, terms that Roberta Krueger points out often were used to describe mediaeval romances.[14] Using narrative techniques derived from her background in drama, Inchbald appropriates elements of the mediaeval chivalric romance form to construct tales whose depictions of passion and use of fable-like symbolism suggest dramatic character types with the ostensible didactic purpose of reforming attitudes on education. In the process, she also creates a legitimate, acceptable form of women's writing that circumvents the imputed immorality of the British novel.

In contrast, Hawthorne had no such qualms about the morality of the novel genre. His concern, founded on a longstanding sense of American cultural insecurity, an insecurity that was further reinforced by contemporaries of his like Ralph Waldo Emerson and Henry Wadsworth Longfellow, was that the novel was too British.[15] In the first half of the nineteenth century, the United States remained a relatively young nation, and although the country had emerged triumphantly from both the Revolutionary War and the War of 1812, Americans still worried that British cultural ascendance could weaken the developing identity of the United States as a fully independent nation. Hence, Hawthorne, too, developed his romances with dramatic techniques, symbolic character-types and allegorical potential akin to that used in fables, myths and legends. His desire was the creation, or at least the further development, of a uniquely American literature, as opposed to British literature, so, preferring to call his books *romances*, he avoided the term *novel* nearly as much as Inchbald had done half a century earlier. In a discussion of the French prose romance, Norris Lacy contrasts the mediaeval romance form with the novel, which 'tends generally toward a more linear structure, with direct links between cause and effect, with character providing the main impetus for narrative developments, and with an emphasis, unknown to earlier periods, on individual psychology'.[16] Inchbald's and Hawthorne's experimental sub-genre retains these primary characteristics of the novel – linear structure, clear sequences of cause and effect, emphasis on psychology – but incorporates the idealism, symbolism and moral interest of the traditional mediaeval romance, and even of the French moral tale.

Chapter 3 discusses the evocation of Shakespearean precedent in Inchbald's and Hawthorne's romances, especially in their adaptation of the experimental romance genre of Shakespeare's last plays. The Romantic moral romance form depended heavily on the continuing influence of Shakespearean drama, with which both Inchbald and Hawthorne were intimately familiar, in Anglo-American literature.[17] Both Inchbald and Hawthorne borrowed techniques from *The Tempest*, *Cymbeline* and *The Winter's Tale*, Shakespeare's later plays in which a unique experimental blending of genres, also based on mediaeval chivalric precedent, results in tragicomedy. Through this unusual blend that tends to emphasize the potential for tragic resolution, Shakespeare challenges conceptions of moral order, involving, among other issues, the questioning of patriarchy and the sympathetic depiction of the 'fallen woman' as victim in anticipation of the way that Inchbald and Hawthorne position their characters in *A Simple Story* and *The Scarlet Letter*. The very structures of each of these narratives are tightly controlled, too, so that, just as *The Winter's Tale* can be split into distinct tragic and comedic sections, *A Simple Story* also splits into two halves, as does *The Scarlet Letter*, and this type of binary narrative structure parallels and reinforces the binary relationships between many of the pairs of characters.

As discussed in Chapter 4, Inchbald and Hawthorne go beyond Shakespeare's example to express the concerns of their era by questioning religious tradition and by exploring the issues of sin and guilt at the individual and social levels. Specifically, *Nature and Art* and *The Marble Faun* contrast individual faith or religious belief with religious social practice in Anglicanism, Catholicism and Puritanism, questioning the moral order prescribed by these three established religious traditions. A Catholic who lived in a repressive Anglican state, especially at a time when the French, also officially Catholic, threatened invasion, Inchbald retained an acute awareness of the disparity between the tolerance and love that the Anglican religion taught and the actual practice of that religion in England. Hawthorne experienced no such official religious repression, but as a native of the originally Puritan town of Salem – notorious for the witchcraft trials of 1692 – he did sense the repressiveness and effeteness of Puritanism in providing viable solutions to the problems of mundane existence. With such negative experiences surrounding religious practice in their lives, Inchbald and Hawthorne had ample incentive to question the effectiveness of organized religion in their romances. *Nature and Art* casts the elder William Norwynne, a clergyman, as a foolish political animal who, concerned with nothing more than his own advancement within the Anglican Church, shuns his brother Henry in favour of society dinners that offer him chances to flatter his bishop; William's son, also named William, may be seen as a further indictment of the moral order of his father's Anglicanism because, as a judge, he participates in the secular functions of the Anglican state; and Hannah Primrose's end in a gruesome execution censures the church because both father and son are complicit in her doom. Likewise, *The Marble Faun* declaims against the ineffectiveness of Puritan doctrine since its tenets provide no solace to the innocent Hilda, who witnesses a murder. Even the Italian Catholicism that pervades the book, although it eventually relieves Hilda's guilt, does not provide meaningful answers to how Donatello and Miriam can manage the inherited guilt for the sins of their ancient families.

Inchbald and Hawthorne further expand their experimentation with romance forms in their depictions of the fragmented Romantic psyche, as discussed in Chapter 5. Using the contrast between nature and art in *A Simple Story*, *Nature and Art*, *The Scarlet Letter* and *The Marble Faun*, they construct tetrads of characters whose shallow development casts them as character-types or figures rather than believable human beings. John Stevens and Roberta Krueger note that the traditional romance tended to idealize experience, and Inchbald's and Hawthorne's Romantic moral romance appropriates this idealizing quality to apply to its characters.[18] Inchbald and Hawthorne create simplified figures who represent individual elements of a single psyche, both in dyadic opposition – or conjunction – with one another and in more complex tetradic relationships. These characters exist as deliberately simplified entities whom readers would have difficulty imagining as existing beyond the confines of the texts in which they appear, but their simplicity is deceptive since Inchbald and Hawthorne are interested primarily in how these characters, *in combination*, negotiate their relationships with one another. For instance, contrasting the naturalness of one character with the artfulness of another in *Nature and Art* allows Inchbald to uphold the primacy of nature over art, ostensibly suggesting, as Jean-Jacques Rousseau had done, that the noble savage is superior in many ways to the cultivated, civilized gentleman.[19] Only the juxtaposition of the two characters can reveal the primary motivations behind their actions, allowing a subjective judgement of the superiority of one over the other, but ironically, Inchbald uses the very art that she denigrates to engender these deceptively simplistic figures so that while ostensibly favouring nature, she actually approaches the nature/art dichotomy as a continuum rather than as a simple dichotomy. Hawthorne does the same in his fictions. The fragmentary characters become quasi-allegorical representations of social and political concerns that were contemporary to Inchbald's and Hawthorne's composition of their tales, and the passionate, emotional and often single-minded wilfulness that the characters demonstrate acts as a way for the authors to represent moral 'truth' for the individual in opposition to established social convention. The fragmented Romantic psyche thus becomes a means for both authors to promulgate their own ideas of individual moral order that will allow the full expression of female writing and the development of distinctively American literature.

Finally, a brief conclusion clarifies the tentative definition of the Romantic moral romance advanced in Chapter 2 by presenting a list of specific criteria, as elaborated in Chapters 3, 4 and 5, that help to define the experimental sub-genre. The criteria show that fiction written by Inchbald or Hawthorne was revolutionary in theme and form, that both writers ultimately wrote similar types of fiction, and that the self-reflexivity of the Romantic moral romance questioned the very nature and purpose of literary art. The conclusion also briefly speculates on the way the Romantic moral romance helped to shape subsequent permutations of the novel in English.

Despite the apparent incongruity of pairing Elizabeth Inchbald and Nathaniel Hawthorne for this study of Romantic fiction, in fact, both writers and their works complement one another exceptionally well. Modifying earlier and simpler examples of mediaeval chivalric romance and moral tale, and drawing on Shakespeare's experimentation with the romance form in his last plays, both Inchbald and Hawthorne set out to create a new mixed sub-genre for their own purposes. While their intentions were divergent, their results were remarkably similar as they enacted a metamorphosis of the novel and the romance into a particularly Romantic form of narrative expression in their fiction, recasting the symbolic and allegorical potential of existing genres. The result was a unique type of fiction that blended symbol and allegorical figures for its effect, probing psychological motivation in terms of the divided psyche and the burdens of sin and guilt, and challenging readers' conceptions of moral order on multiple levels. Although Inchbald's and Hawthorne's works lie over half a century apart in terms of publication dates and are separated from one another in both geographical and cultural terms, the two authors' books nevertheless suggest an undeniable transatlantic relationship and connection to the development and traditions of Romantic fiction, acting as important links between eighteenth- and nineteenth-century fiction and the modern, symbolic novel. Indeed, the sub-genre developed by Inchbald and Hawthorne likely helped to deflect the evolution of the modern novel into a more symbolic and more psychologically motivated arena.

1. 'WRITTEN IN A STYLE TO ENDURE': COMMON SOURCES FOR THE ROMANTIC MORAL ROMANCE AND THE IMPACT OF INCHBALD'S TRANSATLANTIC REPUTATION[1]

> I have now a sight of this new world ...
>
> – Charlotte Lennox[2]

Inchbald's and Hawthorne's works complement one another well because of the remarkable similarities in their effects, patterns and resolutions. That the two writers produced experimental texts, in both form and subject matter, should be no surprise since both participated in the intellectual ferment of the Romantic Era, whose ideas began to spread from Britain to the former American colonies during the late decades of the eighteenth century. What may be surprising, however, is the extent of Inchbald's and Hawthorne's parallel development, as they experiment and move beyond the traditional bounds of the novel genre in their works, of such similar fictions in the Romantic moral romance. Each writer experiments consciously with the romance and novel forms for unique reasons, and each is aware of the traditions at issue in their individual reformulations of the revered genres. Nevertheless, despite the differences between the two authors' fictions and their motivations for writing these fictions, the creative consequence is a hybrid sub-genre that uses and adapts features of both the mediaeval chivalric romance and the contemporary bourgeois novel for its unique form. The similarities are prevalent enough to suggest not just some commonality of tradition and purpose but a possible line of influence between the two authors, and although there is no proof that Inchbald influenced Hawthorne directly, the historical evidence suggests a strong possibility. Regardless, the Romantic moral romance connects Inchbald and Hawthorne despite their individual differences and despite the decades and geography that separate them, even as it places them within one contiguous Romantic Period in British and American literature.

This chapter explores some of the cultural associations and literary connections that link Inchbald and Hawthorne so as to describe a common intellectual climate in which their experimental narrative could arise, in parallel development and not merely coincidentally, on each side of the Atlantic Ocean. The first part of the chapter examines how each author's works fit into, respectively, British and American versions of Romanticism. Then, the chapter touches briefly on the chivalric romance as a common source for both writers and on the moral tale as another possible link. The Gothic novel – a more modern form of romance – as another common source is the next focus, with reference to Matthew Lewis's *The Monk*, followed by an examination of the Godwin/Shelley circle as yet another possible link between Inchbald and Hawthorne. Inchbald shared many ideas in common with William Godwin and Mary Wollstonecraft, whose ideas expressed in works like *Caleb Williams* and *A Vindication of the Rights of Woman* exerted tremendous influence on the Romantic Movement; and both Inchbald's and Hawthorne's fictions bear remarkable similarities with Mary Shelley's short tales and *Frankenstein* and with Percy Shelley's *The Cenci*. After exploring these parallels, the chapter moves to a discussion of Inchbald's reputation in Britain and in America – as an actor, a playwright and a prose writer – to establish the extent of Inchbald's international reputation. During the 1780s, theatre managers Thomas Harris and George Colman (the Elder) repeatedly engaged Inchbald as an actor in London, and later, they produced her plays to great public acclaim at the Covent Garden and Haymarket theatres. A significant number of her plays saw the stage at the Drury Lane Theatre as well. Publishers reprinted the plays, sometimes reissuing a given play several times during a single year, and when Inchbald produced *A Simple Story* and *Nature and Art*, the books gained great popularity, in part, as a result of Inchbald's existing reputation with the theatre. Indeed, by the turn of the century, Inchbald had become an established and internationally-recognized figure. While publishers continued to reprint her plays and books, they also sought her contributions to their periodicals and other editorial and critical projects. Inchbald's theatrical and publishing reputations thus ensured her a permanent and influential position in the continuing evolution of British Romantic thought, and that position made her a visible figure in Hawthorne's America, where theatre managers arranged performances of her plays (like *Lovers' Vows*, a version of which Hawthorne saw performed) well into the nineteenth century and where publishers enthusiastically reprinted her plays, fictions and literary criticism. American circulating libraries, for example, held copies of Inchbald's plays and her fictions. Given the high level of cultural permeation in Britain and America of Inchbald's works and of her theatrical reputation during the Romantic Period, Inchbald would have been familiar to most writers of the time, including, no doubt, American authors like Hawthorne, who wrote within a tradition of American Romantic thought that had been profoundly influenced by the long-established British movement.

The Romantic Context

One of the most obvious connections that binds the works of Inchbald and Hawthorne is their emergence from similar literary contexts. Both authors participated in the intellectual ferment of Romanticism that took hold in Britain while making a transatlantic migration to influence American writers.

Scholars once sited the beginning of Romanticism in England around 1798 when William Wordsworth and Samuel Taylor Coleridge published the first edition of *Lyrical Ballads*, but that demarcation has received intense scrutiny in recent decades by scholars who have argued for earlier beginning dates.[3] After all, older definitions of English Romanticism concentrated on the works of the so-called Big Six – William Wordsworth, Samuel Taylor Coleridge, William Blake, Percy Shelley, John Keats and Lord Byron – all male poets. A large body of recent scholarship, however, has tended to agitate for greater inclusiveness of, for example, fiction writers and women writers in the canon. Newer scholarship includes more discussion of poems by the likes of Charlotte Smith or Mary Robinson, of fiction by Elizabeth Inchbald or Ann Radcliffe or of plays by Joanna Baillie or Sophia Lee. The greater inclusiveness of recent scholarship has tended to encourage expansion in the chronology of British Romanticism. Indeed, some scholars have argued in favour of a Romantic century, spanning from 1750 to 1850.[4] This study adopts the dates used by Anne Mellor and Richard Matlak for their mammoth anthology of British Romanticism – 1780 to 1830 – as a convenient means of defining the period chronologically.[5] Inchbald's two books, published in 1791 and 1796, fit well into this range.

The same problem of chronology arises in defining American versions of Romanticism. If American Romanticism developed largely as a result of the migration of British ideas across the Atlantic, and if defining the onset of British Romanticism is problematic, then deciding when to site the beginning of the American Romantic Movement also is a troublesome task – as is deciding on an ending date for the period. In general terms, most scholars agree that American Romanticism reached its apex shortly after British Romanticism had begun to wane, and most agree that the American Civil War (1860–5) effectively ended the period by ushering in a new era of realism. The 1985 Frye, Baker and Perkins *Harper Handbook to Literature* places American Romanticism roughly within the years from 1820 to 1860, while Jeanne Smoot, writing about American Romantic fiction in 2008, suggests 1820 to 1865.[6] As either range of years includes the publication dates of Hawthorne's *The Scarlet Letter* and *The Marble Faun* – 1850 and 1860, respectively – this study will adopt the more recent one to define the period.

Chronological ranges are, however, far from adequate in defining literary periods or the works that fit into those periods. Just because two authors lived or wrote during a particular time does not mean that their works necessarily fit neatly with the works of their contemporaries. Nor does it mean automatically that the two authors' works relate to one another very closely.[7] Jane Austen's novels fit squarely into British Romanticism chronologically, but the sensibilities expressed in them tend to be more Victorian, so Romanticists often exclude Austen's work from their canon. Hence, literary periods are more accurately defined in terms of the features that characterize texts written by the majority of authors whose works have endured into the present. Chronologies come later – after scholars have found the commonalities among authors' works.

The question that still remains is how Inchbald's and Hawthorne's romances fit respectively into British and American versions of Romanticism. That Hawthorne is an American Romantic is a commonplace in American literary scholarship. For example, Frye, Baker and Perkins classify Hawthorne as Romantic along with the likes of Washington Irving, James Fenimore Cooper, Ralph Waldo Emerson, Edgar Allan Poe, Henry David Thoreau, Herman Melville and Walt Whitman.[8] Inchbald, however, sometimes is considered an eighteenth-century writer whose fictions are novels of sensibility. Patricia Meyer Spacks makes a convincing case for such an interpretation of *A Simple Story* in *Privacy: Concealing the Eighteenth-Century Self*, although she argues that the book is more about the concealment of emotion rather than, as in most novels of sensibility, its expression.[9] But despite clear connections with the novel of sensibility, Inchbald's romances exhibit more characteristics of Romantic writing – as do Hawthorne's romances. Frye, Baker and Perkins suggest five general features that characterize both British and American Romantic writing – emphasis on the individual, belief in human goodness and perfectibility, interest in primitivism and the noble savage, belief in egalitarianism and belief in the value of emotion and intuition.[10] Both Inchbald's and Hawthorne's works exhibit all five of these features as dominating characteristics of the narratives. Margaret Drabble's definition of British Romanticism adds other features such as interest in the sublime and emotion, in the infinite and transcendental, in revolution and nonconformity and in progressivism and the processes of creativity.[11] James Hart's definition of American Romanticism in *The Oxford Companion to American Literature* further mentions introspection, idealization of the common and interest in the past, remote places and the Gothic.[12] Essentially, British and American versions of Romanticism shared many of the same characteristics, and Inchbald's and Hawthorne's works exhibit these features in abundance.

The features of Romantic writing are evident throughout *A Simple Story* and *Nature and Art*. In both books, Inchbald symbolically argues in favour of egalitarianism in terms of how protagonists like Miss Milner and Hannah Primrose are treated. She suggests that they deserve greater control over their own fates and that at the cores of their personalities, despite any flaws they may

exhibit, they are essentially good people. Because Miss Milner's negative treatment of Dorriforth is her only means of expressing her desires openly, readers
are meant to sympathize with her plight. At the same time, the characters resist
conventional women's roles in favour of developing themselves as individuals
whose emotions provide greater truths than conventional wisdom. Hannah's
emotional decision not to kill her newborn child legitimizes the child's right
to live despite his illegitimate origin. Inchbald seems to privilege the primitive
and the noble savage in characters like Matilda and especially the two Henrys.
Matilda is so simple-minded that she willingly agrees to become a prisoner in
her own father's mansion in recompense for a crime she did not commit, and
the two Henrys engage in naïve behaviour that clearly links them with the noble
savage. Moreover, both *A Simple Story* and *Nature and Art* engage symbolically
with the creative processes by which they are written, and both privilege progres-
siveness and introspection as well as interest in the past, remote places and even
the Gothic. Lord Elmwood's trip to the West Indies and the Henrys' voyage to
Africa allow Inchbald to evoke the exoticism of foreign lands, while Matilda's
kidnapping by Lord Margrave suggests a hint of Gothicism.

The Scarlet Letter and *The Marble Faun* present readers with the same types
of features. Hester Prynne's refusal to name Pearl's father emphasizes the strength
of her sense of individuality as well as her sense of nonconformity, and Hilda's
willingness to betray her Puritan heritage does the same. Despite the two characters' failings, readers are meant to sympathize with both of them because at
their cores, they are essentially good, and their ill deeds, even when experienced
vicariously as in Hilda's case, are merely nonconformist, emotional attempts to
find some version of 'truth'. Noble savage features appear in the characters of
Pearl and Donatello, both of whom are compared with wild animals or spirits
separated from the conventional sphere of human endeavour. Their personalities
suggest the value of the sublime and of the transcendental. Hawthorne's interest
in the remote past is clear in his use of Puritan culture in *The Scarlet Letter* and in
his emphasis on Italy's past in *The Marble Faun*. Gothicism is present in the latter
book in the scenes set in the catacombs and in the church graveyard, as well as
in the twisted personality of the Model. Finally, both *The Scarlet Letter* and *The
Marble Faun* symbolically privilege egalitarianism as they examine the creative
processes of the American writer who seeks a viable means of self-expression in
response to the tradition of the British novel.

These and other features clearly situate Inchbald's fictions and Hawthorne's as
part of the current of Romantic thought that developed in England from French
and German sources and made its way to America. The discussion in the succeeding chapters will solidify these two authors' placement within Romanticism
by examining these features in more detail while clarifying the extent to which
Romanticism was a transatlantic phenomenon with far-reaching effects. Addi-

tionally, the following chapters' clarifications of these features will help to explain how the Romantic moral romance is a particularly Romantic form of writing.

Common Sources in the Mediaeval Chivalric Romance

In part, British and American versions of Romanticism developed similarly because of their mutual transatlantic influence. In addition, they evolved upon similar lines as a result of common sources for the ideas that defined the literary movements. Both British and American writers tended to idealize the legendary past and to draw upon artistic productions of the distant past, whether fictional or not, to create their own literature. Michael O'Neill describes romance and English Romantic poetry as 'decisively twinned, living one another's life' and discusses the use of romance features in Samuel Taylor Coleridge's *The Rime of the Ancient Mariner* and in Keats's *Endymion, Isabella, The Eve of St Agnes* and *Lamia*.[13] Lord Byron's *Marino Faliero* uses an old story as its basis, as does Percy Shelley's *The Cenci*. All these writers produced their most important work after Inchbald had written her books, so they would not have influenced her writing. However, their reliance on old legends and stories hints at how popular such tales became during the period. Across the Atlantic, Americans were doing the same. Washington Irving and James Fenimore Cooper culled from old legends for their tales, sometimes delving into Native-American lore, and Hawthorne is well known for his borrowing from America's colonial and Native-American past.

For the Romantic moral romance, Inchbald and Hawthorne seem to have reached back to the mediaeval chivalric romance for inspiration. Both authors were aware of the conventions of the chivalric romance, if not directly, then through their reading of the likes of William Shakespeare and contemporary Romantics who borrowed heavily from the chivalric romance tradition. Indeed, the chivalric romance – and an interest in chivalry in general – experienced a resurgence in popularity in England during the Romantic Period, and those ideas retained their importance as Romanticism made its way across the Atlantic. As early as 1784 in London, Jean-Baptiste St-Palaye published *Memoirs of Ancient Chivalry*, a detailed description of the traditions and values associated with knighthood and consequently the romances in which knights appeared.[14] A number of chivalric romances were reprinted during the succeeding years. In 1791, for example, Joseph Ritson edited a collection of *Pieces of Ancient Popular Poetry* and felt it necessary to apologize in his preface for not including chivalric tales about Robin Hood because the plethora of such stories made choosing specific ones difficult.[15] In 1810, Henry Weber published a three-volume edition of 'ancient English romances' like *Richard Coeur de Lion*, and seven years later, Edward Utterson collected two volumes of, as he termed them, 'romances of chivalry'.[16] Utterson's two volumes are even illustrated, including a number of engravings of knights jousting and riding with great pomp on caparisoned horses. Other collections appeared in 1828 with William Thomas's *A Collection of Early Prose Romances*, including tales of knights and of Robin Hood, and in 1848, with George Ellis's *Specimens of Early English Metrical Romances*.[17] Ellis included the popular romances *Guy of Warwick* and *Richard Coeur de Lion* among his selections – both of which had been adapted as plays in Inchbald's England.

In each case, editors acknowledged the Continental origins of many English romances and especially credited the French for providing sources for much of the material. Indeed, in a section of the fifty-volume *The British Novelists* series of 1810 called 'On the Origin and Progress of Novel-Writing', Anna Letitia Barbauld devotes many pages to discussing French fiction and to situating chivalric romance – primarily originating from France and Spain – as the novel's precursor.[18] While some scholars, such as Lennard Davis, would argue that the novel and the romance are separate entities unto themselves, many others argue just the opposite. Davis finds 'a discursive chasm between these two forms' and says that '[t]he romance seems so utterly unlike the novel as to be unrelated'.[19] However, he then concedes that the forms may have influenced one another. Most scholars are more likely to agree with Barbauld.[20] One of the best-known early discussions of romance comes from Clara Reeve's *The Progress of Romance* of 1785, in which the author credits the French with reviving prose romances and flatly states that chivalry is 'the substance of romance'.[21] Reeve distinguishes between novel and romance as separate genres but acknowledges that they share features.[22] In fact, Reeve claims of the romance that 'the modern Novel sprung up out of its ruins'.[23] Writing in 2000, Caroline Jewers casts the mediaeval romance as 'part of the blueprint, if not a vital cornerstone, of the novel's foundation', and Patrick Parrinder, in his 2006 book *Nation & Novel*, links the novel's ancestry solidly with that of the romance and comments that in 'the background to the novel are the romances of knight-errantry'.[24]

Even had Inchbald and Hawthorne not been familiar with sources from the likes of St-Palaye and Ritson, they certainly would have been familiar with romance tropes from the works of their French and English contemporaries, from the works of Shakespeare (discussed in detail in Chapter 3), and from the works of earlier writers. Inchbald was especially interested in French authors – who often used chivalric romance features in their works – and Hawthorne certainly did not neglect them.[25] John Dunkley points out that Voltaire's most popular play, *Zaïre*, a play that Inchbald saw performed in Paris, included mediaeval chivalric elements, as did the plays of Pierre-Laurent Buirette de Belloy, at least one of which Inchbald saw in Paris.[26] Inchbald knew the Shelleys, whose work borrowed romance features, and she acted in numerous productions of Shakespeare's plays, including the late romances. She was familiar with Jean-Jacques Rousseau, whose novel *Julie, ou la nouvelle Héloïse* was still extremely popular – a novel that, as Anna Letitia Barbauld notes, borrowed heavily from romance tradition.[27] Indeed, G. J. Barker-Benfield quotes a letter from John Philip Kemble to Inchbald that clearly indicates a familiarity with chivalric romance in Inchbald's social circles. Barker-Benfield notes,

> When Inchbald first began *A Simple Story* in 1778, Kemble asked her, 'Pray how far are you advanced in your new novel? – what new characters have you in it – what situations? how many distressed damsels and valorous knights? how many prudes, how many coquettes? what libertines, what sentimental rogues in black and empty cut-throats in red?'.[28]

Hawthorne, as voracious a reader as Inchbald, read Shelley's *The Cenci*, was intimately familiar with Shakespeare's work and also read Rousseau, including *La nouvelle Héloïse*.[29] He read the romance-inspired works of Keats and Byron as well.[30] Both authors were likely familiar with Henry Fielding's *Joseph Andrews* (1742), a novel written, according to its title page, 'in Imitation of The *Manner* of CERVANTES', and with Charlotte Lennox's *The Female Quixote* (1752), which, as Deborah Ross argues, merged features of novel and romance even while it satirized the romance form.[31] Indeed, Hawthorne had read the original *Don Quixote*.[32] Despite the later two books' parody of the chivalric romance, based on Cervantes's parody, they employed a large number of romance features themselves. William Godwin's *Caleb Williams* appeared in 1794, and although it, too, questioned the codes of chivalry and romance, it also kept readers aware of the traditions.

Earlier British literature also affected the likes of Inchbald and Hawthorne. Both surely were familiar with earlier English works based on the romance tradition like *Sir Gawain and the Green Knight*, which A. C. Gibbs refers to as 'the supreme English example of the chivalric romance', and Edmund Spenser's famous adaptation of chivalric romance themes, *The Faerie Queene*.[33] Indeed, biographer James Mellow notes that *The Faerie Queene* was among Hawthorne's favourite tales.[34] Moreover, it is certain that chivalric Arthurian legends provided some inspiration for Hawthorne. In an unpublished dissertation, Edlynn Zimmerman traces many Arthurian connections with Hawthorne's work.[35] Indeed, one of Hawthorne's early stories, published in 1843 and entitled 'The Antique Ring', takes as its central image an old ring that supposedly once belonged to Merlin. The tale is set in England, and at one point in the story, the narrator mentions Posthumus and Imogen in what probably is an allusion to Shakespeare's romance play *Cymbeline*.[36] Alan and Barbara Lupack reference the story in *King Arthur in America*, a book that acknowledges the 'tremendous appeal of the Arthurian legends in America'.[37] In England, Arthurian romances were, as Patrick Parrinder refers to them, among the 'central English myths'.[38] Thomas Malory's *Morte d'Arthur* had collected a number of them, and such romances became, Parrinder argues, 'the traditional source of ideas of chivalry for English writers'.[39] Inchbald could not have been unaware of them, and consciously or not, American writers inherited the same source.

Inchbald and Hawthorne clearly were aware of chivalric romance traditions, but perhaps the most important features of the chivalric romance in terms of their own works were the genre's emphases on symbolism and on moral order and individuality. Because the chivalric romance often depicted a knight on a righteous quest that might lead to his own enlightenment or growth as a human being, the genre easily lent itself to symbolic interpretation. Northrop Frye's hint about the genre's allegorical potential is germane here, for the knight's journey could be interpreted as emblematic of the soul's journey through temptations on its way to the afterlife.[40] Indeed, chivalry itself, as Jean-Baptiste St-Palaye argues 'tended to promote order and good morals', and scholar Helen Cooper points out the importance of 'the individual hero's inward thoughts, feelings, and aspirations' in the genre.[41]

As a number of critics have noted, however, the chivalric romance questioned the very moral orders that it ostensibly tried to protect.[42] The chivalric romance's interests in symbolism, in the individual's psychological development and in the development and challenging of moral order are important features of the Romantic moral romance as Inchbald and Hawthorne developed the sub-genre. As subsequent chapters will show, *A Simple Story*, *Nature and Art*, *The Scarlet Letter* and *The Marble Faun*, as Romantic moral romances, borrow these features from the chivalric romance. In all four books, the authors question the existing moral orders to posit alternative, individual moral orders for their characters. To create realistic moral orders for the characters, Inchbald challenges church and state in *A Simple Story* and *Nature and Art,* and Hawthorne challenges the two religious traditions of Puritanism and Catholicism in *The Scarlet Letter* and *The Marble Faun.* All four books also are concerned with the preservation or creation of independent senses of individuality. With Miss Milner and Matilda in *A Simple Story*, for example, Inchbald questions woman's ability to be truly individual without the benefits of education based on reason and logic. For Hawthorne, Hester Prynne from *The Scarlet Letter* challenges her culture's rules about sexual conduct and about the concealment of truth. In the cases of both Inchbald and Hawthorne, the books symbolically interrogate the status of the author – the woman author for Inchbald and the American author for Hawthorne.

Common Sources in the French Moral Tale

The mediaeval chivalric romance, directly or indirectly, provided a common basis for Inchbald's and Hawthorne's experimentation with Romantic fiction, and while the chivalric romance's origins in France provide a Continental connection that binds the two authors' works, yet another genre – the moral tale or *conte moral* – may have provided another common Continental source.

Moral tales certainly were not a new development in Anglo-European thought. Biblical parables had long held an important place, and fables were nearly as important. Indeed, Arnold Kettle classifies John Bunyan's *Pilgrim's Progress* as a moral fable and suggests that it provides 'the link between the medi-aeval allegory and the moral fable of the eighteenth century'.[43] Patricia Meyer Spacks recognizes allegorical features of Bunyan's work in the eighteenth-century novel in English, and F. O. Matthiessen comments of Hawthorne that 'the favorites of his childhood, Spenser and Bunyan, rose again to the surface when he began to write, and helped determine his bias to allegory'.[44] In fact, Robert Stanton suggests that some of the scenes in *The Scarlet Letter* echo similar scenes in *Pilgrim's Progress* and indicates that Hawthorne may have employed John Bunyan's example also in *The House of the Seven Gables* and *The Blithedale Romance*.[45] Inchbald may have read Bunyan's example, and even if not, she was familiar with other types of moral tales. She frequently read sermons, theological treatises and other religious material, so she would have had a ready knowledge of biblical parables at the very least.

Both authors would have been familiar, too, with recent literary developments in France. French literature in general exerted a strong influence on British literature – and, consequently, American literature as well – during the late eighteenth and early nineteenth centuries. Indeed, much earlier, French language and culture profoundly altered the British cultural landscape following the Norman Conquest that began with the Battle of Hastings in 1066. T. G. Tucker argues that the English experienced an intense period of French literary influence, especially from chivalric romances, shortly thereafter between 1100 and 1370.[46] He also cites the years 1660 to 1780 as showing heavy French influence, although Alfred Upham makes a case for strong French influence in the fifteenth and sixteenth centuries as well.[47] One French critic, Paul Morillot, writes that French and English novels exhibited strong characteristics of one another throughout the eighteenth century, especially in terms of the novels' interests in realism, psychology and the moral qualities of art, and he argues that the moral tale essentially developed into the novel.[48]

Critics writing more recently, such as William Calin, have emphasized the mediaeval French influence in England, while others, like Frédéric Ogée, have concentrated on French Enlightenment currents in English literature.[49] Still others, such as Peter Mortensen, have connected the French even more closely with English writers.[50] Mortensen argues, for example, that British author Matthew Lewis was typical of his contemporaries in being 'preoccupied, almost to the point of obsession, with political and literary developments on the European mainland'.[51] Interestingly, Maria Edgeworth, for whose manuscript of *Patronage*

Inchbald suggested revisions in 1814, published her own *Moral Tales* in 1801. Focusing on children, the stories nevertheless hint at the ongoing influence of Continental literature in England. Indeed, Janet Todd comments in *Women's Friendship in Literature*,

> [I]n the eighteenth century there was a back-and-forth relationship across the Channel that brought the two countries almost into one literary realm. Books of one nation were immediately translated and published in the other, creating a climate of mutual literary influence.[52]

In general terms, regardless of the time period, the French and English often borrowed from one another in creating literature and other forms of art. Hence, the probability that the French moral tale affected the Romantic moral romance, either directly or indirectly, is quite high.

Scholars often have compared Inchbald's work, in particular, with French literature, noticing a number of similarities in theme and style. G. L. Strachey notices enough French connections to call *A Simple Story* 'a descendant of the Tragedies of Racine' and to compare the style of *Nature and Art* with that of Stendhal.[53] He further notes of *A Simple Story* that '[t]he spirit of the eighteenth century is certainly present in the book, but it is the eighteenth century of France rather than of England' and classifies Inchbald 'among the followers of the French classical tradition'.[54] Terry Castle similarly argues that Inchbald 'is far more at home in a tradition that includes Prévost, Rousseau, Stendhal, Flaubert, and Proust, finally, than that of English sentimental fiction'.[55] Castle goes on to note that '[t]he influence of Rousseau is particularly striking' and argues that Miss Milner is 'like a character from a French novel who has strayed by accident into an English one'.[56] Indeed, biographer James Boaden reports that Inchbald attempted a translation of Rousseau's *Confessions*, so it is no surprise that a number of critics have compared Inchbald's writing with Rousseau's.[57] French critic Joseph Texte specifically mentions Inchbald as being heavily influenced by Rousseau, as do Samuel Chew and Richard Altick and Joseph Heidler.[58]

Ronald Rosbottom points out that the title of Rousseau's *Julie, ou la nouvelle Héloïse* was meant 'to recall one of Europe's great legends' – that of Héloïse and Abélard – and interestingly, Inchbald's *A Simple Story* has a strong connection to that same mediaeval story.[59] Pierre Abélard was a twelfth-century philosopher and logician who fell in love with his significantly younger student, Héloïse.[60] Eventually they married, but the secrecy with which they cloaked their relationship angered Héloïse's family, who thought Abélard had abandoned her, and they violently mutilated him. As Terry Castle points out, '[t]he charged guardian/ward relationship in *A Simple Story* at times resembles the teacher/pupil dyad of Saint-Preux and Julie in *La Nouvelle Héloïse*; Abelard and Heloise provide the larger intertextual link'.[61] Not only does the guardian/ward relationship between Inchbald's Dorriforth and Miss Milner reflect the teacher/pupil pattern of Héloïse and Abélard, but a large age difference separates Dorriforth from Miss Milner, even as his love similarly is forbidden because of his ecclesiastical profession. Indeed, as early as Chapter 5 of Book 1, Inchbald references the old story directly in *A Simple Story* when Lord Frederick Lawnly expresses his wish that Dorriforth could absolve him of his sins. Dorriforth warns Lawnly not to confess in the presence of ladies (especially Miss Milner) because he might be tempted to 'excite their compassion' by falsely confessing to sins he has not committed.[62] When Miss Milner laughs at Dorriforth's concern, Lord Frederick sarcastically recites the lines, 'From Abelard it came, / And Eloisa still must love the name'.[63] Although Dorriforth seems oblivious to the meaning behind the lines, Miss Milner is so embarrassed and 'shocked' by the implication that she opens a window and leans out to hide her discomfiture. Inchbald's allusion is pointed, for long before she published *A Simple Story*, she mentions in her diaries that she read Alexander Pope's poetic version of the story of Héloïse and Abélard on 27 April 1780, that she read a 'History' of the couple on 11 August 1780, that she read the 'Life of Abelard' on 30 March 1783 and that she finished 'Rousseaus Eloisa' (*Julie, ou la nouvelle Héloïse*) on 7 March 1788.[64] It seems clear that Inchbald had French precedents in mind as she composed her own work.

While mediaeval stories like that of Héloïse and Abélard may have provided some inspiration for Inchbald, and perhaps to a lesser degree for Hawthorne, the French moral tale might also have offered inspiration. Katherine Astbury points out that moral tales became extremely popular in the second half of the eighteenth century after Jean-François Marmontel proclaimed himself the inventor of the genre around the middle of the century.[65] Indeed, their popularity rose markedly after 1761 when Marmontel published *Contes moraux*, a collection of his tales that had been appearing in print individually since 1755. Josephine Grieder concludes, in her study of French translations in England, that Marmontel was the most popular French writer in England, and his 'entire output of fiction was continually translated and retranslated throughout the last four decades of the century'.[66] As Astbury characterizes them, moral tales such as Marmontel's used simplified narratives to provide realistic, practical principles by which readers could improve their lives, often in terms of 'a secularised, humanitarian set of values'.[67] Astbury highlights the didactic nature of the tales with her comment that they were 'specifically designed to illustrate a point and convince the reader of that point's truth'.[68]

Inchbald definitely was familiar with Marmontel's work in a general way, if not with the moral tales themselves. In her diary entry of 10 January 1783, she mentions seeing *The Lord of the Manor* at the theatre.[69] The play was an adaptation by John Burgoyne of Marmontel's *Silvain*, and it went through a number of performances that theatre season. As testament to her interest in Marmontel,

Inchbald borrowed his autobiography from a circulating library in 1807 and spent ten days poring over the volumes.[70] By this point it had been sixteen years since *A Simple Story* had been first published and eleven years for *Nature and Art*. Even so, Inchbald's reading at least hints at the possibility that she was familiar with Marmontel and his work during her earlier years. Indeed, Arnold Kettle refers to Inchbald, along with William Godwin, Maria Edgeworth and Hannah More, as practitioners of the 'moral fable', as he calls it, and he singles out *Nature and Art* as 'an intriguing example of the *genre*'.[71]

Whether Inchbald and Hawthorne had read moral tales is not certain, although the likelihood that they had is high. Both authors read widely, and the moral tale was so popular, particularly during Inchbald's most productive years, that both authors must have at least been aware of the genre. As later chapters will show, features of the moral tale appeared in the Romantic moral romance as Inchbald and Hawthorne developed the sub-genre. Even the title of *A Simple Story* suggests the simplified nature of the book. Both this first book and *Nature and Art* exhibit extremely simplified characterization and plotting that align them with the evolving tradition of the moral tale. Hawthorne's *The Scarlet Letter* and *The Marble Faun* exhibit the same ostensibly simple characteristics. The situations in which Inchbald and Hawthorne place their characters suggest alternative, secular sets of values that are more realistic than the idealized codes of conduct espoused by many of the authors' contemporaries. In a symbolic way, Inchbald and Hawthorne thus attempt to convince their readers that 'truths' – the 'truths' governing the definitions of woman writer and American writer, or the 'truths' governing definitions of proper behaviour – are constructs that can be revised. Even if Inchbald and Hawthorne did not borrow directly from the moral tale, they certainly employed many of the features of the genre in their work.

Common Sources in the Gothic Novel

Another of the important precursors to and links between the fictive works of Inchbald and Hawthorne is the genre of the Gothic novel, which British Romantic writers developed into a sophisticated form. The Romantic moral romance sub-genre often is characterized by an interest in the dark side of human experience, and Gothic novels provided a ready model from which Inchbald and Hawthorne could develop their own fiction. Mystery and terror, secret passages and supernatural phenomena, and violent and disturbing action are typical tropes of Gothic stories.[72] The action took place in gloomy, isolated landscapes, where a dark, tortured male villain subjected a beautiful and innocent maiden to sexual advances, often before discovering – or revealing – that he was the heroine's brother or father. The Gothic emphasis on irrationality focused the reader's attention on the evolving plot rather than on the characters, who rarely received extensive development. Significantly, as James Carson points out, Gothic writers were especially interested in liminal states of existence, and their own works were liminal in combining features of both novel and romance.[73]

Gothic tales began to gain popularity in Britain especially after the 1764 publication of Horace Walpole's *The Castle of Otranto*, a book that attempted a blending of genres and that went through eleven editions by century's end.[74] Walpole claims in the preface to the second edition to have intended to blend ancient and modern romance forms, but Robert Kiely points out that his ancient and modern categories '[correspond] roughly with the usual neoclassical distinction between romance and novel'.[75] The Romantic fascination with the darker side of humanity – including incest, murder, torture, emotional isolation and so forth – ensured the continued success and development of the Gothic genre. William Godwin's well-known *Caleb Williams* of 1794 aspired to be, simultaneously, Gothic romance and moral fiction, and Matthew Lewis's *The Monk*, whose inflammatory subject matter and purported moral purpose caused a sensation in Britain, appeared in 1796. Replete with magic potions, hidden identities, secret underground passages and ghostly apparitions, *The Monk* is one of the best, and best-known, examples of the Gothic genre. Later writers like Mary Shelley continued to develop the genre, and her short tales and novels, most notably *Frankenstein*, incorporated numerous Gothic elements.

Inchbald could hardly have avoided knowledge of popular Gothic novels of this time, and she undoubtedly would have been familiar with the most prominent examples of the genre even if only through conversations with her contemporaries. Indeed, Inchbald acted many times in *The Count of Narbonne*, Robert Jephson's 1781 adaptation of *The Castle of Otranto*.[76] The Gothic was so prevalent in Britain that Inchbald, consciously or not, incorporated Gothic features into her own fictions, and especially in *A Simple Story*. Certainly, Lord Elmwood's interdiction to his household from mentioning his daughter Matilda's name in his presence savours of the Gothic in the intensity of Elmwood's wilful irrationality, while Matilda's imprisonment in her wing of Elmwood House also has a Gothic quality in its relegation of womanhood to a mysterious, hidden cell whose door, in this case, is both locked and guarded by a servant.[77] Matilda's kidnapping and rescue at the end of the story, moreover, are laced with the popular Gothicism of the period. Annibel Jenkins classifies even the settings of books three and four of *A Simple Story* as 'obviously gothic'.[78]

Inchbald's relationship with the Jacobin Gothic writer William Godwin was at its highest point during the composition of *A Simple Story*, and Godwin's suggested revisions to the book likely added to its Gothicism.[79] Likewise, Inchbald's revision work on *Caleb Williams* would have increased her exposure to elements of the Gothic genre. In addition to retaining an awareness of Godwin's works, Inchbald could not have avoided some knowledge of Lewis's immensely popular

The Monk, one of whose main characters is named – significantly – Matilda. Although the book was published the same year as *Nature and Art*, and consequently could not have influenced either of Inchbald's books, *The Monk* does act as another conduit of influence between the British Romantics and their American counterparts, including Hawthorne. Furthermore, Mary Shelley's Gothic tales, although they were written well after *A Simple Story* and *Nature and Art*, serve as yet another British connection with American versions of Romanticism and writers like Hawthorne.

Hawthorne was an ardent admirer of Gothicism in its British and American incarnations, and perhaps more than Inchbald, he borrowed directly from the works of Godwin, Lewis, Mary Shelley and other writers who used Gothic traditions.[80] At an early age, he was an avid reader of Gothic novels, particularly of those written by Ann Radcliffe, Horace Walpole, William Godwin and Charles Brockden Brown (known as the 'Godwin of America').[81] Hawthorne also was familiar with *The Monk*.[82] Not surprisingly, Gothic qualities appear in his romances as another of his many connections to the British Romantic Movement. In *The House of the Seven Gables*, for example, a longstanding family curse ensures that the members of the old Pyncheon family die suddenly with blood oozing from their mouths. The ancient curse, the hidden identity of Holgrave (a descendant of the man who cursed the Pyncheons) and the ancient parchment hidden in a secret compartment in a picture frame are all Gothic devices. Gothic characteristics appear in *The Scarlet Letter*, too, in which Roger Chillingworth hides his true identity so that he can emotionally torture Arthur Dimmesdale and in which Hester Prynne must endure the guilt, self-recrimination and public humiliation associated with her sin – never mentioned by name in the book – of adultery.[83] *The Marble Faun* includes similar Gothicism in the strange meeting between Miriam and the Model in the dark, tortuous catacombs of Rome, in the attachment of some undefined dark curse to Miriam and even in the guilt that pursues her after the Model's murder.[84] Hawthorne had texts like *The Monk* in mind as he created his own romances, and the Gothic tradition certainly is a strong connection between him and the British Romantics.

The quality that links Inchbald and Hawthorne the most, as inheritors of the Gothic tradition, is that tradition's tendency to subordinate character development in favour of a more concentrated focus on plot and character type. Recognizing the Gothic de-emphasis of character development, Joseph Irwin suggests that the characters in Lewis's *The Monk* are 'caricatures of mankind' or 'stock characters'.[85] Indeed, Lewis's characters are substantially one-dimensional, and as demonstrated in succeeding chapters, especially Chapter 5, Inchbald's and Hawthorne's characters exhibit a similar – and intentional – lack of depth. The intentional one-dimensionality allows the characters to become quasi-allegorical representations of the authors' true concerns and serves as one of the defining features of the Romantic moral romance.

Common Sources in the Works of Godwin and Wollstonecraft

As an actor, as a playwright, as a writer of romance and finally as a literary critic, Inchbald enjoyed mass public appeal both in Britain and in America during the late eighteenth and early nineteenth centuries. In consequence, her ideas were part of the intellectual landscapes of both countries. They incorporated themselves firmly into the Romantic Movement from its beginnings in Britain in the heady 1790s, and they then continued to contribute to the development of American versions of Romanticism during the beginning of the nineteenth century. Moreover, Inchbald's association with other well known British Romantics ensured the promulgation of ideas and influences that she shared with them, and these, in turn, influenced American writers like Hawthorne.[86] Inchbald was on friendly terms for many years with William Godwin and, on less amicable terms, with Mary Wollstonecraft, and she influenced these Romantic figureheads long before she became an important intellectual force in the lives of their daughter, Mary, and her husband, Percy Shelley.

Inchbald's relationship with William Godwin lasted for much of her lifetime, even though Inchbald spent many of her later years angry with him, and the two British Romantic writers were significant influences on one another as intellectual collaborators. According to biographer William St Clair, Godwin 'kept memoranda of prominent people he had met and others he wanted to meet, underlining the names of those he knew best'.[87] He underlined Inchbald's name prominently. In fact, Godwin proposed marriage to Inchbald at least once, although she refused his offer. Nevertheless, while working on *A Simple Story*, Inchbald gave Godwin the manuscript and asked him for advice for revisions; she also suggested revisions for Godwin's *Caleb Williams* (1794), whose Gothicism and focus on moral issues certainly influenced her own evolving aesthetics.[88] *Caleb Williams* was, according to editors Handwerk and Markley, 'the most important and influential novel published in Britain during the 1790s', and, significantly, Godwin took Inchbald's advice as he revised the book for the second edition.[89] Even the title of *Caleb Williams*, the full version of which is *Things As They Are; or, The Adventures of Caleb Williams*, may have been suggested in part by the title of Inchbald's play *Such Things Are* of 1787.[90] The intellectual relationship between the two British Romantic writers cooled after Godwin's marriage to Mary Wollstonecraft in 1797, and although their friendship never attained its former level of intimacy, the two continued to correspond and meet occasionally, especially after Mary's death. Godwin, for example, sent Inchbald copies of his books; in 1817, he sent her a copy of *Mandeville* and asked for her marginal comments on the text, and in 1820, he sent *Of Population*.[91] The prolonged interaction with Godwin certainly ensured Inchbald's continuing contributions to the intellectual ferment of Romanticism in Britain and beyond, as it travelled across the Atlantic to inspire American writers like Hawthorne.

Inchbald and Mary Wollstonecraft also influenced one another in important ways and, according to Janet Todd, they 'agreed on much'.[92] Wollstonecraft stood as an example of the emancipated woman who, in her own words from *A Vindication of the Rights of Woman*, refused to be 'legally prostituted' in a marriage that would keep her in a 'state of perpetual childhood' (at least until she became pregnant), while Inchbald remained an equally independent-minded widow who refused a second marriage despite receiving proposals from several eligible men.[93] Both women were willing to experiment with texts that explored woman's place in contemporary British society, that challenged established traditions of moral order and that suggested that women be educated so that they not be subjugated to masculine control through marriage. Specifically, both women writers believed that the dictates of reason should guide the education of women.[94] The struggle for women's empowerment appears, for example, in Inchbald's *A Simple Story*, which contrasts the educational backgrounds of Miss Milner and her daughter Matilda as the two women become mere property in Lord Elmwood's mind.

Inchbald and Wollstonecraft also explored the consequences of unwed motherhood as a volatile issue in women's rights. Wollstonecraft's *Vindication* had addressed the fate of unwed mothers just four years before Inchbald's *Nature and Art* was published, and Wollstonecraft had lamented,

> A woman who has lost her honour imagines that she cannot fall lower, and as for recovering her former station, it is impossible; no exertion can wash this stain away. Losing thus every spur, and having no other means of support, prostitution becomes her only refuge, and the character is quickly depraved by circumstances over which the poor wretch has little power.[95]

The literal prostitution that Wollstonecraft mentions here appears in Inchbald's later romance when *Nature and Art* depicts the struggling Hannah Primrose, who loses her virtue to young William and then slides into a vicious circle of degradation that ultimately leads to her death by hanging.[96] Indeed, even Inchbald's contemporaries linked her with Wollstonecraft, for the prologue to Inchbald's *Every One Has His Fault* of 1793, written by the Reverend Mr Nares, invokes Wollstonecraft to say, '*The Rights of Woman*, says a female pen, / Are, to do every thing as well as Men. / To think, to argue, to decide, to write, / To talk, undoubtedly – perhaps, to fight'.[97] Clearly, Wollstonecraft and Inchbald agreed on the neglected rights of women and the consequences of women's disempowerment. The mutual influence of the two Romantic writers further enhanced Inchbald's importance as part of the British Romanticism that travelled across the Atlantic to influence Hawthorne and his American contemporaries who found Romanticism so compelling.

Connecting Inchbald and Hawthorne through the Shelleys

Wollstonecraft's daughter Mary Shelley and her husband Percy were both connected with Inchbald through Godwin and Wollstonecraft, and because Hawthorne directly admired the Shelleys, they serve as another important conduit of literary influence between Inchbald and American Romantic writers. Mary Shelley referred to Inchbald personally as 'lovely and charming', and she extolled Inchbald's 'talents, her beauty, her manners'.[98] The young Shelley maintained a genuine and continuing admiration of Inchbald's literary abilities, and many of her own stories bear remarkable resemblances to Inchbald's tales. Shelley's *Mathilda*, whose title character's name may have been borrowed from Inchbald's Matilda in *A Simple Story*, depicts an incestuous relationship between father and daughter in the absence of the mother. One of the most pressing questions in Mary Shelley's tale is whether incestuous desires must be acted upon physically before they become sinful, or whether incest can occur simply in the mind. Inchbald's Matilda has a fractured relationship with her widowed father, Lord Elmwood, which borders on incest and raises the same question while evoking features of the Gothic. Elmwood suppresses his emotional attachment to Matilda, but when the two characters accidentally meet one day on the stairs, Elmwood reveals the truth by calling Matilda by her mother's name. Similarly, Shelley's 'Roger Dodsworth: The Reanimated Englishman' concerns itself with a modern noble savage in a way that suggests connections with Inchbald's *Nature and Art*. In Shelley's story, Roger freezes in an Alpine avalanche and, after being thawed 150 years later, comments naïvely on contemporary political and social events in much the same way that Inchbald's young Henry Norwynne does after his return from Africa. In 'Transformation', Shelley creates a pair of diametrically opposed characters in Guido and the imp-like creature who represents the evil facet of Guido's psyche. Shelley's pairing of characters with opposite qualities is reminiscent of Inchbald's treatment in *Nature and Art* of the Henry Norwynnes and the William Norwynnes, who also act as opposites of one another.[99]

Finally, *Frankenstein* (1818), Shelley's best-known fiction, demonstrates an obsession with bifurcated characters and their education that also recalls Inchbald even as it anticipates fictions by Hawthorne. Many critics, such as Mary Thornburg and Christopher Small, see a reflection of Victor Frankenstein's own personality in the creature he engenders.[100] The creature does, after all, reinforce the idea that the two are intimately connected by saying to Victor at one point, 'my form is a filthy type of yours', and at the end of the novel, the creature suggests that his own existence will end after Victor's death.[101] The plot of *Frankenstein* also suggests that the principles of reason must regulate one's education as one of the most important aspects of a human being's growth process. One of Victor's greatest flaws is his irregular education, and likewise, the creature struggles with the limited worldview he has obtained from watching the De Lacey family.[102] *Frankenstein* thus recalls Inchbald's Lord Elmwood and Miss Milner of *A Simple Story*, whose personalities are opposed, yet inextricably bound as a single psyche, and whose educations have not been properly regulated by reason. *Frankenstein* also is reminiscent of Inchbald's *Nature and Art*, in which the two Williams, like Victor Frankenstein, each receive improper education, and the two Henrys, like Victor's creature, serve as symbols of the noble savage. Moreover, the creature's choice of murder to achieve revenge on Victor for the wrong of having created him recalls Hannah Primrose's negative choices – though forced upon her – as a result of a wrong done to her by young Henry. In parallel fashion, *Frankenstein* also anticipates Hawthorne's *The Scarlet Letter*, in which the characters Roger Chillingworth and Arthur Dimmesdale seem to comprise a single entity in symbolic terms, while Pearl innocently embodies the noble savage and Hester Prynne takes the role of the woman in need of an education regulated by reason. Shelley's novel also prefigures Hawthorne's *The Marble Faun*, in which Donatello takes the role of the noble savage, while Miriam and the Model experience an uncomfortable psychological connection akin to that between Victor Frankenstein and his creature. Likewise, Hawthorne's Hilda and Kenyon form a similar, though happier, pair.

Inchbald's connection with Percy Shelley is perhaps less evident since he was primarily a poet rather than a prose fiction writer, but it, too, is nevertheless present. Shelley is well known for 'spiritualizing and idealizing persons', as Andrea Henderson describes it, and that tendency appears in Inchbald's – and Hawthorne's – texts in the idealized main characters, whose actions represent only portions of psyches rather than complete consciousnesses.[103] One of the best instances of this particular line of influence between Britain and America would be Shelley's play, *The Cenci*, which connects significantly with the fictions of both Inchbald and Hawthorne. Shelley's characterization in the play makes Beatrice Cenci and her tyrannical father Francesco opposite 'poles' along a continuum, as Stuart Curran suggests.[104] Essentially, Shelley creates 'a fundamental opposition of characters representing irreconcilable modes of thought', and this difference suggests that Beatrice and Francesco act as fragmentary elements of a single psyche just as Inchbald's or Hawthorne's characters do.[105] Further, Beatrice's story, much like that of Inchbald's Hannah Primrose in *Nature and Art*, is the well worn example of a woman trapped between two moral impossibilities, in her case either tolerating recurrent rape by her own father or killing him.[106] Hannah has to choose between crime and starvation as a result of her illicit liaison with the younger William, but although her choices are significantly different, her moral situation is essentially the same as Beatrice Cenci's. Shelley's play connects even more directly with Hawthorne's *The Marble Faun*, in which the character Miriam has a mysterious association with the Cenci family of mediaeval Italy. Miriam may, in fact, be a Cenci herself, and she, too, finds herself in a difficult situation that severely limits her options because her former model torments her relentlessly until Donatello kills him. From her point of view, she could have chosen to live with the torment or to live with the ensuing guilt over the murder. Like Beatrice Cenci, she is forced to choose what seems to be the lesser of two evils – murder.

As is often the case when Romantic characters are faced with difficult decisions, both Beatrice and Miriam, and even Hannah, choose the option that, as they perceive the situation, provides the most immediate relief by changing the *status quo*. Beatrice chooses murder over rape; Miriam chooses murder over continual emotional terrorism; and Hannah chooses prostitution and counterfeiting over starvation and death. While the dilemmas of these three women may not seem unusual as plot devices, the way the dilemmas are presented in the three texts is unique. In each case, the character involved is fragmentary in nature so that she can act symbolically as part of a larger psyche rather than as a fully developed, independent entity. Each character is tied psychologically to her tormentor – or, in Hannah's case, to her seducer – by a bond that transcends mere social relationships. The resulting symbolic potential allows each Romantic text to engage in social commentary that challenges the reader's conceptions of moral order and that posits an individual moral order that may or may not be superior. Given the moral conflicts presented in *Nature and Art*, *The Cenci* and *The Marble Faun*, as well as their resolutions by fragmented characters, it seems clear that Shelley's play acts as a significant literary connective medium between Inchbald's fictions and those of Hawthorne.

Inchbald's Reputation in Britain

The mediaeval chivalric romance, the moral tale, the Gothic novel and the Godwin/Shelley circle may have provided common sources of revolutionary and experimental ideas for Inchbald and Hawthorne, but a more direct line of potential influence extends from Inchbald to Hawthorne because of Inchbald's acclaim as an actor and writer. In Britain, Inchbald began to garner the public's attention especially in the 1780s. She had left home in 1772 at the age of eighteen to act in London, but limited by a persistent stammer and by physical beauty that attracted the wrong kind of attention, she quickly married and acted instead with her husband in the provinces and in Scotland until his sudden death in 1779.[107] Widowed at twenty-five, she poured all her energies into supporting herself, and the results were surprisingly good. She began acting in London in

1780 at the Covent Garden Theatre and worked there for nearly a decade (interrupted by one season in Dublin), devoting many of her summers to acting at the Haymarket Theatre and even appearing a few times on stage at Drury Lane.[108] In terms of acting skill, Inchbald was not spectacular and could not compare with the most popular actors like Sarah Siddons, who was Inchbald's good friend. However, the confidence of theatre managers in rehiring her so many times is a strong indicator of her popularity, her reliability and her significance as a performer. Because she had invested her earnings so carefully and had been so successful, by the end of the 1789 summer theatre season, Inchbald found that she no longer needed to act to support herself and could, instead, earn her living through her writing.

Inchbald's writing was even more instrumental than her acting in ensuring that she became a well-known figure of the Romantic Period. She began trying to write a novel as early as 1777 but soon switched to producing drama, much of it adapted from French or German sources. By 1780, she had produced at least one piece that she submitted to theatre manager George Colman, though without success.[109] Only in 1784 did Colman agree to produce her play *A Mogul Tale*, but thereafter her writing achieved great success that led to her eventual retirement from acting. As Roger Manvell notes, she was 'in continuous literary and editorial production' from 1787 to 1811 when she worked on her remaining plays, her two books and her literary criticism.[110]

Although Inchbald's plays were performed widely in Britain, London audiences often determined a playwright's success – or failure – so the London theatre provides a good estimation of a playwright's popularity and influence. Charles Hogan's *The London Stage* gives ample evidence of Inchbald's popularity as a writer for London theatre audiences by cataloguing all performances of her plays through the 1799–1800 season at the three patent theatres of London – Covent Garden, Haymarket and Drury Lane. By the turn of the century, the managers had undertaken an astounding 580 performances – 67 at Drury Lane, 171 at the Haymarket and the remaining 342 at Covent Garden.[111] On average, this total indicates that, during the seventeen years between the first Inchbald performance in 1784 and the turn of the century, Londoners had the opportunity to see Inchbald's plays over thirty-four times each year. Statistically, the average amounts to about one play every two weeks. In reality, some seasons were more profitable for Inchbald than others, but the persistent presence onstage of her work kept her ideas and her name in the public eye. Occasionally, one of Inchbald's plays did not succeed, like *All on a Summer's Day*, staged only once at Covent Garden, or *Young Men and Old Women*, presented at the Haymarket only six times, but others achieved extraordinary success. *Lovers' Vows*, by far the most famous of Inchbald's plays, saw a staggering forty-two performances in its first season alone, and *The Midnight Hour*, which appeared thirty-six times in its second season, had seen the stage eighty-five times by the year 1800. William St Clair notes that, in 1793, *Every One Has His Fault*, which ran through thirty-two performances in its first season, 'confirmed her reputation as one of the most talented women of her day, competing with her friend Sarah Siddons in the literary press for the title of Tenth Muse'.[112] The many performances of Inchbald's plays ensured that *Mrs Inchbald*, as she always was known, became a household name in Britain. Indeed, several of the plays received specific royal patronage that helped to boost their popularity and Inchbald's reputation.[113]

Further, Inchbald shrewdly capitalized upon her stage success to publish most of her plays shortly after their first presentation before the public, and many of them went through multiple editions in rapid succession. *Such Things Are*, Inchbald's sixth play, went through thirteen editions in the seventeen years after its first publication in 1788.[114] As evidence of Inchbald's accomplishments, the *British Museum General Catalogue of Printed Books* provides a substantial index of her published plays.[115] *Every One Has His Fault*, for example, went into a seventh edition by 1794, the year after the publisher first issued it. *Lovers' Vows* was especially popular after its initial appearance in 1798, with publication dates ranging well into the late nineteenth century, and *Wives As They Were and Maids As They Are* saw five editions in 1797 alone. Further, editors included many of the plays in collections of British drama of the nineteenth century. Cumberland's *The British Theatre*, published in London between 1825 and 1855, included eight of Inchbald's dramatic pieces, and Dick's *Standard Plays* of 1833 reprinted ten. *The London Stage*, published between 1834 and 1837, reprinted nine of the plays, while *The British Drama* of 1872, much later in the century, reprinted three.[116] Roger Manvell lists Irish editions, as well, for fourteen of the plays.[117] All told, Inchbald published sixteen plays during her lifetime and wrote others, like *The Massacre* and *A Case of Conscience* (published by biographer James Boaden in 1833), that did not go to press until after her death.

Inchbald's popularity as an actor and playwright undoubtedly contributed as well to the appreciation of her prose fiction, *Nature and Art* and *A Simple Story*, in the literary circles of Britain and other countries. After initial publication in 1796, *Nature and Art* was printed again eight times before the end of the next century.[118] A French edition, entitled *La Nature et l'Art*, came from Geneva as early as 1797, as did another French edition in 1830.[119] Inchbald's earlier and more popular book, *A Simple Story*, appeared nine more times before the end of the next century after its first publication in 1791, and Irish editions came out in 1791 and 1804. An English version was available in Paris in 1802 – and again in 1808 – and French translations, entitled *Simple histoire*, came from Parisian presses eight times by the middle of the next century. The catalogue of the Bibliothèque Nationale de France indexes an unusual French translation – in verse – in 1849. Moreover, the catalogue lists *Lady Mathilde* (second edition) as the 'suite de "Simple Histoire"', which suggests that, in some instances, French publishers issued the first and second halves of *A Simple Story* separately. Patricia Sigl reports that a French translator produced a dramatic version of the second half of the book in 1799.[120] Furthermore, one publisher printed a Spanish version in 1837 in Paris. Both *A Simple Story* and *Nature and Art* were available also in German, and both were reprinted together in English as part of *The British Novelists*, edited by Anna Letitia Barbauld in 1810 and reissued in 1823. *A Simple Story* was so popular that, according to the American Library of Congress's *National Union Catalog*, even a Russian edition was available as early as 1794 in Moscow.[121]

As if an impressive list of publications were not enough, publishers courted Inchbald to solicit her contributions to their magazines and other publications. One asked her, for example, to write for the *Quarterly Review,* although she refused the offer. In 1809, however, she further contributed to the intellectual ferment of Romanticism by agreeing to select the plays to be included in a seven-volume series called the *Collection of Farces and Afterpieces*; the opportunity also allowed her to publish three of her own plays as part of the collection. Two years later, she again assumed the influential role of editor. She chose the contents for *The Modern Theatre*, a ten-volume collection into which she incorporated three of her plays. Even more importantly, she agreed to edit *The British Theatre; or A Collection of Plays which Are Acted at the Theatres Royal, Drury Lane, Covent Garden, and Haymarket* (published in London by Longman and company) and also to write prefaces to the 125 plays that were to be included in the twenty-five-volume series. The plays from the *British Theatre* series appeared first individually between 1806 and 1808 and then were collected into volumes. Although Inchbald did not choose the plays for the series, the publisher devoted an entire volume to her work and republished five plays.

With her impressive list of theatrical and literary accomplishments, Elizabeth Inchbald could not but be a significant intellectual presence in the Romantic Movement, and her influence certainly permeated the literary landscape of the British Isles. Indeed, Hawthorne likely encountered Inchbald's influence during his four years living in Liverpool – where Inchbald had once acted – between 1853 and 1857 while he served as American Consul. Regardless, Inchbald's impact upon the British literary landscape is clear in Roger Manvell's comment that she was, during her lifetime, 'one of the most respected of writers in the mainstream of literary output in England'.[122] Leigh Hunt, a radical writer, activist and editor of the *Examiner* – whose politically provocative essays resulted in his incarceration – wrote in his autobiography that his mother expressed 'great admiration of the novels of Mrs Inchbald, especially the *Simple Story*'.[123] Hunt himself believed that *A Simple Story* and *Nature and Art* were Inchbald's 'chief merits' and were 'written in a style to endure'.[124] Even Lord Byron admired Inchbald's writing. In a journal entry dated 7 December 1813, he queried, '[W]hose praise do I prefer? Why, Mrs Inchbald's, and that of the Americans'.[125] High praise from figures like Hunt and Byron, coupled with a series of laudable accomplishments, situate Inchbald as a major figure of British Romanticism, a figure whose influence extended across the Atlantic, with important consequences for the development of American versions of Romanticism and for the writing efforts of authors like Nathaniel Hawthorne.

Inchbald's Reputation in America

While *Mrs Inchbald* was a household name in Britain, the name also crossed the Atlantic to become just as important to the American public long before Hawthorne's birth in 1804, and Inchbald's reputation remained strong well into Hawthorne's adulthood. At that time, Americans still struggled to define themselves and to create a new national identity that, though based on British cultural examples, would be unique. The Continental Congress had signed the American Declaration of Independence as recently as 1776, and the succeeding war against Britain lasted until 1783. Relations between the two countries remained tense, especially when conflict arose again in the War of 1812. The Anglo–American political fracture during the Romantic Period found its way into the nascent literature of the United States, as American authors argued for a literature that would establish their own cultural presence and legitimize the new nation's relatively new status as a sovereign power. However, even as they cultivated an adolescent desire for cultural autonomy, Americans continued to depend on Britain for much of the literature they read. The excuse for their cultural dependence, as Robert Weisbuch describes it, was that the Americans were 'too busy forming a nation and conquering a continent to write [their own] literature', and as Giles Playfair comments flatly, in the early years of the republic, '[n]ative talent was still very scarce'.[126]

American dependence on British culture increased the likelihood that the works of writers like Inchbald would circulate in America, especially since competition with American authors remained at a minimum. Indeed, American copyright laws did not protect British authors' works, which publishers copied freely in the American states since it was easier – and cheaper – to pirate British literature than to pay royalties to American authors for their efforts.[127] The result was the reinforcement of the already existing predilection for British literature like Inchbald's in the new United States. The states of the new country had been British colonies, some of them for over a century, and a mere declaration of political independence could not change the long-term effects of British cultural hegemony in America. Given this context, Inchbald's presence in America as a literary figure is far less surprising than it might first appear.

Inchbald's name first surfaced in America in connection with the theatre. Americans exhibited a conflicted attitude toward the theatre, as with other types of literature, and paradoxically embraced British drama wholeheartedly while agitating for an American literary tradition. Ruth Michael notices the 'commonplace fact that the American theatre during the eighteenth and early nineteenth centuries reflected the contemporary stage in England'.[128] American dependence on Britain was so strong that audiences actually preferred British drama. Michael highlights American cultural dependence with her statement,

> In no other matter were Americans more definitely colonial than in their attitude toward theatric amusements. During the first decades of the nineteenth century in Boston, as in the other towns of America, English actors were performing plays, for the most part written by Englishmen, in a theatre the architecture of which was modeled on one of the two patent playhouses in London, before audiences which liked the assurance that the entertainments had been received 'with unbounded applause' at Covent Garden or Drury Lane.[129]

Any listing of drama performances in America at the time will support Michael's contention. Even the most cursory of glances at the catalogues in George O. Seilhamer's *History of the American Theatre*, for example, reveals scores – nay, hundreds – of performances from British playwrights, whose works overwhelmingly dominated the American theatre.[130] William Shakespeare is conspicuous throughout, and other British playwrights are well represented, including David Garrick, Oliver Goldsmith, Isaac Bickerstaff, Richard Brinsley Sheridan, John Home, Thomas Otway, George Colman and many other writers. The works of women playwrights like Susannah Centlivre and Hannah Cowley are in evidence, too, as are those of Elizabeth Inchbald, which were performed many times in a wide range of cities. In short, American audiences left their desires for cultural independence at the doors of the theatres they attended.

The early and pervasive cultural dependence of America on Britain meant that American theatre managers frequently produced a number of Inchbald's plays in the new nation, even as American publishers reprinted the plays. Thomas Pollock's *The Philadelphia Theatre in the Eighteenth Century* lists at least thirty-nine performances of Inchbald's plays in Philadelphia alone between 1793 and 1799, an average of more than five and a half plays per year in a single American city.[131] Reese D. James examines dramatic performances in Philadelphia during the first thirty-six years of the nineteenth century to list at least fifty-nine performances of Inchbald's drama through 1835, an average of over one and a half performances per year, and Arthur Wilson's study of the Philadelphia theatre from 1835 through 1855 lists ninety-seven performances, or an average of nearly five per year.[132] Reese James also catalogues performances of Inchbald's plays in Baltimore, Washington and Alexandria, while other authors, such as William R. DuBois, note numerous performances of Inchbald's drama in New York and other cities.[133]

American theatres across the country were producing Inchbald's plays, and the theatres in Boston – near Hawthorne's Salem birthplace and where he later lived – were no exception. Ruth Michael's exhaustive two-volume dissertation explores the inception and development in Boston of theatrical performances after the lifting of Puritan bans on drama. Inchbald's name appears frequently in the listings in Michael's appendix of over 500 pages. During the mere twenty-three years Michael's study covers, a staggering total of 134 performances of Inchbald plays saw the stage at the Federal Theatre alone. Statistically, these numbers indicate that the management at this single Boston theatre produced Inchbald plays an average of nearly six times each year.

Although Ruth Michael's survey of the Boston theatre ends in 1816, when Nathaniel Hawthorne was eleven years old, it is nevertheless clear that Inchbald had a well-known theatrical presence in the Boston area during Hawthorne's childhood. Hawthorne, moreover, who spent his early years and much of his adulthood just outside Boston in Salem, liked the theatre, and according to Pat Ryan, as early as age eight or nine, he was a strong supporter of theatrical endeavours in New England.[134] He is known to have visited the Boston Theatre because his sister Louisa notes that he went to Boston on 5 March 1821 to see the English actor Edmund Kean in a performance of *King Lear*.[135] Salem did not have a theatre at the time, although Ryan notes that the inhabitants occasionally performed dramas.[136] In fact, another critic, Milton Hehr, concurs and points out that Salem saw at least four performances of Inchbald's plays in the 1790s – just a few years before Hawthorne's birth.[137] Pat Ryan remarks that, years later, Hawthorne attended 'some of the most notable productions staged in Salem during the theatrically significant decade of 1820 to 1830'.[138] Inchbald's plays were a part of this decade, as indicated in Weldon B. Durham's *American Theatre Companies, 1749–1887*, which lists performances of Inchbald's work in the new Salem Theatre in 1828 and in 1829.[139] Hawthorne may well have seen one or more of these performances.

Inchbald's plays, furthermore, remained popular in America through the nineteenth century and especially during the period when Hawthorne wrote his major works. According to Durham's information, American theatre companies produced Inchbald plays as far south as New Orleans and as far west as Chicago and Kentucky.[140] The plays spiked in popularity in the 1820s when Hawthorne was a young writer (perhaps revived in reaction to the news of Inchbald's recent death in 1821 when Hawthorne was seventeen). Even in the 1870s, well after Hawthorne's death, at least three performances of Inchbald's plays saw the stage.

Hawthorne enjoyed attending the theatre, and one of the most significant plays he saw during his early years was an English rendition of August Friedrich

Ferdinand von Kotzebue's *Das Kind der Liebe*, known to English-speaking audiences as *Lovers' Vows*. On 3 May 1820, when Hawthorne was nearly sixteen, he saw a performance of the play at Washington Hall in Salem, according to biographer Randall Stewart, who calls it 'Mrs Inchbald's *Lovers' Vows*'.[141] Perhaps Inchbald's best known play, *Lovers' Vows* is a free translation of Kotzebue's drama. The play was well known – indeed, infamous – for its radical ideas on women, marriage and social justice. Its subject matter was scandalously liberal in its rebuke of aristocracy, its concern for the welfare of the poor, its claims of hereditary guilt in the aristocracy, and its suggestion that women deserved more freedom and autonomy in making choices about their lives.[142] Inchbald's 1798 adaptation depicts an illegitimate son whose reunion with his father sparks a marriage between his aristocratic father and peasant mother and between his aristocratic half-sister and her penniless tutor – who happens to be a minister. Inchbald's version made the play famous during the early Romantic Period in Britain, where it retained its currency through the early decades of the nineteenth century to find place as a popular and shocking example in Jane Austen's *Mansfield Park* (1814).[143] When Hawthorne saw the play performed in Salem, his impressionable mind certainly would have absorbed some of the Romantic ideals of the play that Inchbald helped to make famous. These ideals in turn would have had their place in the shaping of Hawthorne's Romantic aesthetic for the later American tradition.

Interestingly, the plot of Inchbald's *Lovers' Vows* bears remarkable parallels with the plots of Inchbald's earlier fictions and with Hawthorne's later books. Avrom Fleishman points out, for example, that an argument for 'the natural goodness of man' appears in *Lovers' Vows* and in Inchbald's *Nature and Art*.[144] Likewise, Hawthorne's *The Marble Faun* incorporates the argument of natural goodness and embodies it initially in the innocent character Donatello. The suggestions of the hereditary guilt of the aristocracy in *Lovers' Vows* are present in *Nature and Art* through the two William Norwynnes, while Hawthorne's Miriam in *The Marble Faun* struggles with an analogous inherited guilt in her aristocratic family. *Lovers' Vows* also links Inchbald's *A Simple Story* and Hawthorne's *The Scarlet Letter*. The minister Anhalt's involvement in the play with Amelia, for example, parallels Dorriforth's relationship with Inchbald's Miss Milner as well as Arthur Dimmesdale's relationship with Hawthorne's Hester Prynne. The motif of hidden identity appears in *Lovers' Vows,* in Frederick's ignorance that his father is the Baron Wildenheim, even as Matilda remains concealed in Elmwood House in Inchbald's book, and even as Chillingworth's and Dimmesdale's true identities or roles (Chillingworth as husband and Dimmesdale as adulterer) remain hidden in Hawthorne's text. Baron Wildenheim's guilt over his treatment of Agatha parallels the repressed guilt of Inchbald's Dorriforth over his treatment of Miss Milner and Matilda and Hawthorne's Dimmesdale over his treatment of Hester and Pearl. These similarities could well be more than mere coincidences of plot – Hawthorne may have had Inchbald's version of *Lovers' Vows* in mind as he wrote his fictions, just as Inchbald certainly had her own earlier fictions in mind as she rendered her version of Kotzebue's play.

Performances of Inchbald's plays on the American stage were frequent and recurrently significant, and the possibility that Hawthorne saw several performances of Inchbald's drama during his lifetime is quite high. Records of the publication of Inchbald's plays in America are expectedly less frequent than their performances, but even these are, nevertheless, significant. The *National Union Catalog*, which indexes entries in the catalogue of the Library of Congress, lists publication information for eleven of Inchbald's plays individually in America.[145] The plays were readily available, therefore, were Hawthorne to choose to read them. The libraries of Boston and Salem, where Hawthorne spent much of his time, owned copies, as did the many circulating libraries that proved popular in America. In fact, as early as 1794, John Dabney, who owned a circulating library in Salem itself, published the *Additional Catalogue of Books, for Sale or Circulation, in Town or Country, at the Salem Bookstore*, which lists Inchbald's 'Dramatic Works' in one volume as one of the many books he had available.[146] About fifteen years later, John West's bookstore in Boston sold five of Inchbald's plays individually.[147] In short, access to Inchbald's plays, either in performance or in print, would have been easy for Hawthorne.

More importantly, Hawthorne likely would have been aware of Inchbald's two Romantic moral romances – *A Simple Story* and *Nature and Art*. Both books were successful, and particularly the former, on both sides of the Atlantic. The British *Union Catalogue* and the American *National Union Catalog* list numerous publication dates throughout the nineteenth century for both books.[148] Although American publications of both texts were less frequent than publications in Britain, both remained popular in the United States. *A Simple Story* appeared in Philadelphia in 1793 and then in New York in 1835 and 1847. The *National Union Catalog* also lists publication dates of 1821 and 1822 in New York for *The Mourning Ring: A Simple Story*, certainly a pirated version of *A Simple Story*.[149] *Nature and Art* has a 1796 publication date in Philadelphia. One must remember, also, that texts published in Britain and elsewhere often made their way across the Atlantic to the shelves of avid American book readers, so that many of the British editions of revolutionary literature by writers like Inchbald would have been readily available in the newly formed United States.

Inchbald's Works in American Circulating Libraries

A number of the circulating libraries and bookstores in America to which Hawthorne would have had access also owned – in addition to editions of Inchbald's plays in Salem as mentioned above – British and American editions of Inchbald's two works of fiction and of her theatre criticism. Indeed, Hawthorne is known to have patronized one of the circulating libraries in Salem.[150] Circulating libraries were increasing in popularity during the nineteenth century because they could provide reading material for thousands of readers who could not afford to buy their own books.[151] The price of books was so high that many booksellers and printers chose to lend books to their clients for periodic fees rather than suffer the economic liability of not being able to sell their stock. The circulating library became so popular in Britain that by the beginning of the nineteenth century, as George Raddin comments, they were 'to be found in almost every city and town in the British Isles'.[152] Although Raddin's statement may be somewhat hyperbolic, the circulating library certainly held an important place in Britain, and in America, libraries achieved similar success, especially after the Revolutionary War, when Americans would have admired the democratizing influence of the public circulating library.

Several important circulating libraries in America held copies of Inchbald's books. One of the most important ones was founded in 1797 in New York by Louis Alexis Hocquet de Caritat.[153] Raddin claims that at the time it was founded, 'the circulating library was a familiar institution not only in New York, but in every town and village of importance in the country ... [and was] a dominant influence in the development of an American reading public'.[154] These types of libraries, operated primarily by printers and booksellers, were 'the principal purveyors of the popular informative and entertaining literature of the day'.[155] Interestingly, Caritat's library included, in 1804, *A Simple Story* and *Nature and Art*.[156] Caritat had acquired the volumes as early as 1799, for his *New Explanatory Catalogue* of that year includes both books.[157] Not far away in Maryland, the Baltimore Circulating Library owned a copy of *Nature and Art* in 1807, and the volume seems to have been popular enough that the proprietors had acquired a second copy for their clients by 1812.[158] Closer to Boston, in Providence, Rhode Island, Henry Cushing's catalogue includes both *A Simple Story* and *Nature and Art* in 1800.[159]

Circulating libraries in the Boston area, where Hawthorne lived and wrote, had been available for nearly half a century by the time of Hawthorne's birth. Charles Bolton dates the first Boston bookstore and circulating library from 1765.[160] Bolton provides ample evidence that this type of library 'continued to flourish in Boston' through the nineteenth century.[161] One circulating library in Boston, that of William and Lemuel Blake, lists both of Inchbald's fictions among its many holdings in 1800.[162] During the previous two years, Boston booksellers had offered both books for sale. James White's catalogue of 1798 lists *Nature and Art* as one of the items available in his establishment, while the *Catalogue of Books for Sale by E. Larkin*, published the same year, includes both *Nature and Art* and *A Simple Story*.[163] The catalogues of David West and of Thomas and Andrews during the next year both list Inchbald's two books again, as does another catalogue by E. Larkin a few years later and a more general *Catalogue of all the Books, Printed in the United States*, that Boston booksellers published probably in 1804.[164] Joseph Nancrede's *Fixed-Price Catalogue* of 1803 lists two copies of *Nature and Art*, and a few years later, the catalogue of the defunct West & Blake company lists *Nature and Art* for sale by auction on 29 May 1815.[165] Sale catalogues like these are instructive, especially since the booksellers who produced them may also have loaned books to their clients, but the catalogues that are styled specifically as those of libraries or circulating libraries are more important since, in comparison with books that may have been for sale only, library books potentially reached a much broader base of clientele. Boston's Union Circulating Library lists *A Simple Story* and *Nature and Art* in its catalogues for the years 1806, 1810 and 1815, while the Boston Library has listings for *Nature and Art* in 1807 and 1815.[166] The Shakespeare Circulating Library includes both books in its 1815 catalogue.[167] Similarly, the catalogue of the Washington Circulating Library in Boston also includes both of Inchbald's books in 1817.[168]

By far the most important Boston library, however, was the Boston Athenaeum, founded in 1807, whose first librarian, William S. Shaw, reportedly collected as many books, pamphlets, manuscripts and so forth as he could find.[169] During Hawthorne's tenure at the Boston Custom House from 1839 to 1841 – just a decade before he would publish *The Scarlet Letter* – he spent many hours in the Athenaeum reading room, whose vast collection included Inchbald's works.[170] The 1827 *Catalogue of Books in the Boston Atheneum* [*sic*] lists *Nature and Art* and *The Mourning Ring* (*A Simple Story*) among its many holdings.[171]

Finally, in Salem itself, Hawthorne's home town, John Dabney's circulating library owned *A Simple Story* as early as 1794.[172] Seven years later, Dabney still owned a copy of the book, which appears also in the sale catalogue of books for auction on 8 September 1818, after his death.[173] The 1808 *Catalogue of the Books Belonging to the Salem Athenaeum*, also lists *A Simple Story* as one of the library's many holdings, as does the 1818 catalogue of Thomas Cushing's Essex Circulating Library in Salem.[174] Succeeding libraries in Salem certainly owned copies of Inchbald's texts throughout Hawthorne's lifetime. Given the availability of *A Simple Story* and *Nature and Art* in the United States in general and in the Boston area, particularly in Salem itself in the nineteenth century, Nathaniel Hawthorne and his fellow American authors unquestionably had many opportunities to read both books.

An even more likely source for Inchbald's influence on Romantic writers like Hawthorne would be the *British Theatre* series, the twenty-five-volume survey of British drama that Inchbald edited between 1806 and 1808. Although she did not select the texts herself for the edition, Inchbald did serve as editor, writing authoritative prefaces which combined biographical and critical commentary to accompany each of the 125 plays. The series, which included many of Shakespeare's plays, was readily available in the new United States. The Boston Library, for example, catalogues the series in 1815.[175] According to the records of the Salem Athenaeum, even this small library owned the series.[176] Moreover, George Parsons Lathrop reports that Hawthorne did borrow at least one volume of the series in 1830.[177] Given Hawthorne's voracious reading habits, he probably was familiar with the entire collection – including Inchbald's prefatory commentary on the tradition of British drama.

Inchbald's and Hawthorne's Common Sources

As this chapter illustrates, an indirect line of influence connected Inchbald and Hawthorne through common sources in the mediaeval chivalric romance, in the moral tale, in the Gothic novel and in themes and patterns both writers shared in common with members of the Godwin/Shelley circle. Moreover, a direct link between Inchbald and Hawthorne is distinctly possible. Indeed, while the evidence suggesting that Inchbald herself had a place among Hawthorne's literary influences may be circumstantial, it is difficult to refute and certainly endures as a substantial and compelling possibility. Inchbald was such an important figure in the British Romantic Movement – through her acting, the performances of her plays, the publication of her plays, romances and criticism, and through her association with figures like the Godwins and the Shelleys – that she had a significant impact on the literary landscape of nineteenth-century America. Writing primarily in the 1790s, which many might consider to be the formative years of the Romantic Period in Britain, she attained a popularity that transcended international boundaries and that ensured the incorporation of her ideas into the essential impetus of Romanticism. British Romanticism and its expressions through writers like Inchbald were significant sources of ideas for American Romantic writers like Hawthorne. The evolution of the Romantic moral romance sub-genre in the work of two writers on opposite sides of the Atlantic but nevertheless part of one contiguous intellectual movement is, under these circumstances, both conceivable and provocatively possible.

2. 'FABLE-WORLD[S]' POPULATED BY 'HUMAN CREATURES': TOWARD A DEFINITION OF THE EXPERIMENTAL ROMANTIC MORAL ROMANCE[1]

I must relieve myself by drawing a different picture.

– Mary Wollstonecraft[2]

The historical evidence in support of several lines of influence, indirect and possibly direct, between Elizabeth Inchbald and Nathaniel Hawthorne is strong, and the evidence that they borrowed features from common sources is even stronger. Inchbald's fame as an actor, a playwright, a fiction writer and an editor, along with her social and literary connections with important figures of the British Romantic Period like Godwin, Wollstonecraft and the Shelleys, ensured that her ideas became integral to the very idea of Romanticism, while those ideas were, in their turn, shaped by the works of other writers of the Romantic Era. That Hawthorne, whom the British Romantics strongly influenced, experimented in much the same way that Inchbald did, should be no surprise. Although many critics of the past have casually labelled Inchbald's and Hawthorne's major fictional works novels, not one of them is a novel in the traditional sense. Instead of writing traditional novels, both authors favoured the imaginative, psychological blend of the romance with the novel – a blend that borrows many realistic conventions from the novel but also borrows elements from the mediaeval chivalric romance and the French moral tale to emphasize allegorical potential, symbolic meaning and the tragic resolution of mixed genre. Although their respective fictions demonstrate originality in both style and subject matter, Inchbald and Hawthorne experimented in parallel terms with their own unique sub-genre in the Romantic moral romance. While other writers also experimented with variations of the form, Inchbald and Hawthorne produced exceptional examples that simplify any attempt to characterize the sub-genre.

This chapter will advance a tentative definition, based on Inchbald's and Hawthorne's stated intentions and on their actual practice, of the Romantic moral romance. Any meaningful attempt to define the alternative sub-genre must take into account the tradition against which these two writers worked and into which their own fictions so often have been classified – that of the novel as it evolved through the late eighteenth and early nineteenth centuries in Britain. For Inchbald, the novel represented a male-dominated genre whose accessibility to women had damaged its reputation. As women contributed to the genre in the late eighteenth century, the novel's critics reacted strongly against what they viewed as the potentially immoral nature of the form. Fifty years later in America, the British novel represented an encroaching British cultural presence for Hawthorne and his contemporaries. Having achieved political independence, Americans wanted a literature that they could claim as uniquely American. Inchbald's response to charges of the novel's immorality, and Hawthorne's response to the novel's Britishness, was to avoid the traditional novel and develop the alternative romance sub-genre of the novel.

After establishing Inchbald's and Hawthorne's motivations, based on the reputation and development of the British novel, this discussion turns to the authors' stated intentions in their prefaces and, in the case of Inchbald's *Nature and Art*, which has no preface, to Inchbald's implied intentions based on internal evidence from the text. While Inchbald – in print – deliberately avoided the term *novel* and preferred to call her books stories and tales, Hawthorne actively labelled his books romances in all of his prefaces. The evidence suggests that both authors' apparent avoidance of the novel form was deliberate and carefully premeditated.

Following the discussion of authorial intentions, the focus of this chapter moves to *A Simple Story*, *Nature and Art*, *The Scarlet Letter* and *The Marble Faun* to suggest how the four books represent a unique kind of writing that differs from the traditional British novel. All four books employ dramatically inspired scenes that juxtapose symbolic and flatly constructed characters who amount to little more than character-types or figures, much like those seen in the chivalric romance and the French moral tale. Indeed, Inchbald develops her figures with such simplicity – more so than Hawthorne – that they are easy to confuse with one another, so Figure 3, Character Relationships in Inchbald's Fictions, helps distinguish them. All four books also focus on strong passion – sometimes repressed – as one method by which the authors simplify their characters and highlight their quasi-symbolic nature as figures, psyches or types. And finally, both Inchbald and Hawthorne use the Romantic moral romance to explore alternate conceptions of 'truth'. As this volume will demonstrate, Inchbald and Hawthorne use their constructed character types to examine psychological motivation in a manner that anticipates the modern symbolic novel, and despite their divergent intentions, they developed similar forms of fiction.

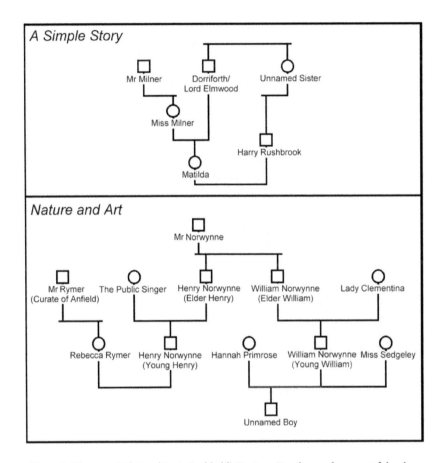

Figure 3, Character Relationships in Inchbald's Fictions. Family-tree diagrams of the character relationships in *A Simple Story* and *Nature and Art*. Squares represent male characters; circles represent female characters. *Diagram by Ben P. Robertson.*

The Context and Motivation for Inchbald's
Experimentation with Fiction

At the time Inchbald published *A Simple Story* in 1791, the novel genre was relatively new as a popular form in English. In fact, as Catherine Gallagher notices in an examination of women's roles in the literary marketplace, fiction itself was a 'new category of discourse' that emerged into the public consciousness.[3] Gallagher acknowledges the existence of fiction for centuries – citing romances, fables, allegories, fairy stories, dramas and narrative poems as examples – but the mid-eighteenth-century novel became the catalyst for a change in the way literary historians viewed fiction. Fiction finally became a legitimate, serious form of discourse that included the new novel along with older forms like fables and romances. As the novel developed, it quickly became the province of male fiction writers. Ian Watt examines Daniel Defoe, Samuel Richardson and Henry Fielding as the three great names in the novel's early evolution in *The Rise of the Novel*, and J. M. S. Tompkins in *The Popular Novel in England* credits Richardson, Fielding, Tobias Smollett, Laurence Sterne and Oliver Goldsmith as the dominant influences during the formative years for the genre in Britain.[4] Michael McKeon includes similar figures in his studies of the novel.[5]

As the form continued to evolve, many lesser novelists simply imitated these men and further reinforced the novel's masculine origins.[6] But as the number of novelists quickly increased, so did objections to the genre. By the time Inchbald wrote, many critics considered the novel, especially novels written by women, to be suspect. They considered the novel, as Gallagher suggests, 'an unruly medium', and they complained about the newness of the genre, about the ease of its production, about its lack of morality, and about its accessibility to impressionable young men and women.[7] Not based on a classical tradition, the novel seemed a bourgeois threat to more respectable literature like poetry, particularly since novelists often wrote openly for profit rather than morally edifying purposes or artistry. Moreover, reviewers thought novels were too easy to produce, as exemplified in a 1781 article in the *Critical Review* that claimed,

> It is indeed a convenient method to writers of the inferior class, of emptying their commonplace books, and throwing together all the farrago of public transactions, private characters, old and new stories, everything, in short, which they can pick up, to afford a little temporary amusement to an idle reader.[8]

The writer's indictment of the 'inferior class' of novelists clearly situates the genre and its practitioners in a questionable position, but the reference to the 'idle reader' is even more censorious. Concerned parents worried that the novel would pervert their children because it could distract them from more appropriate and more useful reading that would prepare them intellectually and morally for adult life. As Gary Kelly notes in a discussion of Romantic fiction, 'Women in particular were supposed to be rendered unfit by novel reading for their domestic character and duties; Kelly also quotes the Reverend Vicesimus Knox, who declared in 1778, "If it is true, that the present age is more corrupt than the preceding, the great multiplication of Novels probably contributes to its degeneracy".[9] The novel's reputation had so eroded that many writers – even male writers – chose to publish anonymously.

Concurrent with the rise of a masculine novel tradition, women adopted the form in increasing numbers, in part because they hoped that the novel's loosely organized structure and emphasis on realism would allow them greater freedom of expression.[10] The new form did not require an education at Oxford or Cambridge – where women could not attend – nor did it, as poetry traditionally had done, require a familiarity with Classical Greek and Roman texts.[11] One result of the unprecedented flexibility of the new novel genre was, as Stuart Curran describes it, 'a flood of women seeking an identity, and sometimes an independence, through writing'.[12] In fact, as the genre of the novel developed, it 'was virtually taken over by women', particularly during the 1790s.[13] Jan Fergus and Janice Farrar Thaddeus record an increase 'by about fifty percent per decade' of women writers in the second half of the eighteenth century, and Curran comments, 'So wholly did the novel come to be identified as a woman's form that by the end of the century women seem to have accounted for well over half the novels written during it'.[14]

Largely excluded from literary endeavours for centuries, women embraced the novel, realizing that it could empower them in new and exciting ways. The fictive nature of the new genre promised the ability to create characters of the imagination who did not correspond to any particular person in reality. These Nobodies, as Gallagher calls them, provided the opportunity for women writers to discourse on sensitive topics, and sometimes to depict questionable behaviour, with near impunity.[15] Consequently, many women took advantage of their new freedom to write novels that foregrounded the plight of women in British society, which Gary Kelly characterizes as 'patriarchal and antifeminist at all levels' and which saw women as 'the weak link in every class confronting a superior male-dominated class'.[16] Curran notes women's appropriation of the new genre to argue

> [T]he emergence of the novel in the early Romantic period as a separatist genre is understandable; and its capacity to encode a separatist agenda, even if the denouement would be the inevitable marriage, can be glimpsed in the prime examples of the kind [...] like Inchbald's *A Simple Story* [...] all of which reveal bright, frustrated, and manipulated young women who have no recourse but themselves to manipulate the males who exert power over them.[17]

In short, women wrote novels about themselves and about their daily frustrations in a patriarchal society that gave them few opportunities for self-expression.

Many of them hoped that their novels would act as positive forces for change in British society by encouraging, for example, education reforms like those that Mary Wollstonecraft advocated in *A Vindication of the Rights of Woman*. Women finally had found a viable medium for their frustrations, an outlet that would allow them to push toward greater autonomy.

The novel's critics, however, disliked novels by women even more than those by men. Curran notes that women had difficulty supporting themselves with their writing and that the professional woman writer's reputation 'was little better than that of mistress, and her precarious financial status indeed seems often to have reduced her to that level'.[18] Even so, Curran acknowledges that during the Romantic Period, countless numbers of women dared to express themselves and explore their identities and independence through writing.[19] Moreover, as Gallagher comments, many women writers 'embraced and feminized' remunerative authorship, and the commodification of the novel further unsettled the genre's critics.[20] Because of the stigma attached to novels and novel writing, novelists – especially female novelists – were 'on the defensive' or 'unnecessarily humble' about their books; for example, when Charlotte Palmer published a book in 1796, she titled it, *It is and it is not, a Novel*.[21] As Leslie Fiedler comments in his discussion of the American novel's origins in Britain,

> One can scarcely open an early example of the genre without finding in the body of the work a condemnation of 'novels', *i.e.*, all *other* novels, and on the title page the claim 'founded in truth' or 'a tale of truth'.[22]

Elizabeth Inchbald wrote her two books in this negatively charged literary atmosphere, so she had ample incentive to avoid the label of *novelist*. She already had written a number of plays, but her efforts to write for the theatre resulted primarily in farces and comedies, in part because she knew they would please the demanding Covent Garden audiences. Only occasionally did she write a more serious drama, like her popular version of *Lovers' Vows*, or *The Massacre*, a tragedy about revolutionary France that was neither performed nor published during her lifetime. Drama, however, was not enough for Inchbald even though she was adept at producing short plays, and the novel genre attracted her because it would allow her greater freedom to present her own revolutionary ideas to the public.[23] However, as a woman with a reputation for virtue, she surely wanted to avoid the imputation of being an immoral novelist. She faced a dilemma; she could write artistic novels, which would incur the wrath of critics who condemned the genre for its bourgeois newness and immorality, or she could write didactic, parable-like romances, which would be less satisfying and less artistic. Her response was to develop a third type of writing.

Inchbald's solution was to develop the Romantic moral romance sub-genre, a form that was similar to the novel in its lengthy prose treatment of primarily realistic action but that deviated from the traditional novel form produced by most of her contemporaries in its simultaneous reliance on characters, or figures, whose personalities were so apparently underdeveloped that they appeared symbolic or allegorical.[24] She perhaps followed the example of Frances Burney, who wrote *Evelina* of 1778 with the intent to '*draw characters from nature, though not from life, and to mark the manners of the times*'.[25] Burney wished to avoid the '*fantastic regions of Romance, where Fiction is coloured by all the gay tints of luxurious Imagination, where Reason is an outcast, and where the sublimity of* the Marvellous *rejects all aid from sober Probability*'.[26] Inchbald wished to do the same, but rather than eschewing the romance altogether, she merged it with the novel form and borrowed features of the mediaeval chivalric romance and French moral tale to write Romantic moral romances. Her fictions demonstrate the 'studied simplicity' that Anne Mellor notices in much women's writing of the Romantic Period.[27] That simplicity, however, is deceptive, for it hides a sophisticated and socially conscious examination of women's issues. As Mellor comments, 'In the Romantic period, women novelists frequently employed the novel as a site of ideological contestation and subversion, exploiting its generic capacity for heteroglossia and dialogism, for disruptive laughter and a sustained interrogation of existing social codes'.[28] Certainly, Inchbald questions social codes through ideological contestation and subversion, and these characteristics are part of what makes the Romantic moral romance particularly Romantic. Like other Romantic writers, she was interested in the 'truth' of emotion (the 'passions' or 'affections' would be the Romantic terms) rather than in realism and verisimilitude, so her works differ considerably from the conception of the traditional novel as it had evolved by the late eighteenth century.[29]

The Context and Motivation for Hawthorne's Experimentation with Fiction

Like Inchbald's works, Hawthorne's books differ also from the traditional conception of the novel. Hawthorne's quarrel with British literary tradition resulted primarily from a sense of cultural insecurity in America, an attitude that permeated the cultural landscape throughout Hawthorne's lifetime and that the author reveals in his own literary efforts. Born on 4 July, the anniversary of the Declaration of Independence, Hawthorne personally developed a strong sense of identification with his country since the nation celebrated on that day, and by the time he published *Fanshawe* in 1828, the United States was a mere fifty-two years old. The relative youth of the nation, coupled with a lack of an independent, longstanding cultural tradition as well as two wars with Britain – the Revolutionary War, which had not ended until 1783, and the more recent

War of 1812 – provided ample incentive for an American sense of antagonism toward British cultural models.[30]

One result of the political and cultural tensions was a plethora of critics who sought an indigenous American literature because they claimed that most of their contemporary American writers were mere imitators of European – and especially British – influences.[31] James E. Rocks, among many other scholars who address American writers' efforts, says that Americans sought 'literary as well as commercial independence in the early nineteenth century', and as Leslie Fiedler suggests, 'Europe is the master from which we have all fled'.[32] Harry Levin comments that at the middle of the nineteenth century, 'criticism grew clamorous in its demands for a national literature commensurate with the size of the country itself, a great American novel which would confound the over-emulated British, a native author who would out-Shakespeare Shakespeare'.[33] In a country that privileged the rights of the individual, critics of Hawthorne's time who declaimed against British literary influences viewed themselves as protectors of the individuality of the nation itself so that the American nature of the literature became a matter of national pride.

In a study of early histories of American literature, Nina Baym concentrates on histories written between 1882 and 1912 to indicate that even at this much later point in America's history, critics still struggled to establish an exclusively American literature. According to Baym, the American Whig party at the time was engaged in an active campaign to establish New England as the origin of the country's culture. As she comments, the 'Whig project of installing New England as the original site of the American nation had been designed to unify the unformed and scattered American people under the aegis of New England by creating a national history anchored in that region'.[34] One consequence of the unification effort was that Nathaniel Hawthorne became a major figure in American literature since he was of New England Puritan descent and since his work, like that of Ralph Waldo Emerson, James Russell Lowell, Henry Wadsworth Longfellow, Oliver Wendell Holmes and John Greenleaf Whittier, 'expressed Puritan values in nineteenth-century terms'.[35] In fact, Baym suggests that these six major authors, whom many critics viewed as the first true American writers, frequently were depicted in literary histories as 'quasi-allegorical personifications', with Hawthorne cast as the Artist, just as Hawthorne's own characters in his romances act as allegorical figures.[36]

However, despite the efforts of literary historians to establish a specifically American literature by emphasizing these New Englanders, many critics felt that American literature still did not exist. In 1820, when Hawthorne was only sixteen, James Kirk Paulding optimistically commented,

This country is not destined to be always behind in the race of literary glory. The time
will assuredly come, when that same freedom of thought and action which has given
such a spur to our genius in other respects, will achieve similar wonders in literature.[37]

Fourteen years later – when Hawthorne was thirty – William Gilmore Simms
claimed that Americans' writings 'might as well be European', and of American
writers, he said flatly, 'They are European'.[38] Even after Hawthorne's death, Walt
Whitman was to suggest in 'Democratic Vistas' of 1871 that America had 'no
literature at all' and that the states of the union were 'entirely held possession of
by foreign lands' in their theology and social standards – including their literature.[39] And as late as 1891, Whitman was still predicting a 'yet to be National
Literature'.[40]

Even as the new nation struggled into the twentieth century and celebrated
over 120 years of existence, critics still lamented American reliance on 'foreign'
culture. In a 1904 essay, Gertrude Atherton lamented the declining tendency
for literature to 'take its cue from the Declaration of Independence'.[41] Atherton goes so far as to suggest that even Hawthorne 'might never have breathed
the free air of a young republic' and exhorts her contemporaries, 'There is only
one way in which man or woman can develop real strength, and that is to fight
unceasingly and to stand absolutely alone'.[42] Americans continued to worry over
European and British influence, so much so that twenty years later in an essay
on the effects of World War I on literature, H. L. Mencken was to suggest that
because the war had negatively influenced European literature, American literature looked all the better.[43] His implication was that European literature still
would have been far superior had the war not occurred. In any case, many Americans held antagonistic attitudes toward Anglo-European literature throughout
Hawthorne's lifetime and long afterward, so Hawthorne worked against British
literary tradition, in much the same way that Elizabeth Inchbald had done over
fifty years earlier, to develop the Romantic moral romance sub-genre.

A concern with writing in opposition to British literature was more than
just a part of the general cultural milieu in which Hawthorne wrote. In fact,
the members of Hawthorne's own social circles evinced their concern repeatedly, and often publicly, and as they advocated a more American literature, they
unwittingly encouraged Hawthorne's desire to develop the Romantic moral
romance.[44] For example, in his well-known 1837 oration, 'The American Scholar',
Hawthorne's contemporary Ralph Waldo Emerson looked forward to the day
when 'our long apprenticeship to the learning of other lands' would end and suggested that Americans had 'listened too long to the courtly muses of Europe'.[45]
Seven years later, he complained in 'The Young American' that Americans' 'reading [is] chiefly confined to the productions of the English press'.[46] Henry David
Thoreau, writing in 1836, argued, 'We are, as it were, but colonies. True, we have

declared our independence, and gained our liberty, but we have dissolved only the political bands which connected us with Great Britain; though we have rejected her tea she still supplies us with food for the mind'.[47] Similarly, Margaret Fuller, who referred to Hawthorne as 'the best writer of the day' in 1846, acknowledged in an essay on American literature that many critics would object to her essay because it dealt with 'that which has as yet no existence'.[48] Herman Melville made the same suggestion in 1850 in 'Hawthorne and His Mosses', an essay in which he called on America to 'prize and cherish her writers' and even to glorify mediocrity over 'literary flunkeyism towards England'.[49]

Similar emphases on the development of a purely American form of literature continued to follow Hawthorne throughout his life, often with his own active participation. At Hawthorne's graduation from Bowdoin College, Henry Wadsworth Longfellow spoke during the ceremony to call for the 'Native Writers' of America to win notoriety, and in a July 1837 review of Hawthorne's *Twice-told Tales* in the *North American Review*, Longfellow, still a 'proponent of native American literature', praised Hawthorne's thematic use in his tales of New England legends.[50] Longfellow approvingly described the stories as 'national in their character'. Years later at a dinner party, when Oliver Wendell Holmes 'began praising both Englishmen and English authors without reservation', Herman Melville defended American writers; James Fields, Hawthorne's publisher, remembered nearly thirty years afterward that Hawthorne had 'stoutly defended the Americans'.[51] Certainly, the circumstance of being American was one of Hawthorne's greatest preoccupations, and one consequence of his deep-seated interest in the nature of American literature was his experimentation with the romance and novel forms that he attempted to develop into a peculiarly American sub-genre in the Romantic moral romance. Just as Elizabeth Inchbald had experimented with genre to mould fiction for her own purposes in an attempt to legitimize her books as texts written by a woman, Hawthorne did the same to legitimize his works as American literature. His subject, developed through his individual form of Romantic moral romance in opposition to the traditional British novel form, was New England, the seat of American civilization. Like Inchbald's experimentation, Hawthorne's, motivated by an increasingly prevalent desire in American literary circles for a uniquely American literature, culminated in a kind of tale that borrows character types, or figures, from the romance and moral tale to examine psychological motivation in allegorical terms.

Inchbald's Expressed Intentions as a Fiction Writer

Now that the contexts in which Inchbald and Hawthorne wrote, and their motives in doing so, are clear, an examination of the authors' expressed intentions is in order, especially as presented in their prefaces. Inchbald's intentions in writing her Romantic moral romances and developing the sub-genre into her unique vehicle are perhaps less clear than Hawthorne's because she left fewer self-reflexive texts in which she examined her own writing. However, some evidence remains to suggest her intentions, particularly within her fictions. The very title of *A Simple Story* implies that the text may be something other than a novel, especially since the plot, with its psychological examination of motives, is far from simple.[52] Further, Inchbald refers to the text pointedly as a story in her preface, and not as a novel, to indicate a clear avoidance of the novel form.[53] Like so many of her female contemporaries, she chooses to denigrate herself in her own introduction. She apologizes to her readers for her supposedly poor efforts at writing and complains that many obstacles have intruded in her creative process, a process that she claims to dislike. Referring to herself in the third person, she acknowledges 'the utmost detestation to the fatigue of inventing, a constitution suffering under a sedentary life, and an education confined to the narrow boundaries prescribed her sex', and she complains that her attempt at a long prose work is a result of her dissatisfaction with thirteen years of barely surviving as an actor because of her speech impediment.[54] In a single sentence, she manages to devalue her own stamina, personality and knowledge and to display the weakness of her stammer. However, in a daring and subversive act of self-promotion, she simultaneously alludes to her own acting and playwriting fame as she refers to the thirteen-year period, and even the reference to her stammer would have reminded her contemporaries, who undoubtedly knew of the limitation, that she had been onstage only a few years earlier.

Inchbald thus legitimizes her own first book by situating it in relation to her earlier theatre career, which she continues as a playwright, so that the book appears to be simply another production of an established actor and writer rather than the first novel of some unknown author. Her ingenious coupling of self-promotion with self-denigration suggests that, in reality, her opinion of herself is much higher than the surface of her text may suggest. In fact, she is proud of her accomplishments and wants her readers to remember them as they read her new book. She then invokes the Muses, but does so, not to thank them for their help, but rather to ask their pardon for not crediting them with helping her to write since 'NECESSITY' has forced her to write to support herself.[55] She embraces the need to write as one might embrace the traditional Muses.

In part, Inchbald's suggestion that she writes out of necessity fits perfectly into the submissive role that women often felt compelled to assume in writing their books. As Tompkins comments,

> Let a woman write to amuse her leisure hours, to instruct her sex, to provide blameless reading for the young, or to boil the pot; moral zeal was an accepted justification and poverty an accepted excuse; but there was one motive which could neither be

justified nor excused – ambition, the 'boast' of conscious power, craving to perform its task and receive its reward.[56]

Countless women writers of these early years of the novel realized the limitation and apologized for their books in their prefaces because they knew that critics would attack them for their temerity if they gave the appearance of writing simply because they wished to express themselves. Frances Burney's *Camilla*, for example, published five years after *A Simple Story* in 1796, begins with a self-deprecating letter to Queen Charlotte Sophia to ask for patronage for the 'humble offering' of the book, which Burney calls 'a production of apparently so light a kind'.[57] Burney further comments that she hopes the text will 'speed the progress of Morality'.[58] Similarly, Mary Hays, in her preface to the *Memoirs of Emma Courtney*, published the same year, suggests that many of her readers may wish to view Emma Courtney's actions 'as a *warning*, rather than as an example'.[59] Both of these books came after *A Simple Story*, however, and their authors may well have used Inchbald's text as inspiration to write prefaces that would disarm hostile critics while more subtly making a serious point about women's issues and women's fictions that both were and were not novels. After all, Hays calls her book 'a simple story' in a possible allusion to Inchbald.[60] Rather than simply appeasing their critics, Burney and Hays more likely followed Inchbald's example to write ironic prefaces whose surface-level text suggested traditional submissiveness but whose metatext suggested Wollstonecraftian pride in their work as they attempted to legitimize their books.

Even Maria Edgeworth praised Inchbald's works and recognized their uniqueness and the extent to which they opposed themselves to the tradition of the popular novel for women that appeared throughout the country. In the 'Advertisement' to *Belinda*, Edgeworth says of her own book,

> The following work is offered to the public as a Moral Tale – the author not wishing to acknowledge a novel. Were all novels like those of madame de Crousaz, Mrs Inchbald, miss Burney, or Dr Moore, she would adopt the name of novel with delight.[61]

Edgeworth praises Inchbald for eschewing the traditional novel form to write a 'Moral Tale' – perhaps a term borrowed from Marmontel's *Contes moraux* or a similar French source. Ostensibly, a moral tale would have a higher purpose than a merely entertaining novel.

Inchbald's writing a book instead of writing another play was a well-conceived plan for infusing her ideas about women's education and empowerment into her cultural milieu. The necessity that she mentions in her preface, although it does refer to her need for money, refers also to the need for a change in the way her contemporaries view women, especially women writers. While thanking her Muse, as Necessity personified, Inchbald makes one request: 'I will not complain

of any hardship thy commands require, so thou doest not urge my pen to prostitution'.[62] Her choice of the word *prostitution* is jarring in the penultimate sentence
of the preface. She gives examples of the prostitution, 'libels' and 'panegyric on
the unworthy', but for Inchbald and her female contemporaries, the word itself is
charged with an emotional intensity tied to women's issues. Beyond its denotation
of a physical sexual act motivated by economic profit, the word also symbolically
connotes many women's social positions at the start of the Romantic Period. The
year after *A Simple Story*'s publication, Mary Wollstonecraft would write *A Vindication of the Rights of Woman*, a book that lamented that women often were
forced into marriages that constituted no more than legal prostitution, and a
book that also flatly stated that women often were forced into literal prostitution
because of a lack of education and freedom. Moreover, Inchbald's *Nature and
Art*, which appeared a mere four years later, depicts Hannah Primrose, a woman
forced into prostitution, among other degradations, to survive, and whose story
Inchbald may have based on the life of her own sister Deborah, who became a
prostitute before dying in poverty in 1794.[63] Hence, Inchbald's preface, a mere
two pages of text that seemingly demonstrate the usual submissive female stance,
expresses both a pride in the author's work and a concern over contemporary
social issues. Inchbald rejects the traditional conception of the Muses to push
aside the inspiration of the traditional patriarchy and claim her own inspiration
in a new kind of Muse – the Muse of possible social change. If one may take
A Simple Story as an example of the Romantic moral romance, then the text's
symbolic contestation of traditional ideologies must be a characteristic of that
romance form. Moreover, that contestation makes the Romantic moral romance
particularly Romantic, as one of the defining features of Romantic thought is its
revolutionary questioning of established order.

Unlike *A Simple Story*, *Nature and Art* has no preface to present Inchbald's
intentions. Nor did Inchbald publish any extended discussion of the text. However, internal evidence from the book, particularly the self-reflexive passages in
which the narrator directly addresses the reader, suggests that, like *A Simple Story*,
Nature and Art is not a traditional novel. Roger Manvell calls the text a 'socio-
political fable rather than a realistic or domestic novel', and Janice Cauwels refers
to *Nature and Art* as a 'moral fable'.[64] More recently, A. A. Markley calls the
book 'fable-like'.[65] In fact, the book's didacticism, combined with its sparse character development, does lend a sense of fable-like simplicity to the text. Jonathan
Wordsworth suggests that the story is 'designed as a fable, at times almost an allegory', and he later refers to the plot as a 'fable-world'.[66] These descriptions recall
descriptions of the mediaeval chivalric romance and the French moral tale.

Rather than being a traditional novel, *Nature and Art* is, instead, Inchbald's
second attempt to develop further the experiment that she had begun in *A Simple Story* in the establishment of an alternative sub-genre into which her writing

could be classified – that of the Romantic moral romance. At no point does Inchbald call *Nature and Art* a novel, but instead, she refers to it much as she did to her earlier book. In a discussion of the elder William and his wife at the beginning of Chapter 7 in Volume 1, the narrator comments, 'They are human creatures who are meant to be pourtrayed in this little book ...'[67] The statement, which appears early in the text, reveals a great deal about Inchbald's intentions. Here, Inchbald makes the first self-reference to the book to call it 'this little book' and differentiate it from a novel. As she does with the word *simple* in the title of *A Simple Story*, she deceptively de-emphasizes the importance of *Nature and Art* with the diminutive word *little*. The statement also reveals that Inchbald's interest lies, not in individual people, but in 'human creatures' in general, which she depicts in characters who amount to little more than caricatures, much like the figures who appear in chivalric romances and moral tales.[68] Indeed, Inchbald's characters generally do not have counterbalancing qualities. Her 'human creatures', who appear in *A Simple Story* and *Nature and Art*, act as another defining element of the Romantic moral romance.

Inchbald's subsequent question about a person's good and bad qualities is ironic, for the elder William in *Nature and Art* really has very few good qualities to counterbalance his bad ones, and his wife, Lady Clementina, possesses even fewer redeeming traits. As figures or types rather than well-rounded characters, they simply cannot be balanced, and their single-sided lack of development underscores the fable-like quality of the text. In a similar discussion of Lord Bendham in Chapter 19, the narrator refers to the text as a 'little history' and calls Bendham a 'creature' who is 'wholly made up of observance, of obedience, of dependance, and of imitation – a borrowed character – a character formed by reflection'.[69] He, too, is a mere caricature, a 'creature', rather than a person, whose individual personality traits are subsumed by the role of his office, Lord of the Bed-Chamber. The word *reflection* often implies thought and consideration, but in this case, it implies simply a thoughtless mirroring of behaviour. When Inchbald calls her book a 'little history' here, she again ironically denigrates it with the diminutive *little*, but she also designates it as part of an important category. The word *history* denotes an exposition of events from the past in a way that conveys the information about those events – the facts – as if they are truth. Hence, when Inchbald calls her book a 'little history', she classifies it as a purveyor of truth. She realizes that history is subjective and that history books can differ widely from one another as to the 'facts'. She also realizes that history has been an overwhelmingly male-oriented field, with truth defined as male action within a male sphere of influence. Thus, when she classifies her book into the history category, she attempts to redefine history – or truth – in female terms and to legitimize her satiric claims about the hypocrisy of the clergy and the judiciary in *Nature and Art* while she traces the sobering story of Hannah Primrose. Hence, the proposition of alternative 'truth', an acknowledgement of the fluidity of what might be considered 'fact', also characterizes the Romantic moral romance.

Inchbald may have had the title of *A Simple Story* in mind as she made the reference to little histories in *Nature and Art*. In French, a language Inchbald had studied extensively and had used during her unsuccessful stay in France with her husband Joseph, the word *histoire* can denote, in translation, either the word *history* or the word *story* depending on its context. Therefore, when Inchbald calls her book a 'little history', she may recall the ambiguity of the French word, particularly since French publishers already had issued *A Simple Story* at least three times as *Simple histoire*.[70] The double meaning of the French word aptly encompasses Inchbald's intentions in writing her book to create both a tale for one's amusement (a story) and a serious examination of truth (a history). The possibility that Inchbald intended the doubling of meaning is reinforced later in the book when she addresses her upper-class readers to warn them that the lower-class Rebecca Rymer and Hannah Primrose are the heroines of 'this little history' and when, in the succeeding paragraph, she refers to the text as 'this story'.[71] Speaking directly to the reader, Inchbald comments here that the book will examine 'the passions which rage in the bosom of the inferior class of human kind'. Essentially, then, Inchbald's interest in *Nature and Art* lies in the examination of truth as expressed through the passions of character types whose allegorical nature allows them to symbolize large segments of humanity. When the two Henrys return from Africa to find Rebecca living with her sisters, the women regale the newly returned travellers with 'the story of poor Hannah's fate'.[72] If, as Inchbald says, Hannah is one of the heroines of the text, and if her fate constitutes a 'story' in Inchbald's terms, then the tale of her seduction and downfall must be seen as an allegory or parable – an alternate kind of 'truth' – that represents the fates of many women.

Hawthorne's Expressed Intentions as a Fiction Writer

While Inchbald struggled against the evolving tradition of the British novel as a woman writer in Britain, Nathaniel Hawthorne, working over half a century later in America, struggled as an American attempting to establish a fictional literature that reflected the uniqueness of the American experience in the mid-nineteenth century. Inchbald left few texts in which she explained her motives for writing, so her intentions must be deduced, in large part, both from the literary climate in which she worked and from the techniques she employs in her texts, ranging from her sparse characterization to her theatrical staging of the characters' actions within plots that ultimately present Inchbald's readers with some moral. If Inchbald's memoirs were available, modern scholars might have a clearer conception of why she wrote as she did, but in the absence of those volumes, reportedly consigned to the flames nearly two hundred years ago, Inchbald's biography and the texts that she wrote must stand as the primary testimonials of her intentions.[73] In contrast, however, Nathaniel Hawthorne left several important texts in which he explicitly examines his own intentions in writing his Romantic moral romances. The prefaces to his books outline a well-conceived approach to the sub-genre – which he simply calls romance – and clearly delineate Hawthorne's conception of the sub-genre as he developed it within the books themselves.[74]

Hawthorne's development of the romance form was deliberate, and he even subtitled his books to indicate their uniqueness. *Fanshawe* is *A Tale* instead of a novel; *The Scarlet Letter* is *A Romance*; and *The Marble Faun* is *The Romance of Monte Beni*. *The Blithedale Romance* announces its unusual romance qualities in its main title rather than a subtitle. Hawthorne's titles make just as bold statements as Elizabeth Inchbald's title of *A Simple Story*. A voracious reader, Hawthorne was familiar with many kinds of writing, and, drawing on his knowledge of varying genres and styles, he consciously constructed his romances to explore issues of psychological motivation through symbolic figures. Richard Chase notes in *The American Novel and Its Tradition* that 'it was in the work of Hawthorne that for the first time the psychological possibilities of romance were realized', and although Chase's statement devalues the contributions that other writers like Inchbald made to the evolution of the novel and romance genres, it does clearly situate Hawthorne's texts outside the traditional novel genre.[75]

The prefaces that Hawthorne prefixed to his romances dissolve any doubt that he consciously developed an alternative to the traditional novel and explicitly outline his intentions with the form. The prefaces also clarify the definition of the Romantic moral romance by directly articulating several characteristics of Hawthorne's texts that Inchbald's texts also share. 'The Custom-House', the 1850 introduction to *The Scarlet Letter*, is the first of these prefaces, and in it, Hawthorne explains his earlier conception of romance as he describes his partially fictionalized adventures in the Custom House and his supposed discovery of a bundle of papers relating Hester Prynne's story. In the second paragraph, the narrator – supposedly Hawthorne – describes himself as the editor rather than the writer and suggests that the story itself is not his own invention but rather a tale whose origins lie in Puritan antiquity.[76] Like a mediaeval chivalric romance, the story reaches back to the legendary past for its basis, and the Puritanism of America's past encourages heavy use of symbolic and allegorical features. Hawthorne connects that Puritan tradition with his own family and takes their shame upon himself in an admission that his Puritan ancestors took part in the witch trials of Salem.[77] Because of his family's involvement in the trials, Hawthorne's love of Salem is bound by concern over moral issues and the questioning of traditional ideologies – concerns that he incorporated into his idea of the Romantic moral romance form just as Inchbald had done. After discovering the bundle of papers about Hester discarded in a dusty corner of the Custom House, the narrator describes finding the scarlet letter, which he believes must have been some sort of important symbol.[78] Symbolism thus infuses the story of Hester Prynne even before the narrator begins his full-scale relation of what he calls a 'legend' or a 'tale'.[79] The heat that he feels when he picks up the scarlet letter is not a supernatural phenomenon but is, instead, a psychological reaction to the symbolic letter, in short, a sensory hallucination that he experiences as a result of his own psychological state. Hawthorne has thus fused the symbolic with the psychological even before beginning the text proper, and as he continues his discussion in 'The Custom-House', he destabilizes the idea of truth to add to his conception of romance. At one point, he says rather facetiously that in writing the book, he has allowed himself so much artistic licence that it may all be fiction; what he does not invent is the general pattern of the facts – of the 'truths' – presented in the tale.[80] While he has retained the facts of the supposed original story of Hester, he has embellished with artistic licence to create something new. The original 'facts' act merely as 'the groundwork of a tale' rather than the truth, but through the new tale, Hawthorne, like Inchbald had done, seeks alternative 'truth'.[81]

After Hawthorne embraces the role of romancer, he describes the stark contrast of moonlight falling on ordinarily familiar objects and suggests that romance similarly creates 'a neutral territory, somewhere between the real world and fairy-land, where the Actual and the Imaginary may meet, and each imbue itself with the nature of the other'.[82] For Hawthorne, then, the romance – or the Romantic moral romance – is a marriage of the real and the imaginary and lies somewhere between truth and falsehood, where it embodies the qualities of both. A page later, he reiterates the idea when he comments that an author who is unable to stray into the realm of the fantastic and unusual – while simultaneously retaining a grasp on realism – should not attempt romances at all.[83] The marriage of real and imaginary occurs in *The Scarlet Letter* in, for example, the letter *A* as it appears on Dimmesdale's bare chest in the penultimate chapter of the text – just before his death in what the narrator calls a 'parable'.[84] Some of the witnesses are not sure they saw the letter, whereas others swear that it was quite visible. Moreover, Pearl embodies Hawthorne's conception of romance. At one point early in the plot, the narrator begins to describe a local legend about Pearl in which the girl meets a wolf who allows her to pat his head one day in the forest. The narrator briefly interrupts himself to note, '[B]ut here the tale has surely lapsed into the improbable'.[85] Hawthorne's choice of the word *tale* is significant since it distinguishes his work from the idea of the standard novel, as does his indication of concern that part of his story has moved into the realm of improbability. His intent, as expressed in the preface and supported here, is for the Romantic moral romance to tread the line between the real and the imaginary without becoming too much of either.

The preface to *The House of the Seven Gables*, published a year later, further describes Hawthorne's methods and explains his rationale. Even though *The House of the Seven Gables* is neither titled nor subtitled a 'romance', Hawthorne makes it clear in the first sentence of the preface that the book is not a traditional novel. In his view, a romance can take greater liberties with the truth than a novel can.[86] A traditional novel, he says, should aim for realism that approximates everyday existence; readers should have no reason to question the veracity of the tale.[87] Hawthorne's recognition of the novel's tendency toward verisimilitude presages the development of the realistic novel during the American Civil War and continuing to the end of the century. Hawthorne, however, wishes to produce romances as a more artistic kind of writing that 'may swerve aside from the truth of the human heart' and that present 'truth under circumstances, to a great extent, of the writer's own choosing or creation'.[88] In short, the romance must blend the real and the imaginary for its effect, and the result, rather than being a novel, is a 'Tale' or 'Legend', as Hawthorne had also recognized in 'The Custom-House' and as Elizabeth Inchbald had realized when she wrote her tales.[89] For both Inchbald and Hawthorne, the Romantic moral romance is a quest for alternative 'truth' revealed through the combination of the real and the imaginary.

As Hawthorne continues his discussion, he calls the romance 'an attempt to connect a by-gone time with the very Present that is flitting away from us' and thereby links the past with the present just as he had done in *The Scarlet Letter* in its reliance on the Puritan past.[90] He also humorously notes that many authors believe a romance should have 'some definite moral purpose' and suggests that he has provided one in *The House of the Seven Gables* so as not to be deficient.[91] He thinks, however, that when romances teach their readers, they should do so through an indirect process that slowly leads readers to the truth rather than preaching to them.[92] Romances should lead their readers through a less obvious learning process that allows for greater artistic expression on the part of the author. Finally, in a last connection of the real with the imaginary, Hawthorne asks his readers to peruse his book purely as a romance that has little to do with concrete reality.[93] Read in combination with 'The Custom-House', the later preface provides considerable insight into Hawthorne's intentions in writing his romances.

The preface to *The Blithedale Romance*, published another year later in 1852, adds even more to Hawthorne's continuously developing aesthetic. He calls the book a 'fancy-sketch' that depicts 'imaginary personages' and suggests that he uses the utopian community of the text, based on the Brook Farm experiment of which Hawthorne himself had been a part, merely to 'establish a theatre' for the story.[94] His choice of the analogy of the theatre for his discussion is interesting since, like Inchbald's texts – and as examples of the Romantic moral romance

– much of his writing retains a distinctly theatrical, or dramatic, quality based on Shakespearean precedent. The characters with whom Hawthorne populates his stage, however, are not well-developed people, but like Inchbald's characters, they are 'creatures of his brain' who have less to do with reality and traditional character development and more relevance to allegorical representation in their 'phantasmagorical antics' as figures or character-types.[95] He later calls them 'beings of imagination'.[96] Hawthorne clearly states that he prefers not to expose them 'to too close a comparison with the actual events of real lives' to suggest that the romancer's work should not be placed 'side by side with nature' since he is allowed 'a license with regard to every-day Probability'.[97]

Hawthorne then makes a direct allusion to one of the problems of American literature in the writings of American authors. He says that romance often includes an 'atmosphere of strange enchantment' that is exactly 'what the American romancer needs' but unfortunately lacks.[98] Because of the historical void in American literary existence, the characters that he creates for his books must 'show themselves in the same category as actually living mortals'.[99] The consequence of the limitation is that the 'paint and pasteboard of their composition [is] but too painfully discernible'.[100] In short, Hawthorne clearly is aware that his characters seem underdeveloped and that they tend to appear more as character-types or figures rather than full-fledged, believable characters who might be conceived of as having an existence beyond the narrative structure of the book. Instead, they exhibit the same deliberate simplicity as Inchbald's characters, and they are 'entirely fictitious'.[101] Hawthorne's reminder about the fictitious nature of his characters counters any suggestions that they resemble the actual people who participated in the Brook Farm experiment on which he based the tale, but Hawthorne is disingenuous here, for Zenobia clearly is a modified version of Margaret Fuller, and other characters have similar real-life counterparts. Hence, the fictitious quality of the characters is more a result of their development and symbolic nature than of their lack of correspondence to real people. Through the development of the example of Brook Farm with the romance form, Hawthorne has created a 'foothold between fiction and reality' in which to situate his fictional characters in *The Blithedale Romance*.[102] They occupy the liminal space as representations of character types.

With each successive preface, Hawthorne added to his conception of fiction to clarify the idea and more clearly delineate his definition of romance. The preface to *The Marble Faun*, published in 1860, is no exception. As in earlier prefaces, he refers to his book as a romance and calls it a 'fanciful story, evolving a thoughtful moral' while he makes it clear that his main character Kenyon is 'entirely imaginary'.[103] In this preface, Hawthorne delivers one of his most quoted passages, in which he claims to set the tale in Italy because, unlike America, it has a dark past that makes writing easier and because '[r]omance and poetry, like ivy, lichens, and wall-flowers, need Ruin to make them grow'.[104] Hawthorne seems equivocal about America here. Clearly, he finds it difficult to write without a longstanding cultural heritage like that of his Anglo-European counterparts. In the preface to a book that contains allusions to the ill-fated Cenci family of Italy's dark past, Hawthorne laments that America does not have antiquity, mystery or any shadowy, guilt-ridden horrors, and without these ills, romance is difficult to write. Margaret Fuller had expressed a similar sentiment in 1846 when she suggested that Americans could not 'have expression until there is something to be expressed'.[105] Despite Fuller's lamentation, however, Hawthorne suggests that a shadowy past unfortunately will develop as the country ages. In the interim, Hawthorne does what Van Wyck Brooks suggested decades later in 1918 when he called for Americans to create a 'usable past' out of their own experiences as a basis for their literature.[106] Hawthorne creates a usable past in Puritan New England, setting most of his romances there and, in the case of *The Marble Faun*, depicting characters whose origins lie in that usable past of Puritan history. If romance and poetry need ruin to make them grow, then the Romantic moral romance must, to be truly successful, build upon some dark portion of human existence, either from one's socio-political environment or from within one's own psyche.

Dramatic Techniques in the Romantic Moral Romance

Hawthorne's prefaces, just like any other author's self-reflexive discussion, are useful in studying his intentions, but the most revealing evidence of an author's intent is the actual text, in which the writer's practice either illustrates or falls short of the expressed intentions. In the cases of Inchbald and Hawthorne, the romances do illustrate the authors' expressed goals while they further help to refine the definition of the Romantic moral romance as a sub-genre. To attain their goals, Inchbald and Hawthorne construct dramatically inspired scenes that examine the psychological motivation of sparsely developed, symbolic character-types. The authors use dramatic staging techniques to focus attention on the human mind, and Inchbald's and Hawthorne's characters exhibit passionate natures that contribute to their one-sidedness and to their symbolic quality. Ultimately, Inchbald and Hawthorne each seek alternative 'truth' – respectively, acknowledgment of women's writing and acknowledgment of indigenous American literature – in opposition to the British novel tradition. These characteristics overlap with other qualities that define the romance form and anticipate the more detailed discussions in Chapters 3, 4 and 5 of the Romantic moral romance's Shakespearean precedents, of its obsession with questions of moral order, and of its reliance on artfully constructed character-types.

   One of the most interesting characteristics of Inchbald's and Hawthorne's books – and of the Romantic moral romance in general – is the texts' dependence upon dramatic convention. In essence, both authors construct metaphorical stages on which to display their stories, and the characters participate in the action just as stage actors might. Consequently, the romances exhibit intentional artificiality that calls attention to the symbolic natures of the characters. Inchbald and Hawthorne, rather than becoming preoccupied with the psychological workings of a single, unified mind, exhibit greater interest in the interactions among several fragments of a mind.[107] Each character thus becomes little more than a single element within a larger psyche that encompasses more than one – perhaps all – of the characters in one story, and the relationships that the characters have with one another reveal psychological motivation.

As an actor and a playwright, Inchbald was acutely aware of the way characters should interact in a convincing manner, for she had both acted and written many roles for the stage. She succeeds in creating convincing dialogue when she wants to do so, but the dramatic staging of action reveals far more about the psychological states of the characters – or symbolic figures – in *A Simple Story*.[108] After Dorriforth becomes Lord Elmwood, staging techniques clarify his relationship with his daughter Matilda. When the two meet accidentally on the stairs one day, Matilda swoons in the arms of her father, whose only response is to call her by her mother's name. Matilda's physical placement in the scene, as she descends the stairs, parallels her relationship with her father. To Lord Elmwood, Matilda is no more than an idea tucked into the far, upper limits of his mind – a negative memory of his marriage to the late Miss Milner. Clearly, at least in Elmwood's mind, Matilda represents her own mother in the scene so that when Matilda descends the stairs, Miss Milner figuratively returns to life – as if descending from Heaven – to intrude upon Elmwood's isolation. Having compartmentalized and ignored his own love for Matilda, Elmwood finds the intrusion disturbing, for it reminds him of the difficulties he experienced in his attempts to control his late wife's behaviour. His response, to call Matilda by her mother's name and then hand the swooning girl to a servant, reveals far more than extensive dialogue could and far more poignantly demonstrates the fractured relationship that exists between father and daughter.

The artificiality of dialogue appears repeatedly throughout the book to emphasize psychological states. Hence, Maria Edgeworth's praise to Inchbald in a January 1810 letter was perceptive when she commented, 'I am of opinion that it is by leaving more than most other writers to the imagination, that you succeed so eminently in affecting it'.[109] In fact, at the beginning of the book, Inchbald openly announces to her readers that the characters' actions will be far more important than their words. After a brief description of Miss Milner, the narrator says, 'And now – leaving description – the reader must form a judgment of her by her actions; by all the round of great or trivial circumstances that shall be related'.[110] This narrative technique is a significant departure from

Inchbald's dramatic productions, in which all of a character's motivation had to be revealed in dialogue and through his or her actions on the stage. Actors, however, thought for themselves and could portray characters in any way they chose, but with *A Simple Story*, Inchbald finally wrote a tale in which she could control, not just the dialogue, but the very physical movements of the figures on its metaphorical stage. For Inchbald, the result was an increased sense of power and control over her own literary production as she examined her characters' psychological motivations.

Just as she does in *A Simple Story*, Inchbald draws from her drama experience in *Nature and Art* to juxtapose characters in ways that de-emphasize the characters' individual identities and make them more symbolic as participants in the Romantic moral romance.[111] One of the most interesting examples of Inchbald's dramatic technique appears in the text when young Henry returns to England to live with his uncle. Conducted by a sailor on whose ship he had sailed, young Henry appears at William's door with no greater advance notice than a letter of introduction from his father that the servant brings to William. After William reads the letter, he orders that the boy be shown into the room, and here, Inchbald reveals her dramatic skill by freezing the characters, for a few moments, into a *tableau vivant* on the metaphorical stage that presents the action of the book.

During the time elapsed as Henry mounts the stairs, the characters in the room, including both Williams and Lady Clementina, do not move, and instead, Inchbald briefly shifts the focus of the story into their minds to display their thoughts just as she, as a playwright, might display the thoughts of characters in a play through the dramatic convention of the aside. Lady Clementina wonders how to receive him in a way that will most flatter her own honour, while young William speculates about how uncouth his cousin will be and notes that the poor boy undoubtedly will be 'surprised, and awed by his superiority'.[112] Inchbald depicts both Lady Clementina and young William as mere types of vanity and pride in the scene by revealing their self-involved thoughts as they await young Henry.[113] They do not care that the boy has endured a long ocean voyage, that he has no money and needs their help, or that he may be ill and malnourished as a result of the voyage. They care, instead, how his presence will reflect upon them and how that presence, combined with its related African background, will support their notions of their own superiority in relation both to him and to their own civilized peers within British social circles.

The elder William, on the other hand, is impatient to see his nephew, and after young Henry enters the room, he is the first to move and speak, for he embraces the boy and exclaims repeatedly, 'I will repay to you, all I owe to your father'.[114] Initially, the elder William's reaction may seem touching, and consequently, it may appear to situate him as a positive figure in contrast to his own wife and son. However, earlier in the story, Inchbald already has established

William's self-involved pride and equated it with Lady Clementina's vanity.[115] In commenting that he will repay young Henry for all that he owes his father, William unwittingly reveals his own limitations since his statement indicates a concern over his being indebted to the elder Henry rather than a concern over young Henry's welfare. He also reveals that, despite any prideful statements to the contrary, he instinctively realizes that he owes the elder Henry a great deal for the financial and moral support that led to his high position in the Anglican Church. Thus, William's impatience at beholding young Henry and his emotional embracing of the boy dramatically indicate William's own pride and self-interest rather than the more noble solicitude for the young man. Inchbald's metaphorical *tableau vivant* acts as a tightly constructed, dramatically motivated device that de-emphasizes the individuality of the characters and helps to turn them into allegorical figures with wider significance.

Just as Inchbald uses dramatic techniques, Hawthorne also incorporates artificial staging into his books to underscore the symbolic nature of the characters of his Romantic moral romances. Like Inchbald, Hawthorne was an avid supporter of the theatre, and he attended many productions of Shakespeare's plays – and perhaps even saw some of Inchbald's plays. Since Hawthorne was not an actor, he did not have the intimate knowledge of the theatre that Inchbald possessed, so he did not rely so heavily on theatrical precedent. However, he did understand the theatre's conventions, and he could, and did, construct scenes within his texts that exhibit marked dramatic qualities.[116] *The Scarlet Letter* includes perhaps the best-known example of Hawthorne's ability to place his characters strategically on a stage in its depiction of Hester upon the scaffold of the pillory at the beginning of the tale – as well as in the middle and at the end in a sort of frame to the story.[117] The book begins at the Boston prison, where Hester makes her dramatic entrance into the story in a procession that leads her to the scaffold. Carrying her child and already bearing the mark of the scarlet letter, she moves through the crowd like a great personage as she takes her place for the three-hour ordeal. Just as a play might last three hours, Hester's drama is introduced officially to the Boston townspeople while she remains onstage, so to speak, during the three-hour punishment. The scarlet letter itself parallels an actor's costume, for it represents Hester's guilt, which she bears like a costume throughout the rest of the plot and removes only once for a few moments.

Although Hester descends from the scaffold, she remains metaphorically onstage throughout the book, where she continuously plays the part of the guilty adulteress who has the eyes of all the town's inhabitants upon her. The Puritan audience stares intensely at the prison door before Hester emerges, and those eyes follow Hester to the scaffold and throughout the plot of the book as she acts her part in the drama of guilt and retribution that Hawthorne constructs.[118] The townspeople even comment upon Hester's fate and suggest alternative – harsher – punishments for her just as a theatre audience might suggest differing endings to a drama.[119]

Ironically, although Hester ascends the scaffold and even wears a sort of costume, she remains, unlike the usual principal actor, relatively silent throughout the text. She speaks only occasionally and reveals little about herself when she does speak. One townsman reveals that Hester remained silent even in the courtroom.[120] But Hester's silence extends beyond the court. Consequently, readers of the book know very little about her beyond the events surrounding her sin with Arthur, and she develops as a one-dimensional character-type like Inchbald's Romantic moral romance characters. She does display, however, an ardent passion in her protection of Arthur's secret since she refuses to expose him to the rest of the townspeople. The social pressure on her to speak is strong, just as Inchbald's Lord Elmwood feels a strong pressure to acknowledge his love for Matilda in the second half of *A Simple Story*, but Hester demonstrates strength of will in her silence. Hence, Hawthorne employs dramatic conventions within a non-dramatic genre to depict a character whose passion situates her as a character-type or figure whose psychological motivations become the focus of the plot as she deals with guilt and its effects. Fittingly, the main action of the plot ends before a crowd on the same scaffold, years later, when Arthur reveals his guilt.

Finally, as the plot of *The Marble Faun* develops, Hawthorne again uses dramatic techniques, just as he had done earlier in *The Scarlet Letter*, to stage the activities of his characters in ways that allow them to reveal their psychological motivations through their actions, rather than through their words.[121] As Inchbald had done in her Romantic moral romances, Hawthorne constructs many scenes that reveal the allegorical nature of the characters and the story itself without extensive dialogue. Donatello, for example, witnesses a disturbing scene in which Miriam, unaware that anyone is watching, has a violent fit of anger.[122] The scene reveals more of Miriam's nature than any dialogue could have done. And later, when Hilda confronts Miriam about the Model's murder, she refers to the look of consent that Miriam gave to Donatello for the deed when she cries, 'A look passed from your eyes to Donatello's – a look –'.[123] Dramatic communication through the eyes rather than with words de-emphasizes the importance of dialogue to heighten the allegorical potential of the characters' actions. A similar dramatic construction is clear in the carnival scene at the end of the book, which situates Kenyon in the middle of a stream of merrymakers. Kenyon stands still, like a character on a stage, as the crowd of loud, dancing people flows past him and taunts him in their merriment. When he feels a rosebud hit him gently on the lips before it falls into his hand, he looks up to see Hilda on the balcony of the adjacent house.[124] She has thrown the flower to attract his attention, and her position above the stage may remind some readers of Shakespeare's Juliet, who reveals her love for Romeo from a similar Italian balcony. Like Shakespeare,

Hawthorne has positioned his characters strategically so that the purity of the woman's love emanates from above in a way that makes that love morally righteous. Again, Hawthorne's dramatic staging emphasizes the one-dimensional nature of the characters with its focus on action rather than dialogue, and it further reinforces the characters' allegorical existence as part of a story that explores psychological motivation in moral terms.

Emphasis on the Truth of Passion in the Romantic Moral Romance

While Inchbald and Hawthorne construct metaphorical stages for their character-types, they also pay careful attention to the passionate natures of the characters. Like other Romantic writers – British and American – Inchbald and Hawthorne were interested in the truth of emotion. They viewed passion, in its multiplicity of definitions, as an alternative purveyor of the truth of human experience in their Romantic moral romances. Consequently, they explore varying kinds of passion in their books, ranging from the passionate love of a woman for a man to a Gothic-inspired passionate hatred or desire for revenge. The passion itself, although it may seem a particularly human expression of emotion, often contributes to the one-sided nature of Inchbald's and Hawthorne's characters because its intensity and single-mindedness, even when repressed, simplify the characters in psychological terms as fragments of larger psyches.

The characters in Inchbald's *A Simple Story* exhibit single-minded passionate love and passionate vengefulness. According to an article in the *Critical Review* in 1791, 'the workings of the passions are inimitably displayed' in the text.[125] More recently, Gary Kelly suggests that Inchbald 'reveals an astonishing penetration into deep psychological disturbance and its symptoms which had to wait over a century for fully scientific exposition', and he further comments that Inchbald 'is really at her best in depicting the struggle to suppress deep feeling'.[126] Similarly, Roger Manvell calls the book 'a study in locked-up emotion and its ultimate need for expression'.[127]

One of the best examples of the repression of emotion in *A Simple Story*, which can help to reveal 'truth' in Romantic moral romance terms, is visible in Dorriforth's refusal to acknowledge his love for Miss Milner and, conversely, Miss Milner's refusal to acknowledge her love for him after the two have had a series of disagreements. Despite their feelings for one another, which both of them have expressed by this point, they barely speak, and Dorriforth, by now Lord Elmwood, decides to leave England to find a wife. Despite obvious signs that the two people are in love, they demonstrate strong passion in their refusal to reconcile, and had not Sandford intervened essentially to force their marriage, they would have separated and prolonged the conflict interminably.[128] In a sense, the first half of the book builds toward the climactic marriage that releases the two main characters' repressed passions.

A similar repression and release occur in the emotional progression toward the climax of the second half of *A Simple Story* in the relationship between Lord Elmwood and his daughter Matilda. Because of Miss Milner's indiscretion during Lord Elmwood's absence in the West Indies, Elmwood refuses to see or speak of either his wife or his innocent daughter Matilda. With surgical precision, Elmwood emotionally compartmentalizes his love for his family and vows to the best of his ability never again to become so emotionally attached to anyone.[129] But although he keeps his resolution for a while, and even though he is so strict with his household that he discharges one of his oldest servants for mentioning the late Miss Milner, he still loves Matilda on some level and cannot avoid expressing that repressed emotion on occasion. Indeed, after Lord Margrave kidnaps Matilda, an armed Elmwood rushes to free her and acknowledges her as his child.[130] The danger of another man's seduction of his daughter forces Elmwood to acknowledge the strong emotion that he has so long repressed.

Like *A Simple Story*, *Nature and Art* also foregrounds the intense passions of its characters to find the alternative 'truth' of the Romantic moral romance in emotion. When Rebecca's father discovers that she is caring for a child in her attic room, he demands to know the identities of the child's parents. Initially, Rebecca declares 'the simple truth' – that young Henry found the child in the woods and brought him to her for protection – but her family members do not believe her explanation.[131] Finally, she lies to her father when she tells him that the child is hers and that Henry is his father. Mr Rymer's passionate response parallels Lord Elmwood's attitude toward Miss Milner and Matilda: "'Go, go out of my sight!" said her father. "[...] neither I, nor any of your relations, shall ever see or hear of you more".[132] Like Lord Elmwood, Mr Rymer loves his daughter, but he banishes her from his sight forever, and the intensity of his passion reveals much about the book as a whole and much about the truth that Inchbald wishes to demonstrate with the story.

Like Miss Milner and Matilda, Rebecca is powerless in the face of her father's anger since he is the patriarchal centre of the family who controls even the family's perception of truth. His refusal to accept Rebecca's explanation, coupled with his angry threats that she confess her guilt, forces Rebecca into a false confession. In fact, when Mr Rymer discusses the situation with the elder William, the dean has young William draw up an affidavit in which Rebecca and young Henry acknowledge being the child's parents.[133] Henry prevents Rebecca from signing the document and endangering her soul by swearing to a falsehood only through his own false confession. When the elder William hears young Henry's confession, his response is similar to Mr Rymer's:

'Henry Norwynne, your first guilt is so enormous; your second, in stedfastly denying it, so base; this last conduct so unaccountable! That from the present hour you must never dare to call me relation, or to consider my house as your home'.[134]

William's passion is just as strong as Mr Rymer's. Interestingly, neither Rebecca's mother nor Lady Clementina (as young Henry's surrogate mother) is involved in any of the activity surrounding the discovery of the baby. Instead, the men from both families rush to control the situation – to ascertain the truth as they see it and then codify that truth with a legal document. It seems that the truth, as Inchbald perceives it here, is that women have very little power and that women's involvement might have made the ordeal less painful for Rebecca and Henry. Moreover, Inchbald suggests that codified truth – of any kind – may not be truth at all, especially since, in Rebecca's case, the men involved are controlled as much by their passions as – if not more so than – the women. Ultimately, Inchbald hints, just as she had done five years earlier in *A Simple Story*, that both women and men should receive educations based on the dictates of reason rather than emotion so that they can avoid situations that compromise their integrity or their ability to support themselves.

Strong passion, just as important for Hawthorne as for Inchbald, plays an important role in Hawthorne's Romantic moral romances, too. In *The Scarlet Letter*, for example, Hester Prynne exhibits passionate love for Arthur Dimmesdale, but she cannot openly express her desire without implicating Arthur in her sin. Despite public exhortations to reveal her partner, despite her experiences in jail and with the pillory and despite her punishment with the scarlet *A*, Hester remains obstinately silent. Her resolution is an expression of passion, and in Hester's case, that passion protects Arthur and his reputation at the expense of Hester's own happiness. Her willingness to endure public humiliation, rather than causing Arthur's downfall with a revelation of the truth, confirms the intensity of Hester's emotion and legitimizes that passion as a form of 'truth' greater than the legislated truth of the Puritan Bostonians.

Likewise, Arthur and Roger Chillingworth demonstrate passion in their unwillingness to expose one another as, respectively, adulterer and self-proclaimed avenger. Like Inchbald's Lord Elmwood, they both exert extreme willpower to repress their own emotions. Roger reveals his strength of will when he first speaks to Hester after her experience in the pillory to proclaim that he will spare no efforts to discover the father of her child.[135] His proclamation is prophetic, for he does discover Arthur's secret, but Roger represses the urge to expose his enemy in favour of the emotional torture he inflicts upon the minister. Arthur, too, must exert his own strength of will to avoid exposing himself to Boston's inhabitants and to protect himself from Roger's emotionally terroristic attacks, but the effort he must use to maintain this emotional control takes its toll both psychologically and physically. Even Roger recognizes the symptoms when he gleefully observes Arthur's pain.[136] In any case, both men exhibit incredible strength of will in their efforts to repress emotion, and their willpower in repressing the truth of that strong emotion provides Hawthorne with a viable means of examining psychological motivation as part of his Romantic moral romance.

In *The Marble Faun*, Hawthorne again employs intense passion to elicit the truth of human experience. Donatello, for example, evinces a strong love for Miriam from the beginning of the text. When he tells her he loves her, however, she hears his declaration without showing any emotion of her own.[137] Despite Miriam's indifference, and despite her calling him a 'foolish boy' because of his love, Donatello cultivates the emotion and refuses to heed Miriam's indifferent rebuffs. The intensity of Donatello's love helps Hawthorne to examine the dynamics of the interaction between him and Miriam while keeping both characters on the level of character-types whose one-sided nature will not allow them to change their minds about one another or to interact in a reasoned manner.

After the Model's murder, Miriam and Donatello exhibit strength of will to an even greater extent as they repress their natural emotional urges to reveal their crime. For Donatello, in particular, the concealment of the secret has dire emotional consequences, and when Kenyon mentions Miriam to him one day, the narrator remarks that Donatello's face transforms into a gruesome image of horror.[138] However, despite the agonizing guilt that tortures the two and threatens to drive them to self-destruction, they silently cling to life. When Kenyon mentions suicide during a visit to Donatello's ancestral home in the Apennines, Donatello rejects the possibility outright.[139] His strength of will is so strong that even the despair over the murder does not make him lose his will to live although he feels compelled to conceal his evil deed. Through his character-types' narrowly focused one-mindedness, Hawthorne achieves an examination of human behaviour and the psychological motivation that initiates the behaviour.

Alternate 'Truth' for the Author in the Romantic Moral Romance

Inchbald and Hawthorne do not limit their writing to a search for psychological or moral truth in the Romantic moral romance, for they also seek a truthful means of self-expression in opposition to the traditional British novel. The act of writing romances is part of that truth since the romance allows Inchbald to call for better education for women and the acknowledgment of women writers while it also allows Hawthorne to transform fiction writing into what might legitimately be called American literature. Hence, Inchbald's books exhibit an overt preoccupation with women's education, while Hawthorne's books focus on the circumstance of being American.

In *A Simple Story*, lack of an education based upon the dictates of reason is the primary cause for much of the conflict among the characters. Inchbald's emphasis of the education issue, particularly for women, makes her Romantic moral romance a symbolic manifesto for women's rights. For Inchbald, her contemporaries' hostility – especially male hostility – toward women writers is a symptom of deficient education, so she advocates improvements for both sexes, not just her own. Without an education that will allow her to become self-supporting, Miss Milner must depend upon Dorriforth. And although Dorriforth is educated well enough to support himself and Miss Milner, clearly he does not possess an education based on reason – from Inchbald's point of view – since he engages in dictatorial and repressive behaviour that disempowers Miss Milner.

Late in the book, the danger of another man's seduction of his daughter forces Elmwood to admit how he feels toward her, and Inchbald, who illustrates Elmwood's emotional release so effectively, suggests that his actions are no more reasonable than those of the ill-educated Miss Milner, whose emotional manipulation so infuriated the earlier Dorriforth. In fact, based on the illustrations in the plot of *A Simple Story*, Inchbald believes that neither men nor women receive educations properly based on reason, so when the book ends with the statement that Mr Milner would have been better off bestowing 'A PROPER EDUCATION' on Miss Milner, Inchbald indicts the dominant male half of British society for not using reason to see that women would be better served with appropriate education.[140] Hence, just as the book's preface takes an ironic approach to Inchbald's own writing, the book's conclusion similarly approaches the issue of women's education. The deceptive simplicity of *A Simple Story* hides a sophisticated examination of the psychological motivations of Inchbald's characters that reveals an inherent imbalance in British society in favour of masculine pursuits even though such pursuits may not be motivated by reason. The imbalance is the tradition Inchbald works against as she eschews the traditional British novel to develop the Romantic moral romance sub-genre.

In *Nature and Art*, Inchbald addresses the education issue less directly, but she incorporates it fully into the text. Had Mr Rymer and the elder William received educations based on reason, in Inchbald's terms, they perhaps would not have committed the grievous error of condemning and banishing Rebecca and young Henry and of attempting to codify a falsehood with a legal document. Hannah has a child after being seduced by young William, who refuses to acknowledge the child, and although the elder William knows that his son is the father, he suppresses that information and allows Hannah to appear to have been seduced by someone else. As Mary Wollstonecraft pointed out in 1792, however, a woman's virtue was one of her most prized possessions, and, if the dictates of reason did not guide her education, as soon as she lost that virtue, she often would be left with no other recourse than prostitution.[141] In fact, prostitution is exactly where Hannah must turn since, after her parents die, she is unable to find work and since the two Williams simply assume that she needs nothing and make no effort to alleviate her financial concerns. Ultimately, she engages in counterfeiting, the primary source of her income at the time that she is arrested, convicted and then executed.

In portraying Hannah's difficult situation and eventual hanging, Inchbald makes a clear statement, just as she had done in *A Simple Story*, about women's education and about the education of the man responsible for Hannah's death. Both were inadequate. For Inchbald, the passions are instrumental in the way they reveal truth, but reason should govern the majority of one's actions while acknowledging the truth of emotion. The narrator describes young Henry's reunion with Rebecca after his absence of many years as joyful, but Inchbald undoubtedly viewed the scene with more circumspection as she wrote it. After all, Rebecca has not changed, so she has not progressed intellectually at all, and if Henry cannot recognize that lack of progress, then he, too, lacks critical acumen.[142] More importantly, Rebecca could just as easily have taken Hannah's place in the streets of London, in the brothel and finally on the gallows if Hannah had not finally acknowledged her son to correct the patriarchal conception of truth as the elder William had established it. Thus, Rebecca's freedom, the limited freedom that comes with the intactness of one's virtue, is a matter of mere chance and not of reasoned thought. Inchbald surely realized the distinction as she contrasted Rebecca's happy life with Hannah's torrid downfall so that, in a sense, Rebecca's story is nearly as unfortunate as that of Hannah. Hence, the two women become allegorical representations of two different types of women in Inchbald's Britain, those who retain their virtue on the terms of the established patriarchy and those who do not, and the ways the men in the book respond to Hannah and Rebecca act as similarly symbolic means of examining contemporary gender relations. When reason does not guide women's education, women must depend on men for their existence, but when the men, themselves, possess deficient educations, even submissive women – not just those, like Hannah, who transgress – become victims of the patriarchal system. As discussed in greater detail in Chapter 5, Inchbald's female characters, denied power and self-expression, represent the British woman author in quasi-allegorical terms.

Like Inchbald, Hawthorne employed dramatic techniques, combined with allegorical representation, to examine moral truth and psychological motivation through character-types or figures. The general descriptions of his books, as they help to define the Romantic moral romance, quite easily could be modified to describe Elizabeth Inchbald's books in many respects; however, Hawthorne's fictions differ from Inchbald's in terms of an important feature – their emphasis on the experience of America. Hawthorne's fictions all are strongly rooted in America and in American culture as a means of subverting the traditional 'truth' that fiction was the purview of the British. *Fanshawe*, for example, is set in New England, and its action surrounds the institution of Harley College, which Hawthorne likely modelled on his own *alma mater*, Bowdoin College, in Maine.[143] Hawthorne sets *The Scarlet Letter* in Boston, Massachusetts, not far from his own native town of Salem, and the story itself draws extensively from Puritan tradition, which Hawthorne explicitly recognizes in 'The Custom-House' when he acknowledges his Puritan forbears.[144] Moreover, the narrator of *The Scarlet Letter* repeatedly uses the word *our* to describe features of the New England setting and the Puritan ancestors who once lived there.[145] Hawthorne's use of the word *our* reflects a formalized authorial presence within the text, but it also encompasses the reader to imply a kinship between reader and author as New Englanders. Hawthorne similarly uses *our* to describe the New England setting, probably in Salem, of *The House of the Seven Gables*, where the Maule and Pynchon families still bear enmity toward one another because of a lost – or rather, hidden – deed to a significant tract of Maine real estate.[146] Hawthorne also stages *The Blithedale Romance* in New England, specifically in Massachusetts.

Finally, *The Marble Faun*, although set in Italy, acts as one of Hawthorne's most consciously American tales to question the British novel further. He sets his other texts in New England and draws on his own Puritan heritage for their effects, but in *The Marble Faun*, Hawthorne reaches a new level of self-reflexiveness in a more consciously tailored text that, while relying on Italian legends, is a significantly American endeavour. Among the four major characters, Donatello clearly is an Italian, but Miriam seems to have ties with America even though she seems also tied to the notorious Cenci family of Italy. In contrast, Kenyon clearly is American and has definite ties with his native country. During his visit to Donatello's family estate, he watches an Italian sunset one evening with his host and compares it with colourful American sunsets – which he finds far superior.[147] Hawthorne seems to suggest here that America defies proper artistic portrayal as if he seeks an excuse for the lack of an indigenous American literature that his contemporaries so ardently lamented. Later, in the simple act of eating a peach at Donatello's estate, Kenyon compares it with his own memories of enjoying American peaches and favours the American variety.[148] Hilda, too, holds strong ties with America. She acknowledges her Puritan origins, and the narrator refers to her as a New Englander both by birth and in terms of her cultural origins.[149] When an old German artist realizes Hilda's innocence, he tells her to go back to her own country for the fresher air.[150] The American innocence and inexperience that she represents seemingly do not belong in Italy.

Perhaps one of the most interesting American features of *The Marble Faun*, like that of *The Scarlet Letter*, is the narrator's attitude toward the reader. In *The Marble Faun*, the reader again is addressed as a New Englander with Hawthorne's all-encompassing *our*, which again makes the reader complicit in Hawthorne's scheme to legitimize American culture.[151] In discussing a dance that Miriam and Donatello witness in a glade, the narrator uses the word 'our' in reference to a fellow American in the crowd who refuses to participate.[152] Later, discussing Italian weather, the narrator switches to the word *we* to make a comment, which he believes the reader will understand without explanation, about the difference between New England weather and that of Italy.[153]

In the final chapter of *The Marble Faun*, the narrator wonders whether to label the book as a romance or as a history, and his indecision paradoxically marks Hawthorne's intentions quite clearly.[154] Just as Inchbald attempted to rewrite history in women's terms by calling her texts both stories and histories, Hawthorne also recognizes the need to establish American literature as a significant part of accepted history by referring to his own books in similar terms. When he claims to have wanted to situate Donatello 'between the Real and the Fantastic', he implies that, as a writer, he attempts to create a 'usable past', in Van Wyck Brooks' terms, that combines elements of the real and the imaginary, and from which American literature can develop more fully.[155] That usable past, for Hawthorne, is securely rooted in New England, where he sets most of his tales and on whose colonial Puritan history he draws for the background material of his stories. The idea of America, then, is important to Hawthorne, particularly since he decides to address his readers as New Englanders. Like Inchbald, he experiments with the romance and novel forms, but unlike her, he tries to establish the legitimacy of American literature through his texts with American settings and legends as his sources and even, perhaps, with a rhetorical transformation of his reader into a New England native.

The reader's transformation into an American finds parallels in the fates of some of Hawthorne's characters. The transformative loss of innocence of Arthur Dimmesdale and Roger Chillingworth, for example may symbolize what Hawthorne sought – the metamorphosis of American colonial literature into independent American literature. Suggesting that Arthur and Roger represent American literature may seem odd since both characters end the book on a negative note. However, one must remember that Hawthorne believed romance needed ruin to flourish. Specifically, truly great literature demanded a loss of innocence.

Just as Roger and Arthur transform (while paradoxically remaining one-sided figures), Donatello undergoes a similar loss of innocence after murdering the Model. In fact, the book's British title was *Transformation*, which emphasized Donatello's change from the innocent, natural faun of the American version's title into an intelligent and thoughtful man.[156] But like the two enemies in *The Scarlet Letter*, Donatello simply shifts from one type to another rather than undergoing a meaningful change in terms of actual human emotion and intelligence. Donatello, more than any other of Hawthorne's characters, symbolizes the transformation of American literature. His association with European legend suggests that the mature Hawthorne – according to Christof Wegelin and others – believed in the alternative 'truth' that Americans should not ignore European cultural models altogether but should build a new literature upon them.[157]

A Tentative Definition of the Romantic Moral Romance Sub-Genre

Given the way Hawthorne constructs *The Marble Faun* and *The Scarlet Letter* and given Elizabeth Inchbald's unique handling of narrative and character development in *A Simple Story* and *Nature and Art*, it seems clear that both authors developed a similar kind of writing as they produced their texts. Inchbald and Hawthorne each sought individual truth other than that which could be expressed through the traditional model of the British novel. Inchbald wanted a form of fiction that would welcome women writers and recognize them as legitimate authors, while Hawthorne sought a truly American form of expression so that his own country's literature could attain notoriety and legitimacy. Struggling for different reasons against the British novel tradition, they produced similar results within a distinctive sub-genre – the Romantic moral romance. In fact, although many critics have labelled Inchbald's and Hawthorne's fictions as novels, the books are not novels in the traditional sense. Each is, instead, a sophisticated romance form – a hybrid between novel and romance – that evolved as a precursor to the modern symbolic novel and that, by employing elements similar to those used in mediaeval chivalric romances and French moral tales, provides an important literary and aesthetic link between British and American versions of Romanticism.

The Romantic moral romance can be defined based on these authors' expressed intentions and based on the way the texts themselves are constructed. Although, like any sub-genre, it has characteristics that overlap with other forms, the Romantic moral romance does exhibit features that, in combination with one another, make this form of writing unique. While a tentative definition of the sub-genre is possible now, the conclusion of this volume will provide more specific features after the discussions in the intervening chapters of the sub-genre's Shakespearean precedents, revolutionary questioning of moral order and use of fragmentary figures. In brief, the Romantic moral romance form examines psychological motivation in text that exhibits a fable-like simplicity based on dramatic precedents, particularly regarding the characters, whose underdevelopment, combined with tendencies to exhibit strong passion (even if repressed), are calculated choices on the author's part to make them representative of quasi-allegorical character-types, figures or psyches. The sub-genre employs symbolism to contribute to a definite moral purpose behind the story; it usually treats subjects of the past that, if the romance is to be truly successful, are based on one or more of the darker aspects of human existence; and finally, it takes a certain licence with reality, moulding it into something between the actual and the imaginary as a better way of portraying moral 'truth'.

3. ADAPTING THE 'GREAT VOICER OF TRUTH': SHAKESPEAREAN LIMINALITY IN THE ROMANTIC MORAL ROMANCE[1]

Oftentimes at least
Me hath such strong entrancement overcome
When I have held a volume in my hand,
Poor earthly casket of immortal verse,
Shakespeare, or Milton, labourers divine!

– William Wordsworth[2]

Elizabeth Inchbald and Nathaniel Hawthorne developed the Romantic moral romance sub-genre for different reasons, but, as argued in the previous chapter, their results exhibit remarkable similarities. In part, the similarities arise because both authors wrote in opposition to the tradition of the British novel, which they tried to recast into a type of fiction that would more accurately reflect their goals as writers. In Inchbald's quest for the woman's niche in British literary history and in Hawthorne's quest for a uniquely American literature, these Romantic writers eschewed the traditional novel in favour of a form that combined elements of the romance and the novel. But while they resisted imitating writers like Samuel Richardson and Henry Fielding, they unhesitatingly borrowed from writers like William Shakespeare.[3] Indeed, Inchbald and Hawthorne held Shakespeare in high regard, perhaps because they respected Shakespeare's reputation for capturing the truth of human experience in his writing. Moreover, Shakespeare's last plays, now known as the romances, experimented with alternate definitions of genre and with challenges to established convention in ways that appealed to Romantic writers like Inchbald and Hawthorne. When Inchbald and Hawthorne developed their Romantic moral romance fictions, they borrowed themes and structures from the later Shakespeare plays whose characteristics complemented their own artistic goals – *The Tempest*, *Cymbeline* and especially *The Winter's Tale*. Inchbald's and Hawthorne's adaptations of Shakespeare's models provide further evidence that the Romantic writers attempted parallel reorientations of contemporary fiction and suggest that the transatlantic development of the Romantic moral romance was not coincidental.

This chapter explores the relationships between Shakespeare and his Romantic admirers, Inchbald and Hawthorne, and especially between Shakespeare's later plays and the Romantic moral romance. The chapter first examines Inchbald's and Hawthorne's extensive personal connections with Shakespeare's works to suggest that both Romantic writers sufficiently admired their Renaissance forebear that they came to borrow themes and structures from his plays. Inchbald acted in the plays, while Hawthorne read them and attended American performances. Additionally, both Inchbald and Hawthorne sustained friendships with important figures related to Shakespearean theatre, and both discussed Shakespeare's texts in their own writings in ways that bespeak intimate familiarity with the drama. After this discussion of Inchbald's and Hawthorne's connections with Shakespearean drama, the chapter examines, in turn, *The Tempest*, *Cymbeline* and *The Winter's Tale* as they relate to Inchbald's *A Simple Story* and Hawthorne's *The Scarlet Letter*. Dozens of critics, writing on the later Shakespeare plays, acknowledge their experimental mixed-genre nature, their use of stock characters, their quasi-allegorical qualities, their interest in moral questions, their self-consciousness as works of art and their use of traditional chivalric romance features.[4] Shakespeare's romance plays demonstrate a preoccupation with liminality that anticipates similar liminal qualities in *A Simple Story* and *The Scarlet Letter*. From *The Tempest*, the character Prospero symbolically represents an artist figure who prefigures Inchbald and Hawthorne and their liminal positions as, respectively, a female writer and an American writer. From *Cymbeline*, and indeed from all of Shakespeare's romance plays, Inchbald and Hawthorne perhaps borrowed the liminality of the dramatic genre, which was situated between comedy and tragedy and which closely paralleled the Romantic moral romance's position between romance and novel. Shakespeare's development of the potential for tragic resolution in *Cymbeline*, especially as it relates to the liminal existence of the 'fallen woman' figure, also anticipates *A Simple Story* and *The Scarlet Letter*. Finally, the structural balance of *The Winter's Tale* may have suggested similarly balanced narrative structures to Inchbald and Hawthorne, who also used romance elements and stock-character figures like those found in Shakespeare's works. Throughout this chapter, the discussion emphasizes the experimental nature of all five texts to suggest that Inchbald and Hawthorne employ themes and structures similar to those of Shakespeare and to suggest a common source in Shakespeare's later plays for the Romantic moral romance.

Inchbald's Knowledge of Shakespeare

The close personal ties to Shakespeare's canon that Inchbald and Hawthorne maintained throughout their lives suggest ample motivation for the authors' incorporation of Shakespearean themes and structures into their own works. The

Romantic writers' high levels of exposure to Shakespeare's drama ensured that each gained a ready knowledge of the plays that certainly influenced their writing. Even before starting her acting career, Inchbald, as an ardent proponent of the theatre, read Shakespeare avidly and attended performances of his plays. As a child, she hoped that she could someday portray Shakespeare characters onstage, and her family even had play recitals and would read plays aloud for entertainment in addition to their visits to the theatres in the towns of Norwich and Bury.[5] Roger Manvell notes that despite her stammer, Inchbald's 'ambition was to become an actress' at an early age, perhaps because, as James Boaden notes, '"stage declamation, being a raised and artificial thing, afforded more time for enunciation"'.[6] Acutely self-aware of her speech impediment, she often copied large passages from plays and then memorized and recited them to overcome her stammer. Her favourite characters for this activity included Cordelia from *King Lear* and, more importantly for this discussion, Hermione from *The Winter's Tale*.[7] When Inchbald wrote *A Simple Story* and *Nature and Art* years later, she borrowed themes and structures from Shakespeare's drama, especially, as discussed later, from *The Winter's Tale*. Moreover, when Inchbald ran away from home to London in 1772, she took copies, not surprisingly, of some of the Bard's plays with her and spent much of her free time studying them. Roger Manvell mentions *Othello* and, significantly, *The Tempest* as important reading material for the young woman and suggests that 'she fancied herself as both Desdemona and Miranda'.[8] Inchbald's study of *The Tempest* and of Miranda's role undoubtedly contributed also to her later development of the Romantic moral romance sub-genre as she experimented with mixed genre as Shakespeare had done and perhaps also envisioned herself as a Prospero figure. Her frequent visits to the theatre in London certainly compounded the general influence that drama would have later on her fiction, along with the specific influence of Shakespeare's example.

A general rise in the popularity of Shakespeare's plays during Inchbald's lifetime further boosted Inchbald's interest in the Bard's drama and helped her to begin the acting career that would significantly shape her writings. Earl R. Wasserman notes that 'Shakespeare was attaining the role that Homer and Virgil had occupied in the Renaissance' during the eighteenth century, and Jonathan Bate says that 'the Romantics worshipped Shakespeare'.[9] With the rise of Shakespeare's popularity, Inchbald focused more of her intellectual energy on Shakespeare's drama, especially since her acting experience began with roles from those plays. Indeed, her first professional role onstage was Cordelia in *King Lear*. Inchbald's later roles included Shakespeare characters such as one of *Macbeth*'s witches, Anne Boleyn, Lady Anne, Lady Percy, Desdemona and Juliet. Significantly, Inchbald also played roles in the three Shakespearean romances discussed later in this chapter, namely, Miranda of *The Tempest*, Imogen of *Cymbeline* and Hermione of *The Winter's Tale*.[10]

The experiences with Shakespeare's characters, memorizing the lines and then acting the characters' parts onstage – even such difficult roles as that of Hamlet – certainly gave Inchbald an intimate knowledge of the Bard's themes and structures so that when she retired from acting in 1789, she could legitimately consider herself an expert on Shakespeare.[11] She had a strong enough grasp of Shakespeare's texts and their interpretation that it seems only logical that she incorporated elements from the plays into her own texts.[12] As she played Miranda, Imogen and Hermione, Inchbald came to appreciate the experimental nature of Shakespeare's romance plays, and when she began her writing career, she drew upon the experiences to craft her own compositions. Roger Manvell, for example, notes Inchbald's reliance upon Shakespearean precedent in her plays, *Such Things Are, Lovers' Vows, The Wise Man of the East, A Case of Conscience* and *To Marry or Not to Marry* to say, 'Once again, Shakespeare offered a model in his more serious, later comedies, such as *Measure for Measure* and *All's Well that Ends Well*.'[13] Adapting Shakespearean themes and structures worked well in her plays, so it should be no surprise that Inchbald incorporated similar elements into her Romantic moral romances. However, her romances were more experimental than her plays, so she relied more heavily on Shakespeare's later drama, which was more experimental than his earlier writings, as she developed her fiction.[14]

Hawthorne's Knowledge of Shakespeare

As a Shakespeare actor, Inchbald probably would have had difficulty excluding Shakespeare's influence from her own writing had she wanted to do so. In contrast, Hawthorne would not have had as much difficulty. Although critics have made much of Hawthorne's familiarity with Shakespeare and of his reliance upon Shakespearean precedent, Hawthorne was neither an actor nor a playwright, and he had few direct connections with the theatre community in comparison with Inchbald.[15] However, he did have a strong love of attending theatre performances and of reading Shakespeare's plays, and his appreciation for Shakespeare drama undoubtedly influenced his writing of *The Scarlet Letter, The Marble Faun* and other works, just as the plays had influenced Inchbald. Moreover, Shakespeare was just as important to the American Romantics in general as he had been to the English Romantics, as testified by F. O. Matthiessen's statement that Herman Melville 'made the response of his era in considering Shakespeare primarily as a great voicer of truth'.[16] As evidence of the importance of Shakespeare to Hawthorne and his family, Hawthorne's sister Elizabeth once wrote, 'As soon as we could read with ease, we began to read Shakespeare', and Pat Ryan says Hawthorne was 'an avid student of the Bard's works' by the age of eight or nine.[17] Moreover, Hawthorne's family encouraged the future writer's interest in Shakespeare at home, especially since Elizabeth 'worshiped' the playwright.[18] Hawthorne read many of Shakespeare's plays 'on rainy days in Maine' during his youth, and he also had access to the plays in Salem.[19] Just as Inchbald's early memories of reading Shakespeare undoubtedly influenced her as she developed her Romantic moral romances, Hawthorne surely experienced the same type of influence.

In addition to reading Shakespeare's drama, Hawthorne attended dramatic performances of the plays when the opportunity arose. In a letter to his mother on 6 March 1821, at the early age of sixteen, Hawthorne mentions having seen a performance of *King Lear*, starring Edmund Kean, which 'was enough to have drawn tears from millstones' and which made him almost lose himself in his own contemplations about the play.[20] The performance was part of a celebrated tour of America in which Kean was participating at the time. Kean, who had inherited John Philip Kemble's place as 'the foremost English actor of the day', was then at the height of his reputation, and his presence in America incited a renewed interest in Shakespeare's drama.[21] In fact, John O. Rees, Jr, notes that 'Shakespeare's immense American prestige was at its peak' during Hawthorne's lifetime.[22] Kean's tour brought him to Boston twice, and Hawthorne saw Kean perform during the first Boston visit, which Giles Playfair describes as 'particularly glamorous'.[23] The presence of a well-known actor, an actor whom Hawthorne saw perform at an early – and impressionable – age, helped fuel the emerging romance-writer's interest in Shakespearean themes and structures.

As Hawthorne grew older – and began to develop his version of the Romantic moral romance – he maintained his interest in Shakespeare's work. According to George Lathrop, the records of the *Salem Athenaeum* indicate that Hawthorne, or at least someone in his family, borrowed one volume of Inchbald's *The British Theatre* in 1830.[24] The collection included twenty-four of Shakespeare's plays along with several of Inchbald's. Marion Kesselring's catalogue of Hawthorne's reading, gleaned directly from the Athenaeum's charge-books, notes that Hawthorne borrowed Volume 1 from 26 February 1831 to 1 March of the same year.[25] It included five of Shakespeare's plays, namely, *The Comedy of Errors, Romeo and Juliet, Hamlet, King John* and *King Richard III*. *The Winter's Tale, Cymbeline* and *The Tempest* appeared in Volumes 3, 4 and 5, respectively, and Hawthorne may have read them. Well into his adulthood, Hawthorne often read Shakespeare aloud in the evenings, especially during his wife Sophia's pregnancy with Una in 1844, six years prior to his publishing *The Scarlet Letter*.[26] Hawthorne's appreciation of Shakespeare drama, which continued throughout his life, made him well aware of Shakespeare's themes and structures, which he, just as Inchbald had done, modified for his own purposes in his Romantic moral romances.

Shakespeare in Inchbald's Social Circles

While Inchbald and Hawthorne cultivated their own appreciations for Shakespeare's drama – Inchbald for professional reasons and Hawthorne for personal reasons – both Romantic writers also established social connections that further enhanced their esteem of their Renaissance forebear. Inchbald's friendships with other Shakespeare actors and Hawthorne's friendships with Shakespeare critics provided social support structures that encouraged Inchbald and Hawthorne to use Shakespearean precedents to construct their own tales. Inchbald, for example, counted the two famous siblings Sarah Siddons and John Philip Kemble among her many friends and even lived with them for a short time.[27] Siddons, who had worked with actor David Garrick, performed such Shakespeare roles as Lady Macbeth, Desdemona, Rosalind, Queen Katharine and Isabella. Brander Matthews refers to Siddons as 'probably the greatest actress the world has ever seen', and indeed, her popularity was so widespread and she was so esteemed that stage managers trusted her with such demanding roles as that of Hamlet.[28] Annibel Jenkins notices the importance of the Siddons/Kemble family and their connection with Inchbald by pointing out that 'Sarah Siddons and her brother John Philip dominated the theatres in London from 1782 until 1815, and Mrs Inchbald was a leading playwright for Covent Garden from 1784 until 1805'.[29] Indeed, Celestine Woo argues that Siddons and Kemble contributed significantly to the elevation of Shakespeare to 'near-godhood' during the years around the turn of the century.[30] Significantly, Siddons also played some of the same Shakespearean romance roles that Inchbald played and that likely influenced Inchbald's writing, including Imogen of *Cymbeline* and Hermione of *The Winter's Tale*. When Inchbald and Siddons met in Liverpool in 1776, just after Inchbald's return from France, they undoubtedly discussed the Shakespeare roles that both of them had played. Surely they shared their thoughts with one another about the themes and structures of the plays and about how their performances of characters like Imogen and Hermione differed. The lifelong friendship with Siddons certainly bolstered Inchbald's appreciation of Shakespeare's drama and encouraged her to draw from Shakespearean precedent in her own fictions.

Inchbald's relationship with Siddons's brother Kemble likewise encouraged her to use Shakespeare as a model in her writing. Like his sister, Kemble was highly praised as a Shakespeare actor in his lifetime, and audiences considered him second in ability only to the famous David Garrick, who died in 1779.[31] As manager of the Drury Lane Theatre and then of the Covent Garden Theatre, he certainly held an influential position in the theatre community in general and with Inchbald in particular. Inchbald met Kemble the year after meeting Siddons and immediately established a close and enduring friendship with him. In fact, after her husband Joseph's death, Inchbald seems to have wanted more than just a friendship with Kemble, and many of their friends expected them to marry.[32] Inchbald appeared in Kemble's *Belisarius* in 1778 and asked for his advice on her early drafts of *A Simple Story*, whose character Dorriforth may have been modelled on him. As an important figure in Romantic theatre circles where Shakespeare remained popular, Kemble undoubtedly gave advice that helped to shape *A Simple Story* more directly in theatrical terms, and he must have encouraged Inchbald to rely on Shakespeare's example.

The extent to which Inchbald herself associated Kemble with Shakespeare roles is clear in her remarks for *The British Theatre*, where she mentions him repeatedly and approvingly. As Manvell notes about the remarks, 'Above all, she enjoys celebrating John Philip Kemble, whose performances shine again through the energy of her prose, and span the whole series of volumes. He excels, she claims, in Shakespeare, being second only to Garrick'.[33] Inchbald's admiration for Kemble, coupled with Kemble's own professional investment in Shakespeare drama, bolstered Inchbald's fascination with the Bard. She praises Kemble's performances in *As You Like It*, *Coriolanus*, *King John* and *King Richard III* with repeated references to his genius, and she admires his ability to make the moral points of *Measure for Measure* and *Macbeth*.[34] Relationships with actors like Siddons and Kemble encouraged Inchbald's already healthy esteem for Shakespeare's plays and for the literary examples the plays provided.

In addition to nurturing close relationships with Siddons and Kemble, Inchbald unquestionably was well acquainted with the reputation and history of Mary Robinson, an author and actor who had been introduced to the stage opposite David Garrick and who had played many important Shakespeare roles. The most important of her roles, which also included Ophelia, Rosalind, Viola and Lady Macbeth, was Perdita from *The Winter's Tale*. The scandal that began with her 3 December 1779 performance as Perdita ensured that Shakespeare's play remained at the forefront of her contemporaries' minds, and Inchbald, who could not have avoided some knowledge of the scandal, undoubtedly remembered it as she composed her own fictions. Thus, Inchbald's decision to adopt themes and structures from *The Winter's Tale* originated, not just in her own experiences with the play, but also in the publicity surrounding the drama as the source of a public scandal. During Robinson's performance as Perdita, the Prince of Wales became enamoured with her, and he later proposed that she become his mistress. Despite initial hesitation – notably because she was married – Robinson eventually consented and exchanged, with the Prince, 'passionate letters in the guise of Perdita and Florizel', the two young lovers from *The Winter's Tale*.[35] Perdita and Florizel indulge a forbidden passion for one another, so the Prince and Robinson's adoption of the characters' names clarifies their awareness of the transgressive nature of their relationship. Eventually, Robinson gave up her acting career, and even her rocky marriage, because she thought that her financial future was secure in the Prince, who had promised her the sum of £20,000 on his coming of age. The relationship excited public curiosity – and condemnation – and Robinson came to the forefront of negative public commentary at the time.[36] Unfortunately, the Prince, who was only seventeen when he first saw Robinson, soon turned his attentions elsewhere and abandoned the now unemployed actor. Fearful of becoming destitute, she threatened to publish the Prince's letters when the Royal Family attempted to rescind the promise of £20,000. The conflict fuelled further public interest in Robinson, and as Jonathan Wordsworth notes, publicity surrounded 'every stage of the affair', so much so that King George III himself became involved before the well-known politician Charles Fox managed to negotiate a settlement.[37] Even after the settlement, however, Robinson remained in the public eye, and as Judith Pascoe comments, 'Robinson, already the subject of public fascination, became the butt of cruel caricatures and the debased heroine of a series of fictional accounts of her love affairs cast in pornographic terms'.[38]

Because Robinson had been a public figure for so long and because her notoriety began with her role as Perdita, she became known as Perdita Robinson, and the very name *Perdita* became associated with adulterous and scandalous activity. Moreover, well before Robinson's affair, the name Perdita had been associated with dishonour because King Leontes of *The Winter's Tale* initially – though erroneously – considers his daughter Perdita an illegitimate child. Hence, the theme of the fallen woman, particularly a fallen woman associated with the name *Perdita*, meaning *the lost one*, was present in Inchbald's social circles well before Inchbald wrote her books.[39] Robinson's notoriety, and particularly its origins in a performance of *The Winter's Tale*, undoubtedly helped to keep Shakespeare drama at the forefront of Inchbald's mind. Inchbald created fallen-woman figures whose fates, in some respects, parallel the downfall of Perdita's mother Hermione.

Shakespeare in Hawthorne's Social Circles

While Inchbald's friendships with Shakespeare actors encouraged her to use Shakespeare's plays as models for developing the romance form, Hawthorne received similar encouragement from two Shakespeare critics. Specifically, Hawthorne's acquaintance with the two self-proclaimed Shakespeare scholars, Jones Very and Delia Bacon, encouraged him to borrow from Shakespeare. Very's and Bacon's enthusiasm for their subject undoubtedly fuelled Hawthorne's existing love of Shakespeare to keep the Bard's plays more current in Hawthorne's mind. Hawthorne met Very, who 'wrote mystical sonnets and had "ideas" about Shakespeare', through the Peabody family in Salem and encountered him often at the homes of Susan Burley and Caleb Foote.[40] In an interesting side note that further illustrates Hawthorne's familiarity with Shakespeare, he called Burley's frequent social gatherings the 'Hurley-Burley', probably in reference to the first scene of *Macbeth*, in which the witches agree to meet again 'When the hurly-burly's done, / When the battle's lost and won'.[41] Jones Very was a frequent guest at the 'Hurley-Burley', where Hawthorne's wife Sophia grew to admire him and where he certainly made known his theories about the Bard. Very's 'ideas' about Shakespeare surely prompted Hawthorne to reconsider his own impressions of the Bard and may have helped him to realize the uniqueness of the Shakespearean romances that would influence his own fiction writing. However, Very suffered from a mental illness and, convinced of his own divinity, began blessing and offering to baptize the people of Salem, including Hawthorne. Very spent time in the Charlestown Asylum, but nothing prevented his writing a lengthy 'dissertation on Shakespeare', which he subsequently sent to Ralph Waldo Emerson.[42] Despite Very's mental illness, the scholar certainly bolstered Hawthorne's awareness of Shakespeare's genius and encouraged Hawthorne to borrow from Shakespeare's plays as he developed his form of Romantic moral romance.

Like Very, Delia Bacon also heightened Hawthorne's awareness of Shakespeare's plays in a way that may have inspired him to draw from Shakespeare's Renaissance example in writing his fictions. Reportedly, after promulgating her theories about Shakespeare largely with Hawthorne's help, Bacon 'went insane'.[43] Hawthorne himself referred to her as 'a monomaniac' and suggested that the obsession with Shakespeare had 'completely thrown her off her balance'.[44] Bacon believed that Francis Bacon, with whom she claimed kinship, had written Shakespeare's plays with the help of Sir Walter Raleigh and Edmund Spenser. Few scholars credited her theories, so she spent much of her time attempting to persuade authorities in England to open Shakespeare's tomb, where she believed (based on evidence from Lord Bacon's letters) that a will and several other documents that would prove her theory were hidden.[45] Hawthorne met Bacon in England while he was the American Consul in Liverpool. Although Hawthorne 'cared nothing for her theories' about the promulgation of Shakespeare's plays, he did respect her intellectual ability and found Bacon's interpretations of the plays compelling enough to agree to fund the publication of her book, *The Philosophy of the Plays of Shakspere Unfolded*.[46] As evidence of his commitment to the Shakespeare scholarship that Bacon represented, Hawthorne even took the time to write a preface to Bacon's book and convinced his own publisher to make it available in America.[47] The book's failure supposedly prompted Bacon's psychological imbalance, and Hawthorne supported her until one of her relatives took her back to the United States. Despite her psychological imbalance, Delia Bacon was an important figure in Hawthorne's life, even if only briefly. Biographer James Mellow suggests that Hawthorne was '[t]ouched by her intensity and dedication'.[48] Indeed, Hawthorne's support of Bacon demonstrates, not just Hawthorne's concern for a fellow American living in England, but a belief in the importance of Shakespeare scholarship. Clearly, Jones Very and Delia Bacon, in spite of their personal problems, contributed to Hawthorne's appreciation for Shakespeare, much as Siddons, Kemble and Robinson had done for Inchbald, by encouraging him to think about the Bard's texts in unique and unprecedented ways.

Inchbald's Writing about Shakespeare

While Inchbald and Hawthorne remained connected to Shakespeare drama through their personal interests and through their social contacts, they further demonstrated their interest in Shakespeare by incorporating elements of Shakespeare's plays into their critical and personal work. Specifically, Inchbald wrote critically about Shakespeare's plays while Hawthorne alluded to them in important ways in his writings. The easy familiarity that the Romantic writers exhibit in relation to Shakespeare's drama provides one final piece of evidence of the likelihood that they borrowed Shakespeare's themes and structures for their own fictions. Since Inchbald and Hawthorne were so willing to allude to and to discuss Shakespeare directly, they undoubtedly also were willing to borrow indirectly from him in more general terms.

Inchbald's work as a drama critic, especially the prefaces she wrote for *The British Theatre*, admirably demonstrate the themes that she found most compelling, and most likely had borrowed for her own fictions, from Shakespeare's plays. Although Longman released the first play in *The British Theatre* series in 1806, ten years after Inchbald had published *Nature and Art* and fifteen years after *A Simple Story*, Inchbald's remarks about the plays remain relevant. As Roger Manvell states,

> In particular, her comments were valuable because they revealed in virtually every instance the knowledge and experience of an actress who over a number of years had enjoyed the privilege of working with and observing at the closest range the performances of the best players of the time, not now and then but on hundreds of occasions, behind the scenes and on the stage, as a participant and as member of an audience in the theatres of London and the provinces.[49]

In her comments, Inchbald reveals an admiration for plays that engage in examinations of moral questions, that preserve at least some measure of verisimilitude, that excite the passions as a way of revealing 'truth' and that take fables and legends as their precedents. In fact, she often uses the word *fable*, rather than the word *plot*, in reference to Shakespeare's plays, perhaps as a way of calling attention to their allegorical potential as they examine moral 'truth' through the passions.[50] Moreover, the fable, while it retained a certain level of improbability, could have its basis in historical reality, and readers could apply its lessons to their daily lives in much the same way that readers might learn from chivalric romances and moral tales. The qualities that Inchbald admired in Shakespeare's plays were the qualities that she had incorporated into her Romantic moral romances, and the qualities that she disliked in the Bard's plays – like excessive use of 'improbabilities' – were the ones she had tried to correct in her fiction writing.[51] In fact, in the remarks about her own plays, Inchbald faults herself for some of the same flaws she sees in Shakespeare's work, although she praises her plays when they achieve the effects that she admires in Shakespeare's drama.

Inchbald's discussion of Shakespeare's plays in *The British Theatre* indicates her admiration of Shakespeare's ability to combine entertainment with moral questioning while relying on verisimilitude and evoking the truth of human experience through the passions. In her view, the *Henry IV* tetralogy, which begins with *Richard II* and ends with *Henry V*, offers good moral instruction.[52] Among the tragedies, *Macbeth* also offers an impressive moral lesson, and she finds useful examinations of the passions in *Coriolanus, King Lear, Romeo and Juliet* and *Othello*.[53] *Coriolanus, Romeo and Juliet* and *Othello* she finds realistic and probable, but she questions the verisimilitude of *King Lear*. Among the comedies, Inchbald complains that *The Comedy of Errors, Measure for Measure, The Merchant of Venice, Much Ado about Nothing* and *The Merry Wives of Windsor* are too improbable.[54] She offers similar complaints about *The Winter's Tale, Cymbeline* and *The Tempest* because they do not adequately examine the truth of human passions, although she believes that Shakespeare's art overpowers such defects.[55] Despite pointing out the flaws in Shakespeare's romance plays, Inchbald admired them enough to borrow extensively from their themes and structures for *A Simple Story* and *Nature and Art*. As Inchbald wrote her own tales, she improved upon Shakespeare's example by preserving a greater sense of verisimilitude in the Romantic moral romance than Shakespeare had done in his drama. In her prefaces to Shakespeare's plays in *The British Theatre*, Inchbald clearly demonstrates her concern with the very issues that help to define the Romantic moral romance as she had developed it in previous years. Evocation of the passions to reveal 'truth', along with a concern with moral questions and with the probability of plots based on precedent genres of improbable fable and legend, constitute significant aspects of Shakespearean drama that reappear in the Romantic moral romance.

Hawthorne's Writing about Shakespeare

Although Hawthorne personally knew Shakespeare critics, he was not one himself and did not produce Shakespeare criticism as Inchbald had done. Nevertheless, he read Shakespeare's plays often and saw them performed by Kean and other actors so that he retained a strong familiarity with the texts. He quoted easily from them in his writing and alluded to them frequently – including *The Tempest, Cymbeline* and *The Winter's Tale*. Indeed, his readily familiarity with the drama may have prompted his contemporaries to compare him with the Bard.[56] In a letter to his sister on 1 October 1824 at age twenty, he quotes Clarence from *King Richard III*, to write, 'I would not live over my college life again, "though 'twere to buy a world of happy days"'.[57] Hawthorne's ability and willingness to quote Shakespeare's work readily in something so mundane as a letter to his sister aptly demonstrates the pervasiveness of Shakespeare's influence in his life and evokes the tacitness with which he might have modelled his Romantic moral romances on Shakespearean precedent. As in the letter to his sister, Hawthorne similarly alludes to *Hamlet* when he mentions 'sandal-shoon' in a letter to Henry Wadsworth Longfellow on 4 June 1837.[58] Years later, he mentions in the *American Notebooks*, alluding to *The Winter's Tale*, that he sees his 'little wife rounding apace' as her pregnancy progresses.[59] He recalls *The Tempest* to describe his son Julian eating as a baby with his mouth open 'wide enough, almost, to swallow the great globe itself', and in a discussion of a friend's marriage, he mentions that the groom married 'this pretty little Miranda'.[60] Even the title of one of Hawthorne's early collections of short stories, *Twice-told Tales,* derives from *King John* (III. iv.108), and the epigraphs to three of the ten chapters of *Fanshawe* are quotations from Shakespeare.

Some of the most significant evidence of Hawthorne's admiration of Shakespeare appears in *The English Notebooks*, written about Hawthorne's experiences in England as American Consul. Beginning with an apocryphal account of Shakespeare's death in a ditch after overindulging at a revel, Hawthorne mentions the Bard repeatedly through *The English Notebooks*.[61] The section about Hawthorne's visit to Stratford is most instructive since it includes his description of Shakespeare's house. Hawthorne describes the building in extreme detail and mentions standing in the chimney in imitation of Shakespeare.[62] He complains about not being emotionally impressed with Shakespeare's house because visiting such a place reminds him of the mundane humanity of the man and of his human flaws.[63] However, the experience remains current in his mind, for he later compares the houses in Gloucester to Shakespeare's, and when he visits the birthplace of Robert Burns, Hawthorne again mentions Shakespeare's house in comparison.[64] When Hawthorne visits the British Museum, he carefully notes seeing the 'strange scrawl of Shakspeare's autograph' in an English translation of Montaigne, and the city of Warwick impresses him because it 'is said to have been founded by Shakspeare's King Cymbeline, in the year *One* of the Christian era'.[65] He speculates that 'Imogen and Posthumus may have strayed hand-in-hand through the country-lanes about Warwick'.[66] Finally, Hawthorne mentions in *The Blithedale Romance*, whose similarity to the Brook Farm experiment he calls an attempt to 'establish a theatre' – another connection to drama – that the character Zenobia often reads from Shakespeare, and in *The Marble Faun*, Hawthorne directly alludes to *The Tempest* when he mentions Prospero and Miranda in a digression on art.[67] The prevalence of allusions to Shakespeare and his plays in Hawthorne's writings indicates a strong admiration of Hawthorne's Renaissance forebear, so Hawthorne's appropriation of Shakespearean thematic and structural precedent is no surprise.

The Artist's Liminal Role from *The Tempest*

Inchbald and Hawthorne certainly were familiar with Shakespeare's plays, including the three late plays that most closely anticipate the Romantic moral romance, namely *The Tempest*, *Cymbeline* and *The Winter's Tale*. Juxtaposed with *A Simple Story* and *The Scarlet Letter*, their themes and structures suggest that the five texts in question exhibit an unusual preoccupation with varied manifestations of the idea of liminality. Inchbald's and Hawthorne's romances are so closely allied with Shakespeare's plays that it seems the relationship is not coincidental. Indeed, it is highly probable that Inchbald and Hawthorne used Shakespeare's late plays as common sources and templates when they wrote their own tales. From *The Tempest*, they borrowed the liminality of the position of the artist-figure Prospero; from *Cymbeline*, they adapted the liminal 'fallen-woman' figure to embody their roles as literary artists; and from *The Winter's Tale* they borrowed Shakespeare's structural balance and his use of romance elements and stock-character figures. Indeed, from all three Shakespeare precedents, Inchbald and Hawthorne borrowed the overall liminality of the tragicomedy genre to modulate their own liminal sub-genre and establish themselves as legitimate artists.

In *The Tempest*, Inchbald and Hawthorne found precedent examples of liminality that significantly influenced their work with the Romantic moral romance.[68] Specifically, *The Tempest* is liminal both in terms of its genre and in terms of the characters' positions within the plot of the drama. Rather than falling into one of the two traditional categories of drama – tragedy or comedy – *The Tempest* lies somewhere between the two.[69] Shakespeare experimentally blended both tragic and comic elements in the play to write what scholars now call tragicomedy. In fact, *The Tempest* is so unique that modern Shakespeare scholars generally classify it separately as a romance, along with Shakespeare's other late plays, *Pericles*, *The Two Noble Kinsmen*, *Cymbeline* and *The Winter's Tale*.[70] *The Tempest's* unusual nature, a characteristic that challenged traditional assumptions about dramatic genre, anticipated Inchbald's and Hawthorne's experimentation with their sub-genre during the Romantic Period. Just as Shakespeare situated his romances in the liminal space between the tragic and the comic to help develop the tragicomic form, Inchbald and Hawthorne situate their texts between the traditional romance and novel to develop the Romantic moral romance form. Recognizing the unique experimental nature of *The Tempest*, Inchbald and Hawthorne adapted its features for their own purposes.

More important to Inchbald and Hawthorne, perhaps, than Shakespeare's challenge to genre classification was his treatment of the character Prospero and specifically the liminality of Prospero's position in *The Tempest*. When Inchbald and Hawthorne read *The Tempest* and saw it performed, they must have identified with Prospero because their own artistic endeavours paralleled Prospero's victimized political situation. At the beginning of *The Tempest*, Prospero is politically powerless. His brother Antonio has usurped Prospero's role as Duke of Milan, and the play follows Prospero's attempts to regain his political position. Initially, before the play begins, Prospero is Antonio's victim, but although Prospero has no political power, he does retain his supernatural powers, especially through his ability to control Ariel. Prospero uses his magic to bring his enemies to the island and to orchestrate the series of events that results in the restoration of his power and in the marriage of Ferdinand and Miranda. Symbolically, Prospero may be interpreted as an emblem of the artist – the dramatist, the novelist. David Bevington calls him a controlling 'artist-figure' and an 'artist-king and patriarch' over the imaginary world of the island, while Joan Kirkby refers to Prospero as an artist obsessed with 'order and control'.[71] Inchbald and Hawthorne undoubtedly sensed Prospero's artist qualities and recognized the parallels between their own efforts and those of Prospero. The Romantic writers felt that the tradition of British literature – and especially the British novel – had stripped them of the possibility of any serious recognition as writers, in a symbolic parallel to the way Prospero had lost his political power to Antonio. Inchbald worked in opposition to the patriarchal nature of British literature that had devalued women's contributions and forced women writers into subordinate roles. Similarly, Hawthorne worked against the tradition of British literature in general, which retained its hegemony in the new United States and forced American writers into subordinate roles. And while Inchbald and Hawthorne may have viewed themselves as subject to the overwhelming influence of the British novel, they were not powerless and used their artistic literary talents to challenge traditional British literature, just as Prospero had used his magic on the island to restore his own power. Inchbald and Hawthorne draw from their experiences with *The Tempest* – Inchbald had played Miranda, and Hawthorne was familiar with the play as well – to construct fictions whose characters collectively mimic the liminality of Prospero's role. Inchbald and Hawthorne did not merely imitate Shakespeare's example. While Shakespeare reaffirmed traditional patriarchal order by restoring Prospero's power in *The Tempest*, Inchbald and Hawthorne questioned the literary order that circumscribed their works and attempted to develop a new tradition with the Romantic moral romance.

As they drew upon the example of *The Tempest*, Inchbald and Hawthorne took advantage of the allegorical potential of the Romantic moral romance to incorporate, symbolically, their own artistic agendas into their works through their characters' identities. In Inchbald's *A Simple Story*, Miss Milner and Matilda symbolize the marginal space of the repressed female author in Britain, who must struggle to find acceptance despite the patriarchal literary tradition embodied in Dorriforth/Lord Elmwood. Inchbald symbolically posits an ideal woman writer who occupies the balanced liminal space between masculine ecclesiastical and aristocratic control (represented by Dorriforth and Lord Elmwood, respectively) and traditional feminine defiant and submissive responses to masculine control (represented, respectively, by Miss Milner and Matilda). Knowing the difficulties that women writers faced in Romantic Britain, Inchbald does not position any of her characters as symbols of the ideal woman writer. Instead, through the symbolic roles of Miss Milner and Matilda, she condemns the positions in which women writers are placed by the masculine tradition in which the women try to write. In decrying the reception given to women's literary endeavours, Inchbald positions herself as the ideal woman writer. In contrast, Hawthorne actively situates one of his characters as a symbol of the ideal American writer in *The Scarlet Letter*. Pearl occupies the liminal space between complete rejection and complete acceptance of British cultural constructs, which symbolize British literary tradition. In Hawthorne's model, Hester Prynne and Arthur Dimmesdale represent the American author who accepts the influence of British literature, symbolized by the Puritan moral codes of Boston. Roger Chillingworth is their opposite – absolute rejection of Puritan moral codes, and, symbolically, British literature. Pearl is the ideal because she chooses her own path and neither rejects nor accepts Puritan morals. Inchbald's and Hawthorne's identification with the marginalized nature of Prospero's character thus finds expression in the Romantic writers' own characters.

In *A Simple Story*, Inchbald's two primary female characters represent the two alternatives that Inchbald believes British female writers usually choose in response to the patriarchal tradition of the British novel – defiance or submission.[72] The respective fates of the two characters suggest that neither approach provides adequate autonomy for the female writer because defiance brings fierce opposition from masculine centres of power while submission merely provides those centres with an acknowledgment of their power. As Jo Alyson Parker suggests, Miss Milner and Matilda essentially 'have no real choice'.[73] Inchbald indirectly suggests that the more balanced liminal space between defiance and submission – the role that Prospero occupies as an exiled, yet powerful, ruler – can provide a more successful arena for the female writer. In *A Simple Story*, Miss Milner is a quasi-allegorical representation of the defiant woman writer. She disrupts the patriarchal order by disobeying Dorriforth on several occasions and being unfaithful to him, just as a writer might defy the conventions of the British novel. Dorriforth's response – to banish and ignore her completely – represents the defiant female author's fate. Miss Milner's open defiance dooms her to oblivion because she does not, as an individual, embody the liminality that Prospero possesses.

In contrast to Miss Milner's defiant nature, Matilda represents the submissive female author, but her fate is no more encouraging than her mother's. Dorriforth, now Lord Elmwood, punishes Matilda for her mother's transgression by refusing to accept her. Matilda's total submission ensures that she achieves practical nonexistence in relation to traditional centres of power in the same way that a female author can relinquish her artistic integrity through submissiveness to the expected norm. Through Miss Milner and Matilda, Inchbald suggests that neither complete defiance nor complete submission is appropriate for the truly good female author, and although Inchbald does not directly suggest an alternative, her own practice as a writer does. Inchbald blends defiance with submission as she co-opts the liminal space between the traditional novel and romance, just as Shakespeare had co-opted the liminal space between tragedy and comedy in *The Tempest*. Inchbald uses traditional elements of each as a means of demonstrating her acceptance of some elements of the established tradition, but her merger of the two genres in the Romantic moral romance demonstrates her defiant independence as she situates herself – along with her book – in the intervening liminal space.[74]

Like *A Simple Story*, Hawthorne's *The Scarlet Letter* depicts a symbolic challenge to an established British literary tradition and suggests the superiority of liminality akin to that depicted in *The Tempest*. Hester Prynne and Arthur Dimmesdale embody the qualities of American writers who attempt to declare their literary independence, but who, discouraged by the reception of their works, submit to the established tradition. Symbolically, the Puritan moral codes of Boston, rather than a particular individual as in the case of Lord Elmwood in *A Simple Story*, represent British literature. Hawthorne, whose own ancestors were Puritan, did not trust the moral codes promulgated by the Puritan faith, and the British origins of American Puritanism provided further incentive for Hawthorne's distrust. Puritanism, like the British literature that Hawthorne found threatening, was a British cultural construct, so any challenge to its authority in *The Scarlet Letter* represents also a symbolic challenge to British literature. Hester and Arthur choose to transgress against the moral codes of their Boston community because, on some level, they realize that its ideologies are not compatible with their own. Their transgression is a particularly Romantic expression of identity and individuality, for Hester and Arthur follow their own consciences despite the condemnation of Boston society. When the Puritan elders accuse Hester of adultery, their action symbolizes an indictment of American literature, which has tried, like Hester, to achieve its own sense of identity in opposition to the established British tradition. Although the elders do not include Arthur in their indictment, notably because they are unaware of his guilt, Arthur still suffers from the effects of their disapproval. He and Hester feel compelled to maintain their silence and to counterfeit submission to their community's mores, even when they secretly disagree with the elders. For Hawthorne, the repressive atmosphere of Puritan control paralleled his own situation as an American writer who wished to assert the individuality of American literature. Just as the Boston elders enforced Puritan ideologies in *The Scarlet Letter*, many writers and literary critics ensured the continuing superiority of British literature by devaluing the efforts of aspiring American writers.

Despite symbolically questioning the tradition of British literature in *The Scarlet Letter*, Hawthorne does not propose literary anarchy in which writers abandon completely any reliance upon preceding generations of British writers and traditions. Rather, Hawthorne proposes an alternate, liminal literary order that draws upon British traditions but recognizes the uniqueness of American literature in the same way that Shakespeare's *The Tempest* drew from both comic and tragic dramatic traditions. In *The Scarlet Letter*, Roger Chillingworth embodies the anarchic principle of departing so far from tradition that one completely loses one's sense of identity. Obsessed with revenge, Roger abandons Puritan precepts so completely that he becomes little more than a savage, unthinking beast much like Shakespeare's Caliban. David Bevington equates Caliban with the Romantic noble savage figure while ignoring the character's malevolent qualities, but according to Howard Felperin, Caliban possesses no human nobility at all because he is 'subhuman'.[75] By extension, complete rejection of the established tradition of British literature would result in productions that are sub-literary.

If Arthur and Hester represent one option for the American writer in relation to British literature, the option that inextricably links itself with and submits to the traditions of its predecessor (embodied in Puritan morality), then Roger may symbolize the opposite option that completely rejects British literary precedents (symbolized by the same morality). Neither option, however, offers an adequate solution for the American writer who seeks literary recognition because neither one embraces the liminality that is necessary for the American author's success. Roger and Arthur die while Hester ends *The Scarlet Letter* as a recluse who still wears her badge of shame for having transgressed. The only character who ends the book on a positive note is Pearl. Like Shakespeare's Ariel of *The Tempest*, she is amoral, for she seems to have no interest in moral questions at all.[76] When Mr Wilson, the minister, asks her who made her, the narrator says she replies that she was plucked from a rose bush.[77] Like Ariel, and somewhat like Inchbald's Matilda, Pearl seems to have an existence separate from that of the other characters in the book, and in fact, Hawthorne even refers to her in supernatural terms as an elf, an imp or a demon-child. She exists as a contrast to the other characters so that their deep concern with moral issues seems even stronger when set beside her own indifference. Pearl exists in the liminal space, the neutral territory, between symbols of ostensible morality (Hester and Arthur) and immorality (Roger). Pearl represents Hawthorne's idea of the American author's ideal approach to writing. Rather than relying heavily on British precedent or eschewing British precedent altogether, the American writer should compose with a similar indifference toward British literature that Pearl evinces toward morality. In short, American writers should use the aspects of the British literary tradition that seem most appropriate to them, not because those features are part of the tradition, but because they seem useful at the time. They should not eschew those conditions completely, either, but they should feel free to discard the features that do not support their artistic goals.

The idea of a liminal existence, between two opposites, was exactly what Inchbald and Hawthorne used as the basis for their books, and Shakespeare's *The Tempest* provided a model on which the Romantic writers could found their own Romantic moral romances. Based on Shakespearean precedent, Inchbald and Hawthorne symbolically created liminal spaces for themselves as writers in books that occupied similar spaces between the genres of romance and novel. David Bevington says of *The Tempest*, 'Even its location juxtaposes the "real" world with an idealized landscape: like Plato's New Atlantis or Thomas More's Utopia, Shakespeare's island is to be found both somewhere and nowhere'.[78] Likewise, in a statement that more directly recalls Hawthorne's obsession with situating his romances in the liminal space between the real and the imaginary, Robert W. Uphaus comments, 'The world of *The Tempest* [...] is both old and new, both real and imagined'.[79] *A Simple Story* and *The Scarlet Letter* occupy similar liminal positions in literary history – as do *Nature and Art* and *The Marble Faun*.

The Fallen Woman Figure from *Cymbeline*

While *The Tempest* likely provided some impetus for Inchbald's and Hawthorne's experimentation with the liminality of the genre they developed and of their own positions as writers, *Cymbeline* may have suggested additional lines of experimental inquiry while reinforcing those that appear in *The Tempest*. The sense of liminality that Inchbald and Hawthorne borrowed from *The Tempest* appears also in *Cymbeline*, whose genre likewise lies between comedy and tragedy and incorporates a liminal sense into its characters. David Bevington calls *Cymbeline* an experiment that 'must be viewed as innovative and unique', and he further suggests that one may describe the play with terms such as 'romance, tragicomedy, and the comedy of forgiveness'.[80] He notes, moreover, that the play uses '[m]any conventional features of romantic narrative – wandering and return, loss and rediscovery, apparent death and rebirth'.[81] Certainly, *Cymbeline*, like *The Tempest*, does blend genres, starting with the serious and tragic, involving Posthumus's exile, Imogen's perceived lack of fidelity, Cloten's gruesome death and even the battle between the British and the Romans. However, the outcome of *Cymbeline* is comic, in the traditional sense of the term, since Posthumus and Imogen are reunited, as are Cymbeline and his two abducted sons, Guiderius and Arviragus. Impressed with Shakespeare's masterful blending of tragedy and comedy – with which Inchbald was familiar because she had acted the part of Imogen, and with which Hawthorne was familiar through his reading – Inchbald and Hawthorne adopted the same strategy to develop the potential for tragic resolution in the Romantic moral romance.[82] Perhaps using Shakespeare's Imogen as their example, they focus the potential for tragedy upon women whose virtue is in question.

The issue of a woman's virtue was not a particularly innovative topic, even for Shakespeare. The motif of the 'fallen woman' – a woman whose sexual virtue has lapsed – has been an important literary trope for many centuries. Traditionally, when a woman's virtue came into question, an author provided one of two possible outcomes to any investigation into her activities. Either the woman was guilty, or she was innocent. In *Cymbeline*, Imogen falls into the latter category. Bevington calls her 'a virtuous woman who responds to her undeserved tribulations with forbearance.'[83] As the play unfolds, Posthumus's suspicion, aroused by Iachimo's deceit, lights on Imogen and results in a series of incidents in which Imogen's life is placed at risk. Her response is forbearance, as she disguises herself as Fidele and ultimately offers her services to Caius Lucius. Appropriately, her alias recalls the English word *fidelity* to belie Iachimo's accusation against her loyalty to Posthumus and reveal her true nature. Neither Inchbald nor Hawthorne was content with a simplistic resolution to the question of a woman's virtue in their books. Instead, they created characters who were guilty, but they complicated the question of guilt by providing their fallen women with mitigating circumstances that suggest, on some level, innocence. Like the books themselves as a genre, the characters occupy liminal spaces, in this case, between guilt and innocence. The characters alternately partake of both guilt and innocence as Inchbald and Hawthorne lead their readers through stories that partake of both the comic and the tragic.

From the beginning of *A Simple Story*, and perhaps with the story of Mary Robinson's difficult life in mind, Inchbald emphasizes the potential for tragic resolution that surrounds Miss Milner's life. David Bevington says that the 'tragic possibilities are manifold' in *Cymbeline*, and the same type of tragic potential follows Miss Milner, and later her daughter Matilda, through Inchbald's book.[84] As the story progresses, Miss Milner begins to display an independent spirit, in response to Dorriforth's tyrannical behaviour, that suggests a potential for another kind of tragedy – her assumption, like Imogen, of the role of the fallen woman.[85] Each time Miss Milner incurs Dorriforth's wrath, she increases the potential that Dorriforth will disown her completely and initiate her tragic downfall. For example, when Dorriforth insists that Miss Milner marry, he requires that she marry the man of his choosing. Miss Milner loves Dorriforth himself, so she refuses his choices of potential husbands. As Dorriforth tries to control his ward and marry her to one of his friends, and as Miss Milner resists Dorriforth's control and attempts to hold his interest as a potential mate, both characters become progressively frustrated with one another – Dorriforth because he cannot understand Miss Milner's seemingly illogical behaviour, and Miss Milner because she cannot elicit the emotional response she desires from Dorriforth. Indeed, both characters' complaints about one another are legitimate. Dorriforth simply cannot understand Miss Milner's intractability, and as Jo Alyson Parker comments, 'Although we cannot applaud the despotic power that Miss Milner wields [as she resists Dorriforth's control], we can appreciate it as a gesture of resistance'.[86] At the end of Volume 2, Sandford marries the couple in a comic resolution to a story whose events include both tragic elements and tragic potential.

Unfortunately, the ring Dorriforth and Miss Milner use to seal their marriage vows is a mourning ring whose significance does not become clear until the second half of the book when Miss Milner, now Lady Elmwood, truly becomes a fallen woman through her infidelity with Lord Frederick Lawnly. Her life ends tragically since she dies in isolation while still in exile from Elmwood House and since her death receives no more than a passing glance from Lord Elmwood, who treats the event more as a business transaction than as the end of his wife's life. Hence, Lady Elmwood's story begins in tragedy, with the death of her father, before moving into comic themes that resolve in, once more, tragedy. Inchbald glosses over the final tragedy, however, by keeping Miss Milner at arm's length from the narrative, hidden away in a small house with Matilda. Like Shakespeare's Imogen, Miss Milner finds her fidelity to her husband in question, but unlike Imogen, Miss Milner does not obey her male advisors, and in fact, her virtue really has been compromised by the end of the tale. But she is simultaneously guilty and innocent.[87] Inchbald does not condemn Miss Milner because, as Miriam Wallace comments, 'there are numerous hints that Elmwood is implicated in her guilt'.[88] Indeed, Inchbald seems to suggest that Miss Milner's sin is largely the result of circumstances she cannot control.

The story of Matilda's life in the second half of *A Simple Story* follows the opposite pattern to Miss Milner's while retaining the liminality of the first half of the book. Matilda's tale begins with comic elements, moves into tragedy and then resolves itself in comedy. Although Matilda is innocent of wrongdoing, she embodies the guilt of her mother, particularly in Elmwood's mind, so, like her mother, Matilda occupies the liminal space between guilt and innocence.[89] Terry Castle suggests, 'Matilda is indeed in many respects a surrogate for the novel's original heroine [Miss Milner] and takes her mother's place, in the reader's mind as well as in the narrator's, with remarkable celerity'.[90] The potential for tragedy remains high since Matilda must so carefully hide herself from her father, and indeed, when she accidentally stumbles upon him on the stairs one day, he banishes her from the house. Like her mother, Matilda once again must live in exile, isolated from the man she loves. Matilda's exile, itself a tragic element, heightens the potential for further tragedy since the young woman has no male protector. Aware of Matilda's vulnerability, Lord Margrave introduces a Gothic trope into the tale by kidnapping her with the intent to seduce her. However, the book resolves in a comic turn when Lord Elwood rescues Matilda from Margrave's mansion and finally accepts her as a legitimate member of the family. He even agrees to her marriage with Harry Rushbrook. Hence, *A Simple Story* blends the tragic and comic in a way that legitimizes its classification as a Romantic moral romance, based on tragicomic precedent like *Cymbeline*, rather than a traditional novel.

Like Inchbald, Hawthorne also privileged liminality like that modelled in *Cymbeline* and complicated it for his own purposes. He avoided writing simplistic tales in which the woman whose virtue came into question was either clearly innocent or clearly guilty. In *The Scarlet Letter*, no reader questions whether Hester has transgressed against the laws of her community, but whether Hester's actions were justified is not so clear. Despite her obvious culpability before the community, Hester's case is unique in that she perhaps believed her husband to be dead before she became involved with Arthur Dimmesdale. She has lived in Boston as long as two years without hearing from Roger at all, so Hawthorne seems to suggest, as Inchbald had done with Miss Milner and Matilda, that Hester's predicament is partially a result of circumstances.[91] Even so, to have a child out of wedlock was a serious crime in Puritan Boston. Moreover, without proof that Roger is dead, the Boston elders choose to believe that he is alive, so they brand Hester as an adulteress. The scarlet *A* that she wears is a symbol of her sin, and it marks her as a fallen woman throughout the tale. Unlike Miss Milner, she chooses a passive approach that parallels Matilda's response to Lord Elmwood. Hester accepts her punishment with as much grace as she can muster, for she even defiantly embroiders her scarlet letter to transform it into an ornament. Just as Imogen deals with the false imputation of her dishonour, Hester exhibits forbearance as she quietly accepts her punishment. Shakespeare's version, however, ends in full comic mode, essentially with a happy ending like the second half of Inchbald's *A Simple Story*, while Hawthorne's romance takes a darker tone and only hints at possible happiness while keeping Hester confined in the role of guilt-ridden adulteress.

Like *Cymbeline*, *The Scarlet Letter* is a blend of genres in the liminal space between comedy and tragedy and has many sources of potentially tragic resolution. One of the greatest tragedies of the book, Hester's assumption of the role of fallen woman, occurs before the story begins.[92] Roger makes his view of Hester's situation clear when he calls her a 'faithless woman' during their first conversation after his appearance in Boston.[93] The potential for further tragic resolution continues throughout the book as Roger vengefully manipulates the guilty conscience of the repentant Arthur. The intensity of Roger's desire for revenge recalls that of Shakespeare's Posthumus and, even more so, Inchbald's Lord Elmwood. Posthumus orders Imogen's death, and Lord Elmwood banishes Lady Matilda from his sight forever, but Roger, initially not knowing the identity of Pearl's father, chooses to keep his own identity hidden as he watches the Bostonians' behaviour to identify the man who cuckolded him. When he realizes that Arthur is the culprit, Roger could decide to expose the minister's sin to the townspeople to discredit him and place him in a position similar to that of Hester. Aware of the potential for further tragedy, Hester remains silent to protect Arthur, but her silence merely delays the inevitable and allows other situations to become potentially tragic. In the central scene of the book, for example, Roger witnesses Hester, Arthur and Pearl's standing together on the scaffold of the pillory one evening. Roger could have confronted the three on the occasion to expose his own identity to Arthur and bring the sequence of events to a climactic point that might have ended tragically. However, Roger chooses simply to observe the three quietly before offering to lead Arthur home. Similarly, when Reverend Wilson catechizes Pearl at Governor Bellingham's home, the young girl responds heretically so that the elders who are present feel even more strongly that she should be isolated from her sinful mother for her own moral good. Only Arthur's intervention prevents their potentially tragic plan from its realization.

The end of *The Scarlet Letter* includes probably the most tragic event in the book in Arthur's death on the scaffold after years of enduring Roger's emotional torture. In some respects, his death is more tragic, in the traditional sense, than even Hester's downfall because of his respected position as a prominent citizen and member of a theocratic culture. Hester's subsequent continued isolation reinforces the tragic elements of the text since she is unable, or unwilling, to move beyond her identity as an adulteress to start her life anew after Arthur's demise. Ultimately, however, a sense of the comic merges with the tragic end of the tale, particularly in respect to Pearl. Apparently, Pearl marries well into an aristocratic family of foreign origin, and herein lies the comic element that balances the tragedy of Arthur's death and of Hester's own guilt-ridden isolation. The story ends with hope for joy in the future, and perhaps of present joy in a faraway land, despite its dark beginnings, and Hawthorne's merger of the comic and tragic elements, based on Shakespearean precedent that probably included *Cymbeline*, helps to define the Romantic moral romance that he developed in parallel terms with Inchbald's form. According to David Bevington, Shakespeare used 'boldly experimental means' in crafting *Cymbeline* as a tragicomic play, and Hawthorne, familiar with Shakespeare's patterns, modified the tragicomic form for the Romantic moral romance.[94]

For both Inchbald and Hawthorne, the fallen woman figure, perhaps borrowed from *Cymbeline*, occupies a liminal role. In legalistic terms, Miss Milner and Hester are both clearly guilty, but Inchbald and Hawthorne suggest mitigating circumstances that call into question the justice of their punishments. As these romances suggest in symbolic terms, the woman author and the American author are similarly guilty of transgressing against the British novel tradition. But just as Miss Milner and Hester may have mitigating circumstances that excuse their transgressions, the woman writer and the American writer also may be excused for their transgressive desires for literary autonomy.

Narrative Structures, Romance Elements and Simple Characters from *The Winter's Tale*

While *A Simple Story* and *The Scarlet Letter* seem to have inherited Shakespearean elements from such plays as *The Tempest* and *Cymbeline*, they have even closer ties to another of Shakespeare's tragicomedies, *The Winter's Tale*.[95] Jonathan Wordsworth suggests that Inchbald takes *The Winter's Tale* 'as her guide' for *Nature and Art*, and it seems clear that *A Simple Story*, along with *The Scarlet Letter*, benefited from the same influence.[96] In fact, J. M. S. Tompkins says that *A Simple Story* was designed 'on the model of *Winter's Tale*', and James Boaden notices the connection as well.[97] Shakespeare's *The Winter's Tale* exhibits the same kind of liminality that appears in *The Tempest* and *Cymbeline*; it merges the tragic and comic so that the drama occupies the liminal space between the two genres that critics traditionally considered opposed to one another, tragedy and comedy.[98] However, unlike Shakespeare's other romance plays, *The Winter's Tale* is more consciously constructed in a way that emphasizes its opposition of comic and tragic elements by breaking the narrative structure of the play near its middle.[99] Bevington calls *The Winter's Tale* a text with an 'almost symmetrical division into two halves of bleak tragedy and comic romance'.[100] Tragedy governs the first half of the play until the revelation of Hermione's faithfulness by the Delphic Oracle in the third act, while comedy governs the second half of the play, which culminates in Hermione's reunion with Leontes. Frank Kermode refers to the second half of *The Winter's Tale* as being so different from the first half that it might 'seem to be another play'.[101] The strength of the play does not lie uniquely in its tragic half or in its comic half; rather its strength lies in the interplay between the two opposed halves.[102] What perhaps interested Inchbald and Hawthorne most was the idea of the interaction between opposites in the liminal space between the two.[103] They saw in the interplay the opportunity to further their own artistic agendas and chose to modify it for their own purposes as they situated their works between the novel and the romance and themselves as writers between the traditional British novel and their own ideals. Consequently, like Shakespeare, they also wrote tales whose tightly controlled narrative structures would call attention to the uniqueness of the narratives.

Structurally, *A Simple Story* and *The Scarlet Letter* are symmetrically balanced, much like *The Winter's Tale*. Inchbald's romance splits neatly in the middle so that the first two volumes detail Miss Milner's experiences with Dorriforth while the second two volumes follow Matilda's life in relation to Lord Elmwood.[104] In fact, Inchbald even includes a seventeen-year gap between the first and second halves of her book, which parallels the sixteen-year gap in Shakespeare's play and further solidifies the relationship between the two texts. The comic and tragic elements of Inchbald's tale, however, are more integrated with one another than are those in *The Winter's Tale*, and Inchbald's classification of what constitutes the comic or the tragic consequently becomes more ambiguous. Miss Milner's marriage at the end of the first half seems a comic resolution to her conflict with Dorriforth/Lord Elmwood, but the mourning ring that seals their marriage foreshadows Miss Milner's tragic banishment and demise. Likewise, the tragedy that seems to follow Matilda ends with her comic marriage, but Inchbald hints that Matilda pays for her happiness with a tragic relinquishment of her independence as a woman.[105] Because Inchbald more closely integrates the comic and the tragic in *A Simple Story* than Shakespeare does in *The Winter's Tale*, *A Simple Story* emerges as a text that more directly confronts the idea of liminality. Inchbald's book incorporates both comic and tragic elements just as it includes characteristics of the traditional novel and romance.

Hawthorne structures *The Scarlet Letter* with a similar attention to balance and to the liminal possibilities of treating comedy and tragedy within the same framework. Like *A Simple Story*, *The Scarlet Letter* is divided into two halves, but unlike Inchbald's book, Hawthorne's does not include a narrative break in the middle with a radical shift in the story.[106] The centre of *The Scarlet Letter* is the night-time scene in which Roger watches as Arthur, Hester and Pearl mount the scaffold in the centre of Boston. The scene incorporates a potential for tragic resolution and for a consequent structural break like that in the middle of *The Winter's Tale* or *A Simple Story*, but because Roger chooses not to expose Arthur's sin, the scene passes uneventfully. Nevertheless, the scene acts as a marker in the narrative because of its strong potential for tragedy. As Roger watches, he receives more proof that Arthur is the man who cuckolded him. Moreover, because Arthur meets Hester and Pearl, and because Arthur sees the meteor creating a great *A* in the sky, he experiences an unsettling 'psychological state' that makes him suspect that Roger may be malevolent.[107] Despite experiencing revelations about one another, Roger and Arthur remain silent so that, for the moment, the comic spirit of the story prevails. Hawthorne integrates the comic with the tragic so closely that a break in the story is not necessary. Instead, the scaffold scene marks the potential breakage point – a point analogous to the climactic scene of a Shakespeare play – and its importance is emphasized by the framing presence of the story's two other scaffold scenes at the beginning and the end. Hawthorne has merged the comic and the tragic so that *The Scarlet Letter* occupies the same liminal space as *A Simple Story*, and his use of the central marking scene recalls the central break in *The Winter's Tale* and, perhaps, that in *A Simple Story* as well.

Inchbald and Hawthorne gave their books symmetrical structures because they wished to call attention to their experimental nature in the same way that

Shakespeare had called attention, structurally, to the experimental nature of *The Winter's Tale*. Likewise, the Romantic writers borrowed elements from the romance tradition, perhaps because Shakespeare had done the same, to emphasize the experimental qualities of their books even further. For example, in *Shakespearean Tragedy as Chivalric Romance*, Michael Hays points out that Shakespeare and his contemporaries were familiar with the chivalric romance and finds features of the genre in *Macbeth*, *Hamlet*, *Othello* and *King Lear*.[108] In *Shakespeare's Late Work* of 2007, Raphael Lyne connects romance history, a significant influence on Shakespeare's later plays, with 'medieval chivalric poems'.[109] David Bevington notices several 'typical devices of romance' in *The Winter's Tale*, including 'a babe abandoned to the elements, a princess brought up by shepherds, a prince disguised as a swain, a sea voyage, and a recognition scene'.[110] The romance devices echo similar elements in *The Tempest* and *Cymbeline*, such as Prospero's abandonment at sea with Miranda, Antonio's recognition of Prospero at the end of the play, Imogen's disguise as Fidele, and Cymbeline's reunion with his two kidnapped sons. Indeed, Norman Sanders points out that all of Shakespeare's romance plays share typical characteristics of traditional romance, including 'large time-spans, riddles, shipwrecks, the strange loss and recovery of children, rural and court settings, extremes of characterization, happy endings embracing incipient tragedy, and so on'.[111] Frank Kermode is more specific in his statement,

> All the Romances treat of the recovery of lost royal children, usually princesses of great, indeed semi-divine, virtue, and beauty; they all bring important characters near to death, and sometimes feature almost miraculous resurrections; they all end with the healing, after many years of repentance and suffering, of some disastrous breach in the lives and happiness of princes, and this final reconciliation is usually brought about by the agency of beautiful young people; they all contain material of a pastoral character or otherwise celebrate natural beauty and its renewal.[112]

A Simple Story and *The Scarlet Letter* incorporate similar romance elements, though modified for the authors' purposes. Miss Milner starts *A Simple Story* as an orphan, and although she is not abandoned to the elements, she is exposed to the vicissitudes of Dorriforth's arbitrary will in much the same way that Perdita is exposed to the indifferent will of nature. Also like Perdita, Matilda spends a significant part of her early life separated from her father, although Lord Elmwood actively shuns her, whereas Leontes supposedly searches for Perdita. Likewise, a recognition scene occurs when Matilda reunites with Lord Elmwood to reaffirm her identity as Elmwood's daughter. A similar recognition occurs at the end of Hawthorne's *The Scarlet Letter* when Arthur Dimmesdale reveals his identity as Hester's partner in sin to the inhabitants of Boston, and an earlier recognition scene occurs on the scaffold of the pillory when Hester's gaze alights on Roger Chillingworth standing in the crowd.[113] Moreover, Pearl, as the product of an adulterous relationship, parallels Perdita's role in *The Winter's Tale* when Leontes believes her to be Polixenes's daughter rather than his own. In fact, Pearl apparently is born while Hester is in prison, just as Hermione bears Perdita while incarcerated. The difference is that Pearl really is the product of adultery, whereas Perdita is not.

Even the sea voyage that appears in *The Winter's Tale* has its parallels in Inchbald's and Hawthorne's romances. Inchbald sends Lord Elmwood on a lengthy voyage to his estate in the West Indies, which physically separates him from Miss Milner, while Hawthorne uses a similar voyage to separate Roger and Hester. The separation in Inchbald's text lasts nearly three years, while that in Hawthorne's lasts about two years.[114] In both cases, however, the separation is long enough that it prompts adulterous activity on the parts of both women, neither of whom hears news of her husband, and both of whom decide that they must continue their lives as if their husbands are deceased. The unfortunate truth, however, dooms the two women when their husbands return to find that they have been replaced by men who, although they do not fill the role of husband, certainly have acquired the tangential roles of companion and lover. Hence, *A Simple Story* and *The Scarlet Letter* read much like fables in the vein of *The Winter's Tale*, and their mixed-genre narratives evoke the liminality of Shakespeare's precedent.

While the narrative structures and the romance elements of *A Simple Story* and *The Scarlet Letter* call attention to the liminal qualities of the books, the characters within the tales further reinforce the liminality of the Romantic moral romance through their one-sided nature. As has already mentioned in Chapter 2, and will be discussed at length in Chapter 5, Inchbald and Hawthorne created characters whose personalities seem simple, flat or one-sided because they do not exhibit the full range of qualities one would expect in an actual human being. Readers have difficulty imagining the characters' existing beyond the confines of the texts in which they appear. The characters, or figures, symbolically represent single facets of personalities, and within the Romantic moral romance, Inchbald and Hawthorne juxtapose the single-faceted figures in opposition to one another to explore the interaction between the two – the activity that occurs in the liminal space in which they meet. *The Winter's Tale* acts as precedent for Inchbald's and Hawthorne's use of symbolic figures since Hermione fills the role of the wrongly accused woman while Leontes acts as the stereotypical jealous husband. Although Shakespeare's characters in *The Winter's Tale* may not be traditional stock characters, their origins do lie in the tradition of the stock character, with which Shakespeare was familiar and which he used freely. Sir John Falstaff, who appears most notably in *I Henry IV*, and characters like Malvolio and Sir Toby Belch from *Twelfth Night* are typical Shakespearean stock characters. Their personalities are each dominated by a single characteristic that sometimes is encoded even in their names.

Inchbald and Hawthorne were well aware of Shakespeare's reliance upon the stock character tradition. Perhaps using Shakespeare's precedent as their guide, they adopted the stock character but modified it for the Romantic moral romance sub-genre.[115] Unlike Shakespeare's stock characters, whose primary purpose often was to incite laughter, Inchbald's and Hawthorne's one-dimensional figures are imbued with a quasi-allegorical symbolism that allows them to represent serious social and cultural issues of the Romantic Period.[116] Rather than functioning merely as representations of excess, as Shakespearean stock characters often did, Inchbald's and Hawthorne's characters exhibit one-dimensionality as a means of calling attention to the liminal spaces between the characters. Symbolically, the spaces represent the liminality of the very texts in which the characters appear – between the traditional romance and novel – as well as the liminal literary space that Inchbald and Hawthorne claim for themselves as writers between British literary tradition and their own ideals. The apparent simplicity of the Romantic moral romance and its characters is deceptive since the genre symbolically encodes its characters and, through its reliance upon Shakespearean precedent that exploited the merger of the comic and the tragic, appropriates the liminal space between romance and novel.

The Liminal Qualities of the Romantic Moral Romance

Given the parallels between Shakespeare's *The Tempest, Cymbeline* and *The Winter's Tale* on one hand, and Inchbald's *A Simple Story* and Hawthorne's *The Scarlet Letter* on the other hand, it seems clear that Inchbald and Hawthorne, drawing from their own love of Shakespeare's plays, based their own Romantic moral romance forms on Shakespearean precedent. Specifically, Inchbald and Hawthorne transformed the liminality of Shakespeare's romance plays for their own purposes. They borrowed the liminal nature of Shakespeare's fusion of tragedy and comedy to shape their own tales as texts that fused elements of the traditional romance and novel. Their use of character types further enhanced their exploration of liminal space by focusing attention on the interaction among characters rather than upon each one as a single entity. And finally, they borrowed Shakespeare's principle of controlled narrative structure to give their own tales tightly controlled formal structures that would further call attention to their experimental nature. Despite the uniqueness of each of their works and despite a divergence in their intentions, Inchbald and Hawthorne drew on similar literary precedents to develop similar forms. Just as Shakespeare used experimental techniques in writing his dramatic romances, Inchbald and Hawthorne dared to reinvent Romantic fiction with similar boldness. The result of their efforts was the Romantic moral romance.

4. 'I WILL NOT ACCEPT YOUR MORAL!': PROPOSITIONS OF AN ALTERNATIVE, INDIVIDUAL AND LIMINAL MORAL ORDER FOR INCHBALD AND HAWTHORNE[1]

Thou art a symbol and a sign
To Mortals of their fate and force;
Like thee, Man is in part divine,
A troubled stream from a pure source.

– George Gordon, Lord Byron[2]

In addition to sharing Shakespearean precedent as a common source for the Romantic moral romance sub-genre, Elizabeth Inchbald and Nathaniel Hawthorne both drew on the conventions of religious belief and socially driven religious practice as they experimented with their alternative form of fiction. Incorporating elements of legends and fables, the form blended allegorical potential and symbolic meaning in a way that, while it examined character motivation in psychological terms, questioned established conventions of moral order and, in some cases, proposed alternatives to that order. Inchbald's *Nature and Art* and Hawthorne's *The Marble Faun* are particularly relevant to the examination of religious concerns since they directly engage the traditions of Anglicanism, Catholicism and Puritanism as defining elements of prevailing cultural identity. In particular, *Nature and Art* and *The Marble Faun* examine the response of religious tradition to sin and guilt at the individual and social levels to suggest that the religious response often fails to provide adequate solutions to the harsh reality of the individual's experience. Again, however, the two authors did not treat their subjects in an identical manner. As a Catholic, Inchbald was concerned with the influence of Anglicanism on her characters' lives in England, while Hawthorne chose to examine Puritanism and Catholicism as the two religious traditions operated in the lives of his characters in Rome. Despite the divergence, however, both authors treat the subject of religion similarly by incorporating its multi-faceted socio-cultural influence into their texts in ways that challenge traditional assumptions while suggesting alternatives to the established moral order.

This chapter examines Inchbald's *Nature and Art* and Hawthorne's *The Marble Faun* to suggest that these books' preoccupation with the nature of right and wrong – with the moral order – exemplifies a didactic subtext accessible in the Romantic moral romance on a symbolic, quasi-allegorical level.[3] Inchbald's and Hawthorne's fictions constitute challenges to the tradition of the British novel, but they simultaneously challenge the conventions of moral order as established by religious doctrine. Infractions against the moral order of established religion, which is how *sin* is defined in this chapter, reveal much about how Inchbald and Hawthorne view religion. In particular, the Romantic authors reveal their own attitudes by depicting their characters' techniques for coping with guilt, the emotional self-recrimination for sin. Rather than alleviating the characters' guilt, religion, as the definer of that guilt, exacerbates it and places the characters in untenable moral dilemmas. Consequently, as an alternative to the religious moral order, Inchbald's and Hawthorne's romances propose an individual moral order situated in the liminal space between absolute rejection of religious precepts and absolute, unthinking obedience to them.[4] The chapter begins with a brief overview of Romantic attitudes toward religion combined with a discussion of Inchbald's and Hawthorne's personal experiences and views. Prevailing contemporary attitudes that challenged organized religion, combined with Inchbald's and Hawthorne's own views, suggest that both authors had ample motivation for questioning the efficacy of religious doctrines in their works. Then, the discussion examines Inchbald's *Nature and Art*, and particularly its focus on clerical hypocrisy, to suggest the corruption that Inchbald believed to be problematic to adherents of the Anglican Church. Finally, the chapter turns to Hawthorne's *The Marble Faun* to show how its depiction of the effects of family guilt on subsequent generations exposes the corruption of Catholicism and, less directly, Puritanism. As Inchbald and Hawthorne unveil the corrupted nature of religion in its response to sin and guilt, they suggest an alternate moral order that reveals 'truth' on the individual's terms. Their alternate moral order neither fully rejects nor fully embraces religious belief but suggests compromise that selectively accepts and rejects religious beliefs based on the truth of the individual's experience and conscience.[5] Appropriately, the alternate, individual moral order parallels Inchbald's and Hawthorne's proposed literary order since its liminal nature parallels the liminal quality of the Romantic moral romance.

Inchbald's and Hawthorne's Attitudes toward Religious Creeds

At the time Inchbald and Hawthorne wrote, and especially in Inchbald's England, traditional religious institutions faced multilateral challenges to their validity and efficacy. As a result, Inchbald and Hawthorne would have experienced pressure to question religion just as their contemporaries were doing, even if they had not possessed their own motivations for doing so. As M. H. Abrams explains in his seminal work, *Natural Supernaturalism*, 'It is a historical commonplace that the course of Western thought since the Renaissance has been one of progressive secularization'.[6] Abrams explains that, as part of the general trend toward secularization, the Romantic poets – and, it seems, fiction writers, as well – were engaged in a campaign to reformulate the 'Judeo-Christian culture' in which they wrote.[7] Abrams argues,

> The tendency in innovative Romantic thought (manifested in proportion as the thinker is or is not a Christian theist) is greatly to diminish, and at the extreme to eliminate, the role of God, leaving as the prime agencies man and the world, mind and nature, the ego and the non-ego, the self and the not-self, spirit and the other, or (in the favorite antithesis of post-Kantian philosophers) subject and object.[8]

He explains that within this system 'it is the subject, mind, or spirit which is primary and takes over the initiative and the functions which had once been the prerogatives of deity', and he also comments that in general, Romantic writers tended 'to naturalize the supernatural and to humanize the divine'.[9]

Another critic, Henry Chadwick, reiterates Jean-Jacques Rousseau's far-reaching influence and his belief in the conscience and instinct as the ultimate arbiters of right and wrong.[10] Moreover, Chadwick asserts the existence of

> a fundamental, uncriticized presupposition of a growing number of thinkers of the Romantic age, namely, that the value of any given affirmation about man and the meaning of his existence lies in subjective sincerity, in the inward conviction with which it is held.[11]

He summarizes the prevailing Romantic view of religion by commenting, 'In one form or another an interest in the subjective act of believing rather than in the nature of the object of faith comes to dominate almost all the principal religious thinkers of nineteenth-century Europe'.[12] Indeed, Robert Ryan, in *The Romantic Reformation,* interprets Romantic literature as 'a conscious attempt by a group of writers to influence the religious transformation that was taking place in their society'.[13] As Abrams, Ryan and other scholars have noted, rather than rejecting religion altogether, the Romantics tended to challenge the assumptions of established religion in favour of a type of faith grounded in individual human experience and conscience. Their alternative faith was more relevant to their daily lives than were the centuries-old pronouncements of traditional creeds. Abrams explains that the Romantics

> undertook to save the overview of human history and destiny, the experiential paradigms, and the cardinal values of their religious heritage, by reconstituting them in a way that would make them intellectually acceptable, as well as emotionally pertinent, for the time being.[14]

John Randall comments, 'Romanticism stood primarily for a religious interpretation of the universe which would make man's interests central in the cosmos'.[15] Inchbald matured as a writer during the height of Romantic challenges to religion, and Hawthorne lived in an intellectual climate in America that had inherited much of the same scepticism. Surrounded by other writers who questioned established religion, Inchbald and Hawthorne remained aware of the difficulties involved in revising one's belief system and came to question their own through their writing.

In addition to the motivation provided by the intellectual climate, Inchbald had ample personal motivation to challenge religion in *Nature and Art* and in her other writings. William McKee suggests that Inchbald moved through three periods of religious practice, the first ending in the 1770s, the second ending around 1810 and the third extending until her death in 1821.[16] During the first and last periods, she depended more heavily on her faith, attending to her religious duties regularly, but she was 'the least fruitful in religious zeal' in the middle period, the time of her most concentrated literary output. In support of his argument, McKee quotes extensively from James Boaden's *Memoirs of Mrs Inchbald*, noting that Inchbald went 'frequently' to morning prayers, was a 'constant visitor' at church and 'faithfully attended' to her religious duties along with her husband Joseph in the early period.[17] During Inchbald's third period, she was a 'sincere penitent', McKee claims, suggesting that the two interests that dominated her life were 'her religion and her charity' and quoting Boaden extensively again to note, for example, that she 'seldom went abroad except to attend Mass'.[18]

In the middle period, however, Inchbald's attendance at Mass was apparently more sporadic, for she relinquished it altogether for long periods, particularly in London, where she attended only occasionally and where she could be seen periodically at Anglican services.[19] At one point, her Catholic friends became concerned about her religious life and wrote about the matter to Dr Alexander Geddes, who responded with advice for helping Inchbald back onto the path toward righteousness. Likewise, Roger Manvell notes that Inchbald 'began to entertain doubts concerning the dogmas of her Church' in the 1780s, particularly after the deaths of her mother and her husband Joseph, both of which 'disturbed her faith'.[20] McKee implies, with good reason, that Inchbald's relationships with Thomas Holcroft and William Godwin, both of whom were staunch sceptics, may have weakened her hold on the tenets of Catholicism. McKee, whose argument seems bent on establishing Inchbald's piety, nevertheless makes a valid point in remembering 'the grave difficulty encountered by English Catholics of the eighteenth century who wished to practice their religion', reminding his readers that at times, 'there was no Mass to attend'.[21] Whatever the reasons for her struggle with her faith, that struggle inspired her writing, and religious and moral issues move to the forefront of *A Simple Story* and then *Nature and Art*.

Although Inchbald questioned Catholicism in *A Simple Story*, by the time she wrote *Nature and Art*, she had turned her attentions to the Anglicanism that provided her with even greater incentive for a direct challenge. The very inception of Anglicanism in opposition to the Pope's wishes in the 1530s had opened a rift between the English and Catholics. Events just before and during Inchbald's lifetime further complicated the relationship and may have encouraged Inchbald's scepticism about her Anglican compatriots. Repeated political uprisings by Irish Catholics in the eighteenth century already had aggravated the relations between Catholics and Anglicans by Inchbald's lifetime.[22] Each rebellion resulted in a stronger Anglican prejudice against Catholics, and the British government continued to enact 'harsher laws against Catholic priests or Catholic laymen, who were deprived of the few rights of citizenship which eighteenth-century governments accorded to their people'.[23] In fact, Catholics could neither purchase nor inherit land until 1778 when the First Catholic Relief Act restored some of their rights and protected priests from prosecution.[24] The anti-Catholic Gordon Riots of 1780 in London reaffirmed many Anglican prejudices so that the Second Catholic Relief Act, which finally allowed Catholics to worship publicly, did not become law until the early 1790s when Inchbald was writing. In an acknowledgement of the connectedness of church and state, the second act also 'allowed Catholics a freer position in practicing professions, provided they took an oath of loyalty'.[25] Refusal to follow Anglican doctrines often implied disloyalty to the current monarch, who held the title Defender of the Faith. For Catholics like Inchbald, not following the official state religion meant that they constantly had to contend with persecution from Anglicans and with having their loyalty questioned. Moreover, Catholicism was the dominant religion of France, which threatened England with invasion during much of the 1790s (after declaring war in 1793) and further exacerbated the religious schism.

Although Inchbald 'was reared in a Catholic household and lived in a community in which many of the families of good birth were also Catholic', she certainly was aware of the anti-Catholic sentiment that was so prevalent in England, and she could not ignore it.[26] In fact, when she married her husband Joseph, who also was Catholic, the couple had two marriage ceremonies, one Catholic and the other Anglican.[27] The Anglican ceremony, held the day after the Catholic rites, officially legalized their union under English law, which did not recognize the Catholic ceremony. Throughout Inchbald's early life and during her most productive years, Catholicism remained a religion that most of the English viewed with suspicion, if not open hostility, and Inchbald consequently remained at odds with Anglicanism throughout her life. Indeed, her diary of 1780 mentions her concern over the Gordon Riots, accounts of which she followed in the newspapers.[28] Developing the Romantic moral romance to challenge religious moral order, particularly the Anglican order depicted in *Nature and Art*, allowed Inchbald to express her views on the Anglican dissonance between religious belief and socially driven religious practice.[29]

Hawthorne may not have experienced the kind of social prejudice that inflected Inchbald's religious experiences, but he cultivated an awareness of moral issues that similarly prompted religious scepticism and that inspired him to confront moral and religious issues in his writing.[30] Public religious controversy during his lifetime, combined with negative experiences with religion in college, probably occasioned Hawthorne's avoidance of churches and clerics in his adulthood. The debate between Unitarians and Trinitarians rose to a 'most decided and heated controversy' during Hawthorne's youth, and as a student at Bowdoin College, Hawthorne was required to attend religious services regularly and frequently.[31] According to John Frederick, the students 'were routed out at six daily, all through the long Maine winters, for morning prayers and were required to attend another service on weekday evenings and three services on Sundays'.[32] The young man chafed under such strict rules, often feigning sickness on Sundays, and Frederick suggests that these services 'account in large measure for both his nearly unbroken record of nonattendance at religious services during the rest of his life and his persistent distrust and dislike of the clerical profession in general'.[33] Mark Van Doren comments that Hawthorne 'was to go with no fashion in religion or philosophy' and claims that '[i]f Hawthorne entertained any dogma, nobody was aware of it'.[34] Hawthorne's attitude is clear in the journal entry for 30 August 1842, in which he writes that his faith in clerics, for whom he finds little use, continuously diminishes and in which he calls for the creation of a vibrant new set of moral codes to replace the worn platitudes of tradition.[35] Earlier that month, he had referred to several religious texts, including sermons, as 'all such trash'.[36]

Despite wanting a revised set of moral guidelines, Hawthorne seems always to have maintained a faith in God and a belief in the redemptive value of sin and guilt. However, Hawthorne's faith remained independent of particular denominational doctrines. He believed that established religious doctrines needed reinvention – perhaps on the individual's terms – so that religious belief and social religious practice would more accurately correspond with one another. As Margaret Moore comments, while critics disagree on the exact nature of Hawthorne's religious views, he seemed to imbibe from 'a great many doctrines, but found little meaning in such precise formulations', and although he distrusted organized religion, he nevertheless maintained the conviction that it was 'significant' while retaining his own faith in God.[37] Likewise, Frederick calls Hawthorne a 'consistent theist' and suggests that he might be described as a Unitarian who believed in 'the reality of evil and in the pervasive and permanent effect of sin' while he doubted the divinity of Christ.[38] Edward Wagenknecht says of Hawthorne, 'He believed in God. He believed in immortality. He believed in Divine Providence. He believed in the infinite value of every human soul'.[39] Wagenknecht acknowledges, however, that Hawthorne exhibited an 'indifference to the church as an institution'.[40] Hawthorne himself made several entries in his journals that suggest a non-religious faith. On one occasion, he mentions the beautiful weather and comments that its beauty makes him think humanity must be immortal, and similarly, as his mother lay dying, he wrote that some sort of afterlife must exist because if it did not, then all of life's trials would be pointless.[41]

In his fiction, Hawthorne most often examined the disjunction between belief and practice in the Puritanism that circumscribed his own ancestry. Well read in Puritan texts, he was aware of the theocratic nature of Puritan society and of the Puritan tendency, because of a belief in predestination, to exhibit arrogant self-assurance of moral righteousness.[42] His own ancestors, who would have faulted him for being a morally deficient story writer, had participated in the witchcraft trials of Salem in 1692, a fact that he acknowledges with shame in 'The Custom-House'.[43] During the trials, a group of young girls accused several Salemites of participating in satanic rituals and haunting other colonists in the form of spectres.[44] The Puritan elders, fearing that the colony was under attack by Satan's minions, arrested the accused and hanged over twenty of them before the scare had run its course. Even in the early stages of the witchcraft scare, many of the colonists realized that it had surpassed the bounds of believability, and one of the accused consequently refused to enter a plea before the court. He was subsequently tortured to death by having stones placed on him until he died, and still other innocent victims died in prison while awaiting trial. As further evidence of the wrong-headedness of the Puritan theocracy at the time, the trials stopped only after several prominent citizens, including the governor's wife, were accused. To Hawthorne, the trials demonstrated Puritanism's limitations since the moral order, despite its self-assurance, failed to divert the irrational brutality of the witchcraft scare.

Although Hawthorne liked to examine Puritan influences because of his ancestry, and although *The Marble Faun* is perhaps his most concerted departure from his usual focus, the book more accurately portrays Hawthorne's attitudes toward organized religion in general. Hawthorne's tenure as American Consul in Liverpool had provided increased opportunity to interact with adherents to Anglicanism, and he spent several months in Italy, the seat of the Catholic Church, before completing the book.[45] With an increased awareness of the differences among religions, Hawthorne chose to confront Catholicism in *The Marble Faun*, a choice that he made, not simply because the book's setting is Italy, but because he saw a potential for forgiveness in Catholicism that Puritanism did not offer. The Puritan doctrine of predestination made individual acts of sin and atonement essentially irrelevant because it denied Puritans a real choice between right and wrong, between salvation and damnation. And while Hawthorne was interested in inherited guilt that paralleled the Puritan idea of natural depravity, he believed that the individual's choices were relevant and that the distinction between guilt and innocence could not always be clearly defined.[46] Catholicism appealed to Hawthorne because of its inclusiveness, because it attempted to address human needs in a way that Hawthorne 'found lacking in the Protestant institutions he had known in England and America' and because it offered absolution from sin and guilt in the confessional in a way that no Protestant religion did.[47] Catholicism seems to have been closer to Hawthorne's ideal of individual moral order than Puritanism, but it clearly was not perfect. Throughout *The Marble Faun*, Hawthorne challenges Catholic assumptions about moral order and exposes the hypocrisy and corruption of Catholicism's adherents. In doing so, Hawthorne suggests that even liberal Catholicism provides inadequate responses to the sin and guilt of the individual. As this chapter will demonstrate, Hawthorne is content only with an individually constructed moral order.

Clearly, Inchbald and Hawthorne had particular interests in religious issues, which touched their daily lives in a myriad of ways and which offered differing methods for coping with guilt and sin. The two authors integrated religious issues into their fictions as a means of questioning established conventions of moral order – and, symbolically, questioning the literary order of the British novel.

Challenges to Anglicanism in *Nature and Art*

A few lines from the end of *Nature and Art*, young Henry Norwynne apparently summarizes the theme of the book by commenting that 'it is not upon earth we are to look for a state of perfection – it is only in heaven'.[48] On the surface, young Henry's comment seems to support the Anglican doctrines that underlie nearly every scene in the text. The statement comes at the end of a speech in which young Henry notes that physicians may not be skilful, soldiers may not be courageous, lawyers may not be honest and ministers may not always have good fortune. It seems to excuse the behaviour of the two upper-class William Norwynnes, who, throughout the book, embody hypocrisy and political deviousness on a grand scale. It seems, also, to have been written to appease Inchbald's more conservative readers, and consequently, many critics consider the ending of *Nature and Art* to be the book's weakest feature. They complain that Inchbald retreats from her more revolutionary attitude at the beginning of the tale, thereby undermining the integrity of her own narrative.[49]

However, scholars who believe that the conclusion weakens Inchbald's tale have overlooked the words young Henry uses to complete his thought. The book does not end with young Henry's assertion that one can find perfection only in heaven, for he continues, 'and there, we may rest assured, that no practitioner in the professions I have named, will ever be admitted to disturb our eternal felicity'.[50] In his list of professions, young Henry includes lawyers like his own cousin William and, more significantly, ministers like his uncle, the elder William. In a statement that contrasts shockingly with his meek, submissive attitude earlier in the tale, young Henry consigns his cousin and uncle to hell. By relating young Henry's scandalous words, Inchbald concludes *Nature and Art* with a caustic reminder of the divergence between religious belief and socially driven religious practice. Far from weakening the conclusion of the tale by appeasing conservative readers, young Henry's words pointedly condemn the hypocrisy of his cousin and uncle and recognize the far-reaching effects of their sins upon the other characters in the book.[51]

As the story in *Nature and Art* develops, Inchbald focuses her attention intensely upon the elder William. In particular, she highlights the disjunction between William's religious beliefs and his actual social religious practice as revealed in his relationships with the other characters. She suggests that William's hypocrisy and corruption as a minister have trans-generational consequences since young William becomes equally hypocritical and corrupt in religious terms.[52] Inchbald then condemns the Williams' hypocrisy by demonstrating its consequences in the fate of Hannah Primrose. Symbolically, Inchbald suggests that if the Anglican Church can allow its members – even its leaders – to become catalysts for the fates of people like Hannah, then that religion needs re-evaluation.[53] Young Henry's injunction to have faith, combined with his dismissal of lawyers and ministers like the Williams, suggests that Inchbald proposes an alternate individual moral order unrelated to religious doctrines. Significantly, young Henry asks for individual faith, not better adherence to the precepts of a particular religion.

The Elder William's Poor Example

The last profession that young Henry mentions in his final words is that of the minister, the most problematic profession for Inchbald in the book. From the beginning of the tale, she characterizes the elder William as hypocritical, corrupt, arrogant and prideful. William is a mere sycophant who seeks advancement within the Anglican Church. Inchbald begins with a sharp contrast between William and his brother, the elder Henry. Henry supports his brother's bid to become a clergyman by playing his violin, but William regards his brother's self-sacrificing efforts with disdain because he finds the music profession demeaning and undignified. William's discomfort becomes so intense that the narrator comments, 'the very agent of his elevation was now so odious to him, that he could not cast his eyes upon the friendly violin, without instant emotions of disgust'.[54] But that violin helps Henry establish a social connection that ensures William's entry into the ministry.

Eventually, William is appointed to a deanship, but he remains an exceedingly prideful and hypocritical example of the Anglican clergy. He continues to treat his brother rudely and even derogates Henry's wife by expressing shock at her singing profession.[55] William himself marries Lady Clementina, a socialite with no redeeming personal qualities whom he chooses because of her family 'connections'.[56] Lady Clementina is hardly a suitable minister's wife, for her most obvious personality characteristic is vanity.[57] Had William's social religious practice conformed to his stated beliefs, he would not have chosen Clementina, whose priorities centred on herself, and neither would he have denounced his loving brother's wife in a way that eventually alienated Henry. As the narrator comments, however, 'That, which in a weak woman is called vanity, in a man of sense is termed pride – make one a degree stronger, or the other a degree weaker, and the dean and his wife were infected with the self-same folly'.[58] William's pride and his obsession over his position in the social hierarchy exemplify the corruption of the Anglican clergy; his social religious practice does not correspond with his stated religious beliefs.

The discrepancy between the elder William's actions and his beliefs becomes more pointed in *Nature and Art* when young Henry returns from Sierra Leone to live with his uncle. Untutored in the conventions of the civilized world, young Henry expresses wonder at many of the traditions of British society and innocently comments upon them in ways that annoy his uncle because they unintentionally expose the older man's hypocrisy. Inchbald uses young Henry as a noble savage figure, as discussed further in Chapter 5, to contrast with the civilized, elder William and condemn, in symbolic terms, William's hypocritical actions.

One of the first contrasts between young Henry and his uncle involves William's wig. William arrogantly explains to the curious Henry that the wig acts as 'a distinction between us and inferior people'.[59] Young Henry accepts his uncle's explanation but damningly responds to the announcement that wigs 'are worn to give an importance to the wearer' by commenting, 'That is just as the savages do; they stick brass nails, wire, buttons, and entrails of beasts all over them to give them importance'.[60] As Eleanor Ty comments, young Henry's 'association of the dean's hairpiece with the ornaments of the Africans enables Inchbald to make a telling statement about the "savagery" of certain English practices'.[61] Later, in one of Inchbald's most humorous passages in the book, Henry catches William before he has donned his hairpiece and decides to bow first to his uncle and then to the lifeless wig.[62] Henry's obeisance to the wig acknowledges its symbolism of political and ecclesiastical power, but it also deflates William's importance by equating the man with the lifeless wig.

As *Nature and Art* progresses, young Henry continues to act as the foil whom Inchbald uses to expose the elder William's foibles as a minister. On more than one occasion, for example, the uncle and nephew discuss the differences between the rich and the poor in England, and the elder William's corruption and greed emerge from each discussion as indictments of Anglicanism and its clergy. The elder William suggests one day that the basic function of the poor is to serve the rich, but he further comments that in the afterlife, everyone will be equal.[63] The confused Henry wonders how God could ordain a distinction between the rich and the poor on earth and yet make the distinction after death.[64] Later, when the elder William comments that hundreds of poor people in England are starving, young Henry again experiences confusion because he has read his uncle's pamphlet claiming that there is enough food for everyone in England.[65] Henry further exposes the hypocrisy of his uncle and his friends by congratulating Lord Bendham for giving the poor just enough charity to them to keep them from revolting when he says, 'I thought it was prudent in you to give a little; lest the poor, driven to despair, should take all'.[66] Henry's naïve comments once more delineate a significant distinction between William's stated religious belief and his socially driven religious practice.

While the elder William's professed beliefs suggest an egalitarian view of humanity, his actions indicate otherwise as he attempts to establish himself and his family as the superiors of those around them. For example, he suggests that his son marry Miss Sedgeley, and although young William at first resists the idea because of his attachment to Hannah Primrose, he relents when the elder William explains 'what great connections, and what great patronage' the marriage would bring to the family.[67] To advance his career, the elder William ingratiates himself with the bishop by allowing the publication of his own work under the bishop's name and by attributing his own ideas to the bishop. All the while, William preaches against pride and ambition to suggest that happiness comes from *'contempt of all riches and worldly honours in balance with a quiet conscience'* and to claim that the greatest happiness is found *'under an humble roof with heaven in prospect'.*[68] Inchbald carefully draws distinct contrasts between William's words and his actions, however. Even his own son does not give much credence to William's preachments. He comments one day, "'My father is a very good man [...] and yet, instead of being satisfied with an humble roof, he looks impatiently forward to a bishop's palace'".[69] The elder William eventually does become bishop, but his hypocritical nature never changes. In a scathing indictment of William's hypocrisy, Henry has difficulty understanding why the new bishop, whom he is told one should not disturb, should receive more respect than God, whom one might disturb at any time with prayer.[70]

Inchbald displays the elder William's hypocritical nature as a clergyman particularly well in his dealings with Hannah Primrose. Rather than supporting her and her illegitimate child either financially or emotionally, William responds with anger, for he believes that she should have been 'pursued, apprehended, and committed to prison'.[71] Much later, William learns the truth – that his own son, young William, seduced Hannah and then abandoned her. Although William claims that the inquiry 'must be done openly' when Hannah begins to confess the truth, he changes his mind and decides to hear her confession in private after she hints that young William is involved.[72] Rather than acknowledging Hannah's innocence, he chooses 'to hush the affair up'.[73] He takes advantage of Hannah's untenable financial situation to manipulate her into silence, and eventually the two Williams simply forget about her rather than honouring their agreement to support her. Inchbald does not condone the Williams' actions and considers their treatment of Hannah reprehensible and immoral. The narrator comments knowingly that Hannah 'mistook the appearance of moral excellence, for moral excellence itself'.[74] Hence, despite his ecclesiastical position, the elder William does not demonstrate Christian charity and chooses, instead, to preserve his own family's reputation at the expense of Hannah Primrose's livelihood, and eventually of her very life, by concealing the truth. He was ready to pursue Hannah and incarcerate her for her fornication, but he does nothing at all to his own son and hypocritically uses his power to protect the young man from any consequences.

Inchbald finds the elder William's behaviour as an Anglican minister so corrupt and so hypocritical that she denigrates him even after his death. As his funeral procession passes before the two Henrys, who have just returned from Africa, they notice that among the crowd of villagers, 'not one afflicted countenance appeared, not one dejected look, not one watery eye'.[75] When young Henry asks about Lady Clementina, a poor woman relates the story of her illness and miserable demise 'with a hearty laugh', and in fact, many of the spectators leave the funeral 'with smiling faces'.[76] One labourer hints that the elder William did not go to Heaven, and when Henry takes offence, the man says that William 'was above speaking to poor folks – unless they did any mischief, and then he was sure to take notice of them'.[77] Asked what William did for the poor, the labourer responds, 'Nothing at all', and comments that when the poor asked William for help, he sent them to '[B]ridewell, or the workhouse'.[78] The labourer even claims that William's dogs 'fared better than we poor'.[79] The encounter is disturbing for the elder Henry, who, although he has been absent for many years, still loves his brother despite any disagreements they may have had. However, it does provide Inchbald's readers with a clearer sense of the elder William's character and emphasizes the fact that his pride and hypocrisy as a clergyman do not change with age.

Young William's Continuation of the Legacy of Hypocrisy

While the elder William remains a negative representative of the clergy throughout *Nature and Art*, his legacy, embodied in young William, is just as villainous. By following the second generation of the family, Inchbald demonstrates the far-reaching effects of the elder William's corrupt nature as reflected in young William.

Essentially, young William inherits his father's guilt in a way that is reminiscent of Matilda's inheritance of her mother's guilt in *A Simple Story*. Unlike Matilda, however, young William embraces and perpetuates his father's corruption. Linking the two Williams as corrupt father and son allows Inchbald to suggest the trans-generational potential of religious hypocrisy and its negative effects.

When Inchbald has young Henry mention lawyers in his list of professionals who will not enter Heaven, she undoubtedly has his cousin William in mind. Young William's legal profession is secular, but it has collateral religious significance since lawyers and judges were to uphold the mandates of the British monarch – the Defender of the (Anglican) Faith. The divergence between religious belief and social practice in young William's life is evident from his first appearance in the story when he exhibits prideful superiority in meeting his cousin young Henry, but Inchbald's most serious indictment of young William's hypocrisy occurs after he becomes a judge. Near the end of the tale, after her arrest for counterfeiting, Hannah is brought before young William's 'righteous judgment-seat' for her trial.[80] Inchbald's words *righteous judgment-seat* allude to biblical prophesy to remind her readers of Judgement Day and to link young William, ironically, with God. Indeed, young William is far from righteous, for he is the catalyst, earlier in the book, for Hannah's downfall. Predictably, the jury pronounces Hannah guilty, but when William rises to pass the death sentence, Hannah exclaims, 'Oh! Not from *you*!'.[81] Hannah accepts – even expects – harsh punishment. Her objection is not to the punishment itself but to young William's being the judge who bestows it upon her. On a symbolic level, Hannah's words acknowledge the irony and hypocrisy of young William's position since he seduced Hannah years earlier and precipitated the desperation that forced her into prostitution and counterfeiting. And although he feels remorse when he learns Hannah's identity after her execution, young William quickly returns to his old ways and again forgets about her.[82] Years later when the two Henrys stumble upon the elder William's funeral procession, the elder Henry asks whether young William is at his father's palace and is told, 'Oh yes, you'll find master there, treading in the old man's shoes, as proud as Lucifer!'.[83]

Inchbald uses Hannah's downward spiral as a quasi-allegorical object lesson for her readers as she questions the moral order of Anglicanism to propose an alternative individual moral order.[84] Although Hannah clearly is guilty of the sin of fornication – and later, of prostitution and counterfeiting – Inchbald implies that the nature of Hannah's guilt is not so simple.[85] Indeed, she suggests that the two Williams share Hannah's guilt and are responsible for her fate. Hannah loses her virtue because young William's social religious practice does not correspond with his stated religious belief, and her fate worsens with the elder William's involvement because he exhibits hypocritical behaviour as well. If young Henry's final words in *Nature and Art* represent the theme of the book, and it seems they do, then Inchbald wishes to propose an alternative moral order that replaces Anglicanism with the 'truth' as expressed through individual experience. Although the doctrines of Anglicanism may promote the compassion and support that Hannah needs, the structured ranks of the clergy and the codified nature of the religion provide Anglicans with a comfortable sense of moral superiority that breeds intolerance. In contrast, Inchbald proposes an individualized moral order that acknowledges one's limitations but offers support for those in need. Above all, Hannah needs a viable means of redemption and acceptance, but the church offers no more than an excuse for the citizens of Anfield to shun her – to turn away the support structures she needs to rebuild her life. For Inchbald, individual experience like that of Hannah reveals more 'truth' in human terms than any religious creed. Indeed, Hannah may be interpreted as a symbol of the repressed female writer in England who needs an alternate literary order for self-expression.[86]

Challenges to Catholicism in *The Marble Faun*

While Inchbald challenges the moral order established in England by Anglicanism in *Nature and Art*, Hawthorne similarly grapples symbolically with Italian Catholicism in *The Marble Faun*.[87] Inchbald's most representative Anglicans are hypocritical, corrupt and self-absorbed, and the actual social practice of Anglicanism fails to provide meaningful support to the likes of Hannah Primrose. Likewise, Hawthorne's book reveals the corruption of Catholicism, but Hawthorne also acknowledges its potential for good. Hawthorne distrusted religious institutions, particularly the Puritanism that circumscribed his ancestry, but as *The Marble Faun* demonstrates, he believed that the moral order established by the individual could employ religion for positive ends. Just as Inchbald does in *Nature and Art*, Hawthorne incorporates the ideas of sin and guilt into his book in ways that allow him to examine religious responses to them and challenge traditional religious ideologies. For Hawthorne, just as for Inchbald, individual experience often reveals the 'truth' of moral order far better than any religion.[88]

Fittingly, Hawthorne decided to set *The Marble Faun* in Italy – mostly in Rome – and doing so allowed him more easily to focus much of his attention on Catholicism. Rome is the seat of the Catholic Church, and Hawthorne implies that Italy consequently retains a reputation for sanctity unlike any other nation. The narrator acknowledges that the religious reach of the Catholic Church ranges far beyond Italy's borders in referring to Saint Peter's Basilica and to the Pope as important symbols for the entire world.[89] Within Italy, especially in rural areas, religious shrines appear everywhere, along with black crosses that symbolize Christ's suffering.[90] Moreover, Hawthorne constantly reminds his readers of the Catholicism that pervades Roman existence. During one of their many strolls, the four protagonists see scores of church domes rising above the city, and even below their feet, the ancient catacombs, where Miriam first meets the Model, bear memories of Christian martyrs who tried, in vain, to conceal themselves in the tortuous passageways.[91] Inside the Coliseum, a structure in which many Christians were martyred in ancient times, shrines line the building to commemorate the many stages of Christ's passion and suffering.[92] Additionally, the opening scene of *The Marble Faun* occurs 'in the Capitol' in Rome, and although the term refers specifically to the Capitoline Museum, it alludes to the idea of a *capitol* as the meeting place of a governing body like that of the Catholic Church.[93] Throughout the book, Hawthorne constantly reminds his readers of the pervading Catholicism in Rome and in Italy at large.

Although Hawthorne acknowledges the pervasiveness of Catholicism, he does not give credit immediately to its potential benefits. Indeed, most of *The Marble Faun* roundly condemns Catholicism as a corrupted religious tradition whose established nature is particularly inadequate for providing meaningful responses to sin and its accompanying guilt. Noting that Italy is 'priest-ridden', the narrator reveals the wide-ranging influence of the Catholic Church while simultaneously implying its ineffectiveness.[94] As early as Chapter 1, the narrator comments that the churches of Rome are 'built on the old pavements of heathen temples, and supported by the very pillars that once upheld them'.[95] While the statement implies the strength and stability of Catholic churches in replacing pagan traditions, it simultaneously suggests that the ideological foundations of the churches may, in fact, be more pagan than Christian and upholds the narrator's comment much later in the book that Rome is filled with 'perverted Christianity'.[96] The narrator likewise notes that Rome's churches are 'lined with the gorgeous marbles that were originally polished for the adornment of pagan temples'.[97] Even the aforementioned catacombs are not as sanctified as one might expect. Although they were the haven of persecuted Christians, they once hid an unbeliever who betrayed the Christians.[98] Additionally, Kenyon once mentions 'Papal despotism', as if Catholic doctrines are too strict and too arbitrary, and Miriam claims that Roman justice, which one might expect to be both egalitarian and tempered by mercy, 'above all things, is a by-word'.[99] She later says that 'there is no such thing as earthly justice, and especially none here, under the Head of Christendom!'.[100] When Donatello returns to his family estate from Rome, the peasants lament that, contrary to what they might expect from a visit to the holy capital, Donatello has been 'sadly changed' by the trip.[101] Much later, when Hilda remembers her 'sad wanderings from gallery to gallery, and from church to church' as she sought relief from the guilt that tortured her, the narrator wonders how she could possibly find peace when 'from the Pope downward, all Christendom was corrupt'.[102] If all Christendom is corrupt, then Catholicism certainly emerges from this tale as a corrupt institution.

As Hawthorne's story develops, Hilda becomes a symbol of Catholic corruption because, while she serves as the caretaker of the Virgin's shrine in her tower, she also assumes pagan qualities. As long as the lamp in the shrine burns, the tower and the land upon which it is built will remain in the possession of the family that has passed the estate from one generation to the next, but if the lamp ever is extinguished, the land and the building will become the Catholic Church's property.[103] Local legends suggest that the tower itself will fall to the ground if the lamp is extinguished. Consequently, to prevent the calamities from befalling the tower's owners, a young woman is chosen to keep the lamp burning, and oddly enough, Hilda holds that position. Hilda is not Catholic, and she does not revere the Virgin, as the person charged with the shrine's maintenance should, so her presence in tending the Virgin's lamp is heretical. Additionally, the reasons for the shrine's very existence are far from pious since its purpose is not truly to revere the Virgin but to keep family lands from reverting to the Church. Hilda's major focus in Rome is her work as a copyist, and the narrator notes that 'the spirits of the Old Masters were hovering over Hilda' and that in copying the paintings of these men, 'she wrought religiously, and therefore wrought a miracle'.[104] Hilda's work as a painter occupies a religious position in her life, and if her copies are the miracles that the narrator suggests, then Hilda must assume deistic – or pagan – qualities. Although Hilda acknowledges that the shrine has 'a religious significance', that significance is neither Catholic nor, despite Hilda's background, Protestant.[105] The significance is, perhaps, of a pagan religious nature, with Hilda, 'The Dove' who wears white gowns, as its sacrificial virgin figure.[106] By placing Hilda in a religious role, Hawthorne questions the moral order of a corrupt Catholicism.

While Hilda's role at the Virgin's shrine implies corruption in the Catholic Church, so does Kenyon's view of the religious establishment based on Donatello's ancestral home in the Apennines. At one point, Kenyon suggests converting Donatello's banquet hall into a chapel because of the allegorical frescoes that line the walls.[107] Suggesting a new chapel to replace, or at least to supplement, the old one implies that the existing chapel is not adequate on a spiritual level, especially since the frescoes that inspire Kenyon's suggestion are pagan.[108] Later in Donatello's private tower, Kenyon finds that, in a cell where a famous monk was once confined, Donatello has established an oratory, a makeshift chapel complete with a crucifix and holy water.[109] Although Donatello has created his chapel with elements of his family's Catholic faith, he has replaced the official family chapel. Moreover, other aspects of the oratory suggest corruption. The room was once used as a prison for the unnamed famous monk, who was burned at the stake five centuries earlier in a punishment that suggests either martyrdom or, more likely since his ghost reportedly haunts the tower, heresy. Furthermore, an alabaster carving of a human skull lies below the crucifix as a grim reminder of death and of the inherited guilt in Donatello's family. Kenyon's proposal of a new chapel at Donatello's estate, coupled with an already existing alternate chapel in the tower, implies that the official family chapel is inadequate. In fact, at the beginning of Chapter 31, the narrator comments that like the chapels in many similar country homes, the official family chapel of Monte Beni is unused and has fallen into a state of disrepair.[110] Kenyon unexpectedly discovers the old family chapel one rainy day while exploring the large mansion and finds it dark, dusty and filled with spider webs.[111] The marble vase at the entrance holds 'hardened mud' rather than holy water, and a spider has woven a web across its brim in a symbolic gesture of the chapel's decay.[112]

Along with Hilda's involvement with the Virgin's shrine and the corruption suggested in Donatello's family mansion, the identity of Miriam's Model emerges as another significant contributor to Hawthorne's challenge to Catholicism in *The Marble Faun*. After the Model's death, the four major characters in the story discover his body to be the object of a funeral service in a Capuchin church. He wears the trappings of a Capuchin monk, and if he is, indeed, the monk he seems to be, then the religious corruption suggested in Hilda's shrine and Donatello's mansion pales in comparison since the Model embodies the guilt and violence that haunt Miriam and Donatello. Other evidence in the book suggests that, regardless of whether the Model really is a monk, he represents Catholic devotion at its most basic level – and its most corrupt. On one occasion, Hilda is surprised to see the Model moving in prayer from shrine to shrine at the Coliseum, and one of the group of protagonists comments without knowing his identity that he must be devout.[113] Hawthorne reaffirms the Model's symbolism as a challenge to the church and clergy when the group of young people observes the figure of a demon in a painting one day. Donatello instantly recognizes the demon as the Model.[114] From Miriam's point of view, the Model is an 'evil spirit', and the narrator comments that 'there had been nothing, in his lifetime, viler than this man'.[115] In fact, when the Model appears at the Trevi Fountain and taunts Miriam on one occasion, she flings water at him as an 'old form of exorcism' as she conjures him to vanish.[116] She refers to him – directly to his face – as a 'Demon'.[117] Earlier in the book, when the other characters confront Miriam about meeting the Model in the catacombs, Miriam replies that she knew that he was an 'old infidel' and that she had begun a conversation with him in hopes of 'converting him to the Christian faith'.[118] Miriam's story is but subterfuge so that she can avoid answering too many questions about her background, but the very suggestion that the Model might need conversion implies that he lives in a depraved state despite his appearance later in a monk's garb. His presence in the catacombs also links him with the pagan spy who betrayed the Christians who lived and worshipped in the underground passages in ancient Rome.

The Model's negative image certainly casts the Catholic Church in a villain-ous role in *The Marble Faun*, and those dark associations transfer to the church building in which his funeral is held and in which he is buried so that the building itself also represents the corrupted Catholic Church. The narrator describes the building's dirty floor as giving the place 'as little the aspect of sanctity as a ken-nel'.[119] Further, Hawthorne's description of the cemetery over which the church is built suggests a dearth of spiritual power. According to the sacristan, the soil in which the monks are buried has been imported from Jerusalem so that the bones can rest in consecrated ground. However, the cemetery, covering only the same small area as that of the church above, is quite small, so it has literally overflowed as the monks have all tried to accommodate one another with burial plots in the sacred earth during the past centuries. Their solution to the overcrowding prob-lem, when one of their number dies, is to disinter the longest-buried skeleton and bury the new body in its place. Symbolically, the disinterment may represent res-urrection, but the fate of the disinterred bones – to become horrifyingly Gothic decorations for the building – may also imply a sublunary fate that has nothing to do with a spiritual afterlife.[120] The narrator sees only death and decay and sug-gests that even the soil's lack of plant life implies that those buried therein may not have continued into an afterlife.[121] If the cemetery is so dead, and if the souls of the bodies buried therein have not risen to heaven, then the Model's burial place and the church above it emerge as representations of Catholic corruption. The only faint praise that Hawthorne can provide for the cemetery is the nar-rator's comment that it has no foul odour.[122] If, as the narrator suggests, Paradise has no place in the foundation, then it seems unlikely that Paradise has any place in the church either, particularly since Miriam's Model, clearly a vile and detest-able creature, is to be buried in the sanctified earth. Symbolically, the Capuchin church represents the Catholic Church in general to imply an internal decay and a lack of spirituality at its foundations.

Miriam's and Donatello's Responses to Sin and Guilt

While Hawthorne expends much effort in *The Marble Faun* to depict the corrupt nature of the Catholic Church, he also gives careful attention to the consequences of that corruption. Just as Inchbald delineates the consequences of Anglican hypocrisy in Hannah Primrose's fate, Hawthorne similarly positions Miriam and Donatello as victims of Catholic corruption.[123] Focusing closely on sin and its associated guilt in the lives of his characters, Hawthorne suggests that the religious response to their sin and guilt is inadequate. He suggests that his characters in *The Marble Faun*, like Inchbald's Hannah Primrose and his own Hester Prynne, are simultaneously guilty and innocent and that the delineation between guilt and innocence is not so clear as religious doctrine might suggest.[124]

In Miriam's experience, social religious practice has not corresponded with stated religious belief, and the result, for her, has been the inheritance of an oppressive generational guilt.[125] The Model's identity as a monk should be evidence enough of the disjunction in *The Marble Faun* between belief and practice since he tortures Miriam with what one might term emotional terrorism. However, Hawthorne chooses to sharpen the disjunction by linking the Model with Miriam's past and with guilt for a sin so shocking that he never names it in the book. Hawthorne cloaks Miriam's identity and past experiences with a conspicuous obscurity that heightens the intensity of her guilt to suggest that corrupt Catholicism has offered her no solace. Her obscure background becomes more critical as the book progresses since she, in conjunction with the Model, acts as catalyst for the guilt that Donatello and Hilda experience. Throughout the text, the narrator refuses to reveal Miriam's family name in any definitive way or any concrete information about her early life.[126] Even on the last page of the book, in a postscript to the primary action of the plot, the narrator intrudes to ask Kenyon to reveal the truth about Miriam's shadowy past.[127] Kenyon drops a few dark hints that Miriam's past is shrouded in guilt and pain, but beyond that, he flatly refuses to talk.[128]

A few pages earlier, during Kenyon's hunt for Hilda in which he meets Miriam and Donatello in a countryside excavation of Roman ruins, Miriam reveals the most information that she ever provides about herself, but Hawthorne conceals most of it from his readers. When Kenyon asks Miriam about her life, she responds by vaguely describing herself as part English, part Jewish and part Italian royalty.[129] She then reveals the name of her Italian family, but only to Kenyon and not to Hawthorne's curious readers. Rather than reporting the name, the narrator describes Kenyon's shocked reaction to hearing it and then vaguely reports that the name was associated with some horrible and notorious crime in recent history.[130] Miriam explains that her refusal to marry prompted the crime and that she was suspected of being involved in some way that she never reveals.[131] No religion provided her with appropriate means of managing her guilt and its consequences, so she fled her home and left behind clues that suggested she had killed herself. When she meets her Model in the catacombs of Rome early in *The Marble Faun*, what she really meets is her own dark past that simply will not allow her any respite.[132] Despite tantalizing readers with clues about Miriam's past, Hawthorne resolutely keeps her identity – and her alleged crime – hidden to intensify his readers' perceptions of her guilt and to establish that Catholicism has not offered Miriam any appropriate means of managing her guilt.[133]

While Hawthorne hides the facts about Miriam's past, he also offers obvious hints about it to suggest that Miriam may be related to the ill-fated Cenci family. Hawthorne's hints serve the dual purpose of questioning the rightness of condemning Miriam while further obscuring the truth about her background. One of the first hints is Hawthorne's reference to a painting of Beatrice Cenci that Hilda, Kenyon and Miriam all admire and that Hilda, as a copyist, is painting. According to the old Italian story, Beatrice's father murdered her brothers and physically abused her, including raping her, before she began to plot his death, the crime for which she herself was later executed.[134] Hawthorne's characters sympathize with her because her crime was the result of negative and uncontrollable circumstances in her life, and they consider her essentially innocent.[135] Likewise, when Miriam worries that the revelation of the facts of her life will alienate Kenyon, he claims that she is innocent in the crime associated with her family.[136] If Miriam is guiltless in the same way as Beatrice Cenci, then her guilt also parallels that of Inchbald's Miss Milner and Hannah Primrose and Hawthorne's Hester Prynne, all of whom find themselves trapped in situations from which they can extricate themselves only by committing further sin. From a Catholic point of view, Miriam, like the other characters, is guilty, but by associating Miriam with Beatrice, Hawthorne acknowledges the involuntary nature of her decision to commit her crime – if, in fact, she committed a crime at all. Hawthorne suggests that while Miriam technically may be guilty of a crime, she may be guiltless like Beatrice. Miriam ignores the Catholic moral order to recognize her own individual moral order based on her own experiences just as Beatrice did.

Hawthorne makes several other connections with the Cenci story in *The Marble Faun*. One of the most significant occurs when Miriam asks Hilda, in a request that suggests more than mere coincidence, to deliver important papers for her to the Palazzo Cenci. Even Miriam's paintings hint at a connection with the Cenci family, for they repeatedly depict 'the idea of woman, acting the part of a revengeful mischief towards man' in much the same way that Beatrice did.[137] When Miriam paints, she always includes a minor figure in each canvas, either peeking from the shrubbery or inconspicuously looking through a frosted window or a similar out-of-the-way place at the main subject of the piece of art.[138] The minor figure resembles Miriam, and it always has an expression of 'deep sadness', much like the expression in the famous painting of Beatrice Cenci that the artists admire.[139] Later, in relating parts of a conversation that Miriam has with her Model, the narrator says that an 'odour of guilt, and a scent of blood' surround the two.[140] The dark Italian roots of Miriam's family, combined with obvious hints about Beatrice Cenci, imply that Miriam's name also is Cenci and that the ill fortune of the original family has followed subsequent generations.[141] Indeed, after confronting Miriam about the Model's murder, Hilda claims – naïvely – that she finally understands how sin and guilt can have trans-generational consequences.[142] Moreover, much later in the story, during Donatello's trip through the Italian countryside with Kenyon, the sculptor comments on the age of many of the Italian villages to note that the past has a significant influence upon the present in the European setting in a way that it does not in America;

Kenyon wonders whether he would be able to survive under the influence of the longstanding guilt that has accumulated in European culture.[143]

Interestingly enough, Donatello's family, like Miriam's, also participates in a longstanding tradition of inherited guilt, so the association of the two families through the Model's murder does not result, as it at first appears, in the fall of a completely innocent Italian man. Rather, just as it does with Miriam's family, the murder reaffirms the previously established tradition of guilt in Donatello's family and confirms their postlapsarian state. On an individual level, Donatello certainly is innocent initially, but as he explains in Chapter 27, his family is not. In a conversation with Kenyon, Donatello relates the story of an ancestor who tainted the family name with murder. According to legend, the ancestor befriended and fell in love with the water nymph who lived in a fountain on the family estate.[144] One day, however, when the ancestor came to wash his face in the fountain, the water shrank away from him because he was trying to wash away a bloodstain. Donatello notes that his ancestor saw the nymph only once thereafter, and at that time, she had a similar bloodstain on her face that represented the guilt that he tried to wash from his face.[145] Consequently, the statue of the nymph that now stands above the fountain is weeping. The unchanging grief on the statue's face parallels the family's inheritance of guilt, which revisits each generation like the stain on the nymph's face. After the Model's murder, Donatello, who has always been able to call the woodland creatures to him by the fountain, no longer can do so. Just as his ancestor lost the ability to commune with the nymph, Donatello loses his ability to call the animals. Guilt has now become an integral part of Donatello's individual existence, just as it did his ancestor's. He has reclaimed his inherited guilt, just as Miriam has reaffirmed hers, and the two characters – Miriam and Donatello – have now merged their families' traditions of inherited guilt through the Model's murder, which now functions as a binding force between the two individuals and between their families.

The fact that inherited guilt exists for Miriam and Donatello attests to the ineffectiveness of religion, and especially Catholicism, in diffusing guilt and offering absolution. If Catholicism truly helped, the family guilt would not intrude into Miriam's and Donatello's lives. However, as the story progresses, Miriam and Donatello reaffirm their inherited guilt by murdering the Model, and they then become inextricably linked, as do their families, through the new crime. The passion of the crime reveals more 'truth' of human experience than Catholic doctrine ever could. When Donatello learns that the Model stalks Miriam through the Roman streets, he decides, rather chivalrously, to assist her. Miriam initially discourages his intervention, and he complies with her every request. In fact, he takes great care to control his anger during an encounter with the Model at an outdoor dance.[146] However, as time passes, his difficulty in controlling that anger increases, for even at the dance, he exclaims his hatred and offers to strangle the Model, although Miriam prohibits any violence. The scene passes briefly, but it reveals Hawthorne's interest in the expression of 'truth' through passion and begins the series of events that culminates in Donatello's ultimate expression of passion in murder. As the story progresses, Miriam continues to have confrontations with the Model, and each time, the encounter disturbs both her and, if he is witness to the event, Donatello. The instance in which Miriam flings water at the Model and commands him to vanish like a demon provides a good example.[147] Again, in pure rage, Donatello offers his protection, this time by asking Miriam for permission to drown the man.[148] Donatello's passion is so strong that it overcomes his natural passivity in response to the threat he sees in the Model. As usual, Miriam soothes Donatello's anger and prevents him from committing any violence by assuring him that all will be well. However, when the Model reappears at the precipice that Kenyon thinks must have been Traitor's Leap, the situation quickly changes as Donatello grasps the man and holds him threateningly over the edge. As always, Donatello seeks Miriam's approval before committing to any action, and when she gives him a certain look, he releases the man, who plummets to his death. As Donatello explains afterward, he saw consent to murder in Miriam's eyes.[149] Donatello's passion, spurred by Miriam's encouragement, overcomes his usually peaceful nature and reveals the 'truth' of the characters' experiences as victims of the Model's aggressive pursuit.

Because Miriam and Donatello collude in murdering the Model, their guilt merges, but they are unable to find relief through religion. The relationship that develops between Miriam and Donatello, the relationship that replaces Miriam's association with her Model, is another guilt-based connection. It functions as yet another link in the continuing series of sins that binds Miriam's legendary family together across many generations and that now links them with Donatello's family. In an attempt to escape the guilt that haunts them so intensely, Miriam and Donatello separate. Donatello goes back to his ancestral home in the Apennines, but despite the physical distance between the two, they still feel the connection of their shared guilt, enough so that Miriam follows Donatello and secretly lives in a long-disused part of his house. When Kenyon discovers her, she admits that she shares Donatello's guilt and that the connection has an intimacy that she cannot break.[150] The nature of that relationship is further reinforced after Donatello and Kenyon begin their trek through the Italian countryside and witness both the quotidian activities of the Italian peasants and the physical landscape that, in many ways, symbolically reflects the relationships of the characters in the book. At one point, the narrator notices a grape vine wrapped around a tree and suggests that the vine's insidious growth parallels the relationships many Italians have with wine.[151] The symbol extends beyond Kenyon's limited perception and encompasses his companions since the fates of Donatello and Miriam, like the vine and the tree, are now intertwined and completely inseparable. When Donatello meets Miriam, by her contrivance, under the statue of Pope Julius III in Perugia, he challenges her suggestion that they separate forever and suggests that their fates are intertwined.[152] Instinctively realizing that their fates are, indeed, connected, Miriam cannot contradict Donatello's suggestion, but the intensity of their shared guilt prevents her from agreeing with him since that agreement would further legitimize and perpetuate the guilt. Consequently, she and Donatello ask Kenyon, as a more objective observer of their situation, for his thoughts. His response is to tell Donatello and Miriam that he thinks they are so intimately connected that only God could separate them.[153] While both Donatello and Miriam agree with Kenyon's assessment, and although Kenyon is not aware of the full extent of their shared guilt as murderers, he does instinctively recognize that their bond is tainted with some sort of guilt and that their relationship will be one of mutual support and sacrifice rather than of contentment.[154] Miriam and Donatello constitute an inseparable dyad whose two parties share the guilt for the sin of murder, a guilt that, in some sense, is a continuation and reaffirmation of the hereditary guilt of Miriam's and Donatello's own families.

Hilda's Response to Sin and Guilt

The guilt that Miriam and Donatello share does not limit its effects to them, for it has serious ramifications for the innocent Hilda. Through Hilda's experience, Hawthorne symbolically faults his native Puritanism to apprise his readers that Catholicism is not the only creed he challenges in *The Marble Faun*. Rather, Hawthorne questions all organized religion to suggest that the individual moral order provides more relevant 'truth'. Developing concurrently with the fusing of inherited guilt in Miriam's and Donatello's families, the guilt that Hilda feels through her association with Miriam further complicates *The Marble Faun* by introducing the idea of vicariously experienced sin and its resulting guilt. Like Donatello, Hilda participates, on one level, in a longstanding tradition of guilt while remaining essentially innocent individually until the Model's murder. In fact, even after the murder, she remains innocent as an individual because the guilt that she feels is for the sin of Miriam and Donatello and not for her own failings.

Hilda's tradition of guilt comes from her Puritan ancestry in New England. She calls herself a Puritan descendant to acknowledge the Calvinistic background of her ancestry.[155] Even the narrator recognizes her connection with Puritanism, a background whose primary doctrines included the idea that humanity was naturally depraved because of inherited Adamic guilt.[156] According to the doctrine, a person's very existence, his or her birth into the physical world, automatically implicated that person into the shared tradition of sin and guilt as it began in the biblical Garden of Eden. Hilda, who is sensitive enough to guilt to assume it on behalf of her friends, seems to believe in that doctrine of natural depravity.

As an individual, Hilda is innocent.[157] The other artists in Rome refer to her as 'Hilda The Dove' and call her apartment 'The Dove-cote', in part because she usually wears a white robe that reminds them of the doves that gather around her tower.[158] The whiteness, along with Hilda's association with doves, who traditionally represent peace, suggest innocence on Hilda's part, a suggestion that Miriam echoes near the end of the book when she acknowledges Hilda's innocence regarding the Model's murder.[159] But while Hilda remains innocent on an individual level, she vicariously assumes the guilt for a sin she does not commit, just as all of Adam's descendants – all of humanity – assume guilt for the original sin in the Garden of Eden.

Unfortunately, as Hawthorne emphasizes pointedly, Hilda's Puritan background does not provide her with a viable means of managing her guilt. The aftermath of the murder, for example, finds Hilda crying into her pillow in a revolted reaction against the now fully confirmed existence of sin, and, noticing her copy of the portrait of Beatrice Cenci, she wonders whether she now shares a common bond of guilt with Beatrice.[160] The implication is that she does, from her own Puritan point of view, a fact that the narrator later confirms.[161] Hilda's Protestantism offers no absolution. Indeed, in the Puritan terms of the natural depravity of humanity, Hilda does participate in the guilt as a member of the human race because the Puritan tradition of inherited guilt assures her place as one of the sinful in the same way that Beatrice participates unavoidably in the inherited guilt of her family. Even so, on an individual level, Hilda remains innocent. Observing the portrait of Beatrice Cenci, the narrator wonders how anyone could condemn Beatrice, and he then comments that Hilda's face bears the same expression as that of the figure in the portrait.[162] The narrator challenges the Puritan tradition by suggesting that despite any inherited natural depravity, Hilda remains untainted by sin as an individual.

Hawthorne links Hilda with Catholicism several times in the book as a means of suggesting its efficacy in contrast to her Puritanism. As early as Chapter 6, Miriam praises Hilda and her hermitage at the top of her tower to suggest that her living literally above everyone else symbolically suggests that she inhabits a higher moral plane and to claim that she would not be surprised if Hilda were canonized.[163] Miriam even suggests that Hilda's tending the shrine practically makes her Catholic already, but Hilda seems displeased with the statement.[164] Later, however, when Miriam asks if Hilda has ever prayed to the Virgin while tending the shrine, Hilda is forced to acknowledge that she has, and after the Model's murder, Miriam suggests that the Virgin certainly must protect Hilda because of her tending the lamp at the shrine.[165] Hilda kneels before the shrine at the end of Chapter 36, but she receives no solace, and her efforts to find absolution for her vicarious sin are similarly thwarted as she wanders through Rome stopping at every church.[166]

Hawthorne most effectively makes the point that Hilda's Protestantism is inadequate when he depicts her receiving absolution in St Peter's Basilica. Simultaneously, he implies that Catholicism can offer appropriate absolution from guilt, but only on the individual's terms. Despite choosing to confess to a Catholic priest, Hilda remains nominally Puritan, although she chooses her own individual moral order over that imposed by either Puritanism or Catholicism. Her entry into St Peter's Basilica signals a change in her approach to Catholicism, for she finds herself in awe at the magnificence displayed before her. As the narrator exclaims in relating the episode, 'If Religion had a material home, was it not here!'.[167] When Hilda enters the building, she dips her fingers in the holy water and stops short of tracing the sign of the cross on her breast, but as she observes a painting that allegorically depicts Virtue at odds with Evil, the narrator notes, 'The moral of the picture [...] appealed as much to Puritans as Catholics'.[168] Hawthorne thus equates Puritanism and Catholicism as if to suggest that either one – or neither one – is appropriate for Hilda. Hilda finally kneels in earnest before a Catholic shrine and offers a short prayer before nervously moving away from the altar. At that one moment, she experiences a spark of happiness and relief.[169] The relief is fleeting, but she receives a premonition that true relief will come to her before she finishes her visit to the cathedral. She marvels at the inclusiveness of Catholicism as she proceeds through the cathedral, and she notices that, with confessionals assigned to so many different languages, people of any nationality can feel welcome.[170] Even the narrator is impressed at Catholicism's adaptability and at the ceremonies that surround its proceedings.[171] When Hilda sees the relief on the face of a woman who has just confessed her sins in one of these confessionals, she finally decides to do the same. When she anonymously reveals all that she knows about the Model's murder without disclosing any names, an immediate sense of relief fills her, and she returns to her innocent state of existence.[172]

In giving Hilda relief through a Catholic confession, Hawthorne upholds the idea that Catholicism can, in some ways, provide positive responses to sin and guilt. The Protestant approach, on the other hand, and particularly the Puritan approach with which Hilda is familiar, would have been to repress the sin and guilt, to allow the pain to build inside the mind, where it would grow and burn until it drove the person into indifference.[173] Hilda, however, essentially has merged her own Puritan faith with a useful aspect of Catholicism and effectively has created her own individual faith as an amalgam of the two. Immediately after the confession, the priest accosts Hilda outside the confessional, chastises her for taking advantage of the privileges reserved for people of the Catholic faith, and tries to convert her. She resists, however, with the Protestant claim that only God can forgive her, and she unabashedly agrees with the priest's assessment of her as a heretic.[174] Despite the priest's negative approach to Hilda, he blesses her, and she kneels to accept the blessing as she would if she were Catholic.[175] Kenyon witnesses the blessing, and he is concerned that Hilda may be entertaining Catholic propensities, a concern that grows deeper when, while searching for the missing girl later in the book, he hears the Roman matron who supervises the tower comment that Hilda has earned the right to be Catholic through her tending the shrine and when he later meets the priest, who feels confident that Hilda eventually will convert to Catholicism.[176]

Ultimately Hawthorne suggests, through Hilda's experience, that the individual's moral order is superior to any established creed.[177] The individual is more adaptable and can choose to honour the parts of a religious doctrine that appear appropriate at the time rather than complying mechanically with every precept. Hilda succeeds in balancing her needs with the dictates of both Puritanism and Catholicism. She represents Hawthorne's ideal since she does not slavishly follow either religion. Despite Kenyon's worries, Hilda never intends to convert to Catholicism even though she does acknowledge its advantages and speculates that no real reason prevents her conversion to a religion that seems to offer solace to its adherents.[178] Part of Hawthorne's point in having Hilda say these words is that no minister can be above error or pure from all iniquity, so Catholicism can never be a perfect religion – and neither can Puritanism.[179] His object is to highlight the adaptability of Catholicism and to suggest that parts of it, if not all of it, may be useful for the individual. More important than any established religion is a person's faith, and Hilda's statement that she does have faith provides the key to understanding how Hawthorne views religious issues. Hilda herself says she will never again confess to a Catholic priest, and her reasoning is simple – she believes she will never again experience the kind of guilt she felt about witnessing the Model's murder.[180] Her statement suggests that if she does experience a similar trial, she probably will return to the confessional, and Hawthorne would approve of her remedy. His position on the matter would be that a person's faith – one's individual moral order – transcends any established religion but that one should not eschew all aspects of religion to label them categorically as detrimental to one's faith. Rather, one should incorporate into one's faith whichever elements of one or more religions are appropriate for the individual.

At the beginning of the book, Kenyon, in critiquing the sculpture of the Dying Gladiator, comments that 'in any sculptural subject, there should be a moral standstill, since there must of necessity be a physical one'.[181] In a sense, Hawthorne views established religion as a sculptural subject, whose doctrines have been moulded, or sculpted, into an established set of unchanging ideas. The static nature of established religion is what he finds unacceptable since religion creates a moral order that also is unchanging or unadaptive. During Donatello and Kenyon's trip through the Italian countryside, when the narrator describes the peasants as being merely 'parenthetically devout', he implies that their religion has become a mere formality with little meaning, and later, the narrator further reinforces that idea of stagnation by stating that 'their worship, now-a-days, is best symbolized by the artificial flower'.[182] Unlike a living flower that grows and changes, the peasants' Catholicism is unchanging and only superficially beautiful. After the Model's murder, Miriam visits Hilda, whose instinct, formed by a similarly longstanding Puritan belief, is to avoid her erstwhile friend, but Miriam exhorts Hilda, 'Then be more my friend than ever, for I need you more!'.[183] Her point, and Hawthorne's, is that, on some moral level, the idea of banishing a needy friend from one's presence for religious reasons is wrong since that friend needs more support than ever. Likewise, the narrator says later, observing Kenyon smoke his pipe at a roadside shrine, that any act is good if done religiously.[184] Acts of worship should not be confined to prayer or to traditional religious rites but can encompass a wide array of activities that, in themselves, may not be religious, but that may be done in a religious manner. A good example of a religiously completed activity would be the sylvan dance in Chapter 10, during which the narrator notes that, in contrast to Puritan traditions that outlawed dancing, Catholics encourage celebration, including dancing, during their festivals.[185] A person's state of mind and a person's faith ultimately are more important in determining the religious nature of an activity rather than its acceptance as a part of established religion. Indeed, in a statement that reaffirms Hawthorne's own belief in a faith that transcends religions, Kenyon says to Hilda in St Peter's that he is sure some church – though he does not know which one – will bestow sainthood upon her.[186]

At the end of the book, when Kenyon pronounces the moral of Donatello's story, that people like him have no place in the modern world, Hilda vehemently objects, to exclaim, 'I will not accept your moral!'.[187] Kenyon's response, 'Then, here is another; take your choice!', emphasizes the relativism of *The Marble Faun* to imply that, just as religious doctrine should be interpreted by the individual, so too should be the moral of the tale. Hilda's response to Kenyon's second suggested moral is noncommittal, although she responds to Kenyon's discussion of the nature of sin by supporting the idea that one should uphold 'whatever precepts of Heaven are written deepest within us'.[188] Hilda's statement upholds Hawthorne's own approach to moral order to suggest that the individual's construction of morality is superior to any imposed order. Of the three characters in *The Marble Faun* who endure moral dilemmas, Hilda, Miriam and Donatello, only Hilda emerges from the tale with any kind of moral purity.[189] Miriam is still tainted by the hereditary guilt of her family, and so is Donatello, who has merged his guilt with Miriam's. Unlike these two, Hilda has managed, by temporarily merging her own New England Puritanism with Italian Catholicism, to achieve absolution. As a New Englander, she still participates in the hereditary guilt of her Puritan forefathers, but she has been absolved of any responsibility in her vicarious participation in the Model's murder.[190] Hence, the religion of the individual is of little importance as opposed to the faith – the individual moral order – that the individual maintains.

Alternative Moral Order in the Romantic Moral Romance

As they draw on the conventions of religious belief and socially driven religious practice, Elizabeth Inchbald and Nathaniel Hawthorne further develop the Romantic moral romance in their experimental tales, *Nature and Art* and *The Marble Faun*. They question the established conventions of moral order, particularly in relation to the traditions of Anglicanism, Puritanism and Catholicism. Suggesting that the response of the religious moral order to sin and guilt sometimes is inadequate to the experience of the individual, Inchbald and Hawthorne propose an alternative moral order that is individual, adaptable and situated liminally in relation to established creeds. Inchbald, whose background was Catholic, questioned the Anglican tradition in England by pointing out its hypocrisies and suggesting that its influence, in many cases, was damaging rather than being supportive. Writing decades later with a Puritan heritage as his base, Hawthorne questioned not only his own Puritanism, but, more importantly, the Catholicism that he had seen first-hand in Italy. At the individual and social levels, the three creeds – Anglicanism, Puritanism and Catholicism – responded to sin and guilt with a harshness that, while often hypocritical and corrupt in practice, denied the guilty any real chance at redemption in the physical world and blatantly ignored the reality of individual experience. Thus, *Nature and Art* and *The Marble Faun* provide further means of defining the experimental Romantic moral romance sub-genre in their challenges to traditional assumptions about established moral order and in their emphasis on the individual as definer of moral order. Simultaneously, these books themselves challenge the recognized order of the British novel tradition to help Inchbald establish women as serious writers and to help Hawthorne establish Americans as serious writers.

5. FIGURES 'POURTRAYED APART' WITH 'REAL OR WELL-COUNTERFEITED SIMPLICITY': COMPLICATING THE ROMANTIC MORAL ROMANCE WITH SYMBOLIC AND FRAGMENTARY FIGURES[1]

It is the perfection of art to conceal art.

– William Hazlitt[2]

As emphasized in the previous chapters, Elizabeth Inchbald and Nathaniel Hawthorne remained acutely aware of their roles as artists, and they self-consciously constructed their Romantic moral romances to reflect their respective artistic goals – legitimizing women writers for Inchbald and establishing an indigenous American literature for Hawthorne. While Inchbald and Hawthorne borrowed themes and structures from Shakespeare's romance plays and challenged religious conceptions of moral order, they also subverted established practices of character development in the alternative sub-genre. Conventional characters in the British novel revealed their personalities through extended elaboration of their fears and desires, and novelists who wrote in the sentimental British tradition aspired to a degree of realism that would elicit reader identification with the well-developed characters and prompt a sympathetic emotional response. In contrast, Inchbald and Hawthorne preserved their readers' emotional distance by resolutely refusing to develop their characters as realistic human beings and by endowing them with quasi-allegorical symbolism as fragmentary figures. Consequently, readers remain ever aware of the fictional nature of the romances, especially since the figures' simplicity calls attention to itself throughout the tales. Through the symbolism of their fragmentary figures, Inchbald and Hawthorne use the Romantic moral romance to explore the fragmented Romantic psyche and to posit alternative 'truths' for themselves in opposition to the British novel tradition.

This chapter first examines the idea of fragmentation in Romantic literature in general and relates the idea to the Romantics' perceived opposition between nature and art. The chapter then examines all four of the books discussed earlier

– *A Simple Story, Nature and Art, The Scarlet Letter* and *The Marble Faun* – to explore Inchbald's and Hawthorne's use of fragmentary figures in the Romantic moral romance. The major figures in each of these romances exhibit forms of studied simplicity, to borrow a term from Anne Mellor, that endow them with symbolic meaning.[3] Indeed, the figures exhibit qualities of characters in mediaeval chivalric romances or moral tales rather than those one might expect in novels.[4] Rather than being fully realized human characters, each represents a fragment of a psyche, and separate fragmentary figures in each book often mirror one another in paired relationships. Instead of emphasizing the development of several minds or psyches, Inchbald and Hawthorne each focus on a single psyche and the way its fragments, *in combination*, negotiate their relationships with one another. The contrived qualities of the fragmentary figures call attention to the books as art forms, but paradoxically, the stories themselves repeatedly privilege the freedom, spontaneity and simplicity of nature. Although Inchbald and Hawthorne did not wish to mimic the traditional novel form, they needed to avoid the imputation of being simplistic and naïve – and, therefore, sub-literary – because they wished to establish legitimate art on their own terms. Consequently, they drew upon the Romantic dichotomy between nature and art to complicate their fictions while ostensibly simplifying them.

Mentioning several Continental sources that engage their readers with the idea of a split psyche, Ernst Grabovszki notes in 2008 that many Romantic authors were fascinated by the idea of using the split psyche 'as a means to discuss human identity from a psychological point of view'.[5] Inchbald would not have hesitated to borrow from this current of Romantic thought, but Hawthorne might have paused before doing so. His desire for an indigenous American literature might have precluded the borrowing of Anglo-European forms. Indeed, Donald Pease argues in 2005 that *The Scarlet Letter* seeks an independent, democratic ideal that does not compromise with the traditional Anglo-European order.[6] However, earlier critics have argued that in Hawthorne's later, more mature years, he was forced to acknowledge that a complete break with Anglo-European traditions simply was not possible. Christof Wegelin makes such an argument, dating back to 1947, and especially suggests that *The Marble Faun* is Hawthorne's most conciliatory book toward Anglo-European traditions.[7] Indeed, Clare Goldfarb suggests that Hilda and Kenyon are American artists who are too dependent on European models, but she also notes that Hawthorne symbolically acknowledges that America needs Europe as its artistic base.[8] She hints that *The Marble Faun* is Hawthorne's response to 'Emerson's challenge to the American citizen to rely on himself and to the American artist to forge a purely American art'.[9] Moreover, David Kesterson believes that *The Marble Faun* 'epitomizes' a change in the attitude of Americans who began to see Europe as no longer invasive in American culture.[10] Donald Ringe believes that Hawthorne's American characters 'fail to see so deeply as their European counterparts into the mystery of good and evil', while Diane Hoeveler notes that America simply cannot be totally free of the evils and history of Europe.[11] In fact, this chapter's closer look at the fragmentary figures in Hawthorne's books suggests that, not only was Hawthorne conciliatory toward Anglo-European tradition in *The Marble Faun*, but he also was more accepting of the idea of a shared tradition in *The Scarlet Letter*.

Hawthorne's general use of fragmentary figures is well documented. Randall Stewart posits a complicated series of character types that he believes Hawthorne developed in all of his fiction. Stewart argues that 'Hawthorne's leading characters, for the most part, can be divided into a comparatively few large groups and that within each group can be traced a process of development which is both repetitive and cumulative'.[12] Many other critics have noticed the same tendencies in Hawthorne's work. F. O. Matthiessen calls Hawthorne's characters 'emotionally starved and one-sided', and as if recognizing their fragmentary nature, he notes that Hawthorne's characters are isolated so that

> not only do they seem to be cut off from any full participation in society beyond their immediate circle, but, in addition, with the absence of the usual novelist's filling of other people and events, you become conscious of how Hawthorne's customary four or five principals are separated one from another by wide, unoccupied spaces.[13]

Matthiessen's reference to 'usual novelists' indicates his recognition of Hawthorne's fiction as unique. James Mellow also notices Hawthorne's character types and supports Stewart's suggestion that the same ones are used repeatedly when he writes that 'there is a sense in which Hawthorne's social types border on the stereotypical. The same characters appear and reappear in his allegories'.[14] Walter Shear echoes the same sentiment with his comment, 'Almost every critic of the fiction seems to assume, allegory or no, that Hawthorne does work with character types, often recurrent types'.[15] Moreover, Yvor Winters, who believed that Hawthorne was 'essentially an allegorist', complains that 'Hawthorne had small gift for the creation of human beings', and A. N. Kaul suggests that Hawthorne's fiction depicts types rather than fully developed characters.[16]

Inchbald's and Hawthorne's characters – despite their simple development, or perhaps because of their simple development – exhibit complex symbolic relationships in which single characters can symbolize more than one idea. Figure 4, Symbolic Correspondences in Inchbald's and Hawthorne's Fictions, helps to support the arguments in this chapter by providing a visual representation of the characters' positions within the tales and of the symbolic continua that help to define the Romantic moral romance. Each row within the three larger columns in the table represents a continuum, with the endpoints of the continuum represented by the left and right columns and the middle, or liminal, space in the continuum represented by the middle column.[17]

	Impulse to Write Unconventionally	Liminal Space	Impulse to Write Conventionally
	Novel	→ Romantic Moral Romance ←	Romance
	Complexity	→ Complex Simplicity ←	Simplicity
	Art	→ Reconciliation of ← Nature and Art	Nature
	Fragmentation	→ Unified Fragmentation ←	Unity
	Immorality (No Moral Order or Corrupted Order)	→ Amorality ← (Alternative Moral Order)	Morality (Moral Order of Catholicism/ Puritanism/Anglicanism)
	Corruption	→ Reconciliation of ← Purity/Corruption	Purity
	Artistic Falsehood	→ Alternative 'Truth' ←	Didactic Truth
	Defiance of Masculine and Anglo-European Authority	→ Reconciliation of Impulses ←	Submission to Masculine and Anglo-European Authority

		Impulse to Write Unconventionally	Liminal Space	Impulse to Write Conventionally
Inchbald's Literary Art	**A Simple Story**	Miss Milner (Fragment that Is Excessively Defiant)		Matilda (Fragment that Is Excessively Submissive)
		Dorriforth (Fragment that Favours Flawed Ecclesiastical Authority)		
		Lord Elmwood (Fragment that Favours Flawed Aristocratic Authority)	**Ideal Woman Writer** Elizabeth Inchbald	
	Nature and Art	Hannah Primrose (Fragment that Defies Moral Codes)		Rebecca Rymer (Fragment that Submits to Moral Codes)
		Elder William (Fragment that Favours Corrupted Ecclesiastical Authority)		Elder Henry (Fragment that Naïvely Relies Excessively upon Flawed Authority)
		Young William (Fragment that Favours Corrupted Judicial Authority)		Young Henry (Fragment that Naïvely Relies Excessively upon Flawed Authority)
Hawthorne's Literary Art	**The Scarlet Letter**	Roger Chillingworth (Fragment that Defies Expected Norms)	Pearl (Fragment that Unifies Conflicting Impulses in Wild, Amoral Innocence)	Arthur Dimmesdale (Fragment that Submits to Expected Norms Despite a Desire for Independence)
				Hester (Fragment that Submits to Expected Norms Despite Earlier Transgression in Favour of Independence)
			Ideal American Writer Nathaniel Hawthorne	
	The Marble Faun	Miriam (Fragment that Favours Corrupted Catholic Tradition)		Kenyon (Fragment that Submits to Puritanical Norms)
		Donatello after the Murder (Fragment that Accepts Corrupted Catholic Norms) ←		Donatello before the Murder (Fragment that Innocently Relies on Catholic Norms) ←
			Hilda (Fragment that Temporarily Unifies Conflicting Impulses through Acceptance of Corruption and Guilt) ← →	Hilda (Fragment that Innocently Relies on Puritan Norms)
				The Model (Fragment that Operates Excessively within Catholic Norms)

Figure 4, Symbolic Correspondences in Inchbald's and Hawthorne's Fictions. A diagram of several symbolic correspondences in Inchbald's and Hawthorne's major works, showing how the primary characters may represent conflicting fragments of the ideal author's mind. Each row represents a continuum between conventionality and unconventionality. For Inchbald and Hawthorne, the ideal writer should be situated in the central liminal space that reconciles the ends of the continua. *Diagram by Ben P. Robertson.*

The top portion of the table lists major concepts with which Inchbald and Hawthorne engage in their romances. All these concepts may be classified as one of three tendencies, as listed across the top of the table, in an author's artistic work – to write unconventionally, to write conventionally or to write in the liminal space on the continuum between convention and its rejection. For example, novel and romance occupy the endpoints of a continuum whose liminal space is occupied by the Romantic moral romance. The novel is associated with complexity and the romance with simplicity, while a sort of complex simplicity occupies the liminal space in the same way that the Romantic moral romance occupies the space between novel and romance. Art, fragmentation, immorality (or lack of moral order), corruption, artistic falsehood and defiance of masculine and Anglo-European authority fall under the unconventional category along with the novel. Nature, unity, morality (in the form of religious moral order), purity, didactic truth and submission to masculine and Anglo-European authority (that may be flawed) fall under the conventional category along with the romance. And the liminal space between includes artistic works that reconcile nature and art, that create a sort of unified fragmentation, that posit alternative order, that reconcile purity and corruption, that posit alternative 'truth' and that balance the impulses to defy or submit to masculine and Anglo-European literary authority. Some of these concepts at first may not seem to fit together on the same ends of parallel continua, but as later sections of this chapter will show, they actually do fit very well together.

The remainder of the table addresses, first, Inchbald's literary art, specifically *A Simple Story* and *Nature and Art*, and then Hawthorne's literary art – *The Scarlet Letter* and *The Marble Faun* – to show how the characters or figures from the four books fit into the continua as discussed in later sections of this chapter. Miss Milner fits into a continuum that has Matilda at its other end. Miss Milner thus represents art, immorality, defiance of authority and so forth, while Matilda represents nature, morality, submission to authority and so forth. Roger Chillingworth, despite his association with the wildness of nature, fits into *The Scarlet Letter* as an unconventional figure because of his rejection of Puritan moral codes. He is defiant, corrupt and artfully deceptive. Although Arthur Dimmesdale breaks Puritan moral codes and hides his sin, his character lies opposed to Roger's because of his acceptance of Puritan strictures.

Romantic Fragments and the Dichotomy between Nature and Art

One of the most important of the continua listed in Figure 4 is that which includes fragmentation and unity. During the Romantic Era, especially in Britain, authors found themselves particularly interested by the idea of fragmentation. As Britons prepared to enter a new century – the nineteenth century – they became more aware of the fragmented nature of time and history, and many felt a strong sense that a new era was upon them, that a sea change of reform would revitalize and strengthen British culture. They became keenly aware of the fragmented nature of 'truth' as established by history and of the potential for large scale change in political, social and artistic terms. As the early threads of Romantic thought began to emerge, the British Empire itself fragmented when the American colonies rebelled in a successful bid for independence. A few short years later, the French overthrew their monarchy and initiated a long period of conflict that further called into question the divine origins of monarchy and that threatened Britain with invasion and further fragmentation. And while many thinkers in Britain excitedly watched Napoleon's rise to power, thinking he would bring an end to tyranny and oppression, their excitement quickly turned to disappointment as Napoleon brought uncertainty and fear by initiating his military campaigns across the Continent and destabilizing the region even more.

Conceptions of art itself became fragmentary during the Romantic Era. Indeed, it is during the early part of the nineteenth century that Lord Elgin acquired the controversial Elgin marbles, fragmentary sculptures from the Parthenon that, even now in the early twenty-first century, remain on display in the British Museum. While authors like John Keats extolled the marbles' beauty, other authors, like Lord Byron, decried the damage – the fragmentation – that the removal of the marbles effected upon Greek culture. Having the marbles in London helped to reinforce British connections with Classical art and tradition, but Romantic authors were well aware of the constructed – and fragmentary – nature of those connections.

Authors became so interested in fragmentation during the Romantic Era that they began creating fragmentary texts as artistic forms in their own right. Samuel Coleridge's 'Kubla Khan' is one of the most easily recognized literary fragments from the period, as is Lord Byron's *Don Juan*. Elizabeth Harries acknowledges the importance of these two fragments in a long list that also includes William Wordsworth's *The Recluse* and Keats's *Hyperion* fragments.[18] Harries argues that most of the works she discusses are intentionally fragmented – that their fragmentary nature is not accidental, but is a choice made by their authors.[19] D. F. Rauber discusses the poetic fragment as 'the ultimate romantic form' because, in his view, the fragment 'can be viewed as that form which more completely than any other embodies romantic ideals and aims'.[20] In Rauber's terms, the fragment encourages active participation in a literary work because readers will have a tendency to want to complete the work – to imagine the possibilities of its completion – in their minds. The fragment thus appeals to Romantic writers because of the imaginative possibilities inherent in the form. And while scholars writing about Romantic fragments and fragmentation tend to focus their attention upon poetry, fragmentary elements appear in the prose fiction as well. Harries notices fragments and fragmentary writing in novels, sermons, essays and a variety of other genres of the period.[21] Her interest is not exclusively in Romantic fragments because, as she rightly notes, the fragment has a much longer history that extends back to ancient times. The second half of the eighteenth century, however, saw an unusual increase in interest in the form. Harries repeatedly mentions Lawrence Sterne's *Tristram Shandy* (1759–67) as an excellent example of an author's struggle with making sense of fragmentary selves and fragmentary text.[22] And with the waning of the Romantic Period, the fragment did not disappear. Christopher Strathman, in *Romantic Poetry and the Fragmentary Imperative* of 2005, points out fragmentary elements that more recent authors such as James Joyce appropriated from Romantic thought.[23] Again, the emphasis is on the imaginative possibilities that the fragment makes available to readers.

An especially important source of fragmentation for Romantic-era writers, both in Britain and those in America, was the profound schism between what they classified as nature and what they classified as art. One of the best known discussions of these concepts comes from Carl Woodring, whose book *Nature into Art: Cultural Transformations in Nineteenth-Century Britain* examines the ramifications of the concepts for British literature. Woodring quotes from American writer Ralph Waldo Emerson to help define the terms; "'*Nature*, in the common sense, refers to essences unchanged by man; space, air, the river, the leaf. *Art* is applied to the mixture of his will with the same things, as in the house, a canal, a statue, a picture'".[24] In describing art, Woodring equates the idea with 'human contrivance', and he establishes nature as that which exists independently of human influence. In an earlier article, he had described the ideas in terms of what is produced versus the materials used in production. In his view, '[A]rt represents all the conscious works of mankind; nature represents all that man works with or works on'.[25]

Like fragmentation and unity, nature and art also can be situated as opposing ends on a continuum, as shown in Figure 4. Inchbald and Hawthorne, as Romantic writers, were well aware of the nature/art dichotomy, particularly since Jean-Jacques Rousseau recently had investigated the issue in such extremely popular books as *Émile, ou l'éducation* of 1762. Lytton Strachey writes in *Landmarks in French Literature*,

> Rousseau was perpetually advocating the return to Nature. All the great evils from which humanity suffers are, he declared, the outcome of civilisation; the ideal man is the primitive man – the untutored Indian, innocent, chaste, brave, who adores the Creator of the universe in simplicity, and passes his life in virtuous harmony with the purposes of Nature.[26]

Rousseau's idea of the noble savage, a natural figure untainted by civilization and flawed human reasoning, permeated Romantic-era thought. Writing in 1928, Hoxie Neale Fairchild notes in *The Noble Savage: A Study in Romantic Naturalism*, that 'a Noble Savage is any free and wild being who draws directly from nature virtues which raise doubts as to the value of civilization'.[27] To the Romantics, art represented old, established ways of interacting with the world, while nature, often embodied by a noble-savage figure, represented fresh, new perspectives. The Romantics often associated nature with alternative approaches to interpreting old ideas and with challenges to established conventions. Nature appears on the same end of a continuum parallel with those of unity and simplicity, while art is aligned with fragmentation and complexity. The primary male characters in Inchbald's second book, significantly entitled *Nature and Art*, exhibit the schism admirably. The two William Norwynnes represent art; they are well educated, civilized, conventional. They symbolize the intellectual establishment, human contrivance and corruption. They approach social situations with calculated self-interest. The two Henry Norwynnes, however, represent nature; they are uneducated, uncivilized, unconventional. They symbolize intellectual freedom, naïveté and innocence. They approach social situations with the interests of others in mind. These characters, Inchbald's other characters, and Hawthorne's characters, may be interpreted as fragments of minds or psyches simultaneously working together and against one another. Hence, the fragmented nature of Romantic-era thought finds expression in Inchbald's and Hawthorne's fictions as the mind itself becomes fragmentary and as the two authors explore how those fragments interact with one another.

Interestingly, Inchbald's use of fragmentary figures anticipates the use of similar figures in Johann Wolfgang von Goethe's *Die Wahlverwandtschaften*, published just a few years afterward in 1809, even as Hawthorne's fictions recall Goethe's example years later. The title of Goethe's work was translated as *Elective Affinities* in English. The term *elective affinities* came from contemporary chemistry and was used to describe the tendencies of certain chemical substances to react differently with one another depending on the conditions present at the time of their combination. In Goethe's tale, the characters mirror one another as fragmentary elements in the vein of Inchbald's and Hawthorne's fragmentary figures, and they similarly assume symbolic meaning as part of Goethe's experimental writing. Goethe's use of fragmentary figures suggests how widespread the interest in fragmentation had become as the first decade of the nineteenth century neared its end, and Goethe himself exerted such a strong influence on the continuing development of Romantic thought that the enduring presence of fragmented figures should be no surprise.

As Goethe's fiction does, Inchbald's and Hawthorne's Romantic moral romances juxtapose characters constructed as opposites – Miss Milner and Matilda, Hannah Primrose and Rebecca Rymer, Roger Chillingworth and Arthur Dimmesdale, Donatello and the Model. The tales and the figures within them masquerade as simplified productions of nature, but they paradoxically demonstrate a sophisticated artistry that distinguishes Inchbald and Hawthorne as practitioners of a unique kind of fiction that must be accepted as legitimate, alternative art.[28] Ultimately, as Figure 4 demonstrates, their alternative artistic productions actually reconcile nature and art, fragmentation and unity, complexity and simplicity and so forth, to suggest the superiority of borrowing from both ends of any of the continua rather than privileging one end or the other.[29] The Romantic dichotomy between nature and art and its relationship with concurrent interest in fragmentation thus add additional layers of complexity to the Romantic moral romance sub-genre through the fragmentary figures that Inchbald and Hawthorne create for their tales.

Inchbald's Fragmentary Figures in *A Simple Story*

Inchbald's experimentation with fragmentary figures surfaces quickly in *A Simple Story*, in which Dorriforth, Lord Elmwood, Miss Milner and Matilda help to distinguish the Romantic moral romance sub-genre from the traditional novel. While Dorriforth and Lord Elmwood actually are the same person, Inchbald's treatment of the character gives Dorriforth/Lord Elmwood the attributes of two separate figures, and this chapter treats them as separate entities – Terry Castle refers to Lord Elmwood as Dorriforth's 'new incarnation'.[30] As G. L. Strachey comments, *A Simple Story* 'is not concerned with the world at large, or with any section of society, hardly even with the family; its subject is a group of two or three individuals whose interaction forms the whole business of the book'.[31] Providing only superficial development of each figure, Inchbald invokes the Romantic dichotomy between nature and art to imbue the figures with a simplicity that implies the superiority of nature but that simultaneously suggests symbolic and artful meaning for the female writer.[32] Inchbald thus finds an alternative approach, in the liminal space between nature and art, that reconciles the two ideas within her fiction, even as her fictions themselves reconcile novel and romance to produce the Romantic moral romance.

Essentially, Inchbald positions her figures to interact thematically in pairs – two gender-mixed pairs (Dorriforth with Miss Milner and Lord Elmwood with Matilda), who exemplify conflicts that the female writer encounters in relation to masculine expectations, and two single-gender pairs (Dorriforth with Lord Elmwood and Miss Milner with Matilda), who exemplify differing approaches to women's writing from masculine and feminine viewpoints. Inchbald's deliberately simplified figures also assume symbolic roles as fragments of the woman writer's psyche and suggest that no traditionally defined approach to writing fiction can be adequate for women. Only an alternative approach that occupies the liminal space between masculine and feminine impulses can provide intellectual and artistic independence and legitimacy for the female writer. As shown in Figure 4, the ideal woman writer, Inchbald herself, stands between the two extremes at the ends of a continuum of conventionality and unconventionality. She incorporates symbolic elements of all four of the characters in her mind, and, through that combination, escapes traditional models.

From the beginning of *A Simple Story*, Inchbald exerts her artistic prerogative to establish Dorriforth as a symbolic and artistic fragment through simplified, superficial descriptions that might be mistaken for the work of an amateur. However, Inchbald's simplified descriptions are deceptive because their apparent proximity to unsophisticated nature conceals the writer's artistic efforts to establish Dorriforth as a symbol rather than as a believable human being. As a priest, Dorriforth is Inchbald's representative of masculine ecclesiastical authority. He is also the fragment of the female writer's psyche that agitates for conformity to masculine guidelines based upon religious precepts that prescribe feminine obedience to patriarchal figures. The narrator's description of Dorriforth on the first page of the story begins Inchbald's concerted effort to deny the man any real personality. His identity is subsumed by his role as priest, and his education in the masculine tradition of the priesthood receives more attention, initially, than the man himself to suggest his symbolism.[33] A few pages later, the narrator pauses to describe Dorriforth but provides little additional information about Dorriforth as a person and concentrates, instead, on his appearance and education. Ultimately, Dorriforth is no more than a fragment for Inchbald to use for artistic purposes as evidenced by her interest in his physical attributes and official role as a priest over his emotional or intellectual capacities.

Dorriforth's reserve may be calculated to hide his feelings, but, despite its intended purpose, it reveals his discomfort with being Miss Milner's guardian. His discomfort with the guardianship and his subsequent ineptitude in managing Miss Milner's behaviour suggest Dorriforth's impotence as a symbol of masculine religious authority as he transitions from suggestions to outright commands – without the desired effect. His inadequacy is clear also in his awkward management of Harry Rushbrook, of Lord Frederick Lawnly (who does not hide his interest in Miss Milner), and even of Mr Sandford (who initially usurps Dorriforth's authority in the household). And despite being a priest, Dorriforth possesses, according to the narrator, 'in his nature shades of evil'.[34] If Dorriforth represents a fragment of the woman writer's psyche that favours adherence to masculine traditions as defined by religion, then his lack of competence suggests that this fragment does not offer women writers adequate forms of expression. Indeed, the masculine traditions themselves, just like Dorriforth, may be flawed.

While Dorriforth remains no more than a symbol of impotent masculine ecclesiastical authority, Lord Elmwood's symbolism superficially seems the opposite in terms of trans-generational aristocratic authority. He wields his power with confidence and will not tolerate challenges to his control. However, like Dorriforth, Lord Elmwood also is a negative symbol of masculine tradition and authority. He is controlling to the point of tyranny, and his friends and relatives fear him. While he is the same man as Dorriforth, his qualities as one of Inchbald's fragmentary figures suggest that he is essentially a different character in the second half of *A Simple Story*. Granted, Dorriforth actually inherits his aristocratic title to become Lord Elmwood at the beginning of Volume 2, but he does not truly become Lord Elmwood – the tyrannical, confident symbol of unyielding masculine power – until Volume 3. The seventeen-year gap between the first and second halves of the book marks Inchbald's shift between the two different types of masculine power – from Dorriforth's inept weakness to Lord Elmwood's oppressive tyranny. The very structure of the narrative supports the idea that the Dorriforth/Lord Elmwood character, while remaining a single person, represents two distinct psychic fragments. Since the four volumes of *A Simple Story* split neatly in the middle, either of the two halves could stand alone, just as Dorriforth and Lord Elmwood can stand separately as different fragmentary figures. Lord Elmwood represents a fragment of the female writer's psyche that, to avoid literary isolation that parallels Matilda's social isolation, wishes to conform to masculine literary expectations as established by the aristocracy. However, like Dorriforth, Lord Elmwood is flawed as a symbol of masculine power, so his connection with masculine literary tradition also is suspect. He is 'a hard-hearted tyrant' whom even Mr Sandford now fears.[35] Elmwood's relationship with Matilda demonstrates, more than any other evidence, his status as a fragmentary figure and a negative symbol of masculine authority – and masculine literary tradition. Even Miss Woodley, whom Elmwood agrees to see despite her being Matilda's governess, notices that Elmwood is 'no longer the considerate, the forbearing character he formerly was; but haughty, impatient, imperious, and more than ever, implacable'.[36] Janet Todd argues that *A Simple Story* makes 'a biting attack on authoritarian patriarchy', and Miriam Wallace suggests that '*A Simple Story* reveals that the patriarch rules or fails to rule through seduction and power, not reason'.[37] Catherine Craft-Fairchild takes a slightly different tack to note that '*A Simple Story* is subversive [...] not because it succeeds in undermining patriarchal authority but because it questions and probes the psychological underpinnings of that authority in subtle and sophisticated ways'.[38] Part of the result is the revelation that Dorriforth/Lord Elmwood does not engage in rational behaviour. Essentially, he fails to rule, to use Miriam Wallace's term, because his heavyhandedness alienates Miss Milner and destroys his relationship with Matilda during her early years. Elmwood reconciles with Matilda only when his own patriarchal control is threatened by Lord Margrave. Indeed, the book is very much about power and control.

While Dorriforth and Lord Elmwood act as fragmentary figures in *A Simple Story*, Miss Milner participates in Inchbald's symbolic scheme as the defiant feminine response to masculine authority.[39] Specifically, one may interpret her as the fragment of the female writer's mind that responds in defiance of the masculine tradition of British literature and that attempts to write artistic novels but then is cast as corrupt, artful and immoral. Like Dorriforth and Lord Elmwood, Miss Milner receives little characterization beyond superficial descriptions of her appearance and social connections. Consequently, she also becomes a fragmentary figure with symbolic meaning rather than a fully developed human being. As with Dorriforth and Lord Elmwood, Miss Milner's simplicity may imply a lack of artistry – and, thus, a closeness to nature – but the simplicity itself is carefully and artistically crafted.

Miss Milner's status as a fragmentary symbol becomes clearer as Inchbald describes her repeatedly in terms that suggest her artfulness. Indeed, Inchbald's interest in the Romantic tension between nature and art moves to the forefront of *A Simple Story* in her descriptions of Miss Milner's actions. Miss Milner's artfulness subsumes other characteristics that might be part of her personality, and she becomes also a symbol of art – human contrivance – used for manipulative purposes. Early in *A Simple Story*, the narrator describes Miss Milner as a lady of fashion and says that her experiences at a Protestant boarding school 'had left her mind without one ornament, except those which nature gave, and even they were not wholly preserved from the ravages made by its rival, *Art*'.[40] Miss Milner's artfulness situates her as a negative symbol. If she represents one possible response of the woman writer to masculine literary traditions, then the artfulness that she displays, as well as its subsequent punishment, suggests that Miss Milner's defiant approach is inappropriate even if readers are meant to sympathize with her plight.[41] Faced with Dorriforth's and Lord Elmwood's two versions of tyrannical control, Miss Milner asserts herself in the only way she believes is possible, but ultimately, she is banned from Lord Elmwood's presence and dies in isolation at the beginning of Volume 3.

Miss Milner seems 'artless' and exhibits 'real or well-counterfeited simplicity'.[42] She is, however, vain, and as her laughter at Mrs Horton's piety indicates, unthinking.[43] Consciously or not, Miss Milner actively employs her artfulness to attain her own ends, particularly in opposition to Dorriforth's wishes. Her artful behaviour confirms her existence as a fragmentary and symbolic figure because the artfulness overshadows other characteristics that might develop her person-ality. She disobeys Dorriforth to attend a ball, for example, flirts insincerely with Lord Frederick and embarks on an artful 'experiment of being beloved in spite of her faults'.[44] Confronted with Sandford's sober criticism one day, Miss Mil-ner feels an 'inward nothingness' as if she is half-conscious of her own lack of development.[45] And even as Miss Milner acts as a fragmentary figure, she experi-ences individual fragmentation as she struggles with the roles of mistress and wife, ward and lover, wife and foster-daughter. The fragmentary nature of her own relationship with Dorriforth parallels the fragmentation, on a greater scale, that casts her role in *A Simple Story* as merely a single shard in the shattered metaphorical glass of the female writer's psyche.

Like her mother, Matilda also is a fragmentary figure. Inchbald describes her only briefly and concentrates, as she does with Dorriforth and Miss Milner, on Matilda's physical attributes rather than on her personality. However, even Matilda's physical description is not uniquely hers, for it derives directly from descriptions of her mother and functions to make Matilda even more simplistic and fragmentary. Miss Woodley pictures her as her mother 'risen from the grave in her former youth, health, and exquisite beauty'.[46] Even Lord Elmwood seems to realize the indissolu-ble bond between mother and daughter when he meets Matilda by accident on the stairs at Elmwood House and addresses her by her mother's name.[47]

In contrast to her mother, Matilda embodies the submissive impulse in the female writer's psyche, the pressure to conform to masculine paradigms and relinquish the desire for self-expression in feminine terms. Symbolically, Mat-ilda is her mother's opposite. While Miss Milner treats Dorriforth with levity in the first half of the book, Matilda, in the second half, views Lord Elmwood with awe. The confined Matilda listens to Sandford's news of her father 'sometimes with tears, sometimes with hope, but always with awe, and terror'.[48] She openly avows to Harry Rushbrook of her father that '"his commands I never dispute"' when she asks Rushbrook to leave her alone.[49] She even kisses Miss Woodley's hand on one occasion because it has touched her father's hand. Furthermore, she stands 'for hours' to look at a full-length portrait of Lord Elmwood, as if worshipping his image, and she watches his carriage from afar when she knows that he is leaving or returning to the mansion.[50] If Lord Elmwood represents aristocratic patriarchal authority and, more pointedly, the masculine literary tradition, and if Matilda represents a potential response of a female writer to that authority, then Matilda's obedience implies feminine acquiescence to mas-culine paradigms.

Matilda's unquestioning devotion contrasts sharply with her mother's disobe-dient tendencies to reinforce the idea that Matilda may represent the submissive impulse of the female writer. Neither woman, however, represents the ideal. Miss Milner is too disobedient and artful, whereas Matilda is too compliant and artless, living in confinement and ending the book as little more than Harry Rushbrook's wife. Matilda is not really the noble-savage figure that one might expect her to be, as her mother's opposite; her education precludes that possibility because of its artfulness. Matilda is, however, closer to being a noble-savage figure than her mother because of her isolation from all but Sandford and Miss Woodley and, more importantly, because she does not demonstrate the superficial artfulness that her mother uses in manipulating Dorriforth. Collectively, mother and daughter represent the conflicting desires of individual fragments of the female psyche that wish to honour masculine traditions and authority figures, both of which represent security and cultural continuity, and that wish to obtain independence from those very figures because of their tendency to stifle feminine self-expression. But since neither Miss Milner nor Matilda achieves true personhood within the book, Inchbald's implication seems to be that neither defiance nor submission can be adequate for the woman writer. Instead, the woman writer should reconcile both desires, borrowing enough of Miss Milner's qualities to assert herself clearly but also borrowing from Matilda's qualities to avoid creating an adversarial attitude that might bring critical oblivion.

Inchbald's Fragmentary Figures in *Nature and Art*

All four of the main characters in *A Simple Story* – Dorriforth, Lord Elmwood, Miss Milner and Matilda – are no more than fragmentary figures, and each one represents a different element within the woman writer's psyche. The male figures may symbolize differing pressures to conform to masculine models of literary production, while the female figures may symbolize two feminine responses to that pressure. Similarly, when Inchbald wrote *Nature and Art*, she again employed fragmentary figures to construct her story in quasi-allegorical terms. However, she placed more direct emphasis on the tension between nature and art – as is evident in the book's title – and complicated her model with six fragmentary figures instead of four. Like the four figures in *A Simple Story*, the six figures in *Nature and Art* exhibit studied, or complex, simplicity that heightens their symbolic potential by limiting them as fragmentary entities. They are emblems of the woman writer's experience, or more specifically, fragments of the woman writer's psyche. Again, Inchbald prevents her fragmentary figures from appearing too realistically human so that she can focus her attention on their relationships with one another rather than on their individual development. Not realizing the symbolic complexity of *Nature and Art*, some scholars have been critical of Inchbald's apparent simplicity. S. R. Littlewood, for example, calls the book a 'sometimes too palpably artificial story', although he rightly notes that the book 'is in its structure rather a formal story' than a novel.[51] And as Janice Cauwels comments, 'Mrs Inchbald's character portrayal in *Nature and*

Art seems one-sided'.[52] As she had done in *A Simple Story*, Inchbald seems to privilege the innocent simplicity of nature, but she does so through particularly artistic means that demonstrate that a woman really can produce serious art. Hence, the truly good woman writer should balance both impulses to borrow from nature and art rather than excessively privileging one over the other.

Although Inchbald says of her 'little history' that 'Rebecca Rymer and Hannah Primrose are its heroines', much of *Nature and Art* focuses on the two Williams and the two Henrys.[53] The four male characters are so flatly constructed, however, that the individual members of each father-son pair are difficult to distinguish, especially since they share the same names.[54] Indeed, the figures are so alike that the two Henrys might even be considered as a single character with the two Williams similarly sharing a role. The two Henrys, whom Inchbald associates with nature, represent the fragments of the woman writer's psyche that would prefer to submit to masculine authority. They are not noble-savage figures in the sense that they defy any kind of authority; instead, they are noble-savage figures in the sense that they are too simplistic and trusting to consider resisting authority. They also represent the simplified, didactic, romance-like moral novel that a woman writer was expected to produce in Britain. Meanwhile, the two William Norwynnes, whom Inchbald associates with art, represent the fragments that wish to exert their own authority. However, the masculine ecclesiastical and judicial authority they represent is corrupted – as the two Williams are corrupted – so they also symbolize the corrupted, immoral novel that women were accused of writing when they did not conform to masculine expectations of didacticism. Hence, Inchbald's unorthodox treatment of her characters, such as her splitting a single character into two figures in *A Simple Story* – Dorriforth and Lord Elmwood – finds expression again in *Nature and Art*, in which the members of each pair of male figures exist together, simultaneously, as fragments of a single psyche and as separate entities.

Despite the distinct similarities between the two Henrys and between the two Williams, Inchbald does not concentrate her attention upon the father-son pairs. Her interest lies, instead, in the interaction and contrasts that emerge in the paired relationships between the two brothers (the elder Henry and the elder William) and between their sons (young Henry and young William). Like many other readers, Patricia Taylor initially finds the elder William and Henry difficult to distinguish from one another, but as the story develops, Inchbald juxtaposes the members of each pair to emphasize emerging contrasts based on the nature/art dichotomy.[55]

As members of the first generation in *Nature and Art*, the elder William and the elder Henry emerge first as negative symbols of masculine classifications of women's writing. They also fill the roles of fragments of the woman writer's psyche that pressure the writer in favour of literary creation on the terms set by masculine literary tradition. Just as she had done with Dorriforth in *A Simple Story*, Inchbald does not characterize William much beyond explaining his vocation and education. His symbolism as a representative of the *art* of the book's title becomes more acute as Inchbald refuses to develop his personality and forces him into his symbolic role. William's status as an 'excellent scholar', for example, associates him with art – and literature – since formal education is an artful endeavour.[56] However, William's immoral qualities suggest that women writers who attempt to develop the artistic innovation and skill that he represents also will be labelled immoral.

In contrast, the elder Henry is no scholar at all, and Inchbald repeatedly links him with the *nature* of the book's title. He openly admits, "'I am no scholar myself'" and assumes a role akin to that of the noble savage, whose simplicity and closeness to the natural world make him a superior creature in Romantic terms.[57] Indeed, Henry continually exhibits a trusting, optimistic attitude and never engages in manipulative and negative behaviour like that of his brother. But the submissive attitude that Henry embodies does not represent a viable alternative for the female writer in contrast to the immorality associated with William. Henry disappears from the main plot of *Nature and Art* during his voyage to Africa and imprisonment on Zocotora Island, and his absence suggests the literary fate – the critical neglect – of the woman writer who authors books in the simplistic, didactic tradition that Henry represents. The two brothers certainly are opposites, but Inchbald's exploration of the interaction between the two fragmentary figures reveals that, ultimately, neither defiance nor submissiveness will provide a useful means of feminine expression within the masculine literary tradition.

In one of Inchbald's more ironic turns of plot, the elder Henry, a symbol of simplistic nature, is more artistic than his brother William, a symbol of sophisticated artfulness. Inchbald perhaps wished to link artistic talent with the freedom, spontaneity and beauty of nature and to disassociate artistic talent from the paternalistic religious law and devious artfulness that William represents. Moreover, by recognizing the artistic production of the elder Henry, a symbol of natural simplicity, Inchbald lends legitimacy to her own deceptively simplistic art in the Romantic moral romance.

While Inchbald uses the nature/art dichotomy to cast the elder William and the elder Henry as fragmentary and symbolic figures, she simultaneously develops their sons into similar psychic fragments. As with the first generation in *Nature and Art*, Inchbald does not concern herself with developing young Henry and young William into fully conceived, believable human beings. Instead, she treats them with the same studied simplicity that she uses to create their fathers, and in doing so, she extends the fathers' symbolic correspondences into the sons' identities. If the elder William and the elder Henry represent, respectively, the immoral and didactic approaches to the novel that women were believed to pursue within the masculine novel tradition, then young William and young Henry represent the same. And whereas the elder Henry and William represent nature and art, respectively, their sons assume the same symbolic roles, although the contrasts between the young men may seem sharper since Inchbald so carefully juxtaposes them.

From the moment that young Henry and young William meet in *Nature and Art*, Inchbald defines the young men in opposition to one another as extensions of their fathers' identities and clearly favours young Henry's example. Like his father, young William is foolish and prideful, concerned mainly with his own advancement and insolently denigrating his cousin Henry. Although Henry is an 'unpolished monster' and a 'beggarly cousin' from young William's point of view, Henry is more handsome, younger looking, more intellectually curious and less self-serving than any of his relatives, and the narrator comments that, in contrast to them, his 'whole faculties were absorbed in *others*'.[58] Nevertheless, the other figures in the tale, including his own father, refer to him repeatedly as savage, ignorant and uncivilized.[59]

The best examples of young Henry's superiority in *Nature and Art* come just after his arrival in England as he explores civilization and begins what the elder William thinks will be his transition from savagery to enlightenment. In a series of social *faux-pas*, young Henry, the 'ignorant savage', innocently exposes the ignorance and narrow-mindedness of his 'civilized' relatives. While these initial experiences establish the wide schism between young Henry and his relatives – and particularly his cousin young William – the two young men's relationships with Rebecca Rymer and Hannah Primrose further intensify the contrast between the cousins. Describing the initial stages of their relationships, the narrator comments that young William 'hoped to make [... Hannah] his mistress' while young Henry watches his own love interest from afar, and does not dare 'to meditate one design that might tend to her dishonour'.[60] The fates of young William and young Henry are opposed in the same way as their fathers' fates to heighten the contrast between the young men and simultaneously de-emphasize the differences between them and their fathers. Inchbald thus ensures that all four figures – the two Henrys and the two Williams – remain fragmentary and symbolic. Her focus remains, rather than any one character, the interaction among the four fragmentary figures and the alternative 'truth' for the woman writer as revealed in those interactions.

While the four primary male characters in *Nature and Art* may represent impulses toward masculine classifications of women's writing in the female writer's psyche, the two primary female characters symbolize the fragments that wish to engage in self expression. They simultaneously represent the fates of women who accept masculine paradigms and write within the masculine tradition. Like Miss Milner and Matilda, who may symbolize opposite ends on a continuum of independence versus obedience to masculine norms in *A Simple Story*, Rebecca and Hannah occupy similarly opposed symbolic roles in *Nature and Art*.

Rebecca, the daughter of the curate of Anfield, symbolizes the female author's impulse to write didactic novels, and her fate parallels the critical fates of women writers who accept the didactic form. As with the male figures in *Nature and Art*, Inchbald refuses to develop Rebecca's character, so Rebecca remains a fragmentary and symbolic figure. Like Miss Milner and Matilda, Rebecca is given a superficial description that casts her character as one dimensional. Inchbald repeatedly reminds her readers of Rebecca's lack of sophistication – her artlessness – as a means of solidifying her symbolism as an emblem of unadulterated nature. For example, when young Henry brings Rebecca the child he finds in the woods, she innocently decides to conceal the baby like a forbidden pet in the attic of her father's house. Rebecca's faith that the baby would not be discovered indicates her innocent simplicity, while the eventual accusation of fornication contrasts so glaringly with the truth that it further confirms her innocent artlessness.

Rebecca represents the woman writer's production of the conventional didactic, moralizing novel because she exhibits the conformity to masculine power that female novelists were expected to embrace in producing didactic fiction. Despite her brief, initial concealment of the baby, Rebecca later abjectly obeys her father's wishes in much the same way that Matilda obeys Lord Elmwood in *A Simple Story*. In relation to her father, Rebecca essentially has no desires of her own, and her identity is not a self-defined construct. Although Rebecca's eventual fate is untroubled by adversity, Inchbald would have condemned it as a dismal existence. By relinquishing her sense of self-fashioning to the men in her life, Rebecca joins the many women who, from Inchbald's point of view, might as well not exist at all. Unable to fulfil their desires independently of masculine control, they become mere puppets of masculine tradition, as do the women writers who choose to write didactic novels. For Inchbald, the woman author who compromises her artistic integrity by writing moralizing, didactic novels achieves critical oblivion. She attains the same position as Rebecca – an existence that is quiet, untroubled, chaste – and unfulfilled.

Given Inchbald's tendency to favour nature over art, Rebecca's fate may seem odd. Indeed, although all of the characters in *Nature and Art* are fragmentary and sparsely developed, Rebecca receives the least attention and plays a much lesser role in the story than do the other figures. Because Rebecca symbolizes the woman author who compromises her artistic integrity, Inchbald devotes less of the story to her in favour of a closer attention to Hannah's fate. Like Rebecca, Hannah represents a kind of female writer and a particular impulse within the female writer's psyche, but Hannah takes the symbolic role of the artistic woman author who refuses to write didactic novels and who subsequently is condemned as immoral for her efforts. Just as women authors endured scorn and challenges to their morality, Hannah's innocent relationship with young William becomes the basis of public censure and, eventually, legal action.

Throughout *Nature and Art*, Hannah is, like Rebecca, no more than a symbolic and fragmentary figure, but unlike Rebecca, Hannah represents the fragmentary impulse of the female author to attempt unfettered artistic expression within the masculine tradition of the British novel. As Inchbald does with Miss Milner and Matilda in *A Simple Story* – indeed, with all of her other figures – she chooses not to give Hannah a realistic human existence and instead constructs Hannah as a symbolic fragment. Inchbald associates Hannah with the two Williams, and young William in particular, to connect her with art. Hannah's art, however, is not the same kind of art as young William's; hers might be referred to as *artistry*, while William's is *artfulness*. William symbolizes artfulness in the sense of conniving social and political manipulation, but Hannah symbolizes artistry in the sense of creative, imaginative human expression. Although William's artfulness and Hannah's artistry both partake of the human contrivance that distinguishes art from nature, Inchbald establishes Hannah's artistry as superior. Like the elder Henry's musical talent, the art that Hannah represents is imbued with innocence and a deep-seated faith in the goodness of humanity. Hers is the art of self-expression and creativity that the woman novelist seeks but that the artfulness of masculine tradition seeks to extinguish. Like many women writers whose works first titillated their readers but were then consigned to critical oblivion for their imputed immorality, Hannah first fascinated William but subsequently was consigned to oblivion for her immorality. Hannah's relationship with young William establishes a sharp contrast that Inchbald uses to draw her readers' sympathies toward Hannah – and symbolically, toward the artistic woman writer. The difficulties that Hannah experiences in acquiring work parallel the artistic female novelist's difficulties in achieving recognition as a serious artist because of imputations of immorality. Essentially illiterate and possessing no useful skills, Hannah tends cattle and eventually moves to London, where she goes 'from service to service' looking for work.[61] In desperation, she finds herself in a brothel – a fate that recalls Inchbald's mention of prostitution as a writer in the preface to *A Simple Story* – where she sinks 'deeper and deeper under fortune's frowns' until she becomes a counterfeiter, the crime for which she ultimately is arrested and condemned to death.[62] In short, many women authors were forced into metaphoric literary prostitution as they created, to quote Inchbald's preface again, 'libels' and 'panegyric on the unworthy' to keep themselves from being ignored completely.[63]

Finally, Hannah's child, although not one of the six major figures in *Nature and Art*, merits a brief critical assessment for his symbolic role. Inchbald characterizes him even less than she does the other characters. She never describes him, and she does not even bother to name him. He never functions as an active participant in the tale but seems merely to take the role of an unwitting plot complication that throws chaos into the lives of the other figures. He appears in the story briefly after his birth but then fades quickly into the background, before dying aged sixteen in Chapter 42. But despite the boy's apparent lack of importance to the plot, he assumes a pivotal role in Inchbald's symbolic scheme. As the progeny of Hannah, emblem of the artistic woman writer, the boy represents artistic women's writing. He is the creative product – the artistic novel – of the female author who attempts artistic expression within a patriarchal system that condemns such creativity as part of the novel genre. After the boy's birth, Hannah panics and contemplates killing him in the same way that a woman writer might consider destroying her novel after realizing the enormity of her transgression against traditions that condemn non-didactic novels by women. Indeed, Dean Norwynne and Mr Rymer are happy only when they can safely manipulate the situation to dissociate themselves and their families from the boy. Hannah's son experiences a fate parallel to that of the potential fates of artistic novels written by women; he is ignored and condemned until his very existence is extinguished.

Through her symbolic fragmentary figures – four in *A Simple Story* and six in *Nature and Art* – Inchbald clarifies the difficulties faced by the woman fiction writer in Romantic Britain. The masculine novel tradition simply had little to no room for women as legitimate artists. Women were expected to produce didactic novels whose sole purpose was the moral edification of their readers, but merely didactic fiction received little critical acclaim because it lacked artistry and depth. However, women writers who attempted artistic novels were labelled immoral and experienced critical disregard. For Inchbald, neither option was acceptable. Knowing the untenable position in which women novelists found themselves, Inchbald chose not to write traditional novels at all in favour of developing the Romantic moral romance sub-genre. Inchbald's romances, and particularly the characters in the tales, appear simplistic and underdeveloped. However, the apparent simplicity conceals a sophisticated symbolic attempt to legitimize women's writing by hinting that a woman writer's best choice might be a combination of submission and defiance.

Hawthorne's Fragmentary Figures in *The Scarlet Letter*

In what cannot be coincidence, Nathaniel Hawthorne attempts the same kind of innovation across the Atlantic in America half a century later. In the same way that Inchbald invests her figures with her own literary concerns, Hawthorne shapes his figures to reflect his unique artistic goals. While Inchbald writes, symbolically, about the legitimization of the female author in *A Simple Story* and *Nature and*

Art, Hawthorne similarly addresses the American author's fate in *The Scarlet Letter* and *The Marble Faun*. Hawthorne adopts the same techniques Inchbald uses when he employs the Romantic dichotomy between nature and art ostensibly to privilege the simplicity of nature but, in reality, to make an important point about his own literary art through particularly artistic means. Although Hawthorne's motivation for writing is different from Inchbald's, both authors focus attention on their own literary art, and Hawthorne creates similar fragmentary figures as he, too, develops a version of the Romantic moral romance sub-genre.

While many scholars have focused their attention on Hawthorne's general use of fragmentary figures, just as many have noticed such figures and their interactions specifically in *The Scarlet Letter*. Malcolm Cowley, for example, acknowledges of the book, 'The action of the novel is completely an *interaction* among four persons in a particular environment that is also presented in its own terms', and A. N. Kaul comments, '*The Scarlet Letter* is a dramatic novel much of whose action is a matter of *interaction* between a few principal characters'.[64] Likewise, F. O. Matthiessen notes, while also acknowledging Hawthorne's use of fragmentary figures, 'Of his four romances, this one [*The Scarlet Letter*] grows most organically out of the interactions between the characters [...]. Furthermore, his integrity of effect is due in part to the incisive contrasts among the human types he is presenting'.[65] Yvor Winters calls *The Scarlet Letter* 'pure allegory' and makes the comment that

> the figures in *The Scarlet Letter* are profoundly unsatisfactory if one comes to the book expecting to find a novel, for they draw their life not from specific and familiar human characteristics, as do the figures of Henry James, but from the precision and intensity with which they render their respective ideas.[66]

Winters's use of the word *figures* rather than *characters* is significant, as is his recognition that *The Scarlet Letter* is not a traditional novel. Additionally, Leslie Fiedler recognizes the fragmentary nature of the figures in *The Scarlet Letter* when he comments that '[a]ll the characters come into existence when the book begins and do not survive'.[67] He notes that each one is a symbolic construct rather than a human being:

> Hester and Dimmesdale are exploited from time to time as 'emblems' of psychological or moral states; but they remain rooted always in the world of reality. Chillingworth, on the other hand, makes so magical an entrance and exit that we find it hard to believe in him as merely an aging scholar, who has nearly destroyed himself by attempting to hold together a loveless marriage with a younger woman; while Pearl, though she is presented as the fruit of her mother's sin, seems hardly flesh and blood at all.[68]

Fiedler also points out one of the most unique features of *The Scarlet Letter* in that 'all passion [is] burned away before the novel proper begins'.[69] Hawthorne does not depict the passion between Hester and Arthur that might humanize them to a greater extent. By withholding the information, Hawthorne makes the figures more symbolic and fragmentary. As James Mellow says, '*The Scarlet Letter* is relentlessly allegorical; it is full of "types" and "symbols"', although he faults the story for being too allegorical when he comments, 'It is one of the flaws of the novel – among its considerable virtues – that the characters remain "types" of the guilty heart, and of fallen human nature, serving out their predetermined roles in the allegory'.[70] John Stubbs pointedly calls Hawthorne's figures in *The Scarlet Letter* 'conventional type characters', and Edward Wagenknecht similarly notices artificiality and symbolism in the characters.[71] Joseph Levi maintains that the four characters represent different aspects of Hawthorne's personality. Arthur is the ego; Chillingworth is the superego; Pearl is the 'id personified'; and Hester is the 'mother ideal'.[72] Comparing Roger with Miriam's model, Randall Stewart writes that Roger 'has no points of contact with real life', and Helen Sutherland sees Roger as little more than a doppelgänger of Arthur.[73] Jane Thrailkill also casts Arthur and Roger as opposites, but she does so in medical and theological terms that suggest that neither science nor theology alone can offer meaningful explanations of reality.[74] Fiedler comments that Pearl 'is so distorted in the interests of her symbolic role that she seems by turns incredible and absurd'.[75] More recently, Cindy Lou Daniels has argued that, through her refusal to accept her community's mores, Pearl also is a symbol of changing women's roles in nineteenth-century America.[76]

In *The Scarlet Letter*, Hawthorne's four major figures – Hester Prynne, Arthur Dimmesdale, Roger Chillingworth and Pearl – symbolize four different fragments of the American author's psyche, as noted in Figure 4. The Puritanism that pervades the book, because of its origins in Britain and because Hawthorne found it such a controlling influence in America, symbolizes the British literary tradition – and, perhaps, a more general Anglo-European literary tradition – against which Hawthorne defines his literary art. The responses of the four major figures to the Puritanism represent four authorial responses to the tradition of the British novel. Hester and Arthur, despite their transgression, ultimately symbolize submission to British literary norms, and Roger embodies the rejection of British models, while Pearl may represent the ideal American writer's response through her indifference. Pearl neither fully accepts nor fully rejects Boston Puritanism but follows her own sense of conscience. As shown in Figure 4, Pearl consequently occupies a more balanced role than the other figures in the tale, and while she stands between the other figures, she also unites them all.[77] Hawthorne occupies the same space; for him, the ideal American writer should embrace the liminal role between opposite ends of the continua of novel/romance, nature/art, rejection/acceptance of Anglo-European models.

Collectively, Hester and Arthur, in their responses to Boston Puritanism, embody the fragments of the American author's psyche that submit to British expectations about writing fiction despite personal preferences for an American tradition. Although both Hester and Arthur are Americans whose simplicity and lack of sophistication might associate them with nature, they also represent American literary art. Hester and Arthur may appear to defy the Puritanism of their community because of their illicit relationship, but their responses to the community's moral indignation suggest otherwise. Both figures accept the judgement that they have sinned, and while Hester agrees to wear the scarlet letter, Arthur decides to conceal his guilt.[78] Both figures decide to hide the truth in the same way that an American author, to achieve literary success, might conceal a desire for independence from British literary tradition. However, Pearl's birth may, on one level, represent the publication of American fiction that does not fit within British expectations. The Puritan traditions of Boston condemn Pearl as an illegitimate, and therefore sinful, child in the same way that British literary tradition and the American public might devalue the writings of authors who attempt to create an indigenous American literature. If Hester symbolizes an American author who transgresses against British expectations by attempting to publish uniquely American fiction – and then accepts the public's judgement – then her fate also must parallel the fates of such authors. Hester experiences popular condemnation for her transgression. The townspeople of Boston are Hawthorne's representatives of the popular American audience that still privileges the patterns and resolutions of the British novel tradition.[79] When Hester publicly rejects the Puritan morality – and, symbolically, the novel tradition – that the townspeople value so highly, she must endure their censure. The scarlet *A* that she wears may symbolize America, or more specifically, American literary art and the American artist.[80]

Hawthorne's development of Hester into a fragmentary figure supports the notion that she represents one response of the American artist to British literary tradition. Rather than making Hester a believable human being, Hawthorne consciously and artistically constructs her identity as a fragment. Hawthorne hardly describes her as a person, and her silence after the trial further isolates and simplifies her as a character. As the narrator points out, Hester undergoes a process of 'giving up her individuality'.[81] She does not have an identity of her own, and as a representative of sin – and perhaps a transgressive challenge to the British novel tradition – she embodies the community's sense of immorality and becomes a figure rather than a fully developed individual.

As *The Scarlet Letter* progresses, Hester's status as merely a fragmentary symbol becomes more acute as her identity becomes intertwined with the symbolic scarlet letter. The letter and its origin develop into legendary proportions for Hester's fellow Bostonians and further reduce any chance that Hester might evolve into a believable human being. The letter's purported glowing at night may symbolize the persistence of American art in developing into a legitimate form despite the metaphorical darkness, in the form of British tradition, that envelops the American artist.[82] The skilful embroidery with which Hester has ornamented the letter may represent American artistry and literary skill. Hester herself represents a failed attempt at the creation of an indigenous American literary art because, although Pearl may symbolize an American publication of which Hawthorne might approve, Hester accepts condemnation for her progeny. At the beginning of the story, as at the end, Hester is no more than a symbol, a one-dimensional, fragmentary figure.

In contrast to Hester, whose scarlet letter advertises her transgression against Puritanism – and, symbolically, the British literary tradition – Arthur conceals his desire to subvert Puritan morality because his popular success is so firmly rooted in the Bostonians' approval. He parallels the American writer whose success is dependent upon a continued public perception that he upholds British traditions. The scarlet *A* that may or may not appear on his skin at the end of the book clearly associates him – along with the illicit affair – with Hester and labels him also as an American artist, or at least a psychic fragment of the American artist. However, Arthur's scarlet letter is hidden under the Puritan – or British – garb that he uses to present himself to the public, so no one is aware of his desire to express himself *as* a symbol of the American artist until his death.

Like Hester, Arthur is a fragmentary figure whose characterization is sparse and whose identity is subsumed by his symbolic role within Hawthorne's story. The narrator's descriptions of Arthur, like those of Hester, concentrate on physical characteristics and largely ignore his personality so that he will not attain a full identity as a human creature. Arthur's downward spiral of emotional and physical deterioration – and his self-loathing for his sin – suggests Hawthorne's stance that American literary art will wither if not publicly acknowledged and legitimized. If Pearl symbolizes an American publication that eschews British models, then Arthur is Hester's authorial collaborator whose identity remains hidden.

In contrast to Hester and Arthur, Roger represents the fragment of the American writer's psyche that openly rejects the British literary tradition as symbolized by Puritanism. Like the other figures in the book, Roger is no more than a fragmentary figure whose identity is limited to his symbolic role in the story. As with Hester and Arthur, the narrator limits the description of Roger to his physical characteristics and conspicuously ignores personality traits that might distinguish him as a human being. The narrator describes Roger as 'slightly deformed', contributing to his symbolic quality since physical disfigurement often represents moral degradation, and stories circulate in Boston, after Roger moves in with Arthur, that Arthur is being haunted 'either by Satan himself, or Satan's emissary, in the guise of old Roger Chillingworth'.[83] Roger represents self-deluded, single-minded rejection of British literary tradition. Roger's only purpose, his only goal, is to torture Arthur once he learns of the minister's sin with Hester. He is a symbol of an authorial response that aggressively attacks anyone – like Arthur and Hester – who might concede the value in British literature. He eschews his former identity to remain the symbol of vengeance and malevolence, the 'leech' who is described in Chapter 9 and whose name, Roger Chillingworth, is but an alias.[84] Roger so completely lacks an identity of his own that readers never explicitly learn his true name and can only speculate that his name must have been Roger Prynne.[85]

Because he refuses to accept the Puritanism of Boston, Roger symbolizes the complete rejection of the British novel tradition by the American author or at least by a fragment of the American author's psyche. Indeed, Roger is an outsider to the Bostonians, who feel so little kinship with him that they decide to lodge him in the local jail, 'as the most convenient and suitable mode of disposing of him', until they can negotiate the terms of his release from his Native-American captors.[86] Although Roger nominally is a prisoner of the Native Americans, he exhibits greater kinship with them and the natural world in which they live than he does with the Puritan Bostonians. Indeed, Roger arrives in town accompanied by a Native American in traditional dress, and his own clothing is a bizarre mix of Native American and English styles.[87] The narrator notes that he has even learned about Native-American remedies and trusts them as much as he does the scientifically garnered European knowledge that the settlers more readily embrace.[88] Rumours even circulate in the town that Roger learned many of his medical skills by participating in occult Native-American rituals that invoked supernatural magic.[89] Roger's association with Native-American peoples suggests that he has relinquished much of his Anglo-European heritage, including a belief in the Puritanism of Boston's inhabitants. If Puritanism represents the British novel tradition in *The Scarlet Letter*, then Roger's rejection of its tenets may symbolize the American author's rejection of the British tradition within his or her psyche. For Hawthorne, complete rejection of the British tradition does not provide a viable base on which the American author can construct a new American literature.

While Hester and Arthur symbolize the fragments of the American author's psyche that submits to British literary tradition, and Roger emblematizes the fragment that rejects the same tradition, Pearl represents the fragment that merges British tradition with an American sense of independence. Pearl neither accepts the Puritanism of her fellow Bostonians, nor rejects it outright. As an amoral creature, she remains indifferent to the moral dilemmas that confront her elders. Hawthorne constructs Pearl symbolically as the American author's psychic fragment that accepts British literary tradition as the foundation for American writing but follows his or her own American instincts to move beyond the British basis for writing. Simultaneously, Pearl serves as a symbol of indigenous American art itself and of the ideal American artist as a whole. Hawthorne does not advocate submission to the British tradition and its judgements as exemplified in Hester and Arthur; nor does he advocate unequivocal rejection of it as embodied in the figure of Roger. For Hawthorne, the balance that Pearl represents provides the solution to establishing a legitimate, indigenous American literature.

Like the other three primary characters in *The Scarlet Letter*, Pearl is a symbolic, fragmentary figure. She embodies the youth and vitality that Hawthorne wishes to see in American literature. The narrator and the other figures in the book recognize Pearl's uniqueness as they repeatedly question her very humanity. She is variously referred to as 'the little elf', 'that wild and flighty little elf', 'a little imp' and the 'elfish child', and the narrator sometimes calls her 'a demon offspring'.[90] Even Hester and Arthur wonder whether Pearl is truly human.[91] A visiting mariner calls her a 'witch-baby', and Pearl's threat to chase his ship with a tempest alludes to Shakespeare's *The Tempest* and Prospero's supernatural Ariel.[92] Pearl is so uncontrollable and so wild that stories of legendary proportions about her circulate in the community. A wolf supposedly once approached her and, recognizing her wildness, 'offered his savage head to be patted by her hand', and during the final scene of the book, a Native-American grows 'conscious of a nature wilder than his own' as he stares into Pearl's eyes.[93] Hester, not knowing what else to do, feels forced to allow Pearl to be 'swayed by her own impulses' – perhaps as American literary artists should be.[94]

Pearl's association with the wild, the untainted, the supernatural, solidifies her connection with America in general, and when she fashions a green letter *A* of eel-grass to wear at the beach, she confirms the relationship by appropriating part of the American landscape as her own symbol. Hester disapproves, proclaiming that the letter is meaningless, but she is mistaken.[95] The letter represents the indigenous American literary art that Pearl embodies. Pearl wears the letter to acknowledge, symbolically, the Puritan – or British – influences that have labelled her mother with the scarlet *A*, but Pearl's *A* is green to evoke the fecund potential of the new American literature that alters old models. Indeed, Leslie Fiedler recognizes the connection that exists between Anglo-European fiction and American fiction when he states,

> To write [...] about the American novel is to write about the fate of certain European genres in a world of alien experience. It is not only a world where courtship and marriage have suffered a profound change, but also one in the process of losing the traditional distinctions of class; a world without a significant history or a substantial past; a world which had left behind the terror of Europe not for the innocence it dreamed of, but for new and special guilts associated with the rape of nature and the exploitation of dark-skinned people; a world doomed to play out the imaginary childhood of Europe. The American novel is only *finally* American; its appearance is an event in the history of the European spirit – as, indeed, is the very invention of America itself.[96]

In short, American literary art simply cannot be independent of Anglo-European influences.

As Inchbald does in *A Simple Story* and *Nature and Art*, Hawthorne juxtaposes his fragmentary figures in *The Scarlet Letter* in ways that allow the figures' interactions with one another to reveal 'truth' in Hawthorne's terms as an American writer. Each figure is connected with the other figures in a complex web of relationships that imply interconnectedness in all human literary activity and that consequently imply symbolically that British and American literature cannot be separated. The four fragmentary figures are so intimately linked that they might even be considered – like Inchbald's earlier figures – as individual impulses within a single psyche, in this case, that of the American artist. Simplicity is the foundation of all four of the major figures in *The Scarlet Letter*, for, like John Bunyan's *Pilgrim's Progress*, to which Hawthorne alludes at the beginning of Chapter 10, *The Scarlet Letter* incorporates symbolic and fragmentary figures.[97]

Hawthorne's Fragmentary Figures in *The Marble Faun*

The Scarlet Letter is a superb example of the Romantic moral romance, especially since Hawthorne seems to privilege nature while artfully crafting a tale that symbolically addresses questions of artistic production. Perhaps recognizing the strength of his own earlier model in *The Scarlet Letter*, Hawthorne constructed *The Marble Faun* with a similar attention to fragmentary figures and the Romantic nature/art dichotomy. As the book follows Miriam, Donatello, Kenyon, and Hilda in their varying levels of involvement in the Model's murder, each character emerges as a simplified, fragmentary figure with multiple levels of symbolic meaning that have broad implications for the American writer.

As Hawthorne had done with Hester Prynne and the other figures in *The Scarlet Letter*, he chose not to provide much information about the personality and origins of each of his figures in *The Marble Faun*. Consequently, as the tale unfolds, each figure remains a fragmentary symbol rather than developing into a believable human being. Merle Brown claims that the figures are more mature human beings than any other of Hawthorne's characters, but most critics argue otherwise.[98] Mellow recognizes their fragmentary nature with his complaint that they are 'too unfocused, too lacking in individuality to be of deep concern to the reader'.[99] Clare Goldfarb calls Hilda and Kenyon 'incomplete human beings and artists' in a recognition of both their fragmentary nature and of their symbolism as representatives of American art.[100] In a discussion of Hilda and Miriam, Leslie Fiedler recognizes their symbolism as being linked with America and Europe, respectively. He states, 'It is Hawthorne who first creates in *The Marble Faun* the international romance, in which the Fair Maiden [Hilda] and Dark Lady [Miriam] come clearly to stand for American innocence and European experience'.[101]

Miriam is the tortured young woman who bears the trans-generational guilt of her family, and because she may be of European origin and is an artist, she symbolizes the fragment of the American writer's psyche that accepts an artistic literary tradition based on Anglo-European models. Her sadness and loneliness suggest that the Anglo-European models are inadequate, in themselves, for the American artist. Even Miriam's paintings all include a figure 'pourtrayed apart' who watches the main subject of the painting from the background and who reflects Miriam's sadness.[102] Additionally, Hawthorne purposely shrouds Miriam's identity and her background in mystery to preserve her status as a fragmentary figure. He provides enough information to individualize Miriam from the other figures within the confines of her constructed caricature-like identity but withholds enough to keep her character from becoming too unique. To be an effective agent within the plot of *The Marble Faun*, Miriam must remain a symbolic construct – an emblem of a writer's potential reliance upon Anglo-European artistic production – rather than a fully developed individual.

In contrast to Miriam, who does not develop in the tale, Donatello begins *The Marble Faun* as an innocent, noble-savage figure associated with nature, but he undergoes a transformation that situates him, ultimately, in the same artfully guilty position as Miriam. Inherited sin and guilt, compounded by his own involvement with the Model's murder, destroys Donatello's chances for true happiness. Like Miriam, he also may represent the American artist's impulse to conform to Anglo-European literary tradition. However, Donatello is not an artist; instead he takes the additional symbolic role of the artist's subject since he is the living example of the marble faun of the book's title and since Kenyon decides to create a sculpture of his head later in the tale. If Donatello takes the symbolic role of the literary artist's subject, then his transformation from the innocent faun associated with nature to the guilt-ridden man associated with art suggests that the Anglo-European literary tradition has become flawed. The inherited sin and guilt of centuries of cultural existence so completely control Anglo-European literary art that the Anglo-European tradition no longer can acknowledge – and, in fact, actively annihilates – the innocent simplicity and naïveté that Donatello embodies at the beginning of *The Marble Faun*. Indeed, at the beginning of the tale, Donatello, associated with Praxiteles, symbolizes the subject of the Anglo-European artist of the past, and his transformation represents the Anglo-European artist's attempt to realign artistic subjects with contemporary culture. However, since contemporary culture is, as suggested in Miriam's experience, infused with the sin and guilt of generations of conflict, the realignment of artistic subjects with contemporary culture destroys the natural beauty of the subjects.

Donatello is the only one of the four primary figures in *The Marble Faun* whose origins are revealed to the reader to a significant extent. However, rather than complicating Donatello's identity and making him appear more fully conceived as a human being, the information about his past confirms his status as a fragmentary figure by calling his very humanity into question. The stories of Donatello's legendary family suggest that he is descended from a faun and situate him as a member of a longstanding Italian tradition that, while it differentiates Donatello from the other figures, subsumes a great measure of his own individuality. Appropriately, as a representative of nature and of the Anglo-European artist's subject, Donatello has no interest in art and rarely offers his opinion about any kind of artwork.[103] Throughout the story, and especially at the beginning, he is referred to variously as a 'simpleton', a 'child', a 'woodland elf', a 'simple boy' and a 'poor simple boy' in recognition of his lack of cultivated – and artful – sophistication.[104] On other occasions, he is a 'hound', a 'pet dog', a 'pet spaniel' and a 'young greyhound'.[105] As a representative of the noble savage, whose lack of sophistication makes him more akin to nature than to art, Donatello is but a fragmentary figure rather than a fully conceived human being.

Interestingly, with the death of Miriam's Model, Donatello undergoes a transformation. The act of murder aligns him with the inherited guilt of his family so that he loses his associations with innocent nature and joins Miriam as a participant in a tradition of inherited guilt (hence, he appears in two places in Figure 4). In a sense, Miriam, as artist, transforms Donatello, her subject, into a mirror image of her contemporary Anglo-European self. The narrator notes, in a chapter called 'The Faun's Transformation', that the pure, simple, animal-like boy is no more.[106] The Model's murder is the catalyst for Donatello's development into true manhood, but the change has come at the expense of his natural simplicity and innocence. The peasants on Donatello's estate lament that he is gloomier since his return from Rome, and the narrator later hints that Donatello has matured into manhood.[107] Near the end of *The Marble Faun*, Miriam describes him as exhibiting '"an inestimable treasure of improvement won from an experience of pain"'.[108] Miriam seems to agree with Hawthorne's own statement in the preface that romance needs ruin to be successful, but the ruin that touches Donatello is too much, for it destroys his innocence.[109]

Like Donatello, the Model is the artist's subject – he has posed on numerous occasions for Miriam – but his negative qualities imply that contemporary Anglo-European art lacks vitality and beauty, perhaps because artists borrow too heavily from a past that is inflected by sin and guilt. If Donatello represents, initially, the Anglo-European artist's subject grounded in the simplicity and innocence of nature, then the Model symbolizes the Anglo-European artist's subject grounded in the sin and guilt of generations of cultural existence. He symbolizes the fragment of an author's psyche that relies heavily on those generations of cultural existence. Like the other figures, he also has a mysterious past whose details are never revealed to the reader, for he is connected to Miriam through the scandalous events that plague her family. The Model's identity is so much subsumed by his symbolic nature that he lacks even a given name, and he is referred to throughout the text simply as 'the Model'. He is referred to only once, after his death, as Antonio by the sacristan of the Capuchin church in which he is to be buried, but the name may merely be an alias, for no one else ever calls him that name, and even his presence in the church seems peculiar.[110] Miriam describes him as a demon or phantom, and the narrator says that in the catacombs, he seems to prefer darkness.[111] The Model remains a symbolic figure who represents evil and its ever-present nature, for even after his death, the repercussions of his demise continue indefinitely for Donatello and Miriam. As a symbol of the artist's subject, he may hold a role that implies excessive Anglo-European reliance on old traditions of sin and trans-generational guilt in fiction.

In contrast to the European figures, the American figures, Kenyon and Hilda, are not haunted by longstanding traditions of sin and guilt. They come from the New World, where Anglo-European culture has re-established itself without the generational sin and guilt that remains connected to Anglo-European artistic endeavours.[112] However, Kenyon's and Hilda's experiences in *The Marble Faun* suggest that American literary art, despite its pristine qualities, is not – on its own – superior to its Anglo-European rival. Indeed, American literary art also lacks vitality and beauty. The traditions that Anglo-European art possesses in excess are the very traditions that American art lacks as a basis for its creations. Kenyon, for example, symbolizes the fragment of the American artist's psyche that is an objective, intellectualized observer – and imitator – of Anglo-European tradition.[113] Unlike the other figures in *The Marble Faun*, Kenyon remains relatively dispassionate throughout the tale. He is unique in that he is the least involved in the sin and guilt that plague his friends, and he acts, on some level, as an impartial observer, who watches the other three figures and comments upon their activities. At one point, for example, he asks Donatello, "'Your head in marble would be a treasure to me. Shall I have it?'".[114] When he makes the request, which Donatello grants, he essentially is asking his friend for permission to preserve an objective essence of the young Italian's identity since such a statue would conceivably, like the Faun of Praxiteles and like the broken marble statue at the end that represents Hilda, last for centuries. Kenyon thus takes the role of interpreter and preserver of the identity of his friend – of the Anglo-European tradition from which his literary ancestors originate. In providing commentary upon the action, he functions as if he were a secondary narrator, and he recedes into the background to give precedence to the other figures in the story. Moreover,

he possesses no inheritance of sin and guilt to inspire his art, and he alone
in the group is a sculptor, whose marble creations project a cold rigidity that
encompasses, as he admits, a 'moral standstill'.[115] Kenyon even calls himself a
'"man of marble"', in reference to his profession as a sculptor, but the term has
more abstract implications since it describes Kenyon's personality.[116] Like the
marble statue that represents Hilda near the end of the tale, and that, except
for the missing limbs, remains essentially unchanged for centuries, Kenyon's
identity also remains unchanged – undeveloped – throughout the story. Hilda
recognizes Kenyon's lack of development when she faults him for not appreci-
ating refinement unless it is 'cold and hard, like the marble in which your ideas
take shape'.[117] As a sculptor, he does shape ideas into marble statues, but Hilda's statement also implies that Kenyon's mind retains a cold, hard, statue-like
rigidity and does not develop, just as his personality does not develop, as the
story progresses. If he symbolizes the fragment of the American author's psyche that relies on Anglo-European literary tradition, then that rigidity implies
lack of progress, lack of development. Like the other characters, he is merely a
fragment, an objectified symbol, rather than a fully conceived human being.

Hilda, also a symbol of American art and of a fragment of the American
artist's psyche, similarly lacks the worldliness that characterizes Anglo-European
art. Like the other figures in the book, she is given minimal characterization so
that she remains fragmentary and thus more symbolic. She is the innocent, virginal figure who experiences the guilt for the Model's murder only collaterally
and is able, ultimately, to shed its effects. Although, like Kenyon, Hilda possesses
the talent to be a magnificent artist, she is a copyist. Her art is limited to the
reproduction of the works of long-dead European masters. Without an American tradition of inherited guilt, Hilda turns to European models for inspiration
in the same way that American novelists turned to Anglo-European models for
their art. Indeed, although a copyist's work requires great skill, the very nature
of the work, producing an exact copy of someone else's artistic endeavours, ultimately is neither creative nor individualizing. In fact, when Hilda does her job
well, no one can distinguish her work from that of the artist whose painting
she has copied, for being a good copyist requires the suppression of one's own
preferences – one's own identity. Rita Gollin calls Hilda's job 'self-abnegating'.[118]
If Hilda, like Kenyon, represents a fragment of the American literary artist's psyche, then her excessive reliance upon European models suggests that part of the
American literary artist's mind also may rely too heavily upon Anglo-European
forms. She is 'Hilda The Dove', who wears a 'customary white robe' that, while
it associates her with the plumage of the doves that flock to her apartment, symbolizes the purity of her identity, an identity whose innocence is clear in Hilda's
naïveté and in her lack of well-defined individuality.[119] Like the American liter-

ary art that she symbolizes, Hilda is a simplistic, innocent, virginal figure who lacks a longstanding tradition of sin and guilt on which to base her identity.

If Miriam's artistic productions, connected with Donatello and the Model, are inadequate, and if Kenyon and Hilda can produce no more than cold sculptures and copies, then neither Anglo-European nor American models of artistic production, in and of themselves, are adequate for the American artist. When Hilda witnesses the Model's murder, she experiences a transformation similar to Donatello's, but the change lasts only until Hilda confesses to a Catholic priest. If Hilda represents Hawthorne's American literary tradition as well as a fragment of the American author's psyche, then her confession can be interpreted as a temporary reliance upon Anglo-European tradition (Figure 4 shows Hilda's move to and retreat from Hawthorne's ideal). The confession represents Hilda's employment of Anglo-European tradition for her own ends as opposed to her usual mimetic approach to painting. Through Hilda's experience, Hawthorne suggests that American authors should neither fully embrace nor fully reject Anglo-European models. Instead, they should rely upon their American experience in their writing, but they also should acknowledge Anglo-European literary tradition as the basis of their writing. As a symbol of one of the American literary artist's impulses, Hilda approaches Hawthorne's ideal in her use of European tradition to alleviate her guilt. However, her reversion to her former self suggests that American literary art has yet to attain complete expression and legitimacy. And because the four major figures may be interpreted as fragments of a psyche – that of the ideal American author – the tale itself artistically mimics the inclusiveness that Hawthorne advocates for the American literary artist. The truly American artist will reconcile the impulses to defy or submit to Anglo-European traditions in favour of an alternate, liminal role between uniquely American and uniquely Anglo-European models. The Romantic moral romance itself becomes a metaphorical representation of the American artist's mind and thus legitimizes American art through its particularly artistic effects.

Throughout *The Marble Faun*, Hawthorne explicitly connects each of his figures with the others in the tale. Doing so allows him symbolically to exhibit the connectedness between American and Anglo-European literary traditions that he believes is necessary for the development of an indigenous American literature. From an Anglo-European point of view – and from the point of view of many Americans – Anglo-European writers produce a sophisticated art, while American writers exhibit simplicity akin to the natural simplicity of the noble savage. Hawthorne, however, believes that American writers should balance nature and art to produce their literature, and the connectedness among his symbolic and fragmentary figures supports his inclusive philosophy. He specifically pairs the figures associated with Europe and then those associated with America to emphasize the differences between their respective symbolic approaches to art, before connecting all four of the figures. A psychic connection occurs between the European figures Donatello and Miriam, for example, when the young Italian sees consent to murder in Miriam's eyes. The result is that Donatello pushes the Model from the cliff. From this point in the text, the two accomplices in the deed experience a strong connection with one another as if the sinful murder has acted as a catalyst for their mutual love and as an acknowledgment of their psychic connectedness. Even at the murder scene, Miriam and Donatello embrace one another as they share the same types of emotions and instantly develop a connection that transcends any of their other relationships.[120] They are aware only of one another, and they feel as if the rest of humanity has simply vanished.[121] Miriam asks Donatello at this point if he is aware of the 'companionship that knits our heart-strings together', and he responds, "I feel it, Miriam. [...] We draw one breath; we live one life!"'.[122] Essentially, Miriam has witnessed the conversion of Donatello into her own image, just as the Anglo-European literary artist appropriates his or her subject and corrupts it with his or her own guilt. Miriam believes that the Model's murder has managed 'to cement two other lives forevermore', and when Kenyon converses with Donatello in the Apennines about Rome, he mentions, in an oblique reference to Miriam, "those friends, whose life-line was twisted with your own".[123] Miriam later acknowledges that she and Donatello share the same guilt, as if they cannot be separated from one another, and Donatello agrees.[124] Certainly, Miriam and Donatello function as psychically connected figures within the book. They spend time apart and attempt to forget their crime, but their psychic connection is so strong that eventually they come together in Perugia, unable to stay away from one another. Similar to the way in which Elizabeth Inchbald's two William Norwynnes merge symbolically as a single character in *Nature and Art*, Miriam and Donatello fuse into a single psychic entity as Hawthorne's book concludes.

Likewise, before the murder, Miriam and the Model, also European figures, seem to have an unusual connectedness that suggests that they function in a paired relationship as psychic fragments. Although Miriam appears to attempt escape from the wild-looking man, she also seems drawn to him while he exerts his influence over her. The common bond of Miriam's family's sin and guilt ties them together, and their identities merge as different aspects of the same consciousness. When Miriam wishes never to have seen the Model in the catacombs, the Model responds that her desires are irrelevant because they two are perpetually connected and would have inevitably met, even if in another place at another time.[125]

The relationship between Hilda and Kenyon, as symbols of American art, is similarly tangled as the two fragmentary figures merge as collateral bearers of Miriam and Donatello's guilt. In the Apennines at Donatello's ancestral home,

Kenyon feels a yearning for Hilda as he looks in the direction of Rome one day.[126] Likewise, Hilda yearns for Kenyon's companionship and wishes that he were with her so that she could unburden her guilt to him and discuss the murder that she witnessed. Ultimately, they marry.[127] Kenyon and Hilda feel such a strong sense of connection that they decide to become one in marriage even though they already participate in a psychic relationship with one another as symbolic fragments of a single psyche.

In the end, all of the characters are connected to one another so that, while they participate in paired relationships with one another, they also exist collectively as fragments of the American writer's psyche – of the impulses within the American writer's mind. In the carnival scene, Kenyon meets Donatello and Miriam, and the three figures stand for a moment together in a moment of shared psychic connection.[128] The circle extends beyond the acknowledged three, for Hilda and the Model are parts of it as well, even though they may be absent from the immediate scene. Indeed, Hilda joins Kenyon shortly thereafter, and the late Model's influence certainly remains an indelible part of the other four figures' identities.

Fragmentary Figures and the Tension between Nature and Art

As Elizabeth Inchbald and Nathaniel Hawthorne wrote their books, both authors developed fragmentary figures rather than fully conceived characters to fill symbolic roles within their texts as they evolved the Romantic moral romance sub-genre. Through the fragmentary figures, both authors employ the Romantic tension between nature and art ostensibly to privilege the simplicity and innocence of nature but simultaneously to produce sophisticated, artistic tales that call for a legitimisation of their art forms. In *A Simple Story*, Miss Milner and Matilda qualify as fragmentary figures, as does Dorriforth/Lord Elmwood, who, though a single character, represents two different identities in the two different halves of the text. In *Nature and Art*, the two Henrys and the two Williams interact as fragmentary elements, as do Rebecca Rymer and the ill-fated Hannah Primrose. For Hawthorne, Hester Prynne, Arthur Dimmesdale, Roger Chillingworth and Pearl fill similar symbolic roles in *The Scarlet Letter*, and *The Marble Faun* incorporates the fragmentary Miriam, Donatello, Hilda, Kenyon and even the Model. In each book, the figures interact with one another in paired groups that suggest either fragments of the same kind of psychic elements, such as the two Henrys in *Nature and Art*, or fragments of opposed psychic elements, such as Donatello and the Model in *The Marble Faun*. In each case, however, even when the characters seem completely opposed to one another in ideological terms, they participate together as fragments of one encompassing psyche as depicted symbolically in each book, for the relationships among them are too complicated to separate cleanly from one another. Indeed, each of the characters exhibits multiple symbolic correspondences to reflect the complexity of Inchbald's and Hawthorne's concerns and to suggest the difficulties an artist encounters in deciding how he or she should write. The fragmentary figures, while allowing an examination of psychological motivation, provide Inchbald and Hawthorne with a means of portraying the fragmented Romantic psyche in a way that subverts the traditional conception of how characters should be developed in novels. The figures' one-sidedness is yet another of the methods used by the two authors as they developed their revolutionary Romantic moral romance sub-genre in parallel terms on opposite sides of the Atlantic Ocean.

CONCLUSION
'IMPRESSION[S] OF VERACITY': ECHOES OF THE ROMANTIC MORAL ROMANCE IN THE MODERN, SYMBOLIC NOVEL[1]

When old age shall this generation waste,
Thou shalt remain ...

– John Keats[2]

In developing the Romantic moral romance sub-genre, Elizabeth Inchbald and Nathaniel Hawthorne attained divergent, yet intimately connected, goals. For Inchbald, the sub-genre offered a legitimate form of fiction for women writers – a form whose deceptive simplicity masked serious artistic work. For Hawthorne, the sub-genre offered an indigenous American literary tradition – a tradition based on European precedents but whose artistry encompassed uniquely American perspectives. While neither author declared absolute independence from the British novel tradition, both constructed fiction in parallel terms that challenged and expanded the existing conventions of the novel.

The introduction to this volume hints that the Romantic moral romance sub-genre anticipated and inflected the evolution of the modern, symbolic novel, especially through the influence of writers like Henry James. This conclusion briefly discusses the Romantic moral romance's afterlife in works like James's, but does not constitute a fully developed analysis of the connection. Rather, this conclusion is meant to hint at one of many possible permutations in the evolution of fiction and to suggest possible avenues for future scholarly research. Indeed, many other writers, both in Britain and America, experimented with fiction in ways that suggest philosophical connections with Inchbald's and Hawthorne's works. In Britain, other women writers who experimented with romance include, among many others, Charlotte Smith, Maria Edgeworth, Ann Radcliffe, Mary Hays, Frances Burney and Susan Ferrier. In America, romances appeared from the likes of Herman Melville, James Fenimore Cooper, Edgar Allan Poe, Washington Irving and of course, Henry James.

In his biographical/critical essay on Hawthorne, James refers to Hawthorne as 'the most beautiful and most eminent representative of a literature' and as 'the most valuable example of the American genius'.[3] Moreover, James praised Hawthorne's books for demonstrating a concern with 'the deeper psychology'.[4] With such a high opinion of Hawthorne, James certainly borrowed some of Hawthorne's themes and patterns in constructing his own novels – novels that so profoundly changed American and British literature. As Tony Tanner comments,

> James's debt to Hawthorne did not diminish with the years: in matters of subject, theme and even technique (particularly with regard to the symbolism in James's late work) the influence of Hawthorne is pervasive. It is quite arguable, indeed, that no other writer influenced James more.[5]

Indeed, in discussing the development of mediaeval romance, John Stevens notices connections with many newer 'works of prose fiction for which the title "novel" seems only partly appropriate: such works as Hawthorne's *The Marble Faun*, Conrad's *Youth*, *The Shadow-Line* and other tales; Melville's *Moby Dick*; Alain-Fournier's *Le Grand Meaulnes*; and Henry James's *The American*'.[6] Laurence Holland comments that 'James's immersion in the writings of Hawthorne is well known', and Malcolm Bradbury makes a similar claim.[7] T. S. Eliot also notices parallels among the works of Hawthorne and James, particularly in their character development, and he describes James's books as being, like Hawthorne's, primarily about the interactions among characters.[8] Through Hawthorne's direct influence on later writers such as James (and perhaps Inchbald's indirect influence through the likes of Hawthorne), the Romantic moral romance sub-genre altered the developmental trajectory of the novel by expanding the genre to include more symbolically and psychologically motivated fiction.

A Final Definition of the Romantic Moral Romance

Chapter 2 provides a tentative definition of the Romantic moral romance sub-genre, and the discussion in the three subsequent chapters elaborates upon and modifies the definition. Before examining James's response to the alternative sub-genre, an enumeration of its characteristics is appropriate to summarize the results of the discussion.

Based on Inchbald's and Hawthorne's expressed intentions and on internal evidence from *A Simple Story*, *Nature and Art*, *The Scarlet Letter* and *The Marble Faun*, nine qualities characterize the Romantic moral romance. (1) Exemplary texts in the sub-genre of Romantic moral romance exhibit near-obsession with multiple forms of liminality. The texts themselves occupy the liminal space between chivalric romance and novel, and their plots and characters often mimic the liminality of the alternative sub-genre. (2) Employing the Romantic nature/

art dichotomy, the Romantic moral romance overtly privileges the simple innocence of nature but exhibits a sophisticated symbolic preoccupation with its own qualities as a form of art. Its self-conscious artistry legitimizes the romance as art. (3) Inchbald's and Hawthorne's sub-genre employs underdeveloped characters whose very simplicity and one-dimensionality cast them as fragmentary figures (often with dominating passions or a tendency to exhibit strong wilfulness), rather than fully developed, realistic people. The figures' simplicity is calculated to enhance their symbolic potential and evoke the fragmented Romantic psyche. (4) The Romantic moral romance examines psychological motivation by juxtaposing its fragmentary figures and scrutinizing the figures' interactions with one another. Consequently, the figures may represent, collectively, individual impulses within a single psyche, and the author's concern may lie, not with the actions of a single character, but with the *interactions* among all of the figures. (5) The narrative structure of the Romantic moral romance embraces a fable-like simplicity because of the genre's connection with dramatic precedent and with the precedents of chivalric romance, French moral tale, fable, legend and even biblical parable. The romance thus acquires a quasi-allegorical nature. (6) The genre employs symbolism to contribute to a definite moral purpose behind the story, a purpose that may operate on multiple levels. The romance may appear to support the established moral order but may simultaneously challenge that order and suggest revolutionary alternatives to it in social, political, economic or individual terms. (7) The Romantic moral romance possesses a narrative structure that is tightly controlled and carefully constructed so that it supports authorial intentions by keeping readers aware of the self-consciously symbolic nature of the text. The carefully crafted structure of the romance exhibits the same balance and control found in such drama as that of William Shakespeare. (8) Inchbald's and Hawthorne's alternate sub-genre often examines the darker aspects of human existence, and in quasi-allegorical terms, the characters and events may symbolize contemporary concerns – including the nature of literary art itself – even when they may be associated with the distant past. (9) Finally, the Romantic moral romance exhibits an authorial willingness to revise conceptions of reality – to mould a story's basis into something between the actual and the imaginary as a better way of portraying 'truth'. Ultimately, the pursuit of 'truth', particularly on the individual level, is the goal of the Romantic moral romance.

These nine characteristics, like those of any sub-genre, overlap with the characteristics of other genres and sub-genres, but it is the unique combination of these traits that distinguishes the Romantic moral romance. The same unique combination situates Inchbald's work squarely within British Romanticism and Hawthorne's within American versions of Romantic thought. In developing the Romantic moral romance, Inchbald and Hawthorne were able to write fiction that represented a significant departure from the traditional form of the British novel but that simultaneously borrowed from that tradition to lend legitimacy to itself.

The Effects of the Sub-Genre on the Modern Novel

Although Henry James did not appreciate the romance form as much as that of the novel, he attempted to define romance in relation to the novel tradition, and his definition may have furthered the influence of the Romantic moral romance on the modern novel form. In his preface to *The American,* James examines romance and attempts to defend it as a viable genre, particularly against the modern novel. Instead of opposing novel and romance as so many previous critics have done, however, James classifies the romance as 'one legitimate type of the novel' and contrasts romance and realism as two modes of novel writing.[9] As William Goetz explains James's conception, 'In realism, the imagination is still anchored to the ground, to the relations of experience, while in romance it is liberated, completely on its own'.[10] James himself comments, in his struggles to define romance,

> The only *general* attribute of projected romance that I can see, the only one that fits all its cases, is the fact of the kind of experience with which it deals – experience liberated, so to speak; experience disengaged, disembroiled, disencumbered, exempt from the conditions that we usually know to attach to it.[11]

In short, James viewed romance as a genre that was not closely related to reality. As Michael Davitt Bell comments, 'For James [...] the essence of romance lies in its moral irresponsibility, its severing of those connections or "relations" between imagination and actuality that characterize the mode for Hawthorne'.[12] However, because he classified the romance as a form of the novel, James helped effect an expansion of the novel genre with Romantic moral romances like Hawthorne's. Indeed, Armin Frank argues that James drew heavily on Hawthorne's romances for *The American,* while T. J. Lustig makes a similar argument for *The Europeans.*[13] Emily Budick suggests that *The Marble Faun* provided 'the very foundations for such novels as Henry James's *Daisy Miller* and *The Portrait of a Lady*'.[14] Harry Levin notices many parallels between the works of Hawthorne and James; he goes so far as to note of *The Scarlet Letter* that '[w]hen we read, in its concluding pages, that she [Pearl] grew up an heiress and traveled abroad, we realize that we can pursue her further adventures through the novels of Henry James'.[15] J. Freedman similarly connects Hawthorne and James to say that 'Hawthorne is everywhere in James' and that 'James does unto his precursor what great writers do to their predecessors – steal'.[16] In the hands of James and other writers, the more traditional novel acquired some of the characteristics of the Romantic moral romance sub-genre, particularly its reliance on symbolism and psychology and its preoccupation with the nature of fiction as art.

Although James did not write about Inchbald and may never have encountered her works, he had the opportunity to read her fictions, and he was very familiar with Hawthorne's works. In reading Hawthorne's fictions, James recognized several of the Romantic moral romance's characteristics. Indeed, he objected to some of the characteristics, and his efforts to avoid them in his own writing helped to mould the nature of the modern novel. James admires *The Scarlet Letter*, but the faults that he detects are some of the qualities that make the book so unique, particularly as an example of the Romantic moral romance. His first concern is the book's lack of realism, which is compounded by, in his view, excessive symbolism and the use of fragmentary figures. James comments,

> The faults of the book are, to my sense, a want of reality and an abuse of the fanciful element – of a certain superficial symbolism. The people strike me not as characters, but as representatives, very picturesquely arranged, of a single state of mind; and the interest of the story lies, not in them, but in the situation, which is insistently kept before us, with little progression, though with a great deal, as I have said, of a certain stable variation; and to which they, out of their reality, contribute little that helps it to live and move.[17]

As Richard Poirier comments in a discussion of James's early fiction, 'Precisely because his mind was saturated with ideas, James feared lest he used characters merely as illustrations of them. In this we find the central dilemma of the early novels'.[18]

James detects similar flaws, from his point of view, in *The Marble Faun*. He comments, 'The fault of *Transformation* [*The Marble Faun*] is that the element of the unreal is pushed too far, and that the book is neither positively of one category nor of another'.[19] Again, his first concern is the realism of the tale, and with *The Marble Faun*, he also realizes the liminal nature of Hawthorne's experiment. Reacting against what he viewed as flaws in the Romantic moral romance, James constructed his novels to be more realistic representations of reality. As Richard Chase notes, James claims in 'The Art of Fiction' of 1884 that 'the novel should give the same impression of veracity as does history itself'.[20] Chase contends that, because of James's influence, the current era is one in which 'all the imaginative dimensions of the novel begin on the operational base of realism'.[21] Essentially, then, writers like Inchbald and Hawthorne significantly shaped the evolution of the modern novel since the rise in the importance of realism in the novel is a logical progression from – or, perhaps, a reaction against – fiction like the Romantic moral romance. In a discussion of American varieties of the romance as nationalist literature, Michael Davitt Bell suggests,

If national romance grew out of native materials, it was no longer primarily the product of the author's 'over-heated imagination.' For all its overtones of imaginative coloring and sentiment, the theory of conservative romance, based on associationist aesthetics and ultimately on American 'reality,' was finally a theory of realism, of rational mimesis.[22]

Despite these critics' emphases on the importance of realism in the novel, modern exempla of the genre, including James's own works, certainly developed the novel's symbolic potential to sophisticated levels. Indeed, James and other writers drew heavily on Anglo-European sources to nurture their own art. The importance of James's connection with European literature is clear in Dorothea Krook's statement that 'it is out of [an] interaction of the American mind with the European that James's grand theme is born – the so-called international theme.'[23] Krook is interested primarily in the plots of James's novels as being international in theme rather than in style, but the transatlantic nature of those plots mirrors the tandem cultural influence of American and Anglo-European literature on James.[24] Indeed, Patrick Parrinder points out that James 'hoped his readers would be unable to tell whether he was an American writing about England or an Englishman writing about America', and James himself, in 'The Art of Fiction', makes reference to 'the English novel (by which of course I mean the American as well)'.[25]

Goethe's work, in particular, inflected James's experimentation with fiction. In an article on Goethe and Henry James, Judith Ryan contends, convincingly, that *Elective Affinities* 'underlies *The Golden Bowl*'.[26] She notes that Goethe's book focuses on a 'set of four characters' in the same way that James's novel does, and, interestingly, in the same way that Inchbald's and Hawthorne's books do.[27] The characters mirror one another as fragmentary elements in the vein of Inchbald's and Hawthorne's fragmentary figures, and they similarly assume symbolic meaning as part of Goethe's experimental writing. James was 'competent in German and familiar with the works of Goethe'.[28] Indeed, he had read *Elective Affinities* and considered it 'as much a part of the German experience as his early morning walks' during his 1860 stay in Bonn, according to Ryan.[29] Given the parallels between Goethe's *Elective Affinities* and the works of Inchbald and Hawthorne, Goethe's example must have given a certain legitimacy to the Romantic moral romance in James's estimation. Goethe's influence gave James yet another reason to adopt some of the characteristics of the Romantic moral romance for his novels.

Although James resisted the symbolic potential of the romance and favoured an approach to writing grounded in realism, later conceptions of the novel fused the rift that James had posited between romance and realism. In fact, the rift fused so well that in 1996, Doody argued in *The True Story of the Novel* that there is no distinction between novel and romance.[30] In her own words, 'Romance and the Novel are one'.[31] Ultimately, the modern novel embraced the focus on symbolism that had emerged from the Romantic Period and, specifically, from the work of such writers as Inchbald and Hawthorne. Indeed, Frank Kermode suggests that the modern symbol is 'the Romantic Image writ large;' and the Romantic moral romance played a significant role in the development of modern fiction.[32] According to some scholars, Romantic and modern – or more precisely, *Modernist* – fiction are but differing aspects of the same movement and should not be separated. Discussing Howard Mumford Jones's *Revolution and Romanticism*, and specifically the difficulties in defining Romanticism, Peter Conrad comments, 'Because it is still happening, romanticism has not yet been satisfactorily defined'.[33] F. X. Shea's statement is more pointed: 'Romanticism [...] is more properly called modernism'.[34] The genre developed by Inchbald and Hawthorne deflected the evolution of the novel into a more symbolic and more psychologically motivated field of inquiry. The Romantic moral romance thus provides a vital connection between earlier Anglo-European conceptions of the novel, especially in the late eighteenth and mid-nineteenth centuries, and later American and British definitions as writers like James developed the novel in English through the latter half of the nineteenth century and into the twentieth.

EDITORIAL NOTES

Introduction: The Romantic Moral Romance: an Alternative Transatlantic Sub-Genre for Elizabeth Inchbald and Nathaniel Hawthorne

1. M. Edgeworth, 'Advertisement', in M. Edgeworth, *Belinda,* ed. K. J. Kirkpatrick (London: Oxford, 1994), p. 3.

2. Unless otherwise noted, all citations from the four books come from E. Inchbald, *A Simple Story* (1791; Oxford: Oxford University Press, 1998), hereafter *SS*; E. Inchbald, *Nature and Art* (1796; Oxford and New York: Woodstock Books, 1994), hereafter *N&A*; N. Hawthorne, *The Scarlet Letter: A Romance,* in *The Centenary Edition of the Works of Nathaniel Hawthorne,* ed. W. Charvat, *et al.,* vol. 1 (1850; Columbus, OH: Ohio State University Press, 1962), hereafter *SL*; and N. Hawthorne, *The Marble Faun, or The Romance of Monte Beni,* in *The Centenary Edition of the Works of Nathaniel Hawthorne,* ed. W. Charvat, *et al.,* vol. 4 (1860; Columbus, OH: Ohio State University Press, 1968), hereafter *MF.* Older editions of the Inchbald books have been used rather than the newer (and well edited) Broadview editions because they reprint the first editions of the books. As for Hawthorne's books, the *Centenary Edition,* despite its age, is still considered the standard.

3. Larry Reynolds argues that since the publication of *The Scarlet Letter,* 'Hawthorne has continued to occupy a central place in the American literary canon' ('Introduction', in L. J. Reynolds (ed.), *A Historical Guide to Nathaniel Hawthorne* (Oxford: Oxford University Press, 2001), p. 3).

4. In discussing the French novel's development, English Showalter Jr notes that '[t]he novel tends to be believable, to deal with ordinary people in familiar settings, to be contemporary or nearly so to show how things really are. The romance tends to appeal to the imagination, to deal with archetypal or allegorical or idealized characters, to show them in remote settings, to show how things might be' (*The Evolution of the French Novel, 1641–1782* (Princeton, NJ: Princeton University Press, 1972), pp. 3–4).

5. John Stevens mentions Coleridge and Keats specifically in the introduction to his *Medieval Romance: Themes and Approaches,* and he also refers to Hawthorne's *The Marble Faun* as a romance ((London: Hutchinson University Library, 1973), pp. 15–16). For recent treatments of Romantic poets' use of romance, see M. O'Neill, 'Poetry of the Romantic Period: Coleridge and Keats', in C. Saunders (ed.), *A Companion to Romance: From Classical to Contemporary* (Malden, MA: Blackwell, 2004), pp. 305–20; J. N. Cox, '*Lamia, Isabella* and *The Eve of St Agnes*: Eros and "Romance"', in S. J. Wolfson (ed.), *The Cam-*

bridge Companion to Keats (Cambridge: Cambridge University Press, 2001), pp. 53–68; A. Stauffer, 'The Hero in the Harem: Byron's Debt to Medieval Romance in *Don Juan* VI', *European Romantic Review*, 10:1 (1999), pp. 84–97.

6.   A. Shealy, 'Romance', in, R. T. Lambdin and L. C. Lambdin (eds), *Encyclopedia of Medieval Literature* (Westport, CT: Greenwood Press, 2000), pp. 442–3. A. B. Taylor refers to the romance as a 'literature of feudalism [which] … was the practical basis of chivalry' (*An Introduction to Medieval Romance* (London: Heath Cranton, 1930), p. 254).

7.   N. Frye, *The Anatomy of Criticism: Four Essays* (Princeton, NJ: Princeton University Press, 1957), p. 304. Frye discusses the characteristics of romance extensively.

8.   John Bunyan's *The Pilgrim's Progress*, for example, presents an allegory of this kind of Christian typology (ed. W. R. Owens (Oxford: Oxford University Press, 2003)). Of Hawthorne's romances, Magnus Ullén argues that Hawthorne uses allegory rather than mere symbolism to explore the liminal region between art and mimesis ('Reading with "The Eye of Faith": The Structural Principle of Hawthorne's Romances', *Texas Studies in Literature and Language*, 48 (2006), pp. 1–36).

9.   Frye, *The Anatomy of Criticism*, p. 305; J. Labbe, *The Romantic Paradox: Love, Violence and the Uses of Romance, 1760–1830* (New York: St Martin's Press, 2000), pp. 33–4.

10.   R. L. Krueger, 'Introduction', in R. L. Krueger (ed.), *The Cambridge Companion to Medieval Romance*, (Cambridge: Cambridge University Press, 2000), p. 1.

11.   Biographer James Boaden refers rather casually to *A Simple Story* as a romance (*Memoirs of Mrs Inchbald*, 2 vols (London: Richard Bentley, 1833), vol. 1, p. 290, hereafter *Memoirs*), and Margaret Drabble's *Oxford Companion to English Literature* does the same ('Inchbald, Mrs Elizabeth', in M. Drabble (ed.), *The Oxford Companion to English Literature*, 5th edn (Oxford: Oxford University Press, 1985), p. 493; 'Nature and Art', idem, p. 688; 'Simple Story, A', idem, p. 905). In terms of contemporary issues, Mary Wollstonecraft wrote in *A Vindication of the Rights of Men* of 1790, 'Whether the glory of Europe is set, I shall not now enquire; but probably the spirit of romance and chivalry is in the wane; and reason will gain by its extinction' (M. Wollstonecraft, *A Vindication of the Rights of Men / A Vindication of the Rights of Woman / An Historical and Moral View of the French Revolution*, ed. J. Todd (Oxford: Oxford University Press, 1993), p. 28).

12.   In recent years, transatlantic studies have assumed an important place in scholarship of the Romantic Period and beyond to show that Romanticism truly was a transatlantic and transnational phenomenon. Some of the better-known studies include B. Lease, *Anglo-American Encounters: England and the Rise of American Literature* (Cambridge: Cambridge University Press, 1981); R. Weisbuch, *Atlantic Double-Cross: American Literature and British Influence in the Age of Emerson* (Chicago, IL and London: University of Chicago Press, 1986); R. Gravil, *Romantic Dialogues: Anglo-American Continuities, 1776–1862* (New York: St Martin's Press, 2000); P. Giles, *Transatlantic Insurrections: British Culture and the Formation of American Literature, 1730–1860* (Philadelphia, PA: University of Pennsylvania Press, 2001); and J. Cass and L. H. Peer (eds), *Romantic Border Crossings* (Aldershot: Ashgate, 2008).

13.   Stuart Curran examines the gendered quality of the novel genre in 'Women readers, Women Writers' in *The Cambridge Companion to British Romanticism* ((Cambridge: Cambridge University Press, 1993), pp. 177–95), as does Gary Kelly in 'Romantic fiction' in the same volume (idem, pp. 196–215). More detailed analyses can be found in J. M. S. Tompkins's *The Popular Novel in England, 1770–1800* (Lincoln, NE: University of Nebraska Press, 1961) and in Catherine Gallagher's *Nobody's Story: The Vanishing Acts*

of Women Writers in the Marketplace, 1670–1820 (Berkeley, CA: University of California Press, 1994).

14. Significantly, Krueger points out that romances or 'romans' were also 'sometimes called "contes" [tales] or "estoires" [stories/histories])' (Krueger, 'Introduction', p. 1).

15. See Emerson's lecture 'The American Scholar', for a well-known example of the expression of that cultural insecurity (reprinted in *The Collected Works of Ralph Waldo Emerson*, intro. and notes R. E. Spiller, ed. Alfred R. Ferguson, vol. 1: *Nature, Addresses, and Lectures* (Cambridge, MA: Belknap Press of Harvard University Press, 1971), pp. 49–70).

16. N. J. Lacy, 'The Evolution and Legacy of French Prose Romance', in R. L. Krueger (ed.), *The Cambridge Companion to Medieval Romance* (Cambridge: Cambridge University Press, 2000), p. 180.

17. See Jonathan Bate's *Shakespeare and the English Romantic Imagination* (Oxford: Clarendon Press, 1986) for an assessment of Shakespeare's influence on the Romantics. E. R. Wasserman's 'Shakespeare and the English Romantic Movement' (in H. M. Schueller (ed.), *The Persistence of Shakespeare Idolatry*, (Detroit, MI: Wayne State University Press, 1964), pp. 77–103) treats the same subject.

18. Stevens, *Medieval Romance*, p. 28; Krueger, 'Introduction', p. 6.

19. Rousseau's *Emile* of 1762, for example, privileges the noble savage (J.-J. Rousseau, *Emile*, trans. W. H. Payne (Amherst, NY: Prometheus Books, 2003)).

1. 'Written in a Style to Endure': Common Sources for the Romantic Moral Romance and the Impact of Inchbald's Transatlantic Reputation

1. L. Hunt, *The Autobiography of Leigh Hunt*, ed. J. E. Morpurgo (London: Cresset Press, 1948), p. 26.

2. C. Lennox, *Euphemia* (Cadell, 1790; Delmar, NY: Scholars' Facsimiles & Reprints, 1989), vol. 2, p. 214.

3. William Harmon, for example, sites the beginning of the period at 1798 ('Romantic Period in English Literature', *A Handbook to Literature*, 10th edn (Upper Saddle River, NJ: Pearson, 2006), pp. 459–60).

4. See, for example, the series of articles in S. J. Wolfson (ed.), 'The Romantic Century: A Forum', *European Romantic Review*, 11:1 (2000), pp. 1–45.

5. A. K. Mellor and R. E. Matlak (eds), *British Literature, 1780–1830* (Boston, MA: Heinle & Heinle, 1996).

6. N. Frye, S. Baker and G. Perkins, *The Harper Handbook to Literature* (New York: Harper & Row, 1985), p. 405; J. J. Smoot, 'Romantic Thought and Style in 19th-Century Realism and Naturalism', in G. Gillespie, M. Engel and B. Dieterle (eds), *Romantic Prose Fiction* (Amsterdam: John Benjamins, 2008), p. 583.

7. See, for example, S. C. Chew and R. D. Altick, *Book IV: The Nineteenth Century and After (1789–1939), A Literary History of England*, gen. ed. Albert C. Baugh, 2nd edn (1948; New York: Appleton-Century-Crofts, 1967), p. 1,122.

8. Frye, Baker and Perkins, *Harper Handbook to Literature*, pp. 403–5.

9. P. M. Spacks, *Privacy: Concealing the Eighteenth-Century Self* (Chicago, IL: University of Chicago Press, 2003), pp. 72–4. Margaret Drabble points out that novels of sentiment or sensibility focus on 'acute sensibility' and 'copious feeling' ('Sentiment, Sensibility, Novel of', *The Oxford Companion to English Literature*, p. 885).

10. Frye, Baker and Perkins, *Harper Handbook to Literature*, pp. 403–5.

11. Drabble (ed.), 'Romanticism', *The Oxford Companion to English Literature*, pp. 842–3.

12. J. D. Hart, 'Romanticism', *The Oxford Companion to American Literature*, 6th edn, rev. Phillip W. Leininger (New York: Oxford, 1995), pp. 572–3.

13. O'Neill, 'Poetry of the Romantic Period: Coleridge and Keats', p. 306.

14. J. B. St-Palaye, *Memoirs of Ancient Chivalry* (London: J. Dodsley, 1784).

15. J. Ritson (ed.), *Pieces of Ancient Popular Poetry* (London: C. Clarke for T. and J. Egerton, 1791), p. x.

16. H. Weber (ed.), *Metrical Romances of the Thirteenth, Fourteenth, and Fifteenth Centuries*, 3 vols (Edinburgh: Constable, et al., 1810), vol. 1, p. x; E. V. Utterson (ed.), *Select Pieces of Early Popular Poetry*, 2 vols (London: Longman, Hurst, Rees, Orme and Brown, 1817), vol. 1, p. xv.

17. W. J. Thomas (ed.), *A Collection of Early Prose Romances* (London: Pickering, 1828); G. Ellis (ed.), *Specimens of Early English Metrical Romances*, rev. by J. O. Halliwell (London: Henry Bohn, 1848; NY: AMS Press, 1968).

18. A. L. Barbauld, *On the Origin and Progress of Novel-Writing* (excerpts of introduction and prefaces from A. L. Barbauld (ed.), *The British Novelists*, 50 vols (London, 1810)).

19. L. J. Davis, *Factual Fictions: The Origins of the English Novel* (New York: Columbia University Press, 1983), pp. 25–6.

20. English Showalter refuses to classify novel and romance as separate categories, and so does Deborah Ross (Showalter, *The Evolution of the French Novel*, p. 4; D. Ross, *The Excellence of Falsehood: Romance, Realism, and Women's Contribution to the Novel* (Lexington, KY: University Press of Kentucky, 1991), pp. 10–14).

21. C. Reeve, *The Progress of Romance* (1785; New York: Facsimile Text Society, 1930), pp. v, x. See also L. C. Ramsey, *Chivalric Romances: Popular Literature in Medieval England* (Bloomington, IN: Indiana University Press, 1983), p. 3; L. Andries, *La Bibliothèque bleue au dix-huitième siècle: une tradition éditoriale*, Studies on Voltaire and the Eighteenth Century 270 (Oxford: Voltaire Foundation, 1989), pp. 9, 106; A. Martin, '"Les amours du bon vieux temps": medieval themes in French prose fiction, 1700–1750', in P. Damian-Grint (ed.), *Medievalism and manière gothique in Enlightenment France*, Studies on Voltaire and the Eighteenth Century, 2006:05 (Oxford: Voltaire Foundation, 2006), pp. 15–36; and L. Andries, 'La *Bibliothèque bleue* et la redécouverte des romans de chevalerie au dix-huitième siècle', in P. Damian-Grint (ed.), *Medievalism and manière gothique in Enlightenment France*, Studies on Voltaire and the Eighteenth Century, 2006:05 (Oxford: Voltaire Foundation, 2006), pp. 52–67.

22. Reeve, *The Progress of Romance*, p. 7.

23. Ibid., p. 8; P. Parrinder, *Nation & Novel: The English Novel from its Origins to the Present Day* (Oxford: Oxford University Press, 2006), p. 29. One of the earliest discussions of the novel and romance forms in English appears in the preface to William Congreve's *Incognita* ('The Preface to the Reader', in *Incognita; or, Love and Duty Reconcil'd*, ed. H. F. B. Brett-Smith (Oxford: Basil Blackwell, 1922), pp. 5–7).

24. C. A. Jewers, *Chivalric Fiction and the History of the Novel* (Gainesville, FL: University Press of Florida, 2000), pp. 4, 7; Parrinder, *Nation & Novel*, p. 29.

25. Inchbald's surviving diaries repeatedly mention her reading French, especially after her trip to France in 1776. As an actor, she was especially interested in plays but read fiction as well. She read works by and about Voltaire and was familiar with the likes of Corneille, Racine and Rousseau. In her diaries, she mentions reading Voltaire's letters as early as 1783, and in early 1788, she was reading Rousseau (E. Inchbald, *The Diaries of Elizabeth Inchbald*, 3 vols, ed. B. P. Robertson (London: Pickering & Chatto, 2007), vol. 2, pp.

172–3, 229, hereafter, *Diaries*). According to biographer James Mellow, Hawthorne likewise read 'Montaigne, Corneille, Racine, Voltaire, and Rousseau' (*Nathaniel Hawthorne in His Times* (Boston, MA: Houghton, 1980), p. 40, hereafter *NHHT*).

26. J. Dunkley, 'Medieval heroes in Enlightenment disguises: figures from Voltaire and Belloy', in P. Damian-Grint (ed.), *Medievalism and manière gothique in Enlightenment France*, Studies on Voltaire and the Eighteenth Century, 2006:05 (Oxford: Voltaire Foundation, 2006), pp. 160, 157, 164–76; Inchbald, *Diaries*, vol. 1, p. 96. Inchbald saw Belloy's *Zelmire*. She was familiar with his work also through Hannah More's adaptation of his *Gabrielle de Vergy* as *Percy* (Inchbald, *Diaries*, vol. 1, p. 319, vol. 2, p. 333).

27. Barbauld, *On the Origin and Progress of Novel-Writing*, p. 15. On the book's popularity, see J. Grieder, *Translations of French Sentimental Prose Fiction in Late Eighteenth-Century England: The History of a Literary Vogue* (Durham, NC: Duke University Press, 1975), p. 53; G. May, *Le Dilemme du Roman au XVIIIe Siècle* (New Haven, CT: Yale University Press; Paris: Presses Universitaires de France, 1963), p. 3; C. Dédéyan, *Jean-Jacques Rousseau et la Sensibilité Littéraire à la Fin du XVIIIe Siècle* (Paris: Société d'Edition d'Enseignement Supérieur, 1966); and R. C. Rosbottom, 'The Novel and Gender Difference', in D. Holier, et al. (eds), *A New History of French Literature* (Cambridge, MA: Harvard University Press, 1989), p. 481.

28. G. J. Barker-Benfield, *The Culture of Sensibility: Sex and Society in Eighteenth-Century Britain* (Chicago, IL: University of Chicago Press, 1992), p. 317.

29. B. Wineapple, *Hawthorne: A Life* (New York: Knopf, 2003), pp. 35, 40, 61, 181.

30. Mellow, *NHHT*, p. 40.

31. H. Fielding, *Joseph Andrews*, ed. S. Copley (London: Methuen, 1987), p. 15; Ross, *The Excellence of Falsehood*, pp. 94–5.

32. Mellow, *NHHT*, p. 40.

33. A. C. Gibbs, 'Introduction', *Middle English Romances* (London: Edward Arnold, 1966), p. 26.

34. Mellow, *NHHT*, p. 21.

35. E. Zimmerman, 'A Puritan Yankee in King Arthur's Court: Deconstructing Hawthorne's Myth America' (PhD dissertation, Claremont Graduate University, 1998).

36. N. Hawthorne, 'The Antique Ring', in *Centenary Edition*, vol. 11, p. 338.

37. A. Lupack and B. T. Lupack, *King Arthur in America* (Woodbridge: D. S. Brewer, 1999), p. xi.

38. Parrinder, *Nation & Novel*, p. 5.

39. Ibid., p. 343. See also D. Pearsall, *Arthurian Romance: A Short Introduction* (Malden, MA: Blackwell, 2003); R. Hurd, 'Letters on Chivalry and Romance', *Moral and Political Dialogues; with Letters on Chivalry and Romance*, 5th edn, 3 vols (London: T. Cadell, 1776), vol. 3, pp. 187–338; and, for chivalric influences from France, W. H. French and C. B. Hale (eds), 'Introduction', *Middle English Metrical Romances*, 2 vols (1930; New York: Russell & Russell, 1964), pp. 1–22. For discussions of the importance of the mediaeval chivalric romance and its later transformations, see, for example, J. C. Isbell, 'Romantic Novel and Verse Romance, 1750–1850: Is There a Romance Continuum?', in G. Gillespie, M. Engel and B. Dieterle (eds), *Romantic Prose Fiction* (Amsterdam: John Benjamins, 2008), pp. 496–516; B. Fuchs, *Romance* (New York: Routledge, 2004); and H. Cooper, *The English Romance in Time: Transforming Motifs from Geoffrey of Monmouth to the Death of Shakespeare* (Oxford: Oxford University Press, 2004).

40. Frye, *The Anatomy of Criticism*, p. 304.

41. St-Palaye, *Memoirs of Ancient Chivalry*, p. 312; Cooper, *The English Romance in Time*, p. 10. Neither Inchbald nor Hawthorne was a stranger to symbolically and allegorically constructed tales. John Bunyan's *Pilgrim's Progress* was one of Hawthorne's favourite books, and both he and Inchbald read Milton and Dante (Mellow, *NHHT*, pp. 21, 355, 217). Inchbald read *Paradise Lost* in the summer of 1783 but – apparently – did not read Dante until 1820 (Inchbald, *Diaries*, vol. 2, p. 163, 170, vol. 3, p. 292).

42. Frye, *The Anatomy of Criticism*, 305; Labbe, *The Romantic Paradox*, pp. 33–4; Krueger, 'Introduction', p. 1.

43. A. Kettle, *An Introduction to the English Novel*, 2 vols (London: Hutchinson's University Library, 1951), vol. 1, pp. 21, 45.

44. P. M. Spacks, *Novel Beginnings: Experiments in Eighteenth-Century English Fiction* (New Haven, CT: Yale University Press, 2006), p. 16; F. O. Matthiessen, *American Renaissance: Art and Expression in the Age of Emerson and Whitman* (London: Oxford University Press, 1968), pp. 243–4.

45. R. Stanton, 'Hawthorne, Bunyan, and the American Romances', *Publications of the Modern Language Association*, 71 (1956), pp. 155–65.

46. T. G. Tucker, *The Foreign Debt of English Literature* (London: George Bell, 1907), pp. 137–8.

47. A. H. Upham, *The French Influence in English Literature: From the Accession of Elizabeth to the Restoration* (New York: Columbia University Press, 1911).

48. P. Morillot, 'Le Roman', in L. P. de Julleville (ed.), *Histoire de la Langue et de la Littérature Française des Origines à 1900*, 8 vols (Paris: Librairie Armand Colin, 1909), vol. 6, p. 474.

49. W. Calin, *The French Tradition and the Literature of Medieval England* (Toronto, ON: University of Toronto Press, 1994); F. Ogée, "Amicable Collision": Some Thoughts on the Reality of Intellectual Exchange between Britain and France in the Enlightenment', in F. Ogée (ed.), *'Better in France?': The Circulation of Ideas Across the Channel in the Eighteenth Century* (Lewisburg, PA: Bucknell University Press, 2005), pp. 13–34.

50. P. Mortensen, 'The Englishness of the English Gothic Novel: Romance Writing in an Age of Europhobia', idem, pp. 269–89.

51. Ibid., p. 271.

52. J. Todd, *Women's Friendship in Literature* (New York: Columbia University Press, 1980), p. 5. For other influences across the English Channel, see M. Cohen and C. Dever (eds), *The Literary Channel: The Inter-National Invention of the Novel* (Princeton, NJ: Princeton University Press, 2002) and C. Bode and F.-W. Neumann (eds), *British and European Romanticisms* (Trier, Germany: Wissenschaftlicher, 2007).

53. G. L. Strachey, 'Introduction', *A Simple Story* (London: Henry Frowde, 1908), pp. iv–v.

54. Ibid., p. iv.

55. T. Castle, *Masquerade and Civilization: The Carnivalesque in Eighteenth-Century English Culture and Fiction* (Stanford, CA: Stanford University Press, 1986), p. 300.

56. Ibid., pp. 300–1. See also P. Mortensen, 'Rousseau's English Daughters: Female Desire and Male Guardianship in British Romantic Fiction', *English Studies*, 83:4 (2002), pp. 356–70.

57. Boaden, *Memoirs*, vol. 1, p. 287.

58. J. Texte, 'Les Relations Littéraires de la France avec l'Étranger au XVIIIe Siècle', in L. P. de Julleville (ed.), *Histoire de la Langue et de la Littérature Française des Origines à 1900*, vol. 6: *Dix-huitième Siècle* (Paris: Librairie Armand Colin, 1909), p. 762); Chew and Altick, *Book IV: The Nineteenth Century and After*, p. 1,197 and J. B. Heidler, *The His-*

tory, from 1700 to 1800, of English Criticism of Prose Fiction, University of Illinois Studies in Language and Literature Series, 13:2 (Urbana, IL: University of Illinois Press, 1928), pp. 94–8.

59. Rosbottom, 'The Novel and Gender Difference', p. 482.
60. For excellent discussions of Héloïse and Abélard, see C. J. Mews, *Abelard and Heloise* (Oxford: Oxford University Press, 2005); *The Letters of Abelard and Heloise* (London: Penguin, 2003); J. Burge, *Heloise & Abelard: A New Biography* (New York: HarperCollins, 2003); and M. B. Shepard, 'A Tomb for Abelard and Heloise', *Romance Studies*, 25:1 (2007), pp. 29–42.
61. Castle, *Masquerade and Civilization*, p. 300.
62. Inchbald, *SS*, p. 22.
63. Ibid.
64. Inchbald, *Diaries*, vol. 1, pp. 136, 164, vol. 2, pp. 139, 229. Peter France points out that *Eloisa* was William Kenrick's translation in 1761 of *Julie, ou La Nouvelle Héloïse* and that it remained the only complete translation for two centuries thereafter, though in multiple editions ('Voltaire and Rousseau', in S. Gillespie and D. Hopkins (eds), *The Oxford History of Literary Translation in English: Volume 3: 1660–1790* (Oxford: Oxford University Press, 2005), pp. 387–8.
65. K. Astbury, *The Moral Tale in France and Germany, 1750–1789*, Studies on Voltaire and the Eighteenth Century, 2002:07 (Oxford: Voltaire Foundation, 2002), pp. 1–3; see also K. Astbury, 'Marmontel and Baculard d'Arnaud's (im)moral tales', in J. Mallinson (ed.), *History of Ideas / Travel Writing / History of the Book / Enlightenment and Antiquity*, Studies on Voltaire and the Eighteenth Century, 2005:01 (Oxford: Voltaire Foundation, 2005), pp. 39–51.
66. Grieder, *Translations of French Sentimental Prose Fiction in Late Eighteenth-Century England*, p. 55.
67. Astbury, *The Moral Tale in France and Germany*, pp. 12–13. See also P. van Tieghem, *Histoire de la Littérature Française* (Paris: Librairie Arthème Fayard, 1949), p. 255.
68. Astbury, *The Moral Tale in France and Germany*, p. 177.
69. Inchbald, *Diaries*, vol. 2, p. 119.
70. Ibid., vol. 3, pp. 64–5.
71. Kettle, *An Introduction to the English Novel*, vol. 1, p. 51. Kettle calls the moral fable 'a development of the allegory' that inculcates moral values (vol. 1, p. 21).
72. See F. Botting, *Gothic* (London and New York: Routledge, 1996), p. 2 and M. Praz, 'Introductory Essay', *Three Gothic Novels* (Harmondsworth: Penguin, 1968), p. 20.
73. J. P. Carson, 'Enlightenment, Popular Culture, and Gothic Fiction', in J. Richetti (ed.), *The Cambridge Companion to the Eighteenth-Century Novel* (Cambridge: Cambridge University Press, 1996), pp. 257–9.
74. See Spacks, *Novel Beginnings*, p. 191.
75. H. Walpole, 'Preface to the second edition of *The Castle of Otranto*', in I. Williams (ed.), *Novel and Romance, 1700–1800: A Documentary Record* (New York: Barnes & Noble, 1970), p. 266; R. Kiely, *The Romantic Novel in England* (Cambridge, MA: Harvard University Press, 1972), p. 5.
76. See A. Jenkins, *I'll Tell You What: The Life of Elizabeth Inchbald* (Lexington, KY: University Press of Kentucky, 2003), p. 259, hereafter *ITYW*, and P. Baines, 'Jephson, Robert (1736/7–1803)', in H. C. G. Matthew and B. Harrison, *Oxford Dictionary of National Biography* (Oxford: Oxford University Press, 2004), vol. 30, pp. 31–3, hereafter *ODNB*. Walpole even attended rehearsals during the play's initial run.

77. P. M. Spacks describes Lord Elmwood as exhibiting 'almost Gothic sadism' (*Desire and Truth: Functions of Plot in Eighteenth-Century English Novels* (Chicago, IL: University of Chicago Press, 1990), p. 199), while Terry Castle accuses him of 'psychic blackmail' (*Masquerade and Civilization*, p. 323).

78. Jenkins, *ITYW*, p. 292.

79. William St Clair discusses Inchbald's and Godwin's intellectual exchanges (*The Godwins and the Shelleys: The Biography of a Family* (New York: Norton, 1989), p. 149). Valerie Henitiuk sees *A Simple Story* as part of the 'gothic romance tradition' and recognizes Matilda's liminal role and the 'important feminist subtext' that surrounds the character ('To Be and Not To Be: The Bounded Body and Embodied Boundary in Inchbald's *A Simple Story*', in Cass and Peer (eds), *Romantic Border Crossings*, pp. 45–6).

80. Arlin Turner suggests that '[v]irtually all the methods and devices peculiar to the Gothic romancers reappear in Hawthorne's romances' ('Hawthorne's Literary Borrowings', *Publications of the Modern Language Association*, 51 (1938), p. 556), and F. S. Frank classifies both *A Scarlet Letter* and *The Marble Faun* as Gothic ('Nathaniel Hawthorne (1804–1864)', in D. H. Thomson, J. G. Voller and F. S. Frank (eds), *Gothic Writers: A Critical and Biographical Guide* (Westport, CT: Greenwood Press, 2002), pp. 165). See also W. Graham, *Gothic Elements in Nathaniel Hawthorne's Fiction* (Marburg, Germany: Tectum Verlag, 1999) and J. Lundblad, *Nathaniel Hawthorne and the Tradition of the Gothic Romance* (New York: Haskell House, 1964).

81. Mellow, *NHHT*, p. 41; R. Stewart, *Nathaniel Hawthorne: A Biography* (New Haven, CT: Yale University Press, 1948), p. 8; G. Handwerk and A. A. Markley, 'Introduction', *Caleb Williams* (Toronto, ON: Broadview, 2000), p. 39.

82. Frank, 'Nathaniel Hawthorne', p. 166.

83. Scholars have used the term in discussing the book, even though it never appears in the book itself. See, for example, L. S. Person, *The Cambridge Introduction to Nathaniel Hawthorne* (Cambridge: Cambridge University Press, 2007), p. 70, and S. B. Wright, *Critical Companion to Nathaniel Hawthorne: A Literary Reference to His Life and Work* (New York: Facts on File, 2007), p. 220.

84. Michael Dunne detects Gothic influences in *The Marble Faun*'s descriptions of the Model, of Roman Catholicism and of Miriam and Donatello's relationship ('"Tearing the Web Apart": Resisting Monological Interpretation in Hawthorne's *Marble Faun*', *South Atlantic Review* 69:3–4 (2004), pp. 23–50).

85. J. J. Irwin, *M. G. 'Monk' Lewis* (Boston, MA: Twayne, 1976), pp. 53, 56.

86. Annibel Jenkins notes that Inchbald knew everyone in the theatre and publishing worlds in London, regardless of whether they were friends (*ITYW*, pp. 3, 348). Hawthorne's love of the British Romantics is well documented. See R. H. Fogle, 'Nathaniel Hawthorne and the Great English Romantic Poets', *Keats-Shelley Journal*, 21–22 (1972–73), p. 220; P. R. Robertson, 'Shelley and Hawthorne: A Comparison of Imagery and Sensibility', *South Central Bulletin*, 32 (1972), p. 239; R. H. Fogle, 'The Great English Romantics in Hawthorne's Major Romances', *Nathaniel Hawthorne Journal*, 6 (1976), pp. 62–8; Matthiessen, *American Renaissance*, p. 203; J. Smith, 'Keats and Hawthorne: A Romantic Bloom in Rappaccini's Garden', *Emerson Society Quarterly*, 42 (1966), pp. 2–12; and J. Harris, 'Reflections of the Byronic Hero in Hawthorne's Fiction', *Nathaniel Hawthorne Journal*, 7 (1977), pp. 305–18.

87. St Clair, *The Godwins and the Shelleys*, pp. 37–8.

88. Ibid., 149.

89. Handwerk and Markley, 'Introduction', p. 9; St Clair, *The Godwins and the Shelleys*, p. 149. Jenkins comments that Godwin revised both *Political Justice* and *Caleb Williams* with a hope 'for a better exposition of "truth"' (*ITYW*, p. 364).

90. Handwerk and Markley, 'Introduction', p. 32.

91. St Clair, *The Godwins and the Shelleys*, p. 441; Inchbald, *Diaries*, vol. 3, p. 294.

92. J. Todd, *Mary Wollstonecraft: A Revolutionary Life* (New York: Columbia University Press, 2000), p. 182.

93. M. Wollstonecraft, *A Vindication of the Rights of Woman*, ed. M. Brody (London: Penguin, 1992), pp. 152, 81.

94. Indeed, Janet Todd points out that '[a]lmost all serious women writers wanted a more rational education for women' (*The Sign of Angellica: Women, Writing and Fiction, 1660 – 1800* (New York: Columbia University Press, 1989), p. 211).

95. Wollstonecraft, *A Vindication of the Rights of Woman*, pp. 167–8.

96. Inchbald, *N&A*, vol. 2, pp. 107–11. Hannah was renamed Agnes in the 1810 edition of the book; interestingly, one of the characters in Matthew Lewis's *The Monk* has the same name.

97. E. Inchbald, *Every One Has His Fault*, in *The Plays of Elizabeth Inchbald*, ed. P. R. Backscheider, 2 vols (New York: Garland, 1980), n.p.

98. W. McKee, *Elizabeth Inchbald: Novelist* (Washington, DC: Catholic University of America, 1935), pp. 16–17.

99. M. Shelley, 'Transformation', in M. Shelley, *The Mary Shelley Reader*, ed. B. T. Bennett and C. E. Robinson (New York: Oxford University Press, 1990), pp. 286–300. Interestingly, the British version of Hawthorne's *The Marble Faun* was entitled *Transformation*.

100. M. K. P. Thornburg, *The Monster in the Mirror: Gender and the Sentimental/Gothic Myth in Frankenstein* (Ann Arbor, MI: UMI Research Press, 1987), pp. 79, 85; C. Small, *Mary Shelley's Frankenstein* (Pittsburgh, PA: University of Pittsburgh Press, 1973), p. 122.

101. M. Shelley, *Frankenstein*, in P. Fairclough (ed.), *Three Gothic Novels* (London: Penguin, 1986), pp. 397, 495.

102. Victor's father calls his reading 'sad trash', and his university professor refers to the books as 'such nonsense' (Shelley, *Frankenstein*, pp. 298, 305, 394).

103. A. K. Henderson, *Romantic Identities: Varieties of Subjectivity, 1774–1830* (Cambridge: Cambridge University Press, 1996), p. 96.

104. S. Curran, *Shelley's Cenci: Scorpions Ringed with Fire* (Princeton, NJ: Princeton University Press, 1970), p. 62.

105. Ibid.

106. Belinda Jack argues that Hawthorne sees Beatrice as essentially sinless and that her story is about the 'clash between individual conscience and the mores of society' (*Beatrice's Spell: The Enduring Legend of Beatrice Cenci* (London: Chatto & Windus, 2004), p. 114). Jack refers to Hester as an Antinomian (Ibid., p. 108). See also C. M. Pages, 'Innocence and Violence: Two Sides of a Face: A Study of Miriam and Hilda in Relation to Beatrice Cenci in Nathaniel Hawthorne's *The Marble Faun*', in W. Wright and S. Kaplan (eds), *The Image of Violence in Literature, the Media, and Society* (Pueblo, CO: University of Southern Colorado, 1995), pp. 453–57.

107. James Boaden notes the oft-repeated anecdote that in an interview with James Dodd, the theatre manager made inappropriate advances, and Inchbald was 'so provoked as to snatch up a bason [*sic*] of hot water and dash it in his face' (*Memoirs*, vol. 1, p. 29). Also, see Jenkins, *ITYW*, p. 2.

108. See C. B. Hogan, *The London Stage, 1660–1800: A Calendar of Plays, Entertainments and Afterpieces together with Casts, Box-Receipts and Contemporary Comment, Part 5: 1776–1800*, 2 vols (Carbondale, IL: Southern Illinois University Press, 1968).

109. Inchbald, *Diaries*, vol. 1, pp. xxviii, 122.

110. R. Manvell, *Elizabeth Inchbald: England's Principal Woman Dramatist and Independent Woman of Letters in 18th-Century London* (Lanham, MD: University Press of America, 1987), p. 35.

111. Hogan, *The London Stage*. These numbers include nine 1791–2 performances of *Cross Partners*, a play attributed to Inchbald but also to Miss Griffiths, and two 1797–8 performances of *An Escape into Prison*, John Cartwright Cross's adaptation of Inchbald's *The Hue and Cry*.

112. St Clair, *The Godwins and the Shelleys*, p. 149.

113. See Boaden, *Memoirs*, vol. 1, p. 224, vol. 2, p. 10; P. Baines and E. Burns, 'Introduction', in P. Baines and E. Burns (eds), *Five Romantic Plays, 1768–1821* (Oxford: Oxford University Press, 2000), p. xxv; Hogan, *The London Stage*, vol. 2, p. 954.

114. S. R. Littlewood, *Elizabeth Inchbald and Her Circle: The Life Story of a Charming Woman (1753–1821)* (London: Daniel O'Connor, 1921), p. 134.

115. *British Museum General Catalogue of Printed Books to 1955*, compact edn (New York: Readex Microprint Corporation, 1967), vol. 12, pp. 1,132–3.

116. Manvell, *Elizabeth Inchbald*, pp. 206–7.

117. Ibid.

118. *British Museum General Catalogue of Printed Books to 1955*, vol. 12, p. 1,132–3; *The National Union Catalog, Pre-1956 Imprints*, 754 vols (London: Mansell, 1968–81), vol. 265, pp. 474–84; Manvell, *Elizabeth Inchbald*, p. 205; F. Moreux, 'Bibliographie Selective d'Elizabeth Inchbald, Auteur Dramatique et Romancière (1753–1821)', *Bulletin de la Société d'Etudes Anglo-Americaines des XVIIe et XVIIIe Siècles*, 13 (1981), pp. 81–105.

119. *British Museum General Catalogue of Printed Books to 1955*, vol. 12, pp. 1,132–3; *The National Union Catalog*, vol. 265, pp. 474–84; *Catalogue Général des Livres Imprimés de la Bibliothèque Nationale* (Paris: Imprimerie Nationale, 1929), pp. 878–9.

120. P. Sigl, 'Elizabeth Inchbald', in P. Backscheider (ed.), *Dictionary of Literary Biography*, vol. 89, *Restoration and Eighteenth-Century Dramatists*, 3rd ser. (Detroit, MI: Gale, 1989), p. 211.

121. *The National Union Catalog, Pre-1956 Imprints*, vol. 265, pp. 474–84.

122. Manvell, *Elizabeth Inchbald*, p. 127.

123. Hunt, The Autobiography of Leigh Hunt, pp. 47, 26.

124. Ibid.

125. G. Gordon, Lord Byron, *Byron's Letters and Journals*, ed. L. A. Marchand, vol. 3: 'Alas! the love of Women!' (Cambridge, MA: Harvard University Press, 1973), p. 236.

126. Weisbuch, *Atlantic Double-Cross*, p. 9; G. Playfair, *Kean: The Life and Paradox of the Great Actor* (London: Reinhardt & Evans, 1950), p. 197.

127. F. Mackinnon, 'Notes on the History of English Copyright', in Drabble (ed.), *The Oxford Companion to English Literature*, p. 1,123, and Wineapple, *Hawthorne: A Life*, p. 76. See also, W. St Clair, *The Reading Nation in the Romantic Period* (Cambridge: Cambridge University Press, 2004), pp. 374–93.

128. R. Michael, 'A History of the Professional Theatre in Boston from the Beginning to 1816', 2 vols (PhD dissertation, Radcliffe College, 1941), vol. 1, pp. 854–5.

129. Michael, 'A History of the Professional Theatre in Boston from the Beginning to 1816', vol. 1, pp. 854–5.

130. G. O. Seilhamer, *History of the American Theatre*, 3 vols (New York: Haskell House, 1969).

131. T. C. Pollock, *The Philadelphia Theatre in the Eighteenth Century* (Philadelphia, PA: University of Pennsylvania Press, 1933).

132. R. D. James, *Old Drury of Philadelphia: A History of the Philadelphia Stage, 1800–1835* (Philadelphia, PA: University of Pennsylvania Press, 1932); A. H. Wilson, *A History of the Philadelphia Theatre, 1835 to 1855* (Philadelphia, PA: University of Pennsylvania Press, 1935), pp. 548, 573, 613, 615, 617, 664, 668.

133. W. R. DuBois, *English and American Stage Productions: An Annotated Checklist of Prompt Books, 1800–1900* (Boston, MA: G. K. Hall, 1973).

134. P. M. Ryan, Jr, 'Young Hawthorne at the Salem Theatre', *Essex Institute Historical Collections*, 94 (1958), p. 243.

135. Ibid., p. 249.

136. Ibid., p. 244.

137. M. G. Hehr, 'Theatrical Life in Salem, 1783–1823', *Essex Institute Historical Collections*, 100 (1964), pp. 3–37.

138. Ryan, 'Young Hawthorne at the Salem Theatre', p. 244.

139. W. B. Durham (ed.), *American Theatre Companies, 1749–1887* (New York: Greenwood Press, 1986), pp. 446–50.

140. See also N. Smither, *A History of the English Theatre in New Orleans* (1944; New York: Benjamin Blom, 1967); Wilson, *A History of the Philadelphia Theatre*; M. S. Shockley, *The Richmond Stage, 1784–1812* (Charlottesville, VA: University Press of Virginia, 1977); G. C. D. Odell, *Annals of the New York Stage*, 15 vols (New York: Columbia University Press, 1927–49).

141. Stewart, *Nathaniel Hawthorne*, p. 8; Pat Ryan disagrees, suggesting that the company presented William Dunlap's adaptation (derived, in turn, from Anne Plumptre's English translation)' ('Young Hawthorne at the Salem Theatre', p. 246). Several versions of the play were available in addition to Inchbald's (see Shockley, *The Richmond Stage* (Charlottesville, VA: University Press of Virginia, 1977), p. 185).

142. For example, Paul Baines and Edward Burns cite Inchbald's contemporaries' shock 'at the forgiveness shown to Frederick's criminal tendency and the privileging of the desires of "a thoughtless young Miss"' in the play (Baines and Burns, 'Introduction', p. xxv).

143. J. Austen, *Mansfield Park*, in J. Austen, *The Complete Novels* (Oxford: Oxford University Press, 1994), pp. 580–9. See also A. Fleishman, *A Reading of Mansfield Park: An Essay in Critical Synthesis* (Minneapolis, MN: University of Minnesota Press, 1967), pp. 27–9; I. Armstrong, *Jane Austen*: Mansfield Park (London: Penguin, 1988), p. 59; S. M. Tave, 'Propriety and *Lovers' Vows*', in H. Bloom (ed.), *Jane Austen's* Mansfield Park (New York: Chelsea House, 1987), p. 39); and S. A. Ford, '"It Is about Lovers' Vows": Kotzebue, Inchbald, and the Players of Mansfield Park', *Persuasions On-Line*, 27:1 (2006), <http://www.jasna.org/persuasions/on-line/vol27no1/ford.htm>.

144. Fleishman, *A Reading of Mansfield Park*, p. 28.

145. *National Union Catalog*, vol. 265, pp. 474–84.

146. J. Dabney, *Additional Catalogue of Books, for Sale or Circulation, in Town or Country, at the Salem Bookstore* (Salem, MA: Osborne [for Dabney], 1794), p. 18, in C. K. Shipton (ed.), *Early American Imprints, 1639–1800* (Worcester, MA: American Antiquarian Society/Readex Microprint, [various dates]), microcard/microfilm, Evans #26,840, hereafter *EAI-1*.

147. *Catalogue of Plays, for Sale at the Bookstore of John West and Co.* (Boston, MA: n.p. [1810]), in American Antiquarian Society (ed.), *Early American Imprints, 1801–1819* (Series II) (New York and New Canaan, CT: Readex Microprint, [various dates]), microfilm, Shaw-Shoemaker #22,022, hereafter *EAI-2*.

148. *British Museum General Catalogue of Printed Books to 1955*, vol. 12, p. 1,133; *National Union Catalog*, vol. 265, pp. 474–84.

149. At the end of Volume 2 of *A Simple Story*, the marriage of Lord Elmwood and Miss Milner is sealed with a 'MOURNING RING' (Inchbald, *SS*, p. 193).

150. Mellow, *NHHT*, p. 41, and M. Van Doren, *Nathaniel Hawthorne* (New York: Viking, 1949), p. 31.

151. See G. G. Raddin, Jr, *An Early New York Library of Fiction: With a Checklist of the Fiction in H. Caritat's Circulating Library, No. 1 City Hotel, Broadway, New York, 1804* (New York: H. W. Wilson, 1940), p. 9, and C. K. Bolton, 'Circulating Libraries in Boston, 1765–1865', *Publications of the Colonial Society of Massachusetts*, 11 (1907), p. 196.

152. Raddin, *An Early New York Library of Fiction*, p. 9. For a more recent assessment of libraries in England, see D. Allan, *A Nation of Readers: The Lending Library in Georgian England* (London: British Library, 2008).

153. Raddin, *An Early New York Library of Fiction*, pp. 9–11.

154. Ibid.

155. Ibid.

156. Ibid., p. 71.

157. H. Caritat, *A New Explanatory Catalogue [of] H. Caritat's General & Increasing Circulating Library* (New York: Davis, 1799), p. 167, in Shipton, *EAI-1*, Evans #35,279.

158. *A Catalogue of the Baltimore Circulating Library* (Baltimore, MD: For W. Munday by John W. Butler, 1807), p. 71, in American Antiquarian Society, *EAI-2*, Shaw-Shoemaker #12,033; *A Catalogue of the Baltimore Circulating Library* (Baltimore, MD: For W. Munday by W. Warner, 1812), p. 28, in American Antiquarian Society, *EAI-2*, Shaw-Shoemaker #24,696.

159. H. Cushing, *Catalogue of Henry Cushing's Circulating Library: At the Sign of the Bible and Anchor* (Providence, RI: B. Wheeler, 1800), pp. 27, 32, in Shipton, *EAI-1*, Evans #38,341.

160. Bolton, 'Circulating Libraries in Boston', p. 196.

161. Ibid., pp. 205–6.

162. W. P. Blake, *Catalogue of W. P. & L. Blake's Circulating Library at the Boston Book-store* (Boston, MA: W. P. and L. Blake, 1800), pp. 29, 35, in Shipton, *EAI-1*, Evans #37,000.

163. *A Catalogue of Books [...] For Sale, Wholesale or Retail, at James White's Book and Stationary-Store [sic]* (Boston, MA: n.p., 1798), p. 21, in Shipton, *EAI-1*, Evans #33,215; *Catalogue of Books for Sale by E. Larkin* (Boston, MA: Larkin, 1798), pp. 33, 41, in Shipton, *EAI-1*, Evans #33,982.

164. *Catalogue of Books, Printed and Published in America, and for Sale at the Bookstore of David West* (Boston, MA: D. West, 1799), pp. 22, 27, in Shipton, *EAI-1*, Evans #36,701; *Catalogue of Books (American Editions) for Sale at the Bookstore of Thomas & Andrews* (Boston, MA: Thomas and Andrews, 1799), pp. 22, 27, in Shipton, *EAI-1*, Evans #36,416; *Catalogue of Books for Sale by E. and S. Larkin* (Boston, MA: E. & S. Larkin, [1802]), pp. 61, 65, in American Antiquarian Society, *EAI-2*, Shaw-Shoemaker #2,503; *A Catalogue of all the Books, Printed in the United States* (Boston, MA: Booksellers, [1804]), pp. 55, 61, in American Antiquarian Society, *EAI-2*, Shaw-Shoemaker #5,987.

165. *Fixed-Price Catalogue* (Boston, MA: J. Nancrede, [1803]), n.p., in American Antiquarian Society, *EAI-2*, Shaw-Shoemaker #2,722; *Catalogue of the Stock of Books of the Late Firm of Blake & West* (Boston, MA: n.p., [1815]), p. 13, in American Antiquarian Society, *EAI-2*, Shaw-Shoemaker #36,542.

166. *Catalogue of the Union Circulating Library* (Boston, MA: Munroe & Francis, 1806), pp. 36, 40, in American Antiquarian Society, *EAI-2*, Shaw-Shoemaker #11,491; *Catalogue of the Union Circulating Library* (Boston, MA: Samuel Avery [for W. Blagrove], 1810), pp. 32, 36, in American Antiquarian Society, *EAI-2*, Shaw-Shoemaker #21,547; *Catalogue of the Boston Union Circulating Library and Reading Room* (Boston, MA: [Parker], 1815), pp. 52, 57, in American Antiquarian Society, *EAI-2*, Shaw-Shoemaker #34,176; *Catalogue of Books, in the Boston Library. Nov. 1, 1807* (Boston, MA: Snelling & Simons, 1807), p. 18, in American Antiquarian Society, *EAI-2*, Shaw-Shoemaker #12,181; *Catalogue, No. 1, of Books, in the Boston Library, October 1, 1815* (Boston, MA: John Eliot, 1815), p. 32, in American Antiquarian Society, *EAI-2*, Shaw-Shoemaker #34,171.

167. *Catalogue of Books in the New Circulating Library* (Boston, MA: Bangs, 1815), pp. 40, 44, in American Antiquarian Society, *EAI-2*, Shaw-Shoemaker #35,911.

168. *Catalogue of the Washington Circulating Library* (Boston, MA: Bangs, 1817), pp. 42, 46, in American Antiquarian Society, *EAI-2*, Shaw-Shoemaker #42,831.

169. [C. K. Bolton], *The Boston Athenaeum, 1807 – 1927: A Sketch* ([Boston, MA: The Athenaeum, 1928]), [p. 2].

170. Mellow, *NHHT*, p. 161 and G. MacLeod, 'Nathaniel Hawthorne and the Boston Athenaeum', *Nathaniel Hawthorne Review*, 32:1 (2006), pp. 1–29.

171. *Catalogue of Books in the Boston Atheneum* [sic] (Boston, MA: W. L. Lewis, 1827), pp. 159, 222.

172. Dabney, *Additional Catalogue*, p. 18.

173. *Catalogue of Books for Sale or Circulation, in Town or Country, by John Dabney, at His Book and Stationary [sic] Store, and Circulating Library, in Salem* (Salem, MA: Dabney, 1801), in American Antiquarian Society, *EAI-2*, Shaw-Shoemaker #376; J. P. Saunders, *Valuable Catalogue of Books Being the Extensive Library Belonging to John Dabney, Esq.* (Salem, MA: Saunders, 1818), p. 42, in American Antiquarian Society, *EAI-2*, Shaw-Shoemaker #46,626.

174. *Catalogue of the Books Belonging to the Salem Athenaeum* (Salem, MA: T. Cushing, 1811), p. 60, in American Antiquarian Society, *EAI-2*, Shaw-Shoemaker #23,864; *Essex Circulating Library: Catalogue of Books, for Sale or Circulation, by Cushing & Appleton* (Salem, MA: T. Cushing, 1818), p. 45, in American Antiquarian Society, *EAI-2*, Shaw-Shoemaker #43,958.

175. *Catalogue, No. 1, of Books, in the Boston Library*, pp. 55–6.

176. *Catalogue of the Books Belonging to the Salem Athenaeum*, p. 39.

177. G. P. Lathrop, *A Study of Hawthorne* (New York: AMS Press, 1969), p. 340.

2. 'Fable-World[s]' Populated by 'Human Creatures': Toward a Definition of the Experimental Romantic Moral Romance

1. J. Wordsworth, 'Introduction', in E. Inchbald, *Nature & Art* (Oxford and New York: Woodstock Books, 1994), n.p.; Inchbald, *N&A*, vol. 1, p. 36.

2. Wollstonecraft, *A Vindication of the Rights of Woman*, p. 139.

3. Gallagher, *Nobody's Story*, pp. xv–xvi.

4. I. Watt, *The Rise of the Novel: Studies in Defoe, Richardson and Fielding* (Berkeley, CA: University of California Press, 1957); Tompkins, *The Popular Novel in England*.

5. M. McKeon, *The Origins of the English Novel, 1600–1740* (Baltimore, MD: Johns Hopkins University Press, 1987); M. McKeon, *Theory of the Novel: A Historical Approach* (Baltimore, MD: Johns Hopkins University Press, 2001).

6. As Tompkins comments, many writers emulated Richardson and Fielding in texts that amounted to 'mechanical imitations' (Tompkins, *The Popular Novel in England*, p. 37).

7. Gallagher, *Nobody's Story*, p. xvii.

8. Qtd. in Tompkins, *The Popular Novel in England*, p. 49.

9. Kelly, 'Romantic Fiction', p. 198, and V. Knox, 'On Novel Reading', in I. Williams (ed.), *Novel and Romance*, p. 304. For other discussions of the dangers of reading novels, see, for example, M. A. Doody, *The True Story of the Novel* (New Brunswick, NJ: Rutgers University Press, 1996), pp. 275, 285; A. W. Cafarelli, 'Rousseau and British Romanticism: Women and the Legacy of Male Radicalism', in G. Maertz (ed.), *Cultural Interactions in the Romantic Age: Critical Essays in Comparative Literature* (Albany, NY: State University of New York Press, 1998), p. 128; May, *Le Dilemme du Roman au XVIIIe Siècle*, p. 8; and items by S. Johnson, J. Beattie and others, on pp. 142–6, 150–9 and 309–27 of Williams (ed.), *Novel and Romance*.

10. See D. Spender, *Mothers of the Novel: 100 Good Women Writers before Jane Austen* (London: Pandora, 1986) and Curran, 'Women Readers, Women Writers', p. 179.

11. Male novelists also recognized this new freedom in the novel genre, for as Watt notes, Defoe and Richardson 'did not take their plots from mythology, history, legend or previous literature' (*The Rise of the Novel*, p. 14).

12. Curran, 'Women Readers, Women Writers', p. 180.

13. Ibid., p. 181.

14. J. Fergus and J. F. Thaddeus, 'Women, Publishers, and Money, 1790–1820', *Studies in Eighteenth-Century Culture*, 17 (1987), p. 191; Curran, 'Women Readers, Women Writers', pp. 181–2.

15. Gallagher, *Nobody's Story*, pp. xvii, 31–4. See also C. Gallagher, 'Nobody's Story: Gender, Property, and the Rise of the Novel', in M. Brown (ed.), *Eighteenth-Century Literary History: An MLQ Reader* (Durham, NC and London: Duke University Press, 1999), p. 31.

16. Kelly, 'Romantic Fiction', p. 202.

17. Curran, 'Women Readers, Women Writers', pp. 182–3.

18. Ibid., p. 179.

19. Ibid., p. 180.

20. Gallagher, *Nobody's Story*, p. xiii.

21. Tompkins, *The Popular Novel in England*, pp. 26, 3, 16.

22. L. A. Fiedler, *Love and Death in the American Novel*, rev. edn (New York: Stein and Day, 1966), p. 44. French authors had long been using their prefaces to deny writing novels, or *romans*, but English Showalter shrewdly notes that '[t]o deny that what follows is a *roman* is in part to promise that it will resemble a *roman*' (Showalter, *The Evolution of the French Novel*, pp. 17–18).

23. Inchbald herself commented, 'The Novelist is a free agent. He lives in a land of liberty, whilst the Dramatic Writer exists but under a despotic government' in the form of the theatre audience (['On the Novel'], in E. Inchbald, *Nature and Art*, ed. S. L. Maurer (London: Pickering & Chatto, 1997), p. 143).

24. J. M. Labbe suggests that 'the apparent need to distinguish between the romance and the novel, and curious inability to do so (manifested by repeated attempts to do so) well

into the nineteenth century, show that, far from being about to die out, the romance was continually resuscitated by critics who seemed anxious they might lose it. Clearly, the genre was viable and deeply significant' (*The Romantic Paradox*, p. 15).

25. F. Burney, 'Preface', *Evelina; or, The History of a Young Lady's Entrance into the World* (Oxford: Oxford University Press, 1998), p. 7.

26. Ibid., p. 8.

27. A. K. Mellor, *Romanticism & Gender* (New York & London: Routledge, 1993), p. 11.

28. Ibid., p. 9.

29. Patricia Spacks refers to Elmwood and Matilda as examining one another's 'behavior to ascertain emotional truth', while Janet Todd remarks that novels (and presumably romances as well) at the end of the eighteenth century tended to be 'psychologically "true"' (Spacks, *Novel Beginnings*, p. 177; Todd, *The Sign of Angellica*, p. 234). Likewise, Deborah Ross argues that many women writers 'used romance to assert the legitimacy of feminine "truth"' (Ross, *The Excellence of Falsehood*, p. 15). The passions were so much an interest during the Romantic Period that Joanna Baillie began a series of plays called *Plays on the Passions*, in each play of which her intention was to present 'the growth of one master passion; while what was dramatized were the often hidden psychological processes giving rise to passionate action' (N. Clarke, 'Baillie, Joanna (1762–1851)', *ODNB*).

30. See Mellow, *NHHT*, p. 427.

31. Robert Weisbuch comments, 'Simply to be alive and thinking in the American nineteenth century consigned one to a place in the struggle with British influence' (*Atlantic Double-Cross*, p. 275). See also S. S. Williams, 'Publishing an Emergent "American" Literature', in S. E. Casper, J. D. Chaison and J. Groves (eds), *Perspectives on American Book History: Artifacts and Commentary* (Amherst, MA: University of Massachusetts Press, 2002), pp. 165–94 and L. Buell, 'Hawthorne and the Problem of "American" Fiction: The Example of *The Scarlet Letter*', in M. Bell (ed.), *Hawthorne and the Real: Bicentennial Essays* (Columbus: Ohio State University Press, 2005), pp. 70–87.

32. J. E. Rocks, 'Hawthorne and France: In Search of American Literary Nationalism', *Tulane Studies in English*, 17 (1969), p. 145; Fiedler, *Love and Death in the American Novel*, p. 367.

33. H. Levin, *The Power of Blackness: Hawthorne, Poe, Melville* (New York: Knopf, 1958), p. 24. Larry J. Reynolds echoes the sentiment to say that, '[l]ike a number of his artistic contemporaries, such as James Fenimore Cooper, Longfellow, and Melville, Hawthorne felt the need to achieve American literary independence from England and to establish an indigenous literature worthy of comparison with the tradition of Shakespeare, Milton, and the immensely popular Sir Walter Scott' ('Introduction', p. 6).

34. N. Baym, 'Early Histories of American Literature: A Chapter in the Institution of New England', *American Literary History*, 1:3 (1989), p. 460.

35. Ibid., p. 460.

36. Ibid., p. 471. Interestingly, James Mellow notes that all five of the other authors attended Hawthorne's funeral (*NHHT*, p. 579).

37. J. K. Paulding, 'National Literature', in G. Hutner (ed.), *American Literature, American Culture* (New York: Oxford University Press, 1999), p. 25.

38. W. G. Simms, 'Americanism in Literature', in C. H. Holman (ed.), *Views and Reviews in American Literature, History, and Fiction*, 1st series (Cambridge, MA: Belknap Press of Harvard University Press, 1962), p. 7.

39. W. Whitman, 'Democratic Vistas', in W. Whitman, *Prose Works 1892: Collect and Other Prose*, ed. Floyd Stovall (New York: New York University Press, 1964), vol. 2, pp. 405, 411.

40. W. Whitman, 'American National Literature', *Complete Prose Works, Complete Poetry and Collected Prose* (New York: Library of America, 1982), p. 1,259.

41. G. Atherton, 'Why Is American Literature Bourgeois?', in G. Hutner (ed.), *American Literature, American Culture* (New York: Oxford University Press, 1999), p. 194.

42. Ibid., pp. 194, 200.

43. H. L. Mencken, 'The American Novel', in H. L. Mencken, *Prejudices: Fourth Series* (New York: Octagon Books, 1977), pp. 278–93.

44. Patricia Ann Carlson suggests that 'Forging a national consciousness through a mythological explanation of the American experience became on of the major goals of the native *belles-lettres*' during Hawthorne's lifetime ('National Typology and Hawthorne's Historical Allegory', *CEA Critic*, 37:1 (1974), p. 12).

45. Emerson, 'The American Scholar', vol. 1, pp. 52, 69.

46. R. W. Emerson, 'The Young American', in R. W. Emerson, *Essays and Lectures* (New York: Library of America, 1983), p. 228.

47. H. D. Thoreau, *Early Essays and Miscellanies*, ed. J. J. Moldenhauer and E. Moser, with A. C. Kern (Princeton, NJ: Princeton University Press, 1975), p. 40.

48. M. Fuller, 'American Literature', in M. Fuller, *The Writings of Margaret Fuller*, ed. M. Wade (Clifton, NJ: Augustus Kelley [by arrangement with Viking Press], 1973), pp. 374, 358.

49. H. Melville, 'Hawthorne and His Mosses', in H. Melville, *The Piazza Tales and Other Prose Pieces, 1839–1860*, ed. H. Hayford, A. A. MacDougall, G. T. Tanselle, *et al.* (Evanston and Chicago: Northwestern University Press and Newberry Library, 1987), vol. 9, pp. 247–8.

50. Mellow, *NHHT*, pp. 34, 80–1.

51. Ibid., pp. 331.

52. Miriam Wallace calls *A Simple Story* a 'particularly fruitful site to examine the development of Romanticism in prose rather than poetry, its connection to Jacobin social critique, and its significance for women's social position' ('Wit and Revolution: Cultural Resistance in Elizabeth Inchbald's *A Simple Story*', *European Romantic Review*, 12:1 (2001), p. 94). She also notices echoes of the romance in Inchbald's book (p. 98).

53. E. Inchbald, 'Preface', in E. Inchbald, *A Simple Story* (Oxford/New York: Oxford University Press, 1988), p. 1.

54. Ibid., p. 1.

55. Ibid., p. 2.

56. Tompkins, *The Popular Novel in England*, p. 116.

57. F. Burney, 'To the Queen', in F. Burney, *Camilla; or, A Picture of Youth*, ed. E. A. Bloom and L. D. Bloom (Oxford: Oxford University Press, 1983), p. 3.

58. Ibid.

59. M. Hays, 'Preface', in M. Hays, *Memoirs of Emma Courtney*, ed. E. Ty (Oxford: Oxford University Press, 1996), p. 4.

60. Ibid.

61. Edgeworth, 'Advertisement', p. 3.

62. Inchbald, 'Preface', in Inchbald, *A Simple Story*, p. 2.

63. Jenkins, *ITYW*, p. 348. See also J. R. Foster, *History of the Pre-Romantic Novel in England* (New York: Modern Language Association, 1949), p. 257.

64. Manvell, *Elizabeth Inchbald*, p. 109; J. M. Cauwels, 'A Critical Edition of *Nature and Art* (1796) by Elizabeth Inchbald (1753–1821)' (PhD dissertation, University of Virginia, 1976).

65. A. A. Markley, *Conversion and Reform in the British Novel in the 1790s: A Revolution of Opinions* (Basingstoke: Palgrave, 2008), p. 4. Markley shrewdly notices that, in true fable form, *Nature and Art* intends to reform its readers, not its characters (Ibid., p. 50).

66. Wordsworth, 'Introduction', in *N&A*.

67. Inchbald, *N&A*, vol. 1, p. 36.

68. Cauwels notes, quite simply, that 'Mrs Inchbald's character portrayal in *Nature and Art* seems one-sided' ('A Critical Edition of *Nature and Art*', p. 246).

69. Inchbald, *N&A*, vol. 1, pp. 119–20.

70. On the other hand, J. Paul Hunter points out that novels often were called histories because they were written about particular people and everyday events ('The Novel and Social/Cultural History', in J. Richetti (ed.), *The Cambridge Companion to the Eighteenth-Century Novel*, p. 9), while John Richetti notes that the terms *romance*, *history*, *true history* and *secret history* often were used interchangeably with that of novel ('Introduction', in J. Richetti (ed.), *The Cambridge Companion to the Eighteenth-Century Novel* (Cambridge: Cambridge University Press, 1996), p. 1).

71. Inchbald, *N&A*, vol. 1, pp. 138–9.

72. Inchbald, *N&A*, vol. 2, p. 192.

73. Biographer Annibel Jenkins echoes James Boaden's comment that Inchbald destroyed her memoirs on the advice of her confessor (Jenkins, *ITYW*, p. 4).

74. Roy Harvey Pearce summarizes Hawthorne's romance theory as 'a moral work; it must be humanly true; it deals with experience in the largest, even in exaggerated, terms' ('Hawthorne and the Twilight of Romance', *Yale Review*, 37 (1948), p. 489).

75. R. Chase, *The American Novel and Its Tradition* (Garden City, NY: Doubleday, 1957), p. 18.

76. Hawthorne, *SL*, p. 4.

77. Hawthorne, *SL*, pp. 9 – 10.

78. Hawthorne, *SL*, pp. 28, 31.

79. Hawthorne, *SL*, pp. 261–3.

80. Hawthorne, *SL*, p. 33.

81. Darrel Abel comments that Hawthorne 'was more concerned to record truthfully and vividly "states of mind" or "truths of the heart" than to paint "the actual scene"' ('"A More Imaginative Pleasure": Hawthorne on the Play of Imagination', *Emerson Society Quarterly*, 55 (1969), p. 65), and Kent Bales believes that Hawthorne seeks multiple truths, not a single one ('Hawthorne's Prefaces and Romantic Perspectivism', *Emerson Society Quarterly*, 23 (1977), p. 74). According to Jesse Bier, 'No one would seriously doubt that moral truth was a prime purpose in Hawthorne's whole career, least of all Hawthorne himself' ('Hawthorne on the Romance: His Prefaces Related and Examined', *Modern Philology*, 53 (1955), p. 22).

82. Hawthorne, *SL*, p. 35–6.

83. Ibid., p. 36.

84. Ibid., *SL*, p. 259.

85. Ibid., *SL*, p. 204.

86. N. Hawthorne, *The House of the Seven Gables*, in *Centenary Edition*, vol. 2, p. 1.

87. Ibid.

88. Ibid.

89. Ibid., pp. 2, 3; Hawthorne, *SL*, p. 43.
90. Hawthorne, *The House of the Seven Gables*, p. 2.
91. Ibid.
92. Ibid.
93. Ibid., p. 3.
94. N. Hawthorne, *Centenary Edition*, vol. 3, *The Blithedale Romance*, p. 1.
95. Ibid.
96. Ibid. Henry James objected to Hawthorne's deliberately simplified characters as being mere states of mind (Matthiessen, *American Renaissance*, p. 299).
97. Hawthorne, *The Blithedale Romance*, p. 1.
98. Ibid.
99. Ibid.
100. Ibid.
101. Ibid., p. 2.
102. Ibid.
103. Hawthorne, *MF*, pp. 1–4.
104. Ibid., p. 3.
105. Fuller, 'American Literature', p. 360.
106. V. W. Brooks, 'On Creating a Usable Past', in G. Hutner (ed.), *American Literature, American Culture* (New York: Oxford University Press, 1999), pp. 213–16.
107. F. O. Matthiessen admits that *The Scarlet Letter* 'grows most organically out of the interactions between the characters' (*American Renaissance*, p. 513). Both Malcolm Cowley and A. N. Kaul are more forgiving and emphasize the interaction among characters in the book ('Five Acts of *The Scarlet Letter*', in Charles Shapiro (ed.), *Twelve Original Essays on Great American Novels* (Detroit, MI: Wayne State University Press, 1958), p. 33; 'Character and Motive in *The Scarlet Letter*', *Critical Quarterly*, 10:4 (1968), p. 375). See also R. Stewart, 'Introduction, Chapter III: The Development of Character Types in Hawthorne's Fiction' in N. Hawthorne, *The American Notebooks*, ed. R. Stewart (New Haven, CT: Yale University Press, 1932), pp. xliv, xlvi.
108. Miriam Wallace contends that the first half of *A Simple Story* 'draws heavily upon dramatic dialogue', and while she is correct, in many cases, as Inchbald herself commented, the dialogue is less important than its dramatic presentation ('Wit and Revolution', p. 97). Emily Patterson describes the book as having 'nimble dialogue and intense drama, which reflect techniques that Mrs. Inchbald had acquired in the theater' ('Elizabeth Inchbald's Treatment of the Family and the Pilgrimage in *A Simple Story*', *Etudes anglaises*, 29 (1976), p. 196). Nora Nachumi notices typical stage gestures in the book, and Anna Lott suggests, 'In many ways, *A Simple Story* is Inchbald's attempt to merge two forms, the novel and the play' ('"Those Simple Signs": The Performance of Emotion in Elizabeth Inchbald's *A Simple Story*', *Eighteenth-Century Fiction*, 11:3 (1999), pp. 317–38; 'Introduction', in E. Inchbald, *A Simple Story*, ed. A. Lott (Peterborough, ON: Broadview Press, 2007), p. 33). For a different view, see D. Osland, 'Heart-Picking in *A Simple Story*', *Eighteenth-Century Fiction*, 16:1 (2003), pp. 79–101.
109. Qtd. in Manvell, *Elizabeth Inchbald*, p. 160. Around the same time, Anna Letitia Barbauld praised the 'dramatic form' of Inchbald's fictions and noted that the most interesting parts are 'carried on in dialogue' (*On the Origin and Progress of Novel-Writing*, n.p.).
110. Inchbald, *SS*, p. 15.

111. After reading over an early fragment of the book, William Godwin complained to Inchbald that 'the drama puts shackles upon you' (Boaden, *Memoirs*, vol. 2, p. 354). Even so, he loved the work.

112. Inchbald, *N&A*, vol. 1, pp. 60–1.

113. Annibel Jenkins refers to Lady Clementina as a 'stereotype' and likens all of the characters in *Nature and Art* to caricatures from popular prints of the time while noting that the book is full of 'dramatic touches' (*ITYW*, pp. 383–5, 373).

114. Inchbald, *N&A*, vol. 1, pp. 61, 63.

115. Ibid., vol. 1, p. 36.

116. F. O. Matthiessen suggests that 'Hawthorne built his important situations as pictures, or rather as tableaux, which were the closest the dramatic inexperience of his milieu could come to a scene' (*American Renaissance*, p. 300).

117. Malcolm Cowley writes a convincing article in which he argues that *The Scarlet Letter* can be divided into five acts like a drama ('Five Acts of *The Scarlet Letter*'). He comments, 'By accident or design he [Hawthorne] had invented a form that was closer to stage drama than it was to ordinary novels' (p. 23).

118. Hawthorne, *SL*, p. 49.

119. Ibid., p. 51.

120. Ibid., p. 62.

121. Matthiessen suggests that in writing about Miriam's mysterious sin, Hawthorne's 'interest was always in the psychological effect rather than in the deed itself' (*American Renaissance*, p. 352).

122. Hawthorne, *MF*, p. 157.

123. Ibid., p. 210.

124. Ibid., p. 451.

125. Qtd. in Manvell, *Elizabeth Inchbald*, p. 92.

126. G. Kelly, *The English Jacobin Novel, 1780–1805* (Oxford: Clarendon Press, 1976), p. 76.

127. Manvell, *Elizabeth Inchbald*, p. 92.

128. Inchbald, *SS*, p. 190.

129. Ibid., p. 202.

130. Ibid., p. 328.

131. Inchbald, *N&A*, vol. 2, pp. 15 – 19.

132. Ibid., vol. 2, p. 21.

133. Ibid., vol. 2, p. 26.

134. Ibid., vol. 2, p. 30.

135. Hawthorne, *SL*, p. 75.

136. Ibid., p. 137.

137. Hawthorne, *MF*, p. 79.

138. Ibid., p. 229.

139. Ibid., p. 260.

140. Inchbald, *SS*, p. 338. H.-S. Lee calls the ending 'ironic, ambiguous, and open' ('Women, Comedy, and *A Simple Story*', *Eighteenth-Century Fiction*, 20:2 (2008), p. 216).

141. Wollstonecraft, *A Vindication of the Rights of Woman*, p. 167.

142. Inchbald, *N&A*, vol. 2, p. 190.

143. N. Hawthorne, *The Centenary Edition*, vol. 3, *Fanshawe*, p. 333.

144. Hawthorne, *SL*, p. 9.

145. Ibid., pp. 108, 66, 82, 103.

146. Hawthorne, *The House of the Seven Gables*, pp. 5, 9. In fact, a literal house of seven gables stood – and still stands – in Salem. A photograph of the house is reprinted in R. S. Levine, 'Genealogical Fictions: Race in *The House of the Seven Gables* and *Pierre*', in J. L. Argersinger and L. S. Person (eds), *Hawthorne and Melville: Writing a Relationship* (Athens, GA: University of Georgia Press, 2008), pp. 227–47.

147. Hawthorne, *MF*, p. 266.

148. Ibid., p. 274.

149. Ibid., pp. 362, 367.

150. Ibid., p. 333.

151. Ibid., p. 63.

152. Ibid., p. 88.

153. Ibid., p. 422.

154. Ibid., p. 455.

155. Ibid., p. 463; Brooks, 'On Creating a Usable Past', pp. 213 – 16.

156. Hawthorne, *MF*, p. 320.

157. C. Wegelin, 'Europe in Hawthorne's Fiction', *Journal of English Literary History*, 14 (1947), pp. 219–45; C. K. Lohmann, 'The Agony of the English Romance', *Nathaniel Hawthorne Journal*, 2 (1972), pp. 219–29; D. B. Kesterson, '*The Marble Faun* as Transformation of Author and Age', *Nathaniel Hawthorne Journal*, 6 (1976), p. 67.

3. Adapting the 'Great Voicer of Truth': Shakespearean Liminality in the Romantic Moral Romance

1. Matthiessen, *American Renaissance*, p. 413.

2. W. Wordsworth, *The Prelude*, in W. Wordsworth, *Selected Poems*, ed. John O. Hayden (London: Penguin, 1994), p. 362.

3. William Hazlitt's 'On the English Novelists' provides a good example of the tendency in English literary circles to privilege such British male writers (in W. Hazlitt, *Lectures on the English Comic Writers and Fugitive Writings*, ed. A. Johnston (London: Everyman, 1963), p. 107). See also Watt, *The Rise of the Novel*; Tompkins, *The Popular Novel in England*; McKeon, *The Origins of the English Novel*; and McKeon, *Theory of the Novel*.

4. For example, see G. W. Knight, *The Crown of Life: Essays in Interpretation of Shakespeare's Final Plays* (London: Oxford University Press, 1947); F. Kermode, *Shakespeare: The Final Plays* (London: Longmans, Green & Co., 1963); S. Wells, 'Shakespeare and Romance', in J. R. Brown and B. Harris (eds), *Later Shakespeare* (New York: St Martin's Press, 1967), pp. 49–79; H. Smith, *Shakespeare's Romances: A Study of Some Ways of the Imagination* (San Marino, CA: Huntington Library, 1972), pp. 6, 20, 162; J. Hartwig, *Shakespeare's Tragicomic Vision* (Baton Rouge, LA: Louisiana State University Press, 1972); D. L. Peterson, *Time, Tide, and Tempest: A Study of Shakespeare's Romances* (San Marino, CA: Huntington Library, 1973); N. Sanders, 'An Overview of Critical Approaches to the Romances', in C. M. Kay and H. E. Jacobs (eds), *Shakespeare's Romances Reconsidered* (Lincoln, NE: University of Nebraska Press, 1978), pp. 1–10; B. A. Mowat, *The Dramaturgy of Shakespeare's Romances* (Athens, GA: University of Georgia Press, 1976); R. W. Uphaus, *Beyond Tragedy: Structure & Experience in Shakespeare's Romances* (Lexington, KY: University Press of Kentucky, 1981); S. Palfrey, *Late Shakespeare: A New World of Words* (Oxford: Clarendon Press, 1997); R. Dutton and J. E. Howard (eds), *A Companion to Shakespeare's Works, Volume IV: The Poems, Problem Comedies, Late Plays* (Malden,

MA: Blackwell, 2003); L. E. Maguire, *Studying Shakespeare: A Guide to the Plays* (Malden, MA: Blackwell, 2004); R. A. Rebholz, *Thirty-Seven Plays by Shakespeare: A Sense of the Corpus* (Lewiston, NY: Edwin Mellen Press, 2006); and C. J. Cobb, *The Staging of Romance in Late Shakespeare: Text and Theatrical Technique* (Newark, DE: University of Delaware Press, 2007).

5.   Boaden, *Memoirs*, vol. 1, pp. 1–18; Manvell, *Elizabeth Inchbald*, pp. 4–5; Littlewood, *Elizabeth Inchbald and Her Circle*, p. 5.

6.   Boaden, *Memoirs*, vol. 1, p. 7; Manvell, *Elizabeth Inchbald*, pp. 4–5.

7.   Annibel Jenkins notes Inchbald's work with the character of Cordelia in her biography of Inchbald (*ITYW*, p. 12).

8.   Manvell, *Elizabeth Inchbald*, p. 3. See also Littlewood, *Elizabeth Inchbald*, p. 13.

9.   Wasserman, 'Shakespeare and the English Romantic Movement', p. 79, and Bate, *Shakespeare and the English Romantic Imagination*, p. 3. See also J. Bate, 'The Romantic Stage', in J. Bate and R. Jackson (eds), *Shakespeare: An Illustrated Stage History* (Oxford: Oxford University Press, 1996), pp. 92–111, and J. Bate (ed.), *The Romantics on Shakespeare* (London: Penguin, 1992).

10. In her diaries, Inchbald also mentions attending 'Florizel & Perditta imitations' on 20 August 1783 (Inchbald, *Diaries*, vol. 2, p. 176). These likely were taken from David Garrick's adaptation of *The Winter's Tale*.

11. Ibid., vol. 1, p. 131.

12. J. M. S. Tompkins suggests that, for women writers of the Romantic Period in general, Shakespeare was seen as an ally in terms of his positive depictions of women (*The Popular Novel in England,* p. 145).

13. Manvell, *Elizabeth Inchbald*, p. 48.

14. Nora Nachumi notes that many writers of the Romantic Period, including Inchbald, were influenced by 'cross-fertilization' between fiction writing and drama, particularly those who had ties with the theatre ('"Those Simple Signs"', p. 318). See also E. H. Anderson, 'Revising Theatrical Conventions in *A Simple Story*: Elizabeth Inchbald's Ambiguous Performance', *Journal for Early Modern Cultural Studies*, 6:1 (2006), pp. 5–30.

15. See A. Warren, 'Hawthorne's Reading', *New England Quarterly*, 8:4 (1935), p. 482; Ryan, 'Young Hawthorne at the Salem Theatre', p. 243; Turner, 'Hawthorne's Literary Borrowings', p. 553; S. Bercovitch, 'Miriam as Shylock: An Echo from Shakespeare in Hawthorne's *Marble Faun*', *Forum for Modern Language Studies*, 5 (1969), p. 385; E. C. Jacobs, 'Shakespearean Borrowings in *The House of the Seven Gables*', *Nathaniel Hawthorne Journal*, 7 (1977), pp. 343–6; J. O. Rees, Jr, 'Shakespeare in *The Blithedale Romance*', *Emerson Society Quarterly*, 19 (1973), p. 84; H. D. Pearce, 'Hawthorne's Old Moodie: *The Blithedale Romance* and *Measure for Measure*', *South Atlantic Bulletin*, 38:4 (1973), pp. 11–15; W. E. Grant, 'Hawthorne's Hamlet: The Archetypal Structure of *The Blithedale Romance*', *Rocky Mountain Review of Language and Literature*, 31 (1977), pp. 1–15; and J. Kirkby, 'The American Prospero', *Southern Review*, 18:1 (1985), p. 90–108.

16. Matthiessen, *American Renaissance*, p. 413.

17. Letter to James T. Fields, [12] December 1870, cited by Randall Stewart, 'Recollections of Hawthorne by His Sister Elizabeth', *American Literature*, 16 (1945), p. 319, and quoted in Ryan, 'Young Hawthorne at the Salem Theatre', p. 243.

18. Mellow, *NHHT*, p. 38.

19. Mellow, *NHHT*, p. 21.

20. Hawthorne, *Centenary Edition*, vol. 15, *The Letters, 1813–1843*, p. 136.

21. C. H. Shattuck, *Shakespeare on the American Stage: From the Hallams to Edwin Booth* (Washington, DC: Folger Shakespeare Library, 1976), p. 37.
22. Rees, 'Shakespeare in *The Blithedale Romance*', p. 84.
23. Playfair, *Kean*, p. 206.
24. Lathrop, *A Study of Hawthorne*, p. 340; M. Kesselring argues that Lathrop may have mistaken the year ('Hawthorne's Reading, 1828–1850', *Bulletin of the New York Public Library*, 53:2 (1949), pp. 55–71, 121–38, 173–94).
25. Ibid., pp. 128, 184.
26. Mellow, *NHHT*, p. 238.
27. Jenkins, *ITYW*, p. 34.
28. B. Matthews and L. Hutton (eds), *The Kembles and Their Contemporaries* (Boston, MA: L. C. Page & Co., 1900), p. 32; According to Roger Manvell, Siddons was 'England's greatest actress in the 18th century' (*Elizabeth Inchbald*, pp. 9, 15).
29. Jenkins, *ITYW*, p. 32.
30. C. Woo, *Romantic Actors and Bardolatry: Performing Shakespeare from Garrick to Kean* (New York: Lang, 2008), p. 1.
31. Garrick's notoriety as the best actor of his time is well documented. See Manvell, *Elizabeth Inchbald*, pp. 9, 15; D. Bevington, 'Shakespeare in Performance', in W. Shakespeare, *The Complete Works of Shakespeare*, updated 4th edn, ed. D. Bevington (New York: Longman, 1997), p. A–63; and C. H. Shattuck, 'Shakespeare's Plays in Performance from 1660 to the Present', in W. Shakespeare, *The Riverside Shakespeare*, ed. G. B. Evans (Boston, MA: Houghton, 1974), pp. 1,803–4.
32. Jenkins, *ITYW*, pp. 62–3. Boaden writes that Inchbald claims Kemble 'never was at any time her *lover*' (*Memoirs*, vol. 1, p. 94).
33. Manvell, *Elizabeth Inchbald*, p. 143.
34. E. Inchbald, remarks on *As You Like It*, in E. Inchbald, *Remarks for The British Theatre (1806–1809)*, intro. C. Macheski (Delmar, NY: Scholars' Facsimiles & Reprints, 1990), n.p., hereafter *Remarks*; idem., remarks on *Coriolanus*, *Remarks*, n.p.; idem, remarks on *King John*, *Remarks*, n.p.; idem, remarks on *King Richard III*, *Remarks*, n.p.; idem, remarks on *Measure for Measure*, *Remarks*, n.p.; idem, remarks on *Macbeth*, *Remarks*, n.p.
35. C. A. Barros and J. M. Smith, 'Mary Robinson', in C. A. Barros and J. M. Smith (eds), *Life-Writings by British Women, 1660–1850: An Anthology* (Boston, MA: Northeastern University Press, 2000), p. 370.
36. See M. Robinson, *Memoirs of the Late Mrs Robinson*, in C. A. Barros and J. M. Smith (eds), *Life-Writings by British Women, 1660–1850: An Anthology* (Boston, MA: Northeastern University Press, 2000), p. 375.
37. J. Wordsworth, 'Introduction', in M. Robinson, *Poems, 1791* (Oxford and New York: Woodstock Books, 1994), n.p.
38. J. Pascoe, 'Introduction', in J. Pascoe (ed.), *Mary Robinson: Selected Poems* (Toronto, ON: Broadview, 2000), p. 29.
39. Inchbald probably discussed Mary Robinson's case with her friend William Godwin, whom William St Clair cites as one of the few friends who did not desert Robinson after the affair with the Prince (*The Godwins and the Shelleys*, pp. 250–1).
40. Mellow, *NHHT*, p. 116.
41. Ibid.; W. Shakespeare, *Macbeth*, in W. Shakespeare, *The Complete Works of Shakespeare*, ed. D. Bevington, p. 1,223.
42. Mellow, *NHHT*, p. 117.
43. Ibid., pp. 441–2.

44. Hawthorne, *The English Notebooks*, ed. R. Stewart, p. 387.

45. Ibid.

46. Mellow, *NHHT*, pp. 441–2.

47. Significantly, Hawthorne notes in his preface that the book was written 'on English ground' and calls England 'our mother-land' before saying that it is 'the land of *our own* PHILOSOPHERS and POETS' ('Preface', in D. Bacon, *The Philosophy of Shakspere Unfolded* (London: Groombridge, 1857; New York: AMS Press, 1970), pp. xii, xiv).

48. Mellow, *NHHT*, pp. 441–2.

49. Manvell, *Elizabeth Inchbald*, p. 145.

50. Like Inchbald, Shakespeare used human feeling, or passion, as a means of examining 'truth'. See Wells, 'Shakespeare and Romance', p. 78; and Peterson, *Time, Tide, and Tempest*, p. 216.

51. See Inchbald, remarks on *Lovers' Vows, Remarks*, n.p.; idem, remarks on *Such Things Are, Remarks*, n.p.; idem, remarks on *To Marry, or Not to Marry, Remarks*, n.p.; idem, remarks on *Wives As They Were, and Maids As They Are, Remarks*, n.p.

52. Idem, remarks on *I Henry IV, Remarks*, n.p.; idem, remarks on *II Henry IV, Remarks*, n.p.; idem, remarks on *Henry V, Remarks*, n.p.

53. Idem, remarks on *Macbeth, Remarks*, n.p.; idem, remarks on *Coriolanus, Remarks*, n.p.; idem, remarks on *King Lear, Remarks*, n.p.; idem, remarks on *Romeo and Juliet, Remarks*, n.p.; idem, remarks on *Romeo and Juliet, Remarks*, n.p.; idem, remarks on *Othello, Remarks*, n.p.; idem, remarks on *Othello, Remarks*, n.p.

54. Idem, remarks on *The Comedy of Errors, Remarks*, n.p.; idem, remarks on *Measure for Measure, Remarks*, n.p.; idem, remarks on *The Merchant of Venice, Remarks*, n.p.; idem, remarks on *Much Ado About Nothing, Remarks*, n.p.; idem, remarks on *The Merry Wives of Windsor, Remarks*, n.p.

55. Idem, remarks on *The Winter's Tale, Remarks*, n.p.; idem, remarks on *Cymbeline, Remarks*, n.p.; idem, remarks on *The Tempest, Remarks*, n.p.

56. In college, Hawthorne's nickname was Oberon, a direct allusion to the King of the Fairies in *A Midsummer Night's Dream*. Herman Melville's 'Hawthorne and His Mosses' compares Hawthorne with Shakespeare: 'Now, I do not say that Nathaniel of Salem is a greater than William of Avon, or as great. But the difference between the two men is by no means immeasurable. Not a very great deal more, and Nathaniel were verily William' (in H. Melville, *The Piazza Tales and Other Prose Pieces, 1839–1860*, ed. H. Hayford, A. A. MacDougall, G. T. Tanselle, *et al.*, vol. 9 (Evanston and Chicago, IL: Northwestern University Press and Newberry Library, 1987), p. 246.). See also T. Woodson, 'Introduction: Hawthorne's Letters, 1813–1853', in Hawthorne, *Centenary Edition*, vol. 15, p. 69; and Mellow, *NHHT*, p. 527.

57. Hawthorne, *The Letters: 1813–1843*, p. 184.

58. Ibid., p. 253.

59. Hawthorne, *Centenary Edition*, vol. 8, *The American Notebooks*, p. 393.

60. Ibid., pp. 401, 537.

61. Hawthorne, *English Notebooks*, p. 100.

62. Ibid., p. 131.

63. Ibid., pp. 132, 344; and Hawthorne, *Centenary Edition*, vol. 5, *Our Old Home*, pp. 99–100.

64. Hawthorne, *English Notebooks*, pp. 368, 508.

65. Ibid., pp. 612, 586.

66. Ibid., p. 586.

67. Hawthorne, *Centenary Edition*, vol. 3, *The Blithedale Romance*, p. 1,106; Hawthorne, *MF*, p. 133.

68. See D. J. Palmer (ed.), *Shakespeare: The Tempest* (Nashville, TN: Aurora Publishers, 1970); D. G. James, *The Dream of Prospero* (Oxford: Clarendon Press, 1967); D. Daniell, *The Tempest* (Atlantic Highlands, NJ: Humanities Press International, 1989); A. D. Nutall, *Two Concepts of Allegory: A Study of Shakespeare's* The Tempest *and the Logic of Allegorical Expression* (New York: Barnes and Noble, 1967).

69. The rest of this chapter uses the words *comedy* and *comic* to refer to Shakespeare's plays and to Inchbald's and Hawthorne's romances, as well as to incidents that occur in the plots of all five texts under scrutiny. The use of the two words is not meant to invoke allusions to humour, but rather, to comedy in the more traditional sense of a happy or satisfactory resolution to conflict.

70. Some critics have suggested alternate classifications. Gerald Schorin, for example, categorizes *The Tempest* as 'tragicomic romance' ('Approaching the Genre of *The Tempest*', in R. C. Tobias and P. G. Zolbrod (eds), *Shakespeare's Late Plays* (Athens, GA: Ohio University Press, 1974), p. 182).

71. D. Bevington, 'The Tempest', in W. Shakespeare, *The Complete Works of Shakespeare*, updated 4th edn, ed. D. Bevington (New York: Longman, 1997), p. 1,526; Kirkby, 'The American Prospero', p. 91. See also Kermode, *Shakespeare*, p. 45; Uphaus, *Beyond Tragedy*, p. 93; and G. W. Knight, *The Shakespearian Tempest* (London: Methuen, 1953), p. 265).

72. Jo Alyson Parker refers to the two opposed stances in the book as 'an active resistance to authority' versus 'a passive acquiescence to it' ('Complicating *A Simple Story*', *Eighteenth-Century Studies*, 30:3 (1997), p. 257). Moreover, she alludes to the book's connection with *The Tempest* by noting that the characters 'undergo a sea change' (p. 256).

73. Ibid., p. 267. According to Catherine Craft-Fairchild, 'Inchbald constructs a complicated and disturbing narrative that exposes defects in the patriarchal system not through explication, but through enactment – showing troubling relationships between men and women and thereby forcing readers to examine the foundations, assumptions, and implications of masculine domination' (*Masquerade and Gender: Disguise and Female Identity in Eighteenth-Century Fictions by Women* (University Park, PA: Pennsylvania State University Press, 1993), p. 120). Candace Ward says that Miss Milner and Matilda 'struggle against – and appear to lose to – mutually exclusive paradigms of proper and improper female behavior', and George Haggerty asserts, 'Inchbald insists that all female power is illusory, even that power she so infamously wields over male desire' ('Inordinate Desire: Schooling the Senses in Elizabeth Inchbald's *A Simple Story*', *Studies in the Novel*, 31:1 (1999), p. 2; 'Female Abjection in Inchbald's *A Simple Story*', *Studies in English Literature, 1500–1900*, 36:3 (1996), p. 670). A revised version of Haggerty's article appears as a chapter in his *Unnatural Affections: Women and Fiction in the Later 18th Century* (Bloomington, IN: Indiana University Press, 1998), pp. 37–51.

74. As Parker suggests, Inchbald is 'practicing an aesthetics of accommodation, one that enables her concurrently to question and affirm the dominant values of her society and thereby reveal their contradictions. In sum, the violation of our aesthetic sensibilities [because of the break in the middle of *A Simple Story*] is a sign that the text is doing its work' ('Complicating *A Simple Story*', p. 265).

75. Bevington, 'The Tempest', pp. 1527–8; H. Felperin, *Shakespearean Romance* (Princeton, NJ: Princeton University Press, 1972), p. 262.

76. Although Leslie A. Fiedler asserts that there are 'no Noble Savages in Hawthorne' only 'warlocks and bestial assassins, demi-devils and demi-brutes', Phyllis W. Barrett disagrees and suggests that Pearl fills the noble savage role (*Love and Death in the American Novel*, p. 197; 'More American Adams: Women Heroes in American Fiction', *Markham Review*, 10 (1981), p. 40).

77. Hawthorne, *SL*, pp. 111–2.

78. Bevington, 'The Tempest', p. 1,526.

79. Uphaus, *Beyond Tragedy*, p. 93. Similarly, Douglas Peterson comments, 'The play's opening scene is an extraordinary instance of the fusion of mimetic and poetic modes', as is the rest of the play, and Howard Felperin contends, '*The Tempest*, more than any other play of Shakespeare's, asks to be seen as glittering illusion or as essential reality, and its cast divides the possibilities of response among them' (*Time, Tide, and Tempest*, p. 219; *Shakespearean Romance*, p. 250).

80. D. Bevington, 'Cymbeline', in W. Shakespeare, *The Complete Works of Shakespeare*, updated 4th edn, ed. D. Bevington (New York: Longman, 1997), p. 1,434. Robert Uphaus sees *Cymbeline* as an experimental 'parody of romance' (*Beyond Tragedy*, pp. 49, 51). Hallett Smith and J. M. Nosworthy acknowledge the play, as other critics have done, as a type of experimental romance (*Shakespeare's Romances*, p. 162; J. M. Nosworthy, introduction to *Cymbeline*, in William Shakespeare, *The Arden Edition of the Works of William Shakespeare* (London: Methuen, 1955), p. 1). Finally, G. Wilson Knight acknowledges also that *Cymbeline* blends comedy and tragedy (*The Crown of Life*, pp. 129–30).

81. Ibid.

82. Additionally, Hallett Smith suggests that *Cymbeline* exhibits 'deliberate artlessness' designed to call attention to itself as an experimental text (*Shakespeare's Romances*, p. 162).

83. Bevington, 'Cymbeline', p. 1,436.

84. Ibid.

85. Jo Alyson Parker writes that Dorriforth's behaviour is 'despotic, even cruel' ('Complicating *A Simple Story*', p. 264).

86. Ibid., 261.

87. Catherine Craft-Fairchild believes that in *A Simple Story*, 'the successful placement of the heroine into the binary of either good or bad is impossible' (*Masquerade and Gender*, p. 80).

88. Wallace, 'Wit and Revolution', p. 104.

89. As Parker comments, readers are forced 'to regard Matilda's "wrong" as a right' ('Complicating *A Simple Story*', p. 263).

90. Castle, *Masquerade and Civilization*, p. 322.

91. Hawthorne, *SL*, p. 62.

92. Interestingly, as Frank Kermode notices about *The Tempest*, 'Shakespeare does not even show Prospero's deposition and banishment on the stage' (*Shakespeare*, p. 11). Perhaps the *in medias res* nature of both *The Tempest* and *The Scarlet Letter* acts as another link between the two.

93. Hawthorne, *SL*, p. 76.

94. Bevington, 'Cymbeline', p. 1,437.

95. See F. Pyle, The Winter's Tale: *A Commentary on the Structure* (New York: Barnes & Noble, 1969); C. Frey, *Shakespeare's Vast Romance: A Study of* The Winter's Tale (Colum-

bia: University of Missouri Press, 1980); K. Muir (ed.), *Shakespeare: The Winter's Tale* (Nashville: Aurora Publishers, 1970).

96. Wordsworth, 'Introduction', in *N&A*.

97. Tompkins, *The Popular Novel in England*, p. 339; Boaden, *Memoirs*, vol. 1, p. 277. Tompkins writes, 'The author designed her book on the model of *Winter's Tale*, a story of wrong and reconciliation in two generations, and it is penetrated with her dramatic experience' (p. 339). Tompkins later comments, '[T]he book that is most penetrated with the experience of the stage is the *Simple Story* of Elizabeth Inchbald [...]. All the important points are made in dialogue, and the action passes before the eye in a series of small and highly-finished scenes' (pp. 348–9). Tompkins calls the book 'entirely dramatic' and concludes, 'nobody before her saw the possibilities of the dramatic treatment so well, or carried them out so consistently' (pp. 350–2). Jenny Davidson points out a number of parallels between *A Simple Story* and *The Winter's Tale* ('Why Girls Look Like Their Mothers: David Garrick Rewrites *The Winter's Tale*', in P. Sabor and P. Yachnin (eds), *Shakespeare and the Eighteenth Century* (Aldershot: Ashgate, 2008), pp. 175–6).

98. Also like *The Tempest* and *Cymbeline*, *The Winter's Tale* occupies the liminal zone between the real and the imaginary. See Peterson, *Time, Tide, and Tempest*, p. 208; and Felperin, *Shakespearean Romance*, p. 216. Felperin goes so far as to contend, 'No play of Shakespeare's (perhaps not even *The Tempest*) so perfectly fulfills the conventions of romance while testing them so rigorously against the touchstone of brazen reality' (p. 242).

99. *The Tempest* and *Cymbeline* also demonstrate a close attention to structure and narrative control, but not in the same way as *The Winter's Tale*. Frank Kermode notices, as have other critics, that *The Tempest* observes 'all the neo-Aristotelian unities', while J. M. Nosworthy says the play exhibits 'technical perfection' (*Shakespeare*, p. 42; introduction to *Cymbeline*, p. 1). G. Wilson Knight calls *Cymbeline* 'a peculiarly studied work' (*The Crown of Life*, p. 129).

100. Bevington, 'The Winter's Tale', in W. Shakespeare, *The Complete Works of Shakespeare*, ed. D. Bevington, p. 1,484. Frank Kermode calls *The Winter's Tale* 'structurally unique' and says that Act 4 has an 'entirely new tone' (*Shakespeare*, pp. 31, 34–5). Douglas Peterson writes that the play demonstrates 'an economy and clarity of structure' (*Time, Tide, and Tempest*, p. 151). Robert Uphaus also refers to the first three acts as tragedy but believes the play continues with romance that possesses a 'comic impulse' (*Beyond Tragedy*, pp. 71, 76, 82).

101. Kermode, *Shakespeare*, pp. 34 – 5.

102. Robert Uphaus comments, 'Not only do the characters frequently contend with one another, but whole sections of the play stand in opposition to one another' (*Beyond Tragedy*, p. 69).

103. See Kelly, *The English Jacobin Novel*, p. 84, and Matthiessen, *American Renaissance*, p. 137.

104. Jo Alyson Parker notes, 'The text divides neatly in half, each half providing a seemingly self-contained story' ('Complicating *A Simple Story*', p. 256). Miriam Wallace suggests that the first half of the book is more indebted to chivalric romance while the second half evokes the Gothic ('Wit and Revolution', p. 99).

105. For Jane Spencer, the second half of the book 'is an attempt to cancel out the boldness of the first' (*The Rise of the Woman Novelist: From Aphra Behn to Jane Austen* (Oxford: Basil Blackwell, 1986), p. 160), and Katherine M. Rogers states flatly that the second half of *A Simple Story* demonstrates a 'failure of nerve' on Inchbald's part ('Inhibitions on Eighteenth-Century Women Novelists: Elizabeth Inchbald and Charlotte Smith', *Eight-*

eenth-Century Studies, 11 (1977), p. 71; K. M. Rogers, 'Elizabeth Inchbald: Not Such a Simple Story', in D. Spender (ed.), *Living by the Pen: Early British Women Writers* (New York: Teachers College Press, 1992), p. 86). Eleanor Ty also faults Inchbald for repressing the 'potentiality of female force' with the second half (*Unsex'd Revolutionaries: Five Women Novelists of the 1790s* (Toronto, ON: University of Toronto Press, 1993), p. 100).

106. James Mellow suggests that *The Scarlet Letter* consists of 'a series of starkly presented tableaux, centering on the three scenes at the scaffold of the pillory', and F. O. Matthiessen goes further to say that Hawthorne uses the tableau technique in all of his romances (*NHHT*, p. 303; *American Renaissance,* p. 300). See also Cowley, 'Five Acts of *The Scarlet Letter*', pp. 23–44).

107. Hawthorne, *SL*, p. 155.

108. M. L. Hays, *Shakespearean Tragedy as Chivalric Romance: Rethinking* Macbeth, Hamlet, Othello, *and* King Lear (Cambridge: D. S. Brewer, 2003), p. 1.

109. R. Lyne, *Shakespeare's Late Work* (Oxford: Oxford University Press, 2007), p. 3.

110. Bevington, 'The Winter's Tale', p. 1,485.

111. Sanders, 'An Overview of Critical Approaches to the Romances', pp. 1 – 2. Sonia Massai notices similar features of the romance ('Romance', in M. Dobson and S. Wells (eds), *The Oxford Companion to Shakespeare* (Oxford: Oxford University Press, 2001), p. 395).

112. Kermode, *Shakespeare,* pp. 7–8.

113. Interestingly, D. H. Lawrence calls *The Scarlet Letter* 'a sort of parable' (*Studies in Classic American Literature* (London: Heinemann, 1964), p. 78). He further comments, 'You *must* look through the surface of American art, and see the inner diabolism of the symbolic meaning. Otherwise it is all mere childishness' (Ibid.).

114. Inchbald, *SS*, p. 196; Hawthorne, *SL*, p. 62.

115. S. R. Littlewood notices stock characters in some of Inchbald's plays (which would have affected her fiction), and James Mellow notes stock characters in Hawthorne's work (*Elizabeth Inchbald*, p. 75; *NHHT*, p. 42).

116. Yvor Winters goes so far as to call *The Scarlet Letter* 'pure allegory' and refers to Hawthorne as 'essentially an allegorist' ('Maule's Curse: Hawthorne and the Problem of Allegory', *American Review,* 9:3 (1937), pp. 339–40). John O. Rees, however, points out that all narratives 'lend themselves to allegorical interpretation' and suggests that Hawthorne, whose symbols shift and never mean 'precisely the same thing twice' was critical of traditional allegory ('Hawthorne's Concept of Allegory: A Reconsideration', *Philological Quarterly,* 54 (1975), pp. 495, 505, 508).

4. 'I Will Not Accept Your Moral!': Propositions of an Alternative, Individual and Liminal Moral Order for Inchbald and Hawthorne

1. Hawthorne, *MF*, pp. 459–60.

2. George Gordon, Lord Byron, 'Prometheus', in G. G. Byron, *Selected Poems,* ed. and pref. S. J. Wolfson and P. J. Manning (London: Penguin, 1996), p. 395.

3. Indeed, as Katharine M. Rogers comments of Inchbald, she 'never misses an opportunity to press home a didactic point' ('Elizabeth Inchbald', p. 88).

4. In an article on politics in *The Scarlet Letter,* Donald Pease notes that Hester's sin is 'productive of a new social order' ('Hawthorne in the Custom-House: The Metapolitics, Postpolitics, and Politics of *The Scarlet Letter*', *Boundary 2,* 32:1 (2005), pp. 53–70).

5. Olivia Gatti Taylor makes an argument for such an interpretation of both *The Scarlet Letter* and *The Marble Faun* in 'Cultural Confessions: Penance and Penitence in Nathaniel Hawthorne's *The Scarlet Letter* and *The Marble Faun*', *Renascence*, 58:2 (2005), pp. 135–52. In her view, Hawthorne saw potential in both Catholicism and Protestantism.

6. M. H. Abrams, *Natural Supernaturalism: Tradition and Revolution in Romantic Literature* (New York: Norton, 1971), p. 13.

7. Ibid. Abrams reminds his readers that 'the later eighteenth century was another age of apocalyptic expectation' (*Natural Supernaturalism*, p. 64) and suggests that the eschatological nature of much Romantic thought may have bolstered challenges to religious institutions. Margaret Anne Doody points out that a number of critics have suggested that the novel arose from the trend toward secularization. She comments, 'In twentieth-century criticism the Novel is seen also as not only displacing but *re*placing myth, or religious narrative, or rather religion – customarily, Christianity – itself. A book like Frank Kermode's *The Sense of an Ending* (1969) is based on that assumption' (Doody, *The True Story of the Novel*, p. 3). She summarizes Erich Auerbach's position in *Mimesis* to say, '*Mimesis* assumes the displacement of (particularly Biblical) myth by realism' (p. 3), and when she mentions Georg Lukács and his book *The Theory of the Novel*, she presents a neat formulation to summarize his stance: 'The Past = Belief in God = Epic; Modernity = Disbelief = Novel' (p. 2).

8. Abrams, *Natural Supernaturalism*, p. 91.

9. Ibid., pp. 91, 68.

10. H. Chadwick, 'Romanticism and Religion', in J. C. Laidlaw (ed.), *The Future of the Modern Humanities* (Modern Humanities Research Association, 1969), p. 22.

11. Ibid., p. 23.

12. Ibid., p. 24.

13. R. M. Ryan, *The Romantic Reformation: Religious Politics in English Literature, 1789–1824* (Cambridge: Cambridge University Press, 1997), p. 7. F. X. Shea outright states, 'The Romantics sought a new religion' ('Religion and the Romantic Movement', *Studies in Romanticism*, 9 (1970), p. 294) and goes on to say, 'It is, then, a religion primarily that the Romantics sought, rather than a faith. And it is a religion feminine in character rather than masculine. But the search no longer demanded absolute commitment and single choice' (p. 295).

14. Abrams, *Natural Supernaturalism*, p. 66.

15. J. H. Randall, Jr, 'Romantic Reinterpretations of Religion', *Studies in Romanticism*, 2:4 (1963), p. 189.

16. McKee, *Elizabeth Inchbald*, p. 104.

17. Ibid., pp. 104–6.

18. Ibid., pp. 111–14.

19. Ibid., pp. 109–10.

20. Manvell, *Elizabeth Inchbald*, p. 29.

21. McKee, *Elizabeth Inchbald*, p. 118. McKee claims that 'religion is treated positively' in *A Simple Story*, but his statement ignores the obvious tyranny and hypocrisy of Dorriforth/Lord Elmwood, as he imposes unreasonable constraints upon Miss Milner and Matilda (p. 121). He argues convincingly that in *Nature and Art*, '[i]t was not religion itself that was bad, but the abuse which certain ecclesiastics made of that religion' (pp. 128, 122). Similarly, Lance Wilcox finds in *A Simple Story* 'a searing and thoroughly Christian study of idolatry' and advances a strong argument that the conflict in the book stems from 'religious errors on the part of the characters involved' ('Idols and Idolaters in *A Simple Story*',

Age of Johnson, 17 (2006), pp. 297, 299). For other similar discussions, see M. Boardman, 'Inchbald's *A Simple Story*: An Anti-Ideological Reading', *Eighteenth Century: Theory and Interpretation,* 37:3 (1996), pp. 271–84 and S. L. Maurer, 'Masculinity and Morality in Elizabeth Inchbald's *Nature and Art*', in L. Lang-Peralta (ed.), *Women, Revolution, and the Novels of the 1790's* (East Lansing, MI: Michigan State University Press, 1999), pp. 155–76.

22. As J. H. Plumb notes, 'each rebellion appeared as a Roman Catholic revolt against a Protestant government' (*England in the Eighteenth Century* (Harmondsworth, England: Penguin, 1950), p. 180). George Haggerty notices that Catholicism eventually became associated with the Gothic genre in Britain ('The Horrors of Catholicism: Religion and Sexuality in Gothic Fiction', *Romanticism on the Net,* 36-37 (2004), <http://www.eru-dit.org/revue/ron/2004/v/n36-37/0011133ar.html>).

23. Plumb, *England in the Eighteenth Century*, p. 180.

24. Manvell, *Elizabeth Inchbald*, p. 72.

25. Ibid.

26. McKee, *Elizabeth Inchbald*, p. 11.

27. Jenkins, *ITYW*, p. 2.

28. Inchbald, *Diaries*, vol. 1, pp. 146–7.

29. Roger Manvell refers to *A Simple Story* as 'the first English Catholic novel' because its main characters, except for Miss Milner, are Catholic (*Elizabeth Inchbald*, p. 72).

30. John Frederick says that an emphasis on 'religious matters is very marked in [Hawthorne's] fiction' (*The Darkened Sky: Nineteenth-Century American Novelists and Religion* (Notre Dame, IN: University of Notre Dame Press, 1969), p. 28), and James Mellow comments of Hawthorne, 'The mystery of sin is what absorbs him' (*NHHT*, p. 58).

31. M. B. Moore, *The Salem World of Nathaniel Hawthorne* (Columbia, MO: University of Missouri Press, 1998), p. 103

32. Frederick, *The Darkened Sky*, p. 34.

33. Ibid., p. 35.

34. Van Doren, *Nathaniel Hawthorne*, pp. 29, 215.

35. Hawthorne, *The American Notebooks*, p. 352.

36. Ibid., p. 339.

37. Moore, *The Salem World of Nathaniel Hawthorne*, p. 122.

38. Frederick, *The Darkened Sky*, pp. 29 – 30.

39. E. Wagenknecht, *Nathaniel Hawthorne: Man and Writer* (New York: Oxford University Press, 1961), p. 185.

40. Ibid., p. 172.

41. Hawthorne, *The American Notebooks*, pp. 393, 429.

42. For example, Hawthorne was familiar with such texts as Cotton Mather's *Magnalia Christi Americana*, a history of American settlement written from a Puritan point of view. He called the *Magnalia* a 'strange, pedantic history, in which true events and real personages move before the reader with the dreamy aspect which they wore in Cotton Mather's singular mind' (Mellow, *NHHT*, p. 40). Hawthorne's statement about Mather sounds reminiscent of his own discussion of romance as a merger of the real and the imaginary in 'The Custom-House', and it seems that Puritanism acted as an important catalyst for the Romantic moral romance form.

43. Hawthorne, *SL*, pp. 9–10.

44. For important discussions of the witchcraft scare, see P. Boyer and S. Nissenbaum, *Salem Possessed: The Social Origins of Witchcraft* (Cambridge, MA: Harvard University Press,

1974); S. G. Drake (ed.), *The Witchcraft Delusion in New England*, 3 vols (1866; New York: Burt Franklin, 1970); A. C. Kors and E. Peters (eds), *Witchcraft in Europe, 1100-1700: A Documentary History* (Philadelphia, PA: University of Pennsylvania Press, 1972); and C. F. Karlsen, *The Devil in the Shape of a Woman: Witchcraft in Colonial New England* (New York: Norton, 1987).

45. Evan Carton comments, 'Everywhere in Italy, the art, history, rituals, and values of Catholicism confronted the New England Hawthornes; they exerted a powerful sensory and intellectual pull on Una [Hawthorne's daughter] and, unsettlingly, rekindled an old and theretofore theoretical fascination in Hawthorne himself. The principles of Hawthorne's identity were too firmly established to be radically altered by these challenging stimuli, but at the same time he was too observant, sensitive, and self-analytical to ignore or repress such challenges altogether' (*The Marble Faun: Hawthorne's Transformations* (New York: Twayne, 1992), p. 11).

46. David Lyttle points out that Hawthorne 'did not believe in human depravity' ('Hawthorne: Calvinistic Humanism', *Studies in Religion in Early American Literature: Edwards, Poe, Channing, Emerson, Some Minor Transcendentalists, Hawthorne and Thoreau* (Lanham, MD: University Press of America, 1983), p. 152). Hawthorne was, however, interested in the idea of natural depravity as a departure point for his examinations of human motivation.

47. Frederick, *The Darkened Sky*, p. 66. Frederick points out Hawthorne's 'conflicting feelings about Catholicism' by noting his antipathy toward clergymen as expressed in *The Marble Faun* and by simultaneously acknowledging that Hawthorne found an 'attractiveness' in the religion. Hawthorne's antipathy toward priests undoubtedly was an extension of his dislike of Protestant ministers, but Frederick points out also that Hawthorne had, himself, preached to an American priest in Liverpool who had spent 'a week's residence in a brothel' and had come to Hawthorne, as Consul, for assistance after running out of money (Ibid.).

48. Inchbald, *N&A*, vol. 2, p. 202.

49. Gary Kelly suggests, 'Perhaps prudence induced Mrs Inchbald to soften the ending', and Patricia Spacks complains that the plot tacitly endorses 'the necessity of dominant maleness' (*The English Jacobin Novel*, p. 104; *Desire and Truth*, p. 201). Eleanor Ty makes similar claims about *A Simple Story* to suggest that Matilda is Inchbald's 'concession to the patriarchal order', and Katharine Rogers complains that both *Nature and Art* and *A Simple Story* make too many concessions to the male order (*Unsex'd Revolutionaries*, p. 88; *Feminism in Eighteenth-Century England* (New York: St Martin's Press, 1982), pp. 196–9).

50. Inchbald, *N&A*, vol. 2, pp. 202–3.

51. As William Hazlitt commented, probably in reference to young Henry's final words, 'The conclusion of *Nature and Art* [...] is a scene of heartless desolation, which must effectually deter any one from ever reading the book twice' ('On the English Novelists', *Lectures on the English Comic Writers and Fugitive Writings*, introd. A. Johnston (London: Everyman, 1963), p. 128). Moreover, Hazlitt recognized Inchbald's condemnation of the two Williams: 'Mrs Inchbald's "Nature and Art" would scarcely have had the same popularity, but that it fell in (as to its two main characters) with the prevailing prejudice of the moment, that judges and bishops were not invariably pure abstractions of justice and piety' (p. 123). Interestingly, later editions of *Nature and Art* had a slightly different ending. The revised ending was less inflammatory and blamed faulty education for the problems of the poor. As Janice Cauwels comments, Inchbald 'probably felt impelled to

change her text to satisfy publishers and readers (sometimes against her better judgment) with a view to increasing the novel's sales' ('Authorial "Caprice" vs. Editorial "Calculation": The Text of Elizabeth Inchbald's *Nature and Art*, *Papers of the Bibliographical Society of America*, p. 170). Cauwels points out other passages that Inchbald revised and notes that some of the changes may have been made 'without her knowledge' (p. 179). Patricia Taylor, however, calls the original ending 'inept' ('Authorial Amendments in Mrs Inchbald's *Nature and Art*, *Notes and Queries*, 25 (1978), p. 69).

52. Indeed, Inchbald condemns all ministers in *Nature and Art*, not just the elder William. For example, Inchbald makes the point that the elder William's hypocrisy symbolically represents that of the Anglican clergy in general when she depicts his search for a job in Chapter 2. Already well educated and able to understand Greek and Latin, William is nevertheless refused a position as servant to a young clergyman because, as the narrator comments, 'he could not dress hair' (Inchbald, *N&A*, vol. 1, p. 7). The young clergyman is sinfully more interested in the worldly issue of his appearance than in William's ability to understand scripture and provide adequate support for his ministerial duties. With the briefly mentioned refusal of work from the young clergyman, Inchbald establishes, early, her position in opposition to Anglicanism and implies that Anglican corruption extends much farther than the elder William.

53. In speculating about why *Nature and Art* has received less critical attention than *A Simple Story*, Dale Spender comments, 'The only conclusion that I can draw is that as Victorian morality became more firmly entrenched, the subject matter of *Nature and Art* became more distasteful, more offensive' (*Mothers of the Novel*, p. 214).

54. Inchbald, *N&A*, vol. 1, pp. 21–3.

55. Ibid., vol. 1, p. 26.

56. Ibid., vol. 1, p. 29.

57. Ibid., vol. 1, pp. 32 – 3; Eleanor Ty says that 'As the wife of a man of religion, Lady Clementina, with her vanity and love of earthly pleasure, sets a bad example for the rest of the community' (*Unsex'd Revolutionaries*, p. 105).

58. Inchbald, *N&A*, vol. 1, p. 36.

59. Ibid., vol. 1, pp. 64–5.

60. Ibid., vol. 1, p. 65.

61. Ty, Unsex'd Revolutionaries, pp. 102–3.

62. Inchbald, *N&A*, vol. 1, p. 73.

63. Ibid., vol. 1, pp. 78–9.

64. Ibid., vol. 1, pp. 78–9.

65. Ibid., vol. 1, pp. 100–3.

66. Ibid., vol. 1, pp. 126–7.

67. Ibid., vol. 1, p. 166.

68. Ibid., vol. 1, pp. 150–1.

69. Ibid., vol. 1, pp. 150–1.

70. Ibid., vol. 1, p. 108.

71. Ibid., vol. 2, p. 28.

72. Ibid., vol. 2, pp. 64–5.

73. Ibid., vol. 2, p. 66.

74. Ibid., vol. 2, p. 109.

75. Ibid., vol. 2, pp. 170, 173–4.

76. Ibid., vol. 2, pp. 174–5.

77. Ibid., vol. 2, pp. 176–7.

78. Ibid.
79. Ibid.
80. Ibid., vol. 2, p. 138.
81. Ibid., vol. 2, p. 143.
82. Ibid., vol. 2, p. 152.
83. Ibid., vol. 2, pp. 178–9.
84. Indeed, Taylor says that 'it is primarily for its didactic qualities that the book [*Nature and Art*] has survived' ('Authorial Amendments', p. 68).
85. As Taylor comments, 'The fallen woman, wanting only to live peacefully and honourably with her child, was [...] shown to be exploited and ostracized by a hypocritically self-righteous society and driven to crime in order to stay alive' (Ibid., p. 69). She later writes, 'Mrs Inchbald constantly stresses that the rustic girl [...] is essentially a pure woman. Like St Agnes she remains unsullied in character, and she only commits crimes because the hierarchical and prejudiced society in which she lives frustrates her every effort to earn a living honestly' (p. 70). Appropriately, Agnes is the name given to Hannah in later editions of *Nature and Art*. Likewise, Eleanor Ty writes, 'Hannah becomes a prostitute in order to save her own life and that of her son's' and clearly assigns blame to the patriarchal order for Hannah's fate (*Unsex'd Revolutionaries*, p. 111).
86. As Eleanor Ty comments, the second volume of *Nature and Art*, where Hannah's story comes to the forefront, is where 'Inchbald comes ideologically closest to outspoken radicals like Wollstonecraft and Hays' (*Unsex'd Revolutionaries*, p. 106). The book 'stands as a powerful critique of eighteenth-century patriarchy' (Ibid., p. 114).
87. Leslie Fiedler writes that Hawthorne is anti-Catholic and sees the Catholic Church as the enemy of the protagonists in *The Marble Faun* (*Love and Death in the American Novel*, p. 138).
88. In a comparison of Hawthorne's conception of 'truth' with that of Herman Melville, Clark Davis notes that while Melville wanted more definite answers to his questions of morality, Hawthorne was much more flexible as to what constituted 'truth' ('Hawthorne's Shyness: Romance and the Forms of Truth', *Emerson Society Quarterly*, 45:1 (1999), p. 33–65). Leland Person sees the book as showing negotiated 'truth' of the heart and feelings, not the mind (*The Cambridge Introduction to Nathaniel Hawthorne*, pp. 73, 34).
89. Hawthorne, *MF*, p. 107.
90. Ibid., p. 297.
91. Ibid., p. 109.
92. Ibid., p. 154.
93. Ibid., p. 5.
94. Ibid., p. 266.
95. Ibid., p. 6.
96. Ibid., p. 412.
97. Ibid., p. 110.
98. Ibid., p. 26.
99. Ibid., pp. 109, 211.
100. Ibid., p. 433.
101. Ibid., p. 238.
102. Ibid., p. 375.
103. Ibid., pp. 51–2.
104. Ibid., pp. 58, 60.

105. Ibid., p. 112.
106. Ibid., p. 56.
107. Ibid., pp. 226–7.
108. Ibid., p. 225.
109. Ibid., pp. 254–6.
110. Ibid., p. 277.
111. Ibid.
112. Ibid.
113. Ibid., pp. 156, 159.
114. Ibid., p. 140.
115. Ibid., pp. 190–1.
116. Ibid., p. 147.
117. Ibid.
118. Ibid., p. 34.
119. Ibid., p. 182.
120. Ibid., p. 193.
121. Ibid., p. 194.
122. Ibid.
123. F. O. Matthiessen comments, 'Not sin, but its consequence for human lives is Hawthorne's major theme' (*American Renaissance*, p. 343).
124. As Emily Schiller points out, 'with the possible exceptions of Ethan Brand and Chillingworth, no character in Hawthorne consciously chooses evil. He/she chooses what seems best at the time' ('The Choice of Innocence: Hilda in *The Marble Faun*', *Studies in the Novel*, 26:4 (1994), p. 378). Hyatt Waggoner comments, 'Hawthorne was more interested in guilt as a necessary human condition than he was in any specific sinful act. So he treated the central action in *The Marble Faun* in such a way that it is [...] impossible to decide that Donatello is really responsible for the murder he committed' ('The Marble Faun', in A. N. Kaul (ed.), *Hawthorne: A Collection of Critical Essays* (Englewood Cliffs, NJ: Prentice-Hall, 1966), p. 165). Not all critics have approved of Hawthorne's relativism, however. Mellow notes that one critic, E. P. Whipple, who was a contemporary of Hawthorne's, liked *The Marble Faun*, but disliked the 'bloodlessness' of the characters, particularly since readers do not feel that Donatello truly has sinned even though he commits murder (*NHHT*, p. 527).
125. David Lyttle, however, comments that while Hawthorne did not 'believe in inherited guilt', he 'did not deny that a person inherits the consequences of good and bad choices of preceding generations' ('Hawthorne', p. 152). Either way, the sins of earlier generations have profound effects on the characters in Hawthorne's works.
126. The narrator only once mentions Miriam's family name as Schaefer, but the name may be an alias. James Mellow rightly argues that Hawthorne intended to keep Miriam's family name a mystery (*NHHT*, p. 521).
127. Hawthorne, *MF*, p. 466.
128. Ibid., pp. 466–7.
129. Ibid., pp. 429–30.
130. Ibid., p. 430.
131. Ibid., pp. 430–1.
132. Ibid., p. 432.
133. Leslie Fiedler writes, 'For Hawthorne, the Faustian man [of whom Miriam is a female representative] is one who, unable to deny the definitions of right and wrong by which

his community lives, chooses nonetheless to defy them. He is the individual, who, in pursuit of "knowledge" or "experience" or just "happiness" places himself outside the sanctions and protection of society. His loneliness and alienation are at once his crime and his punishment; for he commits a kind of suicide when he steps outside of society by deciding to live in unrepented sin; and he can only return to haunt the world of ordinary men like a ghost' (*Love and Death in the American Novel*, pp. 448, 440).

134. Percy Shelley's version of the story in his drama *The Cenci* may have inspired Hawthorne, as discussed in Chapter 1.

135. Hawthorne, *MF*, p. 205. Ronald Paulson interprets Hester from *The Scarlet Letter* similarly and suggests that the community represents evil, not Hester ('Sin/Evil and the Law: The Novel', *Sin and Evil: Moral Values in Literature* (New Haven, CT: Yale University Press, 2007), pp. 124–60).

136. Hawthorne, *MF*, p. 430.

137. Ibid., p. 44.

138. Ibid., p. 46.

139. Ibid.

140. Ibid., p. 97.

141. Leland Person points out that 'Hawthorne identifies Miriam with Beatrice Cenci' (*The Cambridge Introduction to Nathaniel Hawthorne*, p. 109). Diane Long Hoeveler examines Beatrice Cenci's story as a connection among Byron, Shelley, Hawthorne and Melville and suggests that the Americans' use of the story helps to imply their belief in the impossibility of creating a purely independent literary tradition of their own ('Beatrice Cenci in Hawthorne, Melville, and Her Atlantic-Rim Contexts', *Romanticism on the Net*, 38-39 (2005), <http://www.erudit.org/revue/ron/2005/v/n38-39/011670ar.html>).

142. Hawthorne, *MF*, p. 212.

143. Ibid., p. 302.

144. Ibid., pp. 244–5.

145. Ibid., p. 246.

146. Ibid., pp. 90–1.

147. Ibid., p. 147.

148. Ibid., p. 148.

149. Ibid., p. 172.

150. Ibid., pp. 282–3.

151. Ibid., p. 291.

152. Ibid., p. 320.

153. Ibid., p. 321.

154. Ibid., p. 322.

155. Ibid., pp. 54, 362.

156. Ibid., p. 344.

157. Emily Schiller points out, however, that Hilda has no choice but to participate in the depravity that Puritanism posits ('The Choice of Innocence', p. 378). Consequently, Hilda is not so innocent as she at first appears. Indeed, Schiller rightly points out that 'to choose innocence one must no longer be innocent' (Ibid.).

158. Hawthorne, *MF*, p. 56. Otis Wheeler writes, 'Hilda's innocence is emphasized most obviously through the symbolism of the doves and the shrine of the Virgin' ('Love among the Ruins: Hawthorne's Surrogate Religion', *Southern Review*, (1974), p. 559).

159. Hawthorne, *MF*, p. 429. Appropriately, Wheeler says that Hawthorne uses the 'stereotype of the angel in the house' to describe Hilda and calls her the 'moral anchor for Kenyon' ('Love Among the Ruins', p. 559).

160. Hawthorne, *MF*, pp. 204–5.

161. Ibid., p. 329.

162. Ibid., p. 205.

163. Ibid., p. 53.

164. Ibid., p. 54.

165. Ibid., pp. 69, 180.

166. Ibid., pp. 332, 346, 347–8.

167. Ibid., p. 351.

168. Ibid., p. 352.

169. Ibid.

170. Ibid., pp. 354–6.

171. Ibid., pp. 344–5.

172. Ibid., p. 357.

173. Ibid., p. 347.

174. Ibid., p. 359.

175. Ibid., p. 362.

176. Ibid., pp. 368, 405, 415–16.

177. Otis Wheeler summarizes Leonard Fick's argument that 'Hawthorne felt that a viable religion should bring the individual near to God or God near the individual, that religion should be existential rather than doctrinal' ('Love among the Ruins', p. 536). The allusion is to L. J. Fick, *The Light Beyond: A Study of Hawthorne's Theology* (Westminster, MD: Newman Press, 1955).

178. Hawthorne, *MF*, p. 368.

179. According to Randall Stewart, Hawthorne originally intended to have Arthur Dimmesdale confess his sin to a Catholic priest in *The Scarlet Letter* (*Nathaniel Hawthorne*, p. 198).

180. Hawthorne, *MF*, p. 367.

181. Ibid., p. 16.

182. Ibid., pp. 295, 298.

183. Ibid., p. 208.

184. Ibid., p. 298.

185. Ibid., pp. 86–7.

186. Ibid., p. 364.

187. Ibid., pp. 459–60.

188. Ibid.

189. David Lyttle would disagree, for he suggests, as have other critics, that 'human beings are morally profound only by knowing of evil' ('Hawthorne', p. 162). Likewise, Donald Ringe makes the claim that only sin can bring 'true moral progress' ('Hawthorne's Psychology of the Head and Heart', *Publications of the Modern Language Association*, 65 (1950), p. 132).

190. Otis Wheeler condemns Hilda as a 'moral monster' because she is able to relinquish her guilt so easily ('Love Among the Ruins', p. 560).

5. Figures 'Pourtrayed Apart' with 'Real or Well-Counterfeited Simplicity': Complicating the Romantic Moral Romance with Symbolic and Fragmentary Figures

1. Hawthorne, *MF*, p. 46; Inchbald, *SS*, pp. 15–16.
2. Hazlitt, 'On the English Novelists', p. 128.
3. Mellor uses the term 'studied simplicity' to describe the work of women poets during the Romantic Period, but the term may be applied to Inchbald's work, as well as to Hawthorne's (*Romanticism & Gender*, p. 11).
4. Arnold Kettle argues that in traditional romances, '[c]haracters, instead of being realistic, that is to say human, that is to say neither wholly good nor bad, tend to become entirely black or white', while John Stevens makes the point that '[t]he "characters" of romance are white and black, good men and bad men, saints and devils. Wickedness is idealized as well as goodness' (Kettle, *An Introduction to the English Novel*, vol. 1, p. 35; *Medieval Romance*, p. 169).
5. E. Grabovszki, 'Doubling, Doubles, Duplicity, Bipolarity', in G. Gillespie, M. Engel and B. Dieterle (eds), *Romantic Prose Fiction* (Amsterdam: John Benjamins, 2008), pp. 168, 174–6.
6. Pease, 'Hawthorne in the Custom-House', pp. 53–70.
7. Wegelin, 'Europe in Hawthorne's Fiction', pp. 219–45.
8. C. Goldfarb, '*The Marble Faun* and Emersonian Self-Reliance', *American Transcendental Quarterly*, 1:1 (1969), pp. 21–2.
9. Ibid., p. 19.
10. Kesterson, '*The Marble Faun* as Transformation of Author and Age', p. 67.
11. D. A. Ringe, 'Go East, Young Man, and Discover Your Country', *The Kentucky Review*, 10:1 (1990), p. 13; D. L. Hoeveler, 'La Cenci: The Incest Motif in Hawthorne and Melville', *American Transcendental Quarterly*, 44 (1979), p. 258.
12. Stewart, 'Introduction, Chapter III', p. lxvi.
13. Matthiessen, *American Renaissance*, pp. 513, 335.
14. Mellow, *NHHT*, p. 234.
15. W. Shear, 'Characterization in *The Scarlet Letter*', *Midwest Quarterly*, 12 (1971), p. 443.
16. Winters, 'Maule's Curse', pp. 340, 355; A. N. Kaul, *The American Vision: Actual and Ideal Society in Nineteenth-Century Fiction* (New Haven, CT and London: Yale University Press, 1963), p. 142.
17. In an anthropological discussion about initiation rituals and ceremonies, Victor Turner discusses the idea of liminal entities who 'are neither here nor there; they are betwixt and between the positions assigned and arrayed by law, custom, convention, and ceremonial' (*The Ritual Process: Structure and Anti-Structure* (1969; Ithaca, NY: Cornell University Press, 1977), p. 95). Inchbald's and Hawthorne's characters fit into similar roles, as do Inchbald and Hawthorne themselves. Turner includes a list of binaries that show the status of liminality versus the status of being a fully integrated part of the 'system'; his binaries include 'Foolishness/sagacity' and 'Simplicity/complexity' (pp. 106–7). Turner's binaries closely resemble those in Figure 4.
18. E. W. Harries, *The Unfinished Manner: Essays on the Fragment in the Later Eighteenth Century* (Charlottesville, VA and London: University Press of Virginia, 1994), pp. 1–2. Harries refers to 'Kubla Khan' as 'probably the most famous fragment in English' (p. 151).

19. Ibid., pp. 1–2.
20. D. F. Rauber, 'The Fragment as Romantic Form', *Modern Language Quarterly*, 30 (1969), pp. 215, 212.
21. Harries, *The Unfinished Manner*, pp. 1–2. Harries goes so far as to include a chapter on the construction of fragmentary ruins and includes architectural plans and other illustrations that show the considered nature of the fake ruin. Interestingly, she notes that the Romantics and their forebears often associated fragments with femininity (p. 10). For other discussions of fragments and fragmentation in Romantic literature, see L. Kritzman and J. P. Plottel, *Fragments: Incompletion and Discontinuity* (New York: New York Literary Forum, 1981); T. McFarland, *Romanticism and the Forms of Ruin: Wordsworth, Coleridge, and Modalities of Fragmentation* (Princeton, NJ: Princeton University Press, 1981); B. Rajan, *The Form of the Unfinished: English Poetics from Spenser to Pound* (Princeton, NJ: Princeton University Press, 1985); M. Levinson, *The Romantic Fragment Poem: A Critique of a Form* (Chapel Hill, NC: University of North Carolina Press, 1986); A. Janowitz, 'The Romantic Fragment', in D. Wu (ed.) *A Companion to Romanticism* (London: Blackwell, 1999), pp. 442–51; A. Rawes, *Romanticism and Form* (Basingstoke: Palgrave, 2007) and R. Ceserani and P. Zanotti, 'The Fragment as Structuring Force', in *Romantic Prose Fiction*, ed. G. Gillespie, M. Engel, and B. Dieterle (Amsterdam: John Benjamins, 2008), pp. 452–75.
22. Harries, *The Unfinished Manner*, pp. 166–7.
23. C. A. Strathman, *Romantic Poetry and the Fragmentary Imperative: Schlegel, Byron, Joyce, Blanchot* (Albany, NY: State University of New York Press, 2005).
24. C. Woodring, *Nature into Art: Cultural Transformations in Nineteenth-Century Britain* (Cambridge, MA: Harvard University Press, 1989), p. 18.
25. C. Woodring, 'Nature and Art in the Nineteenth Century', *Publications of the Modern Language Association*, 92:2 (1977), p. 195.
26. G. L. Strachey, *Landmarks in French Literature* (London: Thornton Butterworth, 1936), p. 187.
27. H. N. Fairchild, *The Noble Savage: A Study in Romantic Naturalism* (New York: Columbia University Press, 1928), p. 2. Fairchild notices use of the noble-savage figure in works by Godwin, Wollstonecraft, Charlotte Lennox, Charlotte Smith and other writers (pp. 148–60).
28. Allardyce Nicoll points out that Inchbald used figures or types in her drama as well (*A History of English Drama, 1660–1900, vol. 3, Late Eighteenth-Century Drama, 1750–1800* (Cambridge: Cambridge University Press, 1955), pp. 144–54).
29. Leo Marx notices this feature in American literature in general when he argues that '[n]ature is what accounts for the virtue and special good fortune of Americans. It enables them to design a community in the image of a garden, an ideal fusion of nature with art' (*The Machine in the Garden: Technology and the Pastoral Ideal in America* (1964; New York: Oxford University Press, 1970), p. 228).
30. Castle, *Masquerade and Civilization*, p. 294.
31. Strachey, 'Introduction', *A Simple Story*, p. iv.
32. As Catherine Craft-Fairchild comments, 'Inchbald's *A Simple Story*, offering itself as a familiar, straightforward domestic novel, is deceptively titled and compellingly complex' (*Masquerade and Gender*, p. 121).
33. Inchbald, *SS*, p. 1.
34. Ibid., p. 33.
35. Ibid., p. 194.

36. Ibid., p. 230.
37. Todd, *The Sign of Angellica*, p. 228; Wallace, 'Wit and Revolution', p. 111.
38. Craft-Fairchild, *Masquerade and Gender*, p. 77.
39. Jo Alyson Parker suggests, '*A Simple Story* allows Inchbald to test out two versions of female power or influence – that which derives from an active resistance to authority and that which derives from a passive acquiescence to it' ('Complicating *A Simple Story*', p. 257). Miss Milner actively resists, while Matilda acquiesces.
40. Inchbald, *SS*, p. 5.
41. Stuart Curran acknowledges Miss Milner's resistance by classifying *A Simple Story* among the Romantic novels that 'encode a separatist agenda' by revealing 'bright, frustrated, and manipulated young women who have no recourse but themselves to manipulate the males who exert power over them' (Curran, 'Women Readers, Women Writers', pp. 182–3).
42. Inchbald, *SS*, pp. 15–16.
43. Ibid., pp. 19, 17.
44. Ibid., p. 138.
45. Ibid., p. 40.
46. Ibid., p. 221.
47. Ibid., p. 274.
48. Ibid., p. 218.
49. Ibid., p. 239.
50. Ibid., p. 220.
51. Littlewood, *Elizabeth Inchbald and Her Circle*, pp. 94, 88.
52. Cauwels, 'A Critical Edition of *Nature and Art* (1796) by Elizabeth Inchbald (1753–1821)', p. 246. S. L. Maurer points out that some of the characters are one-sided but argues that others, like the elder William, are more complex ('Introduction', in E. Inchbald, *Nature and Art*, ed. S. L. Maurer (Peterborough, ON: Broadview Press, 2005), p. 15).
53. Inchbald, *N&A*, vol. 1, pp. 138–9.
54. Chapter 2, Figure 3, Charting the Relationships among Inchbald's Fragmentary Figures, diagrams the family connections presented in *Nature and Art* – as well as those of *A Simple Story* – to help distinguish the figures from one another.
55. Taylor, 'Authorial Amendments in Mrs Inchbald's *Nature and Art*', p. 69.
56. Inchbald, *N&A*, vol. 1, p. 7.
57. Ibid., vol. 1, p. 55.
58. Ibid., vol. 1, pp. 60–3.
59. Ibid., vol. 1, pp. 51, 54, 84, 151. Young William, Lady Clementina and even the bishop refer to him repeatedly as a 'simpleton', a 'poor silly boy' and an 'ideot' (Ibid., vol. 1, p. 72).
60. Ibid., vol. 1, p. 131.
61. Ibid., vol. 2, p. 106.
62. Ibid., vol. 2, p. 130.
63. Inchbald, 'Preface', *A Simple Story*, p. 2.
64. Cowley, 'Five Acts of *The Scarlet Letter*', p. 33; Kaul, 'Character and Motive in *The Scarlet Letter*', p. 375.
65. Matthiessen, *American Renaissance*, p. 275.
66. Winters, 'Maule's Curse', pp. 339, 355.
67. Fiedler, *Love and Death in the American Novel*, p. 231.

68. Ibid., pp. 436–7.

69. Ibid., p. 25.

70. Mellow, *NHHT*, p. 305.

71. J. C. Stubbs, 'Hawthorne's *The Scarlet Letter*: The Theory of the Romance and the Use of the New England Situation', *Publications of the Modern Language Association*, 83 (1968), p. 1,446; E. Wagenknecht, *Nathaniel Hawthorne: The Man, His Tales and Romances* (New York: Continuum, 1989), pp. 80–1.

72. J. Levi, 'Hawthorne's *The Scarlet Letter*', *American Imago*, 10 (1953), pp. 301–4.

73. Stewart, 'Introduction, Chapter III', p. liii; H. Sutherland, 'Varieties of Protestant Experience: Religion and the Doppelgänger in Hogg, Brown, and Hawthorne', *Studies in Hogg and his World*, 16 (2005), pp. 71–85.

74. J. E. Thrailkill, '*The Scarlet Letter*'s Romantic Medicine', *Studies in American Fiction*, 34:1 (2006), pp. 3–31.

75. Fiedler, *Love and Death in the American Novel*, pp. 230, 437.

76. C. L. Daniels, 'Hawthorne's Pearl: Woman-Child of the Future', *American Transcendental Quarterly*, 19:3 (2005), pp. 221–36.

77. Fred C. Adams acknowledges Pearl as a kind of alternative to the Puritan traditions that Dimmesdale represents, although he points out that Pearl leaves at the end of the book ('Blood Vengeance in *The Scarlet Letter*', *Nathaniel Hawthorne Review*, 32:2 (2006), pp. 1–12).

78. Myra Jehlen points out Hester's submissiveness to Puritan norms in 'The Novel and the Middle Class in America', in M. Jehlen (ed.), *Readings at the Edge of Literature* (Chicago, IL: University of Chicago Press, 2002), pp. 50–67.

79. Leslie Fiedler even calls the Puritan community one of the protagonists in the book (*Love and Death in the American Novel*, p. 438). The suggestion that Americans generally favoured British literature is not as provocative as it might seem. The catalogues of the circulating libraries mentioned in Chapter 1 are filled with works from the likes of William Shakespeare, Samuel Johnson, John Milton, Jonathan Swift and so forth. Fiedler comments that, for example, 'Rousseau's fiction was immensely popular with our readers' and says that 'Goethe was even more widely read' (pp. 105–6).

80. Rosemary Stephens agrees, for she believes that Hester represents the American artist, as symbolized by the *A* ('A is for Art in *The Scarlet Letter*', *American Transcendental Quarterly*, 1:1 (1969), p. 25). Alternatively, Paula White contends that the *A* represents America itself and that the subject of *The Scarlet Letter* is America and its evolving history ('Puritan Theories of History in Hawthorne's Fiction', *Canadian Review of American Studies*, 9 (1978), p. 143).

81. Hawthorne, *SL*, p. 79.

82. Ibid., pp. 87–8.

83. Ibid., pp. 58, 128. Wanda Faye Jones hints at murder in her suggestion that Chillingworth may have poisoned Dimmesdale with scopolamine to elicit a confession of Dimmesdale's guilt ('Scopolamine Poisoning and the Death of Dimmesdale in *The Scarlet Letter*', *Nathaniel Hawthorne Review*, 32:1 (2006), pp. 52–62).

84. Hawthorne, *SL*, p. 118.

85. Wright calls him Roger Prynne, for example (*Critical Companion to Nathaniel Hawthorne*, p. 216).

86. Hawthorne, *SL*, pp. 70–1.

87. Ibid., p. 60.

88. Ibid., pp. 119–20.

89. Ibid., p. 127.
90. Ibid., pp. 92, 115, 98, 156, 99.
91. Ibid., p. 92.
92. Ibid., p. 245.
93. Ibid., pp. 204, 244.
94. Ibid., pp. 91–2.
95. Ibid., p. 178. S. B. Wright refers to Pearl as 'a child of nature' and says the green letter 'signifies truth' (*Critical Companion to Nathaniel Hawthorne*, p. 219).
96. Fiedler, *Love and Death in the American Novel*, p. 31.
97. Hawthorne, *SL*, p. 129.
98. M. E. Brown, 'The Structure of *The Marble Faun*', *American Literature*, 28 (1956), p. 313.
99. Mellow, *NHHT*, p. 524.
100. Goldfarb, '*The Marble Faun* and Emersonian Self-Reliance', p. 21.
101. Fiedler, *Love and Death in the American Novel*, p. 302.
102. Hawthorne, *MF*, p. 46.
103. Ibid., p. 140. Wright calls Donatello, like Pearl from *The Scarlet Letter*, 'a child of nature' (*Critical Companion to Nathaniel Hawthorne*, p. 161).
104. Hawthorne, *MF*, pp. 7, 15, 18, 42, 81, 158.
105. Ibid., pp. 14, 43, 82, 131, 157, 170.
106. Ibid., p. 172.
107. Ibid., pp. 238, 320.
108. Ibid., p. 434.
109. Ibid., p. 3.
110. Ibid., p. 192.
111. Ibid., p. 30.
112. Matthiessen believes that Hawthorne 'could never feel that America was a new world' because of the weight of the past on the present (*American Renaissance*, p. 322), but the evidence from Hawthorne's prefaces and from his other writings suggests otherwise. Indeed, Mellow points out that it is in the museums of Paris – in the Old World – where Hawthorne feels 'the burden of the past' (*NHHT*, p. 482).
113. Randall Stewart classifies Kenyon as a 'detached observer' ('Introduction, Chapter III', p. lxi), and Wright refers to Kenyon as 'the detached observer of life' (*Critical Companion to Nathaniel Hawthorne*, p. 162).
114. Hawthorne, *MF*, p. 228.
115. Ibid., p. 16.
116. Ibid., p. 103.
117. Ibid., p. 105.
118. R. Gollin, 'Hawthorne and the Visual Arts', in L. J. Reynolds (ed.), *A Historical Guide to Nathaniel Hawthorne* (Oxford: Oxford University Press, 2001), p. 128.
119. Hawthorne, *MF*, p. 56.
120. Ibid., p. 174.
121. Ibid.
122. Ibid., p. 175.
123. Ibid., pp. 175, 264.
124. Ibid., pp. 282, 320.
125. Ibid., p. 95, 96.
126. Ibid., p. 343.

127. Ibid., p. 461.
128. Ibid., p. 448.

Conclusion: 'Impression[s] of Veracity': Echoes of the Romantic Moral Romance in the Modern, Symbolic Novel

1. Chase, *The American Novel and Its Tradition*, p. 118.
2. J. Keats, 'Ode on a Grecian Urn', in J. Keats, *Complete Poems*, ed. Jack Stillinger (Cambridge, MA: Harvard University Press, 1982), p. 283.
3. H. James, *Hawthorne* (1887; London: Macmillan, 1967; New York: St Martin's, 1967), p. 22.
4. Chase, *The American Novel and Its Tradition*, p. 71.
5. T. Tanner, 'Introduction', in H. James, *Hawthorne*, p. 2.
6. Stevens, *Medieval Romance*, p. 16.
7. L. B. Holland, *The Expense of Vision: Essays on the Craft of Henry James* (Princeton, NJ: Princeton University Press, 1964), p. 20; M. Bradbury, *Dangerous Pilgrimages: Trans-Atlantic Mythologies and the Novel* (London: Secker & Warburg, 1995), p. 156.
8. T. S. Eliot, 'On Henry James', in F. W. Dupee (ed.), *The Question of Henry James: A Collection of Critical Essays* (New York: Holt, 1945), p. 110.
9. W. R. Goetz, *Henry James and the Darkest Abyss of Romance* (Baton Rouge, LA: Louisiana State University Press, 1986), p. 24. Richard Chase's chapters, 'Hawthorne and the Limits of Romance' and 'The Lesson of the Master' in *The American Novel and Its Tradition* also are of particular use in examining this evolving Jamesian definition. See also James's 'The Art of Fiction', in which James makes the point that there is no need to distinguish between novel and romance (H. James, 'The Art of Fiction', in G. L. Barnett (ed.), *Nineteenth-Century British Novelists on the Novel* (New York: Appleton-Century-Crofts, 1971), p. 248).
10. Goetz, *Henry James and the Darkest Abyss of Romance*, p. 26.
11. Qtd. in Chase, *The American Novel and Its Tradition*, p. 26.
12. M. D. Bell, *The Development of American Romance: The Sacrifice of Relation* (Chicago, IL: University of Chicago Press, 1980), p. 8.
13. A. P. Frank, 'James's *The American*: A Tragedy of Intercultural Bafflement', in A. P. Frank and R. Lohse (eds), *Internationality in American Fiction: Henry James, William Dean Howells, William Faulkner, Toni Morrison* (Frankfurt: Peter Lang, 2005), pp. 19–110; T. J. Lustig, 'Sunspots and Blindspots in *The Europeans*', *EREA*, 3:2 (2005), pp. 6–18. For more recent discussions that link James and Hawthorne, see M. Anesko, 'Is James's Hawthorne Really James's Hawthorne?', *Henry James Review*, 29:1 (2008), pp. 36–53; S. Teahan, 'My Sculptor/My Self: A Story of Reading', *Henry James Review*, 23:3 (2002), pp. 246–54; N. Matheson, 'Intimacy and Form: James on Hawthorne's Charm', *Henry James Review*, 28:2 (2007), pp. 120–139.
14. E. M. Budick, 'Perplexity, Sympathy, and the Question of the Human: A Reading of *The Marble Faun*', in R. H. Millington (ed.), *The Cambridge Companion to Nathaniel Hawthorne* (Cambridge: Cambridge University Press, 2004), p. 236.
15. Levin, *The Power of Blackness*, p. 78.
16. J. Freedman, 'Introduction: The Moment of Henry James', in J. Freedman (ed.), *The Cambridge Companion to Henry James* (Cambridge: Cambridge University Press, 1998), pp. 13, 15.

17. James, *Hawthorne*, p. 111.
18. R. Poirier, *The Comic Sense of Henry James: A Study of the Early Novels* (New York: Oxford University Press, 1960), p. 9.
19. James, *Hawthorne*, p. 154.
20. Chase, *The American Novel and Its Tradition*, p. 118.
21. Ibid., p. 200.
22. Bell, *The Development of American Romance*, p. 19.
23. D. Krook, *The Ordeal of Consciousness in Henry James* (Cambridge: Cambridge University Press, 1962), p. 9. Jonah Siegel also notes Hawthorne's and James's mutual connections with Anglo-European literature in a chapter entitled 'The Museum in the Romance: James with Hawthorne', in *Haunted Museum: Longing, Travel, and the Art-Romance Tradition* (Princeton, NJ: Princeton University Press, 2005), pp. 113–48.
24. Margaret Anne Doody's *The True Story of the Novel* is relevant here in its suggestion of the 'connectedness' of western literature to the literatures of ancient cultures of Greece, Russia, China and Japan, see *The True Story of the* Novel, p. 9). Doody contends that the novel has had a continuous western existence for 2,000 years (p. 1) and argues for a comprehensive interconnection of literary influence across the globe.
25. Parrinder, *Nation & Novel*, p. 2; James, 'The Art of Fiction', p. 254.
26. J. Ryan, 'Elective Affinities', p. 155.
27. Ibid.
28. Ibid., p. 154.
29. Ibid.
30. Doody, *The True Story of the Novel*, p. 1.
31. Ibid., p. 15. In part, Doody is able to merge the novel and romance traditions easily because she provides such a broad definition of the novel form (perhaps because modern permutations of the novel have taken such varied forms). She believes that a novel 'includes the idea of length (preferably forty or more pages), and that, above all, it should be in prose' (p. 10). Later, she refines her definition slightly: 'A work is a novel if it is fictional, if it is in prose, and if it is of a certain length' (p. 16).
32. F. Kermode, *Romantic Image* (1957; London and New York: Routledge, 2002), p. 8.
33. P. Conrad, 'The Religion of Romanticism', *Times Literary Supplement* (23 May 1975), p. 550.
34. Shea, 'Religion and the Romantic Movement', p. 285.

WORKS CITED

Abel, D., '"A More Imaginative Pleasure": Hawthorne on the Play of Imagination', *Emerson Society Quarterly*, 55 (1969), pp. 63–71.

Abrams, M. H., *Natural Supernaturalism: Tradition and Revolution in Romantic Literature* (New York: Norton, 1971).

Adams, F. C., 'Blood Vengeance in *The Scarlet Letter*', *Nathaniel Hawthorne Review*, 32:2 (2006), pp. 1–12.

Allan, D., *A Nation of Readers: The Lending Library in Georgian England* (London: British Library, 2008).

American Antiquarian Society (ed.), *Early American Imprints, 1801–1819* (Series II) (New York and New Canaan, CT: Readex Microprint, various dates).

Anderson, E. H., 'Revising Theatrical Conventions in *A Simple Story*: Elizabeth Inchbald's Ambiguous Performance', *Journal for Early Modern Cultural Studies*, 6:1 (2006), pp. 5–30.

Andries, L., *La Bibliothèque bleue au dix-huitième siècle: une tradition éditoriale*, Studies on Voltaire and the Eighteenth Century 270 (Oxford: Voltaire Foundation, 1989).

—, 'La *Bibliothèque bleue* et la redécouverte des romans de chevalerie au dix-huitième siècle', in P. Damian-Grint (ed.), *Medievalism and manière gothique in Enlightenment France*, Studies on Voltaire and the Eighteenth Century 2006:05 (Oxford: Voltaire Foundation, 2006), pp. 52–67.

Anesko, M., 'Is James's Hawthorne Really James's Hawthorne?', *Henry James Review*, 29:1 (2008), pp. 36–53.

Argersinger, J. L., and L. S. Person (eds), *Hawthorne and Melville: Writing a Relationship* (Athens, GA: University of Georgia Press, 2008).

Armstrong, I., *Jane Austen: Mansfield Park* (London: Penguin, 1988).

Astbury, K., *The Moral Tale in France and Germany, 1750–1789*, Studies on Voltaire and the Eighteenth Century, 2002:07 (Oxford: Voltaire Foundation, 2002).

—, 'Marmontel and Baculard d'Arnaud's (im)moral tales', in J. Mallinson (gen. ed.), *History of Ideas / Travel Writing / History of the Book / Enlightenment and Antiquity*, Studies on Voltaire and the Eighteenth Century, 2005:01 (Oxford: Voltaire Foundation, 2005), pp. 39–51.

Atherton, G., 'Why Is American Literature Bourgeois?', in G. Hutner (ed.), *American Literature, American Culture* (New York: Oxford University Press, 1999), pp. 194–200.

Auerbach, E., *Mimesis*, trans. W. R. Trask (Princeton, NJ: Princeton University Press, 1974).

Austen, J., *Mansfield Park*, in J. Austen, *The Complete Novels* (Oxford: Oxford University Press, 1994), pp. 473–766.

Baines, P., 'Jephson, Robert (1736/7–1803)', in H. C. G. Matthew and B. Harrison, *Oxford Dictionary of National Biography* (Oxford: Oxford University Press, 2004), vol. 30, pp. 31–3.

Baines, P., and E. Burns, 'Introduction', in P. Baines and E. Burns (eds), *Five Romantic Plays, 1768–1821* (Oxford: Oxford University Press, 2000), pp. v–xlvi.

Bales, K., 'Hawthorne's Prefaces and Romantic Perspectivism', *Emerson Society Quarterly*, 23 (1977), pp. 55–69.

Barbauld, A. L., *On the Origin and Progress of Novel-Writing* (excerpts of introduction and prefaces from A. L. Barbauld (ed.), *The British Novelists*, 50 vols (London, 1810)).

Barker-Benfield, G. J., *The Culture of Sensibility: Sex and Society in Eighteenth-Century Britain* (Chicago, IL: University of Chicago Press, 1992).

Barrett, P. W., 'More American Adams: Women Heroes in American Fiction', *Markham Review*, 10 (1981), pp. 39–41.

Barros, C. A., and J. M. Smith, 'Mary Robinson', in C. A. Barros and J. M. Smith (eds), *Life-Writings by British Women, 1660–1850: An Anthology* (Boston, MA: Northeastern University Press, 2000), pp. 369–70.

Bate, J., *Shakespeare and the English Romantic Imagination* (Oxford: Clarendon Press, 1986).

— (ed.), *The Romantics on Shakespeare* (London: Penguin, 1992).

—, 'The Romantic Stage', in J. Bate and R. Jackson (eds), *Shakespeare: An Illustrated Stage History* (Oxford: Oxford University Press, 1996), pp. 92–111.

Baym, N., 'Early Histories of American Literature: A Chapter in the Institution of New England', *American Literary History*, 1:3 (1989), pp. 459–88.

Bell, M. D., *The Development of American Romance: The Sacrifice of Relation* (Chicago, IL: University of Chicago Press, 1980).

Bell, M. (ed.), *Hawthorne and the Real: Bicentennial Essays* (Columbus: Ohio State University Press, 2005).

Bercovitch, S., 'Miriam as Shylock: An Echo from Shakespeare in Hawthorne's *Marble Faun*', *Forum for Modern Language Studies*, 5 (1969), pp. 385–7.

Bier, J., 'Hawthorne on the Romance: His Prefaces Related and Examined', *Modern Philology*, 53 (1955), pp. 17–24.

Boaden, J., *Memoirs of Mrs Inchbald*, 2 vols (London: Richard Bentley, 1833).

Boardman, M., 'Inchbald's *A Simple Story*: An Anti-Ideological Reading', *Eighteenth Century: Theory and Interpretation*, 37:3 (1996), pp. 271–84.

Bode, C., and F.-W. Neumann (eds), *British and European Romanticisms* (Trier, Germany: Wissenschaftlicher, 2007).

Bolton, C. K., 'Circulating Libraries in Boston, 1765–1865', *Publications of the Colonial Society of Massachusetts*, 11 (1907), pp. 196–208.

[Bolton, C. K.], *The Boston Athenaeum, 1807–1927: A Sketch* ([Boston, MA: The Athenaeum, 1928]).

Bosco, R. A., and J. Murphy (eds), *Hawthorne in His Own Time* (Iowa City: University of Iowa Press, 2007).

Botting, F., *Gothic* (London and New York: Routledge, 1996).

Boyer, P. and S. Nissenbaum, *Salem Possessed: The Social Origins of Witchcraft* (Cambridge, MA: Harvard University Press, 1974).

Bradbury, M., *Dangerous Pilgrimages: Trans-Atlantic Mythologies and the Novel* (London: Secker & Warburg, 1995).

Breashears, C., 'Defining Masculinity in *A Simple Story*', *Eighteenth-Century Fiction*, 16:3 (2004), pp. 451–70.

British Museum General Catalogue of Printed Books to 1955, compact edn, 50 vols (New York: Readex Microprint Corporation, 1965–1968).

Brooks, V. W., 'On Creating a Usable Past', in G. Hutner (ed.), *American Literature, American Culture* (New York: Oxford University Press, 1999), pp. 213–16.

Brown, M. E., 'The Structure of *The Marble Faun*', *American Literature*, 28 (1956), pp. 302–13.

Budick, E. M., 'Perplexity, Sympathy, and the Question of the Human: A Reading of *The Marble Faun*', in R. H. Millington (ed.), *The Cambridge Companion to Nathaniel Hawthorne* (Cambridge: Cambridge University Press, 2004), pp. 230–50.

Buell, L., 'Hawthorne and the Problem of "American" Fiction: The Example of *The Scarlet Letter*', in M. Bell (ed.), *Hawthorne and the Real: Bicentennial Essays* (Columbus: Ohio State University Press, 2005), pp. 70–87.

Bunyan, J., *The Pilgrim's Progress*, ed. W. R. Owens (Oxford: Oxford University Press, 2003).

Burge, J., *Heloise & Abelard: A New Biography* (New York: HarperCollins, 2003).

Burney, F., 'To the Queen', in F. Burney, *Camilla; or, A Picture of Youth*, ed. E. A. Bloom and L. D. Bloom (Oxford: Oxford University Press, 1983), pp. 3–4.

—, 'Preface', in F. Burney, *Evelina; or, The History of a Young Lady's Entrance into the World*, ed. E. Bloom (Oxford: Oxford University Press, 1998), pp. 7–9.

Byron, G. G., *Byron's Letters and Journals*, ed. L. A. Marchand, vol. 3: 'Alas! the love of Women!' (Cambridge, MA: Harvard University Press, 1973).

—, 'Prometheus', in G. G. Byron, *Selected Poems*, ed. S. J. Wolfson and P. J. Manning (London: Penguin, 1996), pp. 394–6.

Cafarelli, A. W., 'Rousseau and British Romanticism: Women and the Legacy of Male Radicalism', in G. Maertz (ed.), *Cultural Interactions in the Romantic Age: Critical Essays in Comparative Literature* (Albany, NY: State University of New York Press, 1998), pp. 125–55.

Calin, W., *The French Tradition and the Literature of Medieval England* (Toronto, ON: University of Toronto Press, 1994).

Carlson, P. A., 'National Typology and Hawthorne's Historical Allegory', *CEA Critic,* 37:1 (1974), pp. 11–13.

Carson, J. P., 'Enlightenment, Popular Culture, and Gothic Fiction', in J. Richetti (ed.), *The Cambridge Companion to the Eighteenth-Century Novel* (Cambridge: Cambridge University Press, 1996), pp. 257–9.

Carton, E., *The Marble Faun: Hawthorne's Transformations* (New York: Twayne, 1992).

Cass, J., and L. H. Peer (eds), *Romantic Border Crossings* (Aldershot: Ashgate, 2008).

Castle, T., *Masquerade and Civilization: The Carnivalesque in Eighteenth-Century English Culture and Fiction* (Stanford, CA: Stanford University Press, 1986).

Catalogue Général des Livres Imprimés de la Bibliothèque Nationale, 231 vols (Paris: Imprimerie Nationale, 1924–1981).

Catalogue of Books in the Boston Atheneum [*sic*] (Boston, MA: W. L. Lewis, 1827).

Cauwels, J. M., 'A Critical Edition of *Nature and Art* (1796) by Elizabeth Inchbald (1753– 1821)' (PhD dissertation, University of Virginia, 1976).

—, 'Authorial "Caprice" vs. Editorial "Calculation": The Text of Elizabeth Inchbald's *Nature and Art*', *Papers of the Bibliographical Society of America,* 72 (1978), pp. 169–85.

Cervantes Saavedra, M. de, *Don Quixote,* trans. J. H. Montgomery (Indianapolis, IN: Hackett Publishing, 2009).

Ceserani, R., and P. Zanotti, 'The Fragment as Structuring Force', in G. Gillespie, M. Engel, and B. Dieterle (eds), *Romantic Prose Fiction* (Amsterdam: John Benjamins, 2008), pp. 452–75.

Chadwick, H., 'Romanticism and Religion', in J. C. Laidlaw (ed.), *The Future of the Modern Humanities* (Modern Humanities Research Association, 1969), pp. 18–30.

Chase, R., *The American Novel and Its Tradition* (Garden City, NY: Doubleday, 1957).

Chew, S. C., and R. D. Altick, *Book IV: The Nineteenth Century and After (1789–1939), A Literary History of England,* gen. ed. A. C. Baugh, 2nd edn (1948. New York: Appleton-Century-Crofts, 1967).

Clarke, N., 'Baillie, Joanna (1762–1851)', in H. C. G. Matthew and B. Harrison, *Oxford Dictionary of National Biography* (Oxford: Oxford University Press, 2004), vol. 3, pp. 288–90.

Cobb, C. J., *The Staging of Romance in Late Shakespeare: Text and Theatrical Technique* (Newark, DE: University of Delaware Press, 2007).

Cohen, M., and C. Dever (eds), *The Literary Channel: The Inter-National Invention of the Novel* (Princeton, NJ: Princeton University Press, 2002).

Congreve, W., 'The Preface to the Reader', in H. F. B. Brett-Smith (ed.), *Incognita; or, Love and Duty Reconcil'd* (Oxford: Basil Blackwell, 1922), pp. 5–7.

Conrad, P., 'The Religion of Romanticism', *Times Literary Supplement,* 23 May 1975, pp. 550–1.

Cooper, H., *The English Romance in Time: Transforming Motifs from Geoffrey of Monmouth to the Death of Shakespeare* (Oxford: Oxford University Press, 2004).

Cowley, M., 'Five Acts of *The Scarlet Letter*', in C. Shapiro (ed.), *Twelve Original Essays on Great American Novels* (Detroit, MI: Wayne State University Press, 1958), pp. 23–44.

Cox, J. N., '*Lamia, Isabella,* and *The Eve of St Agnes*: Eros and "Romance"', in S. J. Wolfson (ed.), *The Cambridge Companion to Keats* (Cambridge: Cambridge University Press, 2001), pp. 53–68.

Craft-Fairchild, C., *Masquerade and Gender: Disguise and Female Identity in Eighteenth-Century Fictions by Women* (University Park, PA: Pennsylvania State University Press, 1993).

Curran, S., *Shelley's* Cenci: *Scorpions Ringed with Fire* (Princeton, NJ: Princeton University Press, 1970).

—, 'Women Readers, Women Writers' in S. Curran (ed.), *The Cambridge Companion to British Romanticism* (Cambridge: Cambridge University Press, 1993), pp. 177–95.

Daniell, D., The Tempest (Atlantic Highlands, NJ: Humanities Press International, 1989).

Daniels, C. L., 'Hawthorne's Pearl: Woman-Child of the Future', *American Transcendental Quarterly,* 19:3 (2005), pp. 221–36.

Davidson, J., 'Why Girls Look Like Their Mothers: David Garrick Rewrites *The Winter's Tale*', in P. Sabor and P. Yachnin (eds), *Shakespeare and the Eighteenth Century* (Aldershot: Ashgate, 2008), pp. 165–80.

Davis, C., 'Hawthorne's Shyness: Romance and the Forms of Truth', *Emerson Society Quarterly: A Journal of the American Renaissance,* 45:1 (1999), pp. 33–65.

Davis, L. J., *Factual Fictions: The Origins of the English Novel* (New York: Columbia University Press, 1983).

Dédéyan, C., *Jean-Jacques Rousseau et la Sensibilité Littéraire à la Fin du XVIIIe Siècle* (Paris: Société d'Edition d'Enseignement Supérieur, 1966).

Doody, M. A., *The True Story of the Novel* (New Brunswick, NJ: Rutgers University Press, 1996).

Drabble, M. (ed.), *The Oxford Companion to English Literature,* 5th edn (Oxford: Oxford University Press, 1985).

Drake, S. G. (ed.), *The Witchcraft Delusion in New England,* 3 vols (1866; New York: Burt Franklin, 1970).

DuBois, W. R., *English and American Stage Productions: An Annotated Checklist of Prompt Books, 1800–1900* (Boston, MA: G. K. Hall, 1973).

Dunkley, J., 'Medieval Heroes in Enlightenment Disguises: Figures from Voltaire and Belloy', in P. Damian-Grint (ed.), *Medievalism and manière gothique in Enlightenment France,* Studies on Voltaire and the Eighteenth Century 2006:05 (Oxford: Voltaire Foundation, 2006).

Dunne, M., '"Tearing the Web Apart": Resisting Monological Interpretation in Hawthorne's *Marble Faun*', *South Atlantic Review,* 69:3–4 (2004), pp. 23–50.

Durham, W. B., *American Theatre Companies, 1749–1887* (New York: Greenwood Press, 1986).

Dutton, R., and J. E. Howard (eds), *A Companion to Shakespeare's Works, Volume 4: The Poems, Problem Comedies, Late Plays* (Malden, MA: Blackwell, 2003).

Edgeworth, M., 'Advertisement', in M. Edgeworth, *Belinda*, ed. K. J. Kirkpatrick (Oxford: Oxford University Press, 1999), p. 3.

Eliot, T. S., 'On Henry James', in F. W. Dupee (ed.), *The Question of Henry James: A Collection of Critical Essays* (New York: Holt, 1945), pp. 108–19.

Ellis, G. (ed.), *Specimens of Early English Metrical Romances*, rev. J. O. Halliwell (London: Henry Bohn, 1848; NY: AMS Press, 1968).

Emerson, R. W., 'The American Scholar', in R. W. Emerson, *The Collected Works of Ralph Waldo Emerson, Volume 1: Nature, Addresses, and Lectures,* ed. A. R. Ferguson (Cambridge, MA: Belknap Press of Harvard University Press, 1971), pp. 49–70.

—, 'The Young American', in R. W. Emerson, *Essays and Lectures* (New York: Library of America, 1983), pp. 211–30.

Fairchild, H. N., *The Noble Savage: A Study in Romantic Naturalism* (New York: Columbia University Press, 1928).

Felperin, H., *Shakespearean Romance* (Princeton, NJ: Princeton University Press, 1972).

Fergus, J., and J. F. Thaddeus, 'Women, Publishers, and Money, 1790–1820', *Studies in Eighteenth-Century Culture,* 17 (1987), pp. 191–207.

Fick, L. J., *The Light Beyond: A Study of Hawthorne's Theology* (Westminster, MD: Newman Press, 1955).

Fiedler, L. A., *Love and Death in the American Novel,* rev. edn (New York: Stein and Day, 1966).

Fielding, H., *Joseph Andrews*, ed. S. Copley (London: Methuen, 1987).

Fleishman, A., *A Reading of* Mansfield Park: *An Essay in Critical Synthesis* (Minneapolis, MN: University of Minnesota Press, 1967).

Fogle, R. H., 'Nathaniel Hawthorne and the Great English Romantic Poets', *Keats-Shelley Journal,* 21–22 (1972–73), pp. 219–35.

—, 'The Great English Romantics in Hawthorne's Major Romances', *Nathaniel Hawthorne Journal,* 6 (1976), pp. 62–8.

Ford, S. A., '"It Is about Lovers' Vows": Kotzebue, Inchbald, and the Players of Mansfield Park', *Persuasions On-Line,* 27:1 (2006), <http://www.jasna.org/persuasions/on-line/vol27no1/ford.htm>.

Foster, J. R., *History of the Pre-Romantic Novel in England* (New York: Modern Language Association, 1949).

France, P., and S. Gillespie (eds), *The Oxford History of Literary Translation in English,* 5 vols (Oxford: Oxford University Press, 2005 ongoing).

Frank, A. P., 'James's *The American*: A Tragedy of Intercultural Bafflement', in A. P. Frank and R. Lohse (eds), *Internationality in American Fiction: Henry James, William Dean Howells, William Faulkner, Toni Morrison* (Frankfurt: Peter Lang, 2005), pp. 19–110.

Frank, F. S. 'Nathaniel Hawthorne (1804–1864)', in D. H. Thomson, J. G. Voller and F. S. Frank (eds), *Gothic Writers: A Critical and Biographical Guide* (Westport, CT: Greenwood Press, 2002), pp. 165–76.

Frederick, J., *The Darkened Sky: Nineteenth-Century American Novelists and Religion* (Notre Dame, IN: University of Notre Dame Press, 1969).

Freedman, J., 'Introduction: The Moment of Henry James', in J. Freedman (ed.), *The Cambridge Companion to Henry James* (Cambridge: Cambridge University Press, 1998), pp. 1–20.

French, W. H., and C. B. Hale (eds), 'Introduction', *Middle English Metrical Romances*, 2 vols (1930. New York: Russell & Russell, 1964), vol. 1, pp. 1–22.

Frey, C., *Shakespeare's Vast Romance: A Study of* The Winter's Tale (Columbia: University of Missouri Press, 1980).

Frye, N., *The Anatomy of Criticism: Four Essays* (Princeton, NJ: Princeton University Press, 1957).

Frye, N., S. Baker and G. Perkins, *The Harper Handbook to Literature* (New York: Harper & Row, 1985).

Fuchs, B., *Romance* (New York: Routledge, 2004).

Fuller, M., 'American Literature', in M. Fuller, *The Writings of Margaret Fuller*, ed. M. Wade (Clifton, NJ: Augustus Kelley (by arrangement with Viking Press), 1973), pp. 358–88.

Gallagher, C., *Nobody's Story: The Vanishing Acts of Women Writers in the Marketplace, 1670–1820* (Berkeley, CA: University of California Press, 1994).

—, 'Nobody's Story: Gender, Property, and the Rise of the Novel', in M. Brown (ed.), *Eighteenth-Century Literary History: An MLQ Reader* (Durham and London: Duke University Press, 1999), pp. 27–42.

Gibbs, A. C., 'Introduction', *in Middle English Romances* (London: Edward Arnold, 1966), pp. 1–40.

Giles, P., *Transatlantic Insurrections: British Culture and the Formation of American Literature, 1730–1860* (Philadelphia, PA: University of Pennsylvania Press, 2001).

Goetz, W. R., *Henry James and the Darkest Abyss of Romance* (Baton Rouge, LA: Louisiana State University Press, 1986).

Goldfarb, C., 'The Marble Faun and Emersonian Self-Reliance', *American Transcendental Quarterly*, 1:1 (1969), pp. 19–23.

Gollin, R., 'Hawthorne and the Visual Arts', in L. J. Reynolds (ed.), *A Historical Guide to Nathaniel Hawthorne* (Oxford: Oxford University Press, 2001), pp. 109–33.

Grabovszki, E., 'Doubling, Doubles, Duplicity, Bipolarity', in G. Gillespie, M. Engel and B. Dieterle (eds), *Romantic Prose Fiction* (Amsterdam: John Benjamins, 2008), pp. 168–82.

Graham, W., *Gothic Elements in Nathaniel Hawthorne's Fiction* (Marburg, Germany: Tectum Verlag, 1999).

Grant, W. E., 'Hawthorne's Hamlet: The Archetypal Structure of *The Blithedale Romance*', *Rocky Mountain Review of Language and Literature*, 31 (1977), pp. 1–15.

Gravil, R., *Romantic Dialogues: Anglo-American Continuities, 1776–1862* (New York: St Martin's Press, 2000).

Grieder, J., *Translations of French Sentimental Prose Fiction in Late Eighteenth-Century England: The History of a Literary Vogue* (Durham, NC: Duke University Press, 1975).

Haggerty, G. E., 'Female Abjection in Inchbald's *A Simple Story*', *Studies in English Literature, 1500–1900*, 36:3 (1996), pp. 655–71.

—, *Unnatural Affections: Women and Fiction in the Later 18th Century* (Bloomington, IN: Indiana University Press, 1998).

—, 'The Horrors of Catholicism: Religion and Sexuality in Gothic Fiction', *Romanticism on the Net*, 36–37 (2004), <http://www.erudit.org/revue/ron/2004/v/n36-37/0011133ar. html>.

Handwerk, G., and A. A. Markley, 'Introduction', in W. Godwin, *Caleb Williams* (Toronto, ON: Broadview, 2000), pp. 9–46.

Harmon, W., 'Romantic Period in English Literature', *A Handbook to Literature*, 10th edn (Upper Saddle River, NJ: Pearson, 2006), pp. 459–60.

Harries, E. W., *The Unfinished Manner: Essays on the Fragment in the Later Eighteenth Century* (Charlottesville, VA and London: University Press of Virginia, 1994).

Harris, J., 'Reflections of the Byronic Hero in Hawthorne's Fiction', *Nathaniel Hawthorne Journal*, 7 (1977), pp. 305–18.

Hart, J. D., 'Romanticism', *The Oxford Companion to American Literature*, 6th edn, rev. P. W. Leininger (New York: Oxford, 1995), pp. 572–3.

Hartwig, J., *Shakespeare's Tragicomic Vision* (Baton Rouge, LA: Louisiana State University Press, 1972).

Hawthorne, N., *The Centenary Edition of the Works of Nathaniel Hawthorne*, ed. W. Charvat, *et al.*, 23 vols (Columbus, OH: Ohio State University Press, 1962–1997).

—, *The English Notebooks*, ed. R. Stewart (New York: Russell & Russell, 1962).

—, 'Preface', in D. Bacon, *The Philosophy of Shakspere Unfolded* (London: Groombridge, 1857; New York: AMS Press, 1970), pp. vii–xv.

Hays, M. L., *Shakespearean Tragedy as Chivalric Romance: Rethinking Macbeth, Hamlet, Othello, and King Lear* (Cambridge: D. S. Brewer, 2003).

Hays, M., 'Preface', in M. Hays, *Memoirs of Emma Courtney*, ed. E. Ty (Oxford: Oxford University Press, 1996), pp. 3–5.

Hazlitt, W., 'On the English Novelists', in W. Hazlitt, *Lectures on the English Comic Writers and Fugitive Writings*, ed. A. Johnston (London: Everyman, 1963), pp. 106–32.

Hehr, M. G., 'Theatrical Life in Salem, 1783–1823', *Essex Institute Historical Collections*, 100 (1964), pp. 3–37.

Heidler, J. B., *The History, from 1700 to 1800, of English Criticism of Prose Fiction*, University of Illinois Studies in Language and Literature Series 13:2 (Urbana, IL: University of Illinois Press, 1928).

Henderson, A. K., *Romantic Identities: Varieties of Subjectivity, 1774–1830* (Cambridge: Cambridge University Press, 1996).

Henitiuk, V., 'To Be and Not To Be: The Bounded Body and Embodied Boundary in Inchbald's *A Simple Story*', in J. Cass and L. H. Peer (eds), *Romantic Border Crossings* (Aldershot: Ashgate, 2008), pp. 41–51.

Heydt-Stevenson, J., and C. Sussman (eds), *Recognizing the Romantic Novel: New Histories of British Fiction, 1780–1830* (Liverpool: Liverpool University Press, 2008).

Hoeveler, D. L., 'La Cenci: The Incest Motif in Hawthorne and Melville', *American Transcendental Quarterly*, 44 (1979), pp. 247–59.

—, 'Beatrice Cenci in Hawthorne, Melville, and Her Atlantic-Rim Contexts', *Romanticism on the Net* 38–39 (2005), <http://www.erudit.org/revue/ron/2005/v/n38-39/011670ar. html>.

Hogan, C. B., *The London Stage, 1660–1800: A Calendar of Plays, Entertainments and Afterpieces together with Casts, Box-Receipts and Contemporary Comment*, Part 5: 1776–1800, 2 vols (Carbondale, IL: Southern Illinois University Press, 1968).

Holland, L. B., *The Expense of Vision: Essays on the Craft of Henry James* (Princeton, NJ: Princeton University Press, 1964).

Hunt, L., *The Autobiography of Leigh Hunt*, ed. J. E. Morpurgo (London: Cresset Press, 1948).

Hunter, J. P., 'The Novel and Social/Cultural History', in J. Richetti (ed.), *The Cambridge Companion to the Eighteenth-Century Novel* (Cambridge: Cambridge University Press, 1996), pp. 9–40.

Hurd, R., 'Letters on Chivalry and Romance', *Moral and Political Dialogues; with Letters on Chivalry and Romance*, 5th edn, 3 vols (London: T. Cadell, 1776), vol. 3, pp. 187–338.

Inchbald, E., *The British Theatre; or, A Collection of Plays, which Are Acted at the Theatres Royal, Drury Lane, Covent Garden, and Haymarket. With Biographical and Critical Remarks, by Mrs. Inchbald,* 25 vols (London: Longman, Hurst, Rees and Orme, 1808).

— (ed.), *A Collection of Farces and Other Afterpieces Which are Acted at the Theatres Royal, Drury Lane, Covent Garden, and Hay-Market,* 7 vols (London: Longman, Hurst, Rees and Orme, 1809).

— (ed.), *The Modern Theatre; A Collection of Successful Modern Plays, As Acted at the Theatres Royal, London, selected by Mrs. Inchbald,* 10 vols (London: Longman, Hurst, Rees, Orme and Brown, 1811).

—, *The Plays of Elizabeth Inchbald*, ed. and introd. P. R. Backscheider, 2 vols (New York: Garland, 1980).

—, *Remarks for* The British Theatre *(1806–1809)*, introd. C. Macheski (Delmar, NY: Scholars' Facsimiles & Reprints, 1990).

—, *Nature and Art* (1796; Oxford: Woodstock Books, 1994).

—, ['On the Novel'], in E. Inchbald, *Nature and Art*, ed. S. L. Maurer (London: Pickering & Chatto, 1997), pp. 139–44.

—, *A Simple Story* (1791; Oxford: Oxford University Press, 1998).

—, *Nature and Art*, ed. Shawn Lisa Maurer (1796; Peterborough, ON: Broadview Press, 2005).

—, *A Simple Story*, ed. Anna Lott (1791; Peterborough, ON: Broadview Press, 2007).

—, *The Diaries of Elizabeth Inchbald*, 3 vols, ed. B. P. Robertson (London: Pickering & Chatto, 2007).

Irwin, J. J., *M. G. 'Monk' Lewis* (Boston, MA: Twayne, 1976).

Isbell, J. C., 'Romantic Novel and Verse Romance, 1750–1850: Is There a Romance Continuum?', in G. Gillespie, M. Engel and B. Dieterle (eds), *Romantic Prose Fiction*, (Amsterdam: John Benjamins, 2008), pp. 496–516.

Jack, B., *Beatrice's Spell: The Enduring Legend of Beatrice Cenci* (London: Chatto & Windus, 2004).

Jacobs, E. C., 'Shakespearean Borrowings in *The House of the Seven Gables*', *Nathaniel Hawthorne Journal*, 7 (1977), pp. 343–6.

James, D. G., *The Dream of Prospero* (Oxford: Clarendon Press, 1967).

James, H., *Hawthorne* (1887; London: Macmillan, 1967; New York: St Martin's, 1967).

—, 'The Art of Fiction', in G. L. Barnett (ed.), *Nineteenth-Century British Novelists on the Novel* (New York: Appleton-Century-Crofts, 1971).

James, R. D., *Old Drury of Philadelphia: A History of the Philadelphia Stage, 1800–1835* (Philadelphia, PA: University of Pennsylvania Press, 1932).

Janowitz, A., 'The Romantic Fragment', in D. Wu (ed.), *A Companion to Romanticism* (London: Blackwell, 1999), pp. 442–51.

Jehlen, M., 'The Novel and the Middle Class in America', in M. Jehlen (ed.), *Readings at the Edge of Literature* (Chicago, IL: University of Chicago Press, 2002), pp. 50–67.

Jenkins, A., *I'll Tell You What: The Life of Elizabeth Inchbald* (Lexington, KY: University Press of Kentucky, 2003).

Jewers, C. A., *Chivalric Fiction and the History of the Novel* (Gainesville, FL: University Press of Florida, 2000).

Jones, W. F., 'Scopolamine Poisoning and the Death of Dimmesdale in *The Scarlet Letter*', *Nathaniel Hawthorne Review*, 32:1 (2006), pp. 52–62.

Karlsen, C. F., *The Devil in the Shape of a Woman: Witchcraft in Colonial New England* (New York: Norton, 1987).

Kaul, A. N., *The American Vision: Actual and Ideal Society in Nineteenth-Century Fiction* (New Haven, CT, and London: Yale University Press, 1963).

—, 'Character and Motive in *The Scarlet Letter*', *Critical Quarterly*, 10 (1968), pp. 373–84.

Keats, J., 'Ode on a Grecian Urn', in J. Keats, *Complete Poems*, ed. J. Stillinger (Cambridge, MA: Harvard University Press, 1982), p. 283.

Kelly, G., *The English Jacobin Novel, 1780–1805* (Oxford: Clarendon Press, 1976).

—, 'Romantic Fiction', in S. Curran (ed.), *The Cambridge Companion to British Romanticism* (Cambridge: Cambridge University Press, 1993), pp. 196–215.

Kermode, F., *William Shakespeare: The Final Plays* (London: Longmans, Green & Co., 1963).

—, *Romantic Image* (1957; London and New York: Routledge, 2002).

Kesselring, M., 'Hawthorne's Reading, 1828–1850', *Bulletin of the New York Public Library*, 53:2 (1949), pp. 55–71, 121–38, 173–94.

Kesterson, D. B., '*The Marble Faun* as Transformation of Author and Age', *Nathaniel Hawthorne Journal*, 6 (1976), pp. 67–78.

Kettle, A., *An Introduction to the English Novel*, 2 vols (London: Hutchinson's University Library, 1951).

Kiely, R., *The Romantic Novel in England* (Cambridge, MA: Harvard University Press, 1972).

Kirkby, J., 'The American Prospero', *Southern Review*, 18:1 (1985), pp. 90–108.

Knight, G. W., *The Crown of Life: Essays in Interpretation of Shakespeare's Final Plays* (London: Oxford University Press, 1947).

—, *The Shakespearian Tempest* (London: Methuen, 1953).

Knox, V., 'On Novel Reading', in I. Williams (ed.), *Novel and Romance, 1700–1800: A Documentary Record* (New York: Barnes & Noble, 1970), pp. 304–7.

Kors, A. C., and E. Peters (eds), *Witchcraft in Europe, 1100–1700: A Documentary History* (Philadelphia, PA: University of Pennsylvania Press, 1972).

Kritzman, L., and J. P. Plottel, *Fragments: Incompletion and Discontinuity* (New York: New York Literary Forum, 1981).

Krook, D., *The Ordeal of Consciousness in Henry James* (Cambridge: Cambridge University Press, 1962).

Krueger, R. L., 'Introduction', in R. L. Krueger (ed.), *The Cambridge Companion to Medieval Romance* (Cambridge: Cambridge University Press, 2000), pp. 1–9.

Labbe, J., *The Romantic Paradox: Love, Violence and the Uses of Romance, 1760–1830* (New York: St Martin's Press, 2000).

Lacy, N. J., 'The Evolution and Legacy of French Prose Romance', in R. L. Krueger (ed.), *The Cambridge Companion to Medieval Romance* (Cambridge: Cambridge University Press, 2000), pp. 167–82.

Lathrop, G. P., *A Study of Hawthorne* (1876; New York: AMS Press, 1969).

Lawrence, D. H., *Studies in Classic American Literature* (London: Heinemann, 1964).

Lease, B., *Anglo-American Encounters: England and the Rise of American Literature* (Cambridge: Cambridge University Press, 1981).

Lee, H.-S., 'Women, Comedy, and *A Simple Story*', *Eighteenth-Century Fiction*, 20:2 (2008), pp. 197–217.

Lennox, C., *Euphemia* (London: T. Cadell, 1790; Delmar, NY: Scholars' Facsimiles & Reprints, 1989).

The Letters of Abelard and Heloise, trans. B. Radice, rev. by M. T. Clancy (London: Penguin, 2003).

Levi, J., 'Hawthorne's *The Scarlet Letter*', *American Imago*, 10 (1953), pp. 291–306.

Levin, H., *The Power of Blackness: Hawthorne, Poe, Melville* (New York: Knopf, 1958).

Levine, R. S., 'Genealogical Fictions: Race in *The House of the Seven Gables* and *Pierre*', in J. L. Argersinger and L. S. Person (eds), *Hawthorne and Melville: Writing a Relationship* (Athens, GA: University of Georgia Press, 2008), pp. 227–47.

Levinson, M., *The Romantic Fragment Poem: A Critique of a Form* (Chapel Hill, NC: University of North Carolina Press, 1986).

Lewis, M. G., *The Monk*, ed. H. Anderson (Oxford: Oxford University Press, 1998).

Littlewood, S. R., *Elizabeth Inchbald and Her Circle: The Life Story of a Charming Woman (1753–1821)* (London: Daniel O'Connor, 1921).

Lohmann, C. K., 'The Agony of the English Romance', *Nathaniel Hawthorne Journal*, 2 (1972), pp. 219–29.

Lott, A., 'Introduction', in E. Inchbald, *A Simple Story*, ed. Anna Lott (Peterborough, ON: Broadview Press, 2007), pp. 13–46.

Lukács, G., *The Theory of the Novel* (Cambridge, MA: MIT Press, 1974).

Lundblad, J., *Nathaniel Hawthorne and the Tradition of the Gothic Romance* (New York: Haskell House, 1964).

Lupack, A., and B. T. Lupack, *King Arthur in America* (Woodbridge: D. S. Brewer, 1999).

Lustig, T. J., 'Sunspots and Blindspots in *The Europeans*', *EREA*, 3:2 (2005), pp. 6–18.

Lyne, R., *Shakespeare's Late Work* (Oxford: Oxford University Press, 2007).

Lyttle, D., 'Hawthorne: Calvinistic Humanism', *Studies in Religion in Early American Literature: Edwards, Poe, Channing, Emerson, Some Minor Transcendentalists, Hawthorne and Thoreau* (Lanham, MD: University Press of America, 1983), pp. 152–81.

MacLeod, G., 'Nathaniel Hawthorne and the Boston Athenaeum', *Nathaniel Hawthorne Review*, 32:1 (2006), pp. 1–29.

Maguire, L. E., *Studying Shakespeare: A Guide to the Plays* (Malden, MA: Blackwell, 2004).

Manvell, R., *Elizabeth Inchbald: England's Principal Woman Dramatist and Independent Woman of Letters in 18th-Century London* (Lanham, MD: University Press of America, 1987).

Markley, A. A., *Conversion and Reform in the British Novel in the 1790s: A Revolution of Opinions* (Basingstoke: Palgrave, 2008).

Martin, A., '"Les amours du bon vieux temps": medieval themes in French prose fiction, 1700–1750', in P. Damian-Grint (ed.), *Medievalism and manière gothique in Enlightenment France*, Studies on Voltaire and the Eighteenth Century 2006:05 (Oxford: Voltaire Foundation, 2006), pp. 15–36.

Marx, L., *The Machine in the Garden: Technology and the Pastoral Ideal in America* (1964; New York: Oxford University Press, 1970).

Massai, S., 'Romance', in M. Dobson (gen. ed.) and S. Wells (assoc. gen. ed.), *The Oxford Companion to Shakespeare* (Oxford: Oxford University Press, 2001), p. 395.

Matheson, N., 'Intimacy and Form: James on Hawthorne's Charm', *Henry James Review*, 28:2 (2007), pp. 120–139.

Matthews, B., and L. Hutton (eds), *The Kembles and Their Contemporaries* (Boston, MA; L. C. Page & Co., 1900).

Matthiessen, F. O., *American Renaissance: Art and Expression in the Age of Emerson and Whitman* (London: Oxford University Press, 1968).

Maurer, S. L., 'Introduction', in E. Inchbald, *Nature and Art*, ed. S. L. Maurer (Peterborough, ON: Broadview Press, 2005), pp. 11–31.

—, 'Masculinity and Morality in Elizabeth Inchbald's *Nature and Art*', in L. Lang-Peralta (ed.), *Women, Revolution, and the Novels of the 1790's* (East Lansing, MI: Michigan State University Press, 1999), pp. 155–76.

Maxwell, R., and K. Trumpener, eds. *The Cambridge Companion to Fiction in the Romantic Period* (Cambridge: Cambridge University Press, 2008).

May, G., *Le Dilemme du Roman au XVIIIe Siècle* (New Haven, CT: Yale University Press; Paris: Presses Universitaires de France, 1963).

McFarland, T., *Romanticism and the Forms of Ruin: Wordsworth, Coleridge, and Modalities of Fragmentation* (Princeton, NJ: Princeton University Press, 1981).

McKee, W., *Elizabeth Inchbald: Novelist* (Washington, DC: Catholic University of America, 1935).

McKeon, M., *The Origins of the English Novel, 1600–1740* (Baltimore, MD: Johns Hopkins University Press, 1987).

—, *Theory of the Novel: A Historical Approach* (Baltimore, MD: Johns Hopkins University Press, 2001).

Mellor, A. K., *Romanticism & Gender* (New York: Routledge, 1993).

Mellor, A. K., and R. E. Matlak (eds), *British Literature, 1780–1830* (Boston, MA: Heinle & Heinle, 1996).

Mellow, J. R., *Nathaniel Hawthorne in His Times* (Boston, MA: Houghton, 1980).

Melville, H., 'Hawthorne and His Mosses', in H. Melville, *The Piazza Tales and Other Prose Pieces, 1839–1860*, ed. H. Hayford, A. A. MacDougall, G. T. Tanselle, *et al.*, vol. 9 (Evanston and Chicago: Northwestern University Press and Newberry Library, 1987), pp. 239–53.

Mencken, H. L., 'The American Novel', in H. L. Mencken, *Prejudices: Fourth Series* (New York: Octagon Books, 1977), pp. 278–93.

Mews, C. J., *Abelard and Heloise* (Oxford: Oxford University Press, 2005).

Michael, R., 'A History of the Professional Theatre in Boston from the Beginning to 1816', 2 vols (PhD dissertation, Radcliffe College, 1941).

Milder, R., and R. Fuller (eds), *The Business of Reflection: Hawthorne in His Notebooks* (Columbus: Ohio State University Press, 2009).

Millington, R. H. (ed.), *The Cambridge Companion to Nathaniel Hawthorne* (Cambridge: Cambridge University Press, 2004).

Moore, M. B., *The Salem World of Nathaniel Hawthorne* (Columbia, MO: University of Missouri Press, 1998).

Moreux, F., 'Bibliographie Selective d'Elizabeth Inchbald, Auteur Dramatique et Romancière (1753–1821)', *Bulletin de la Société d'Etudes Anglo–Americaines des XVIIe et XVIIIe Siècles*, 13 (1981), pp. 81–105.

Morillot, P., 'Le Roman', in L. P. de Julleville (ed.), *Histoire de la Langue et de la Littérature Française des Origines à 1900*, 8 vols (Paris: Librairie Armand Colin, 1909), vol. 6, pp. 447–502.

Mortensen, P., 'Rousseau's English Daughters: Female Desire and Male Guardianship in British Romantic Fiction', *English Studies*, 83:4 (2002), pp. 356–70.

—, 'The Englishness of the English Gothic Novel: Romance Writing in an Age of Europhobia', in F. Ogée (ed.), *'Better in France?': The Circulation of Ideas Across the Channel in the Eighteenth Century* (Lewisburg, PA: Bucknell University Press, 2005), pp. 269–89.

Mowat, B. A., *The Dramaturgy of Shakespeare's Romances* (Athens, GA: University of Georgia Press, 1976).

Muir, K. (ed.), *Shakespeare*: The Winter's Tale (Nashville: Aurora Publishers, 1970).

Nachumi, N., '"Those Simple Signs": The Performance of Emotion in Elizabeth Inchbald's *A Simple Story*', *Eighteenth-Century Fiction*, 11:3 (1999), pp. 317–38.

Newberry, F., *Hawthorne's Divided Loyalties: England and America in His Works* (Rutherford, NJ: Fairleigh Dickinson University Press, 1987).

Nicoll, A., *A History of English Drama, 1660–1900*, 6 vols, *vol. 3, Late Eighteenth-Century Drama, 1750–1800* (Cambridge: Cambridge University Press, 1955).

Nosworthy, J. M. (ed.), introduction to *Cymbeline*, in W. Shakespeare, *The Arden Edition of the Works of William Shakespeare* (London: Methuen, 1955), pp. xi–lxxxv.

Nutall, A. D., *Two Concepts of Allegory: A Study of Shakespeare's* The Tempest *and the Logic of Allegorical Expression* (New York: Barnes & Noble, 1967).

O'Neill, M., 'Poetry of the Romantic Period: Coleridge and Keats', in C. Saunders (ed.), *A Companion to Romance: From Classical to Contemporary* (Malden, MA: Blackwell, 2004), pp. 305–20.

Odell, G. C. D., *Annals of the New York Stage*, 15 vols (New York: Columbia University Press, 1927–1949).

Ogée, F., '"Amicable Collision": Some Thoughts on the Reality of Intellectual Exchange between Britain and France in the Enlightenment', in F. Ogée (ed.), *'Better in France?': The Circulation of Ideas Across the Channel in the Eighteenth Century* (Lewisburg, PA: Bucknell University Press, 2005), pp. 13–34.

Osland, D., 'Heart–Picking in *A Simple Story*', *Eighteenth-Century Fiction*, 16:1 (2003), pp. 79–101.

Pages, C. M., 'Innocence and Violence: Two Sides of a Face: A Study of Miriam and Hilda in Relation to Beatrice Cenci in Nathaniel Hawthorne's *The Marble Faun*', in W. Wright and S. Kaplan (eds), *The Image of Violence in Literature, the Media, and Society* (Pueblo, CO: University of Southern Colorado, 1995), pp. 453–7.

Palfrey, S., *Late Shakespeare: A New World of Words* (Oxford: Clarendon Press, 1997).

Palmer, D. J. (ed.), *Shakespeare:* The Tempest (Nashville, TN: Aurora Publishers, 1970).

Parker, J. A., 'Complicating *A Simple Story*: Inchbald's Two Versions of Female Power', *Eighteenth-Century Studies,* 30:3 (1997), pp. 255–70.

Parrinder, P., *Nation & Novel: The English Novel from its Origins to the Present Day* (Oxford: Oxford University Press, 2006).

Pascoe, J., 'Introduction', in M. Robinson, *Mary Robinson: Selected Poems*, ed. J. Pascoe (Toronto: Broadview, 2000), pp. 19–61.

Patterson, E. H., 'Elizabeth Inchbald's Treatment of the Family and the Pilgrimage in *A Simple Story*', *Etudes anglaises*, 29 (1976), pp. 196–8.

Paulding, J. K., 'National Literature', in G. Hutner (ed.), *American Literature, American Culture* (New York: Oxford University Press, 1999), pp. 24–5.

Paulson, R., *Sin and Evil: Moral Values in Literature* (New Haven, CT: Yale University Press, 2007).

Pearce, H. D., 'Hawthorne's Old Moodie: *The Blithedale Romance* and *Measure for Measure*', *South Atlantic Bulletin,* 38:4 (1973), pp. 11–15.

Pearce, R. H., 'Hawthorne and the Twilight of Romance', *Yale Review,* 37 (1948), pp. 487–506.

Pearsall, D., *Arthurian Romance: A Short Introduction* (Malden, MA: Blackwell, 2003).

Pease, D. E., 'Hawthorne in the Custom–House: The Metapolitics, Postpolitics, and Politics of *The Scarlet Letter*', *Boundary 2: An International Journal of Literature and Culture,* 32:1 (2005), pp. 53–70.

Person, L. S., *The Cambridge Introduction to Nathaniel Hawthorne* (Cambridge: Cambridge University Press, 2007).

Peterson, D. L., *Time, Tide, and Tempest: A Study of Shakespeare's Romances* (San Marino, CA: Huntington Library, 1973).

Playfair, G., *Kean: The Life and Paradox of the Great Actor* (London: Reinhardt & Evans, 1950).

Plumb, J. H., *England in the Eighteenth Century* (Harmondsworth, England: Penguin, 1950).

Poirier, R., *The Comic Sense of Henry James: A Study of the Early Novels* (New York: Oxford University Press, 1960).

Pollock, T. C., *The Philadelphia Theatre in the Eighteenth Century* (Philadelphia, PA: University of Pennsylvania Press, 1933).

Praz, M., 'Introductory Essay', in *Three Gothic Novels* (Harmondsworth: Penguin, 1968), pp. 7–34.

Pyle, F., The Winter's Tale*: A Commentary on the Structure* (New York: Barnes & Noble, 1969).

Raddin, G. G., Jr, *An Early New York Library of Fiction: With a Checklist of the Fiction in H. Caritat's Circulating Library, No. 1 City Hotel, Broadway, New York, 1804* (New York: H. W. Wilson, 1940).

Rajan, B., *The Form of the Unfinished: English Poetics from Spenser to Pound* (Princeton, NJ: Princeton University Press, 1985).

Ramsey, L. C., *Chivalric Romances: Popular Literature in Medieval England* (Bloomington, IN: Indiana University Press, 1983).

Randall, J. H., Jr, 'Romantic Reinterpretations of Religion', *Studies in Romanticism*, 2:4 (1963), pp. 189–212.

Rauber, D. F., 'The Fragment as Romantic Form', *Modern Language Quarterly*, 30 (1969), pp. 212–21.

Rawes, A., *Romanticism and Form* (Basingstoke: Palgrave, 2007).

Rebholz, R. A., *Thirty–Seven Plays by Shakespeare: A Sense of the Corpus* (Lewiston, NY: Edwin Mellen Press, 2006).

Rees, J. O., 'Shakespeare in *The Blithedale Romance*', *Emerson Society Quarterly*, 19 (1973), pp. 84–93.

—, 'Hawthorne's Concept of Allegory: A Reconsideration', *Philological Quarterly*, 54 (1975), pp. 494–510.

Reeve, C., *The Progress of Romance* (1785; New York: Facsimile Text Society, 1930).

Reynolds, L. J., 'Introduction', in L. J. Reynolds (ed.), *A Historical Guide to Nathaniel Hawthorne* (Oxford: Oxford University Press, 2001), pp. 3–12.

Richetti, J., 'Introduction', in J. Richetti (ed.), *The Cambridge Companion to the Eighteenth-Century Novel* (Cambridge: Cambridge University Press, 1996), pp. 1–8.

Ringe, D. A., 'Hawthorne's Psychology of the Head and Heart', *Publications of the Modern Language Association*, 65 (1950), pp. 120–32.

—, 'Go East, Young Man, and Discover Your Country', *The Kentucky Review*, 10:1 (1990), pp. 3–20.

Ritson, J. (ed.), *Pieces of Ancient Popular Poetry* (London: C. Clarke for T. and J. Egerton, 1791).

Robertson, P. R., 'Shelley and Hawthorne: A Comparison of Imagery and Sensibility', *South Central Bulletin*, 32 (1972), pp. 233–9.

Robinson, M., *Memoirs of the Late Mrs Robinson*, in C. A. Barros and J. M. Smith (eds), *Life–Writings by British Women, 1660–1850: An Anthology* (Boston, MA: Northeastern University Press, 2000), pp. 369–80.

Rocks, J. E., 'Hawthorne and France: In Search of American Literary Nationalism', *Tulane Studies in English*, 17 (1969), pp. 145–57.

Rogers, K. M., 'Inhibitions on Eighteenth-Century Women Novelists: Elizabeth Inchbald and Charlotte Smith', *Eighteenth-Century Studies*, 11 (1977), pp. 63–78.

—, *Feminism in Eighteenth-Century England* (New York: St Martin's Press, 1982).

—, 'Elizabeth Inchbald: Not Such a Simple Story', in D. Spender (ed,), *Living by the Pen: Early British Women Writers* (New York: Teachers College Press, 1992), pp. 82–90.

Rosbottom, R. C., 'The Novel and Gender Difference', in D. Holier, *et al.* (eds), *A New History of French Literature* (Cambridge, MA: Harvard University Press, 1989), pp. 481–7.

Ross, D., *The Excellence of Falsehood: Romance, Realism, and Women's Contribution to the Novel* (Lexington, KY: University Press of Kentucky, 1991).

Rousseau, J.–J., *Emile*, trans. W. H. Payne (Amherst, NY: Prometheus Books, 2003).

Ryan, J., 'Elective Affinities: Goethe and Henry James', *Goethe Yearbook*, 1 (1982), pp. 153–71.

Ryan, P. M., 'Young Hawthorne at the Salem Theatre', *Essex Institute Historical Collections*, 94 (1958), pp. 243–55.

Ryan, R. M., *The Romantic Reformation: Religious Politics in English Literature, 1789–1824* (Cambridge: Cambridge University Press, 1997).

Sanders, N., 'An Overview of Critical Approaches to the Romances', in C. M. Kay and H. E. Jacobs (eds), *Shakespeare's Romances Reconsidered* (Lincoln, NE: University of Nebraska Press, 1978), pp. 1–10.

Schiller, E., 'The Choice of Innocence: Hilda in *The Marble Faun*', *Studies in the Novel*, 26:4 (1994), pp. 372–91.

Schorin, G., 'Approaching the Genre of *The Tempest*', in R. C. Tobias and P. G. Zolbrod (eds), *Shakespeare's Late Plays* (Athens, GA: Ohio University Press, 1974), pp. 166–84.

Scribner, D., *Hawthorne Revisited: Honoring the Bicentennial of the Author's Birth* (Lenox, MA: Lenox Library Association, 2004).

Seilhamer, G. O., *History of the American Theatre*, 3 vols (New York: Haskell House, 1969).

Shakespeare, W., *The Riverside Shakespeare*, ed. G. B. Evans (Boston, MA: Houghton, 1974), pp. 1,803–4.

—, *The Complete Works of Shakespeare*, updated 4th edn, ed. D. Bevington (New York: Longman, 1997).

Shattuck, C. H., 'Shakespeare's Plays in Performance from 1660 to the Present', in G. B. Evans (ed.), *The Riverside Shakespeare*, (Boston, MA: Houghton, 1974), pp. 1,799–825.

—, *Shakespeare on the American Stage: From the Hallams to Edwin Booth* (Washington, DC: Folger Shakespeare Library, 1976).

Shea, F. X., 'Religion and the Romantic Movement', *Studies in Romanticism*, 9 (1970), pp. 285–96.

Shealy, A., 'Romance', in R. T. Lambdin and L. C. Lambdin (eds), *Encyclopedia of Medieval Literature* (Westport, CT: Greenwood Press, 2000), pp. 442–3.

Shear, W., 'Characterization in *The Scarlet Letter*', *Midwest Quarterly*, 12 (1971), pp. 437–54.

Shelley, M., *Frankenstein*, in P. Fairclough (ed.), *Three Gothic Novels* (London: Penguin, 1986), pp. 256–497.

—, *The Mary Shelley Reader*, ed. B. T. Bennett and C. E. Robinson (New York: Oxford University Press, 1990).

Shelley, P., *The Cenci: A Tragedy, in Five Acts*, in P. Shelley, *Shelley's Poetry and Prose*, ed. D. H. Reiman and S. B. Powers (New York: Norton, 1977), pp. 236–301.

Shepard, M. B., 'A Tomb for Abelard and Heloise', *Romance Studies*, 25:1 (2007), pp. 29–42.

Shipton, C. K. (ed.), *Early American Imprints, 1639–1800* (Worcester, MA: American Antiquarian Society/Readex Microprint, various dates).

Shockley, M. S., *The Richmond Stage, 1784–1812* (Charlottesville, VA: University Press of Virginia, 1977).

Showalter, E., Jr, *The Evolution of the French Novel, 1641–1782* (Princeton, NJ: Princeton University Press, 1972).

Siegel, J., *Haunted Museum: Longing, Travel, and the Art–Romance Tradition* (Princeton, NJ: Princeton University Press, 2005).

Sigl, P., 'Elizabeth Inchbald', in Paula Backscheider (ed.), *Dictionary of Literary Biography*, vol. 89, *Restoration and Eighteenth-Century Dramatists*, 3rd ser. (Detroit, MI: Gale, 1989), pp. 198–215.

Simms, W. G., 'Americanism in Literature', in C. H. Holman (ed.), *Views and Reviews in American Literature, History, and Fiction*, 1st series (Cambridge, MA: Belknap Press of Harvard University Press, 1962), pp. 7–29.

Small, C., *Mary Shelley's* Frankenstein (Pittsburgh, PA: University of Pittsburgh Press, 1973).

Smith, H., *Shakespeare's Romances: A Study of Some Ways of the Imagination* (San Marino, CA: Huntington Library, 1972).

Smith, J., 'Keats and Hawthorne: A Romantic Bloom in Rappaccini's Garden', *Emerson Society Quarterly*, 42 (1966), pp. 8–12.

Smither, N., *A History of the English Theatre in New Orleans* (1944; New York: Benjamin Blom, 1967).

Smoot, J. J., 'Romantic Thought and Style in 19th-Century Realism and Naturalism', in G. Gillespie, M. Engel and B. Dieterle (eds), *Romantic Prose Fiction* (Amsterdam: John Benjamins, 2008), pp. 580–95.

Spacks, P. M., *Desire and Truth: Functions of Plot in Eighteenth-Century English Novels* (Chicago, IL: University of Chicago Press, 1990).

—, *Novel Beginnings: Experiments in Eighteenth-Century English Fiction* (New Haven, CT: Yale University Press, 2006).

—, *Privacy: Concealing the Eighteenth-Century Self* (Chicago, IL: University of Chicago Press, 2003).

Spencer, J., *The Rise of the Woman Novelist: From Aphra Behn to Jane Austen* (Oxford: Basil Blackwell, 1986).

Spender, D., *Mothers of the Novel: 100 Good Women Writers before Jane Austen* (London: Pandora, 1986).

St Clair, W., *The Godwins and the Shelleys: The Biography of a Family* (New York: Norton, 1989).

—, *The Reading Nation in the Romantic Period* (Cambridge: Cambridge University Press, 2004).

Stanton, R., 'Hawthorne, Bunyan, and the American Romances', *Publications of the Modern Language Association*, 71 (1956), pp. 155–65.

Stauffer, A., 'The Hero in the Harem: Byron's Debt to Medieval Romance in *Don Juan* VI', *European Romantic Review*, 10:1 (1999), pp. 84–97.

Stephens, R., 'A is for Art in *The Scarlet Letter*', *American Transcendental Quarterly*, 1:1 (1969), pp. 23–7.

Stevens, J. E., *Medieval Romance: Themes and Approaches* (London: Hutchinson University Library, 1973).

Stewart, R., 'Introduction, Chapter III: The Development of Character Types in Hawthorne's Fiction', in N. Hawthorne, *The American Notebooks*, ed. R. Stewart (New Haven, CT: Yale University Press, 1932), pp. xliv–lxvii.

—, 'Recollections of Hawthorne by His Sister Elizabeth', *American Literature*, 16 (1945), pp. 316–31.

—, *Nathaniel Hawthorne: A Biography* (New Haven, CT: Yale University Press, 1948).

St-Palaye, J.-B., *Memoirs of Ancient Chivalry* (London: J. Dodsley, 1784).

Strachey, G. L., 'Introduction', in Elizabeth Inchbald, *A Simple Story* (London: Henry Frowde, 1908), pp. iii–xv.

—, *Landmarks in French Literature* (London: Thornton Butterworth, 1936).

Strathman, C. A., *Romantic Poetry and the Fragmentary Imperative: Schlegel, Byron, Joyce, Blanchot* (Albany, NY: State University of New York Press, 2005).

Stubbs, J. C., 'Hawthorne's *The Scarlet Letter*: The Theory of the Romance and the Use of the New England Situation', *Publications of the Modern Language Association*, 83 (1968), pp. 1,439–47.

Sutherland, H., 'Varieties of Protestant Experience: Religion and the Doppelgänger in Hogg, Brown, and Hawthorne', *Studies in Hogg and his World*, 16 (2005), pp. 71–85.

Tanner, T., 'Introduction', in H. James, *Hawthorne* (London: Macmillan, 1967; New York: St Martin's Press, 1967), pp. 1–21.

Tave, S. M., 'Propriety and *Lovers' Vows*', in H. Bloom (ed.), *Jane Austen's* Mansfield Park (New York: Chelsea House, 1987), pp. 37–46.

Taylor, A. B., *An Introduction to Medieval Romance* (London: Heath Cranton, 1930).

Taylor, O. G., 'Cultural Confessions: Penance and Penitence in Nathaniel Hawthorne's *The Scarlet Letter* and *The Marble Faun*', *Renascence*, 58:2 (2005), pp. 135–52.

Taylor, P. M., 'Authorial Amendments in Mrs Inchbald's *Nature and Art*', *Notes and Queries*, 25 (1978), pp. 68–70.

Teahan, S., 'My Sculptor/My Self: A Story of Reading', *Henry James Review*, 23:3 (2002), pp. 246–54.

Texte, J., 'Les Relations Littéraires de la France avec l'Étranger au XVIIIe Siècle', in L. P. de Julleville (ed.), *Histoire de la Langue et de la Littérature Française des Origines à 1900*, Vol. 6: Dix–huitième Siècle (Paris: Librairie Armand Colin, 1909).

The National Union Catalog, Pre–1956 Imprints, 754 vols (London: Mansell, 1968–1981).

Thomas, W. J. (ed.), *A Collection of Early Prose Romances* (London: Pickering, 1828).

Thoreau, H. D., *Early Essays and Miscellanies*, ed. J. J. Moldenhauer and E. Moser, with A. C. Kern (Princeton, NJ: Princeton University Press, 1975).

Thornburg, M. K. P., *The Monster in the Mirror: Gender and the Sentimental/Gothic Myth in Frankenstein* (Ann Arbor, MI: UMI Research Press, 1987).

Thrailkill, J. E., '*The Scarlet Letter*'s Romantic Medicine', *Studies in American Fiction*, 34:1 (2006), pp. 3–31.

Todd, J., *Women's Friendship in Literature* (New York: Columbia University Press, 1980).

—, *The Sign of Angellica: Women, Writing and Fiction, 1660–1800* (New York: Columbia University Press, 1989).

—, *Mary Wollstonecraft: A Revolutionary Life* (New York: Columbia University Press, 2000).

Tompkins, J. M. S., *The Popular Novel in England, 1770–1800* (Lincoln, NE: University of Nebraska Press, 1961).

Tucker, T. G., *The Foreign Debt of English Literature* (London: George Bell, 1907).

Turner, A., 'Hawthorne's Literary Borrowings', *Publications of the Modern Language Association*, 51 (1938), pp. 543–62.

Turner, V., *The Ritual Process: Structure and Anti–Structure* (1969; Ithaca, NY: Cornell University Press, 1977).

Ty, E., *Unsex'd Revolutionaries: Five Women Novelists of the 1790s* (Toronto, ON: University of Toronto Press, 1993).

Ullén, M., 'Reading with "The Eye of Faith": The Structural Principle of Hawthorne's Romances', *Texas Studies in Literature and Language*, 48 (2006), pp. 1–36.

Upham, A. H., *The French Influence in English Literature: From the Accession of Elizabeth to the Restoration* (New York: Columbia University Press, 1911).

Uphaus, R. W., *Beyond Tragedy: Structure & Experience in Shakespeare's Romances* (Lexington, KY: University Press of Kentucky, 1981).

Utterson, E. V. (ed.), *Select Pieces of Early Popular Poetry*, 2 vols (London: Longman, Hurst, Rees, Orme and Brown, 1817).

Van Doren, M., *Nathaniel Hawthorne* (New York: Viking, 1949).

van Tieghem, P., *Histoire de la Littérature Française* (Paris: Librairie Arthème Fayard, 1949).

Wagenknecht, E., *Nathaniel Hawthorne: Man and Writer* (New York: Oxford University Press, 1961).

—, *Nathaniel Hawthorne: The Man, His Tales and Romances* (New York: Continuum, 1989).

Waggoner, H. H., 'The Marble Faun', in A. N. Kaul (ed.), *Hawthorne: A Collection of Critical Essays* (Englewood Cliffs, NJ: Prentice–Hall, 1966), pp. 164–76.

Wallace, M., 'Wit and Revolution: Cultural Resistance in Elizabeth Inchbald's *A Simple Story*', *European Romantic Review*, 12:1 (2001), pp. 92–121.

Walpole, H., 'Preface to the second edition of *The Castle of Otranto*', in I. Williams (ed.), *Novel and Romance, 1700–1800: A Documentary Record* (New York: Barnes & Noble, 1970), pp. 265–9.

Ward, C., 'Inordinate Desire: Schooling the Senses in Elizabeth Inchbald's *A Simple Story*', *Studies in the Novel*, 31:1 (1999), pp. 1–18.

Warren, A., 'Hawthorne's Reading', *New England Quarterly*, 8:4 (1935), pp. 480–97.

Wasserman, E. R., 'Shakespeare and the English Romantic Movement', in H. M. Schueller (ed.), *The Persistence of Shakespeare Idolatry* (Detroit, MI: Wayne State University Press, 1964), pp. 77–103.

Watt, I., *The Rise of the Novel: Studies in Defoe, Richardson and Fielding* (Berkeley, CA: University of California Press, 1957).

Weber, H. (ed.), *Metrical Romances of the Thirteenth, Fourteenth, and Fifteenth Centuries*, 3 vols (Edinburgh: Constable, *et al.*, 1810).

Wegelin, C., 'Europe in Hawthorne's Fiction', *Journal of English Literary History*, 14 (1947), pp. 219–45.

Weisbuch, R., *Atlantic Double-Cross: American Literature and British Influence in the Age of Emerson* (Chicago, IL and London: University of Chicago Press, 1986).

Wells, S., 'Shakespeare and Romance', in J. R. Brown and B. Harris (eds), *Later Shakespeare* (New York: St Martin's Press, 1967), pp. 49–80.

Wheeler, O. B., 'Love among the Ruins: Hawthorne's Surrogate Religion', *Southern Review*, (1974), pp. 535–65.

White, P. K., 'Puritan Theories of History in Hawthorne's Fiction', *Canadian Review of American Studies*, 9 (1978), pp. 135–53.

Whitman, W., 'Democratic Vistas', in F. Stovall (ed.), *Prose Works 1892: Collect and Other Prose* (New York: New York University Press, 1964), vol. 2, pp. 361–426.

—, 'American National Literature', in W. Whitman, *Complete Poetry and Collected Prose* (New York: Library of America, 1982), pp. 1,258–64.

Wilcox, L., 'Idols and Idolaters in *A Simple Story*', *Age of Johnson*, 17 (2006), pp. 297–316.

Williams, I. (ed.), *Novel and Romance, 1700–1800: A Documentary Record* (New York: Barnes & Noble, 1970).

Williams, S. S., 'Publishing an Emergent "American" Literature', in S. E. Casper, J. D. Chaison and J. Groves (eds), *Perspectives on American Book History: Artifacts and Commentary* (Ameherst, MA: University of Massachusetts Press, 2002), pp. 165–94.

Wilson, A. H., *A History of the Philadelphia Theatre, 1835 to 1855* (Philadelphia, PA: University of Pennsylvania Press, 1935).

Wineapple, B., *Hawthorne: A Life* (New York: Knopf, 2003).

Winters, Y., 'Maule's Curse: Hawthorne and the Problem of Allegory', *American Review*, 9:3 (1937), pp 339–61.

Wolfson, S. J. (ed.), 'The Romantic Century: A Forum', *European Romantic Review*, 11:1 (2000), pp. 1–45.

Wollstonecraft, M., *A Vindication of the Rights of Woman*, ed. M. Brody (London: Penguin, 1992).

—, *A Vindication of the Rights of Men / A Vindication of the Rights of Woman / An Historical and Moral View of the French Revolution*, ed. J. Todd (Oxford: Oxford University Press, 1993).

Woo, C., *Romantic Actors and Bardolatry: Performing Shakespeare from Garrick to Kean* (New York: Peter Lang, 2008).

Woodring, C., 'Nature and Art in the Nineteenth Century', *Publications of the Modern Language Association*, 92:2 (1977), pp. 193–202.

—, *Nature into Art: Cultural Transformations in Nineteenth-Century Britain* (Cambridge, MA: Harvard University Press, 1989).

Wordsworth, J., 'Introduction', in E. Inchbald, *Nature and Art* (Oxford and New York: Woodstock Books, 1994), n.p.

—, 'Introduction', in M. Robinson, *Poems, 1791* (1791; Oxford and New York: Woodstock Books, 1994), n.p.

Wordsworth, W., *The Prelude*, in W. Wordsworth, *Selected Poems*, ed. J. O. Hayden (London: Penguin, 1994), pp. 307–49.

Wright, S. B., *Critical Companion to Nathaniel Hawthorne: A Literary Reference to His Life and Work* (New York: Facts on File, 2007).

Zimmerman, E., 'A Puritan Yankee in King Arthur's Court: Deconstructing Hawthorne's Myth America' (PhD dissertation, Claremont Graduate University, 1998).

INDEX

www.ingramcontent.com/pod-product-compliance
Ingram Content Group UK Ltd.
Pitfield, Milton Keynes, MK11 3LW, UK
UKHW020356010325
455677UK00021B/490